POLITICS AND TERRITORY

Politics and Territory

THE SOCIOLOGY

OF REGIONAL

PERSISTENCE

IN CANADA

Mildred A. Schwartz

McGill–Queen's University Press   MONTREAL AND LONDON 1974

© McGill-Queen's University Press 1974
International Standard Book Number 0 7735 0166 5
Library of Congress Catalog Number 73-79502
Legal Deposit First Quarter 1974

Design by Mary Cserepy
Printed in Canada by John Deyell Co.

This book has been published with the help of a grant
from the Social Science Research Council of Canada
using funds provided by the Canada Council.

CONTENTS

TABLES

CHARTS

PREFACE

The present volume is a counterpoint to my previously published *Public Opinion and Canadian Identity*. The central concept in that book was national identity, by which I meant citizens' perceptions of their country in its relations with outside powers, internal arrangements for the distribution of resources and rewards, and the symbolic representation of the nation. One of the clearest findings from an examination of public opinion polls over a twenty-year period, was the continuing relevance of where people lived to their outlook on national problems. Since I did not believe this was owing to any form of geographic determinism, I argued that there was an uneven distribution of opinions because certain kinds of people had settled in particular areas and various economic consequences had become associated with regionally differentiated resource potentials and industrial developments. As post facto explanations for the opinion cleavages revealed by a secondary analysis of public opinion data, my conclusions had enough common-sense validity to be satisfying.

While at one level, my explanations for the lack of a uniform definition of the nation were sufficient, at others they provoked many more questions than my data could answer. Transferring my attention from the nation as a whole to its constituent regions, I wondered why they should be so distinctive in outlook. To some extent, I had already answered this question: special combinations of population and resources were interacting in a given place. But I was not convinced that I had fully uncovered the interplay between economy and population. It was apparent that other dimensions of regional differentiation were involved. For example, what kinds of political adaptations had been made within regions? How did locally determined viewpoints emerge and how were they related to the behaviour of residents and the responses of political leaders? Was it possible to discern some emergent properties associated with regionalism itself?

Such questions led me to welcome the opportunity to participate in a study immediately following the 1965 Canadian general election. Supported by grants from the Canada Council and the Committee on Election Expenses, John Meisel, Philip Converse, Maurice Pinard, Peter Regenstreif, and I planned a nation-wide survey to gather basic data on political opinions and behaviour. This gave me the means to collect fresh and more relevant information from a rigorously selected sample about topics that still puzzled me. The 1965 election itself was not of prime importance to me; it merely forms a terminal point for most of my analysis. Whether the 1968 election significantly altered what the following chapters describe is unlikely, given the stability of past experience, but I do consider as many recent developments as seem pertinent. The analysis was completed well before the 1972 election, yet the same qualification applies to it as well.

Each of my colleagues brought quite different interests to the planning of our survey. As far as was possible, our questionnaire attempted to incorporate all of these. It was then intended that we produce a joint work, with each of us also free to publish independently. For various reasons, the joint volume was never produced. This book is my own work and my colleagues are in no way responsible for the ways I have used our data. However, I remain indebted to them for their collaboration in the survey that made this present volume possible.

In addition to support from the Canada Council and the Committee on Election Expenses for the actual costs of the survey, grants to me from the Graduate College Research Board of the University of Illinois at Chicago Circle and the National Science Foundation enabled me to carry out my analysis. Suggestions and criticisms at various stages of writing were generously supplied by Philip Converse, David Easton, Fred C. Engelmann, Michael Hechter, Tom Kent, Fred L. Strodtbeck, Clifford Tiedemann, and James Wiley. Technical assistance was given by Michael Burmester, Don Goldhamer, Kathleen Crittenden, Andrew Rojecki, Chet Juszczak, and Mr. Wiley. No less important was the shepherding of the manuscript through numerous typings. Under the supervision of Lorraine Wallace, this was done by Debbie Goode, Carol Johnson, Carol Genty, Ed Neva, and Hattie Jones. Public acknowledgment of this assistance serves as only a small measure of my appreciation.

CHAPTER

The division into regions

THE UBIQUITY OF TERRITORIAL DIVISIONS

Nature and history have conspired to make geography central to an understanding of Canadian existence. The spatial makeup of Canada compounds every critical social and political problem the country faces. This does not make Canada unique. In any territorially based society, some form of internal variation is always present. With the exception of population diversity related to such attributes as age and sex, most forms of differentiation are not evenly distributed throughout a society. As a result, we can almost always find differences, often of great magnitude, between territorial divisions or regions within a single society. A reading of the popular press immediately calls to mind examples of regionally divided societies—Belgium, Nigeria, Yugoslavia. What is more difficult is finding countries that could *not* be usefully described in regional terms. England?[1] France? Germany? Spain?[2] The answer is no in each instance. In Europe, we would probably be confined to places such

---

1. For anyone who needs convincing, see Donald Read, *The English Provinces, c. 1760-1960, A Study in Influence* (New York: St. Martin's Press, 1964).

2. One of the few contemporary analyses of regionalism from the perspective of modern sociology is contained in Juan J. Linz and Amando de Miguel, "Within-National Differences and Comparisons: The Eight Spains," in Richard L. Merritt and Stein Rokkan, eds., *Comparing Nations* (New Haven: Yale University Press, 1966), pp. 267-319.

as Luxembourg, Monaco, and Lichtenstein. The African experience constantly reminds us of the centrifugal tendencies of tribal societies.[3] The volatility of regional divisions is also sharply apparent throughout Asia. In Latin America, nations themselves are in many ways artificial constructs, lacking a clear-cut national identity, with regional loyalties most prominent. There are regionally distinct climates of opinion in the United States that even large-scale population movements have not eroded.[4]

To many early students of sociology, the relations between individuals and physical locality were a basic component of the primary roots of social existence. Tönnies, for example, linked common habitat with blood ties and shared sacred beliefs as the basis for his concept of *Gemeinschaft*.[5] From his comparative studies of law, Sir Henry Maine argued that there were two principles which might underlie even the most primitive forms of political union: those based on kinship and those on territory. It was his theory of evolution that territorial ties followed those of kinship, yet the former were long present in the history of human society.[6] The anthropologist Lowie disputed this view, arguing for the coexistence, if not the precedence, of territorial bonds.[7] In all of these instances, regardless of disagreements, territory is conceived as a primitive unit of social organization, one of the essential links among disparate individuals. It is a primordial attachment, a means of ascribing a social location to individuals.[8] The problem with this kind of conceptualization, whether or not it is correct, is that it lends itself to tautologies. If territorial attachments are of such a primary nature, then nothing further needs to be said about them. They exist, pervading behavioural responses in much the same way as biological attributes and kinship relations. Yet this is a

---

3. An excellent anthology, already outdated, is Gwendolyn M. Carter, ed., *National Unity and Regionalism in Eight African States* (Ithaca: Cornell University Press, 1966).

4. Two recent studies documenting these differences are: Mildred A. Schwartz, *Trends in White Attitudes Toward Negroes* (Chicago: National Opinion Research Center, 1967); Norval D. Glenn and J. L. Simmons, "Are Regional Cultural Differences Diminishing?" *Public Opinion Quarterly,* 31 (Summer, 1967): 176-93.

5. Ferdinand Tönnies, *Community and Society,* ed. and trans. Charles P. Loomis (New York: Harper Torchbooks, 1963), pp. 42-44.

6. Sir Henry Maine, *Ancient Law* (London: Murray, 1861) ch. 5.

7. Robert H. Lowie, *The Origin of the State* (New York: Harcourt, Brace, & Co., 1927).

8. Primordial is used here in the sense elaborated by Shils. Edward A. Shils, "Primordial, Personal, Sacred and Civil Ties," *British Journal of Sociology,* 8 (1957): 130-45.

most unsatisfying formulation, distracting us from empirical questions about the social relevance of locality.

It could be argued that the conceptions of locality derived from Tönnies or Lowie, to the extent that they do have some empirical content, apply only to simpler societies with minimal population mobility. Knowing where someone lives gives both the participants in the society and the outside observer a crucial insight into the roles he is likely to play. In the case of Tönnies, the concept of *Gemeinschaft* evokes the nostalgia for a less complex world, where the bonds of friends, neighbours, and kin establish a protective environment for the conduct of life. But what happens in complex, mobile societies? One apparent clue to the personal importance of locality can be derived from studies using the Twenty Statements Test (TST), in answer to the question, "Who am I?"[9] In the published studies examined, geographic location barely appears as a category of self-definition. The principal identities that spontaneously emerge are those of family, religion, and occupation.[10] We are, however, unwilling to conclude from these studies that territory is an irrelevant aspect of personal identity. The kinds of samples used, frequently students in Iowa, have a bearing on the absence of territorial identifications. It is probable that, under some circumstances at least, if people in the types of societies mentioned by Lowie and Tönnies were given the same test, they would respond in similar ways. To the extent that territory is a meaningful referent to individuals, it may not normally be evoked among stable population groups. For one thing, it does not have obvious links with behaviour in the same way as do occupational and kinship roles. Nor does it, on the surface at least, lead to the kind of solidarity associated with social groups based on these statuses. It more likely bestows an ascribed status, the salience of which comes to the surface most often when it is challenged. Such challenges may occur when travelling, moving from one area to another, facing competition based on locality, and so on. It is then that pride of place, or perhaps its opposite, will come into play.

From the perspective of the society, the salience of regional divisions is also problematic. It might be thought, from the examples cited at the outset, that all countries manifesting prominent regional divisions would suffer dysfunctional consequences with respect to political stability and peaceful relations among groups. But regional differences need not always be a source of contention. At issue here

---

9. For example, Manford Kuhn, "Self-Attitudes by Age, Sex, and Professional Training," *Sociological Quarterly,* 1 (1960): 39-55.

10. Harold A. Mulford and Winfield W. Salisbury II, "Self-Conceptions in a General Population," *Sociological Quarterly,* 5 (1964): 35-46.

are the conditions under which their recognition becomes linked with political tensions.

Defining Region

The definition of region has been a natural concern of geographers, who have added new refinements as they have become more quantitative. Kevin Cox, for example, would like to encourage more widespread adoption of geographers' tools and concepts for making regions into a set of cleanly defined categories. According to him,

> A region is a group of places analagous to the social class as a group of people. The allocation of places to regions involves the same taxonomic principles as presented above: the aim of regionalization is to allocate places (or the people at places) to regions in such a way as to minimize the within-region variance/between-region variance ratio within the constraint of the number of regions required.[11]

Continuing his analogy, Cox draws a parallel between class intervals and regional boundaries, and between the use of single or multiple indicators of class and region. It is clear from this approach that regional boundaries could easily shift, depending on the attributes to be classified into regional categories. What is more, and this is not so apparent, regions may consist of places homogeneous in some characteristics but not necessarily contiguous.

A sociological view of regions and regionalism was long a major interest at the University of North Carolina.[12] The definitions evolved there emphasized a configuration of shared characteristics, of which Rupert Vance's definition is typical.

> A region is a homogeneous area with physical and cultural characteristics distinct from those of neighboring areas. As a part of a national domain a region is sufficiently unified to have a consciousness of its customs and ideals and thus possess a sense of identity distinct from the rest of the country. The term "regionalism" properly represents the regional idea in action as an ideology, as a social movement, or as the theoretical basis for regional planning; it is also applied to

---

11. Kevin R. Cox, "On the Utility and Definition of Regions in Comparative Political Sociology," *Comparative Political Studies*, 2 (April, 1969): 68-98.

12. See, for example, the work of Howard Odum: *An American Epoch* (New York: Henry Holt & Co., 1930); *The Regional Approach to National Social Planning* (New York: Foreign Policy Association and Chapel Hill: University of North Carolina Press, 1935); *Southern Regions of the United States* (Chapel Hill: University of North Carolina Press, 1936); and with Harry Estill Moore, *American Regionalism* (New York: Henry Holt & Co., 1938).

the scientific task of delimiting and analyzing regions as entities lacking formal boundaries.[13]

In this definition, it is the shared sense of identification with a territorial unit that gives the concept of regionalism its special sociological significance.

The research problem dictates the definition of region employed. In this book, the questions raised are threefold. What are the nature and extent of regional differences? What factors promote their continuity or contribute to their breakdown? What consequences do these differences have for specified areas of life? The first question could be dismissed as a mere cataloguing of differences if it did not require at the outset a decision as to what is meant by region. We must decide whether to fit characteristics into previously established regional boundaries, or to create boundaries as a result of the distribution of these characteristics. In the case of Canada, the second and particularly the third questions determine the choices we make. In examining consequences of regional differences and factors associated with their continuity or decline we focus on the political milieu. It is not necessary to take this approach to regional differences, but its usefulness is evident throughout this book. As a result, for us a region is made up of adjacent areas, so that the entire region is distinguishable in character from others in that society, and can be treated as though it were a political actor. We associate "regionalism" with situations of politically relevant divisiveness and territorial cleavages, often accompanied by some consciousness on the part of residents that they have distinctive, regionally based interests.[14]

It is possible to define Canadian regions in a number of ways, according to ecological, physiographic, climatological, economic, or political criteria. In keeping with the focus on political life in this volume, we use as our principal boundaries those that have political relevance. This means that, for the most part, we concentrate our comparisons on the ten provinces of Canada, excluding the sparsely populated northland. In other words, for our purposes, region and province are often synonymous.[15] Following usage long accepted by geographers and economists, we also frequently compress these ten

13. Rupert B. Vance, "Region," in David L. Sills, ed., *International Encyclopedia of the Social Sciences,* 13 (1968): 377-78.

14. Compare the rationale for establishing regional boundaries in Ira Sharkansky, *Regionalism in American Politics* (Indianapolis: The Bobbs-Merrill Co., 1970), pp. 17-48.

15. Compare Paul W. Fox, "Regionalism and Confederation," in Mason Wade, ed., *Regionalism in the Canadian Community, 1867-1967* (Toronto: University of Toronto Press, 1969), pp. 3-5.

units into five.[16] This is not to say that either the Atlantic region (Newfoundland, Nova Scotia, New Brunswick and Prince Edward Island) or the Prairie provinces (Manitoba, Saskatchewan and Alberta) are completely homogeneous, any more than this is true of single provinces.[17] Yet relative to the rest of the country, the makeup and problems of the constituent provinces are sufficiently alike to make it meaningful to speak of each of them as distinct units. The validity of this aggregation will also be examined in Chapter 2, when economic conditions and population factors are reviewed province by province.

Perhaps the greatest objection to this form of grouping is the loss of independent political units, but this too is not unduly serious. Such agencies as the Atlantic Provinces Economic Council, the Atlantic Development Council, and the Western Grain Growers Association have helped create a larger political identity for these areas. Even more persuasive is the interest in political union within these two regions. In 1965, the legislatures of Nova Scotia and New Brunswick passed resolutions calling for a Maritime Union Study. A study was actually commissioned in 1968, making its report two years later, when Prince Edward Island joined with the two originating provinces.[18] It should be remembered that in 1864, it was just such a Maritime Union that was under consideration when representatives from Canadas East and West came to the Charlottetown meetings to persuade the Maritimers that a broader union was more desirable. While Newfoundland holds aloof now, as it did for different reasons then, it would probably become a reluctant member if a union should come about. The Prairie provinces might appear less likely candidates for political union, but there as well union has become a subject of serious thought.[19]

16. Richard E. Caves and Richard H. Holton, *The Canadian Economy* (Cambridge: Harvard University Press, 1959); Donald F. Putnam, ed., *Canadian Regions,* 2nd ed. (Toronto: J. M. Dent & Sons, 1954); George W. Wilson, Scott Gordon, Stanislaw Judek, *Canada: An Appraisal of its Needs and Resources* (Toronto: University of Toronto Press, 1965); P. Camu, E. P. Weeks, Z. W. Sametz, *Economic Geography of Canada* (Toronto: Macmillan, 1964).

17. For example, a recent examination of structural unemployment indicates that this is present in local areas in all regions, so that the understanding of such unemployment, and most particularly its amelioration, are dependent on the use of smaller territorial units. S. F. Kaliski, "Structural Unemployment in Canada: Towards a Definition of the Geographic Dimension," *Canadian Journal of Economics,* 1 (August, 1968): 552-65.

18. Maritime Union Study, commissioned by the governments of New Brunswick, Nova Scotia and Prince Edward Island (Fredericton, N.B.: 1970).

19. Prairie political union was the subject of a conference sponsored by the University of Lethbridge and the Lethbridge *Herald,* 10-13 May 1970.

Dividing Canada into five regions is common procedure for Canadians, who normally understand what is meant by the Prairies or the Maritime or Atlantic provinces. In a contest for their readers, *Maclean's* magazine asked for the choice of one of four maps that would give the most desirable geographic divisions to the country. The map that came closest to our groupings, but which also allocated the Yukon and Northwest Territories to the provinces and made Toronto and Montreal into separate provinces, was the most favoured by readers, chosen by 41 percent of those who responded. As one reader said, "This map would come about in a natural way without any violence. It would seem to be the natural grouping of people, of commerce, of political boundaries. It would not endanger the mutual trust that one area gives to another."[20]

PROSPECTS FOR DEREGIONALIZATION

It has been argued that processes of social change will bring about a decline in the importance of territory. In his examination of Norwegian politics, Rokkan traces the shift from regional-cultural cleavages to functional-economic ones.[21] This is associated with the development of an urban, industrial society, where the class system reflects the emerging strains. The defence of territorial interests then becomes secondary to conflicts between urban and rural interests and between social classes. With Lipset, Rokkan has extended this perspective to a three-stage model of nation-building. "In the first phase the thrusts of penetration and standardization from the national center increase territorial resistances and raise issues of cultural identity."[22] They cite Robert E. Lee's, "Am I a Virginian or an American?" as a typical response to the dilemmas raised by the contact between national and local interests. The second phase is characterized by the building of alliances, across or within regional lines. In the latter case, when

---

20. "Which Canada Would You Choose," *Maclean's* (October 1969) pp. 76-78; "This Is the Canada that Won Our Contest," *Maclean's* (January 1970), pp. 66-67.

21. Stein Rokkan and Henry Valen, "Regional Contrasts in Norwegian Politics," in E. Allardt and Y. Littunen, eds., *Cleavages, Ideologies and Party Systems* (Helsinki: Westermarck Society, 1964), pp. 162-238; Stein Rokkan, "Geography, Religion and Social Class: Crosscutting Cleavages in Norwegian Politics," in Seymour M. Lipset and Stein Rokkan, eds., *Party Systems and Voter Alignments* (New York: Free Press, 1967).

22. Seymour M. Lipset and Stein Rokkan, "Cleavage Structures, Party Systems, and Voter Alignments: An Introduction," in Lipset and Rokkan, *Party Systems and Voter Alignments,* p. 9.

a number of identities coalesce, as with religion, language, and class, regional loyalties are reinforced. By the third phase, the previously developed alliances become part of the national scene, affecting the distribution of resources and the procedures for political action. If territorial oppositions remain strong, as they can, severe limits are set on the scope of nation-building. In other words, the evolutionary process is not inevitable, but can be halted by what are essentially gaps in modernization.

Kevin Cox, in looking at changes in national voting patterns, makes explicit the foregoing perspective through the concept of "locational evolution." He associates it with four variables which bear on the nature of partisan divisions. These are information flow, resistance to information, birth-death processes, and relocation processes.[23] The relationship among the variables differs according to whether national voting patterns are in the territorial or functional phase of locational evolution. The territorial phase

> is associated with a highly clustered resistance pattern, the population of each region defending old cultural, ethnic and religious interests or emerging economic interests against the conflicting interests of either the nation as a whole or of other regions. Mitigation of the situation is hindered by the low horizontal mobility and highly limited communication characteristic of traditional societies.
>
> . . . The change from territorial politics to a more functional politics appears to be linked to a number of social and economic changes which we associate with industrialization. The emergence of factory industry, the growth of towns, out-migration from rural areas, improved transportation systems promoting increased mobility, the emergence of an educational system promoting the diffusion of information and changes in religious beliefs: either in the form of secularization or sectarianism.[24]

The shift from territorial cleavages to those that are national in scope can refer to a process of change within a society. The kinds of cleavages predominating can also provide the basis for classifying societies according to their stage of development. In either case, there

---

23. Kevin R. Cox, "The Spatial Evolution of National Voting Response Surfaces: Theory and Measurement," Department Of Geography, Ohio State University, discussion paper No. 9, mimeo., p. 3. One of the major proponents of the importance of communication links has been Karl W. Deutsch, for example in, *Nationalism and Communication* (Cambridge: MIT Press, 1953).

24. Cox, "The Spacial Evolution," p. 7.

is a compatability with similar perspectives on individual loyalties as shifting from primordial to national attachments.[25]

The assumption that barriers to modernization are related to the continuity of regionalism seems reasonable. At the same time, it is hardly adequate as an explanation of those situations in the western world where regional divisions are still highly salient. Why does de-regionalization not appear to be an inevitable feature of national development? A search for more specific answers can be approached through Cox's model of the nationalization and deregionalization of voting patterns. Although we are concerned with the total complex of regional relevance, Cox's theory still provides a useful baseline from which to proceed. It is all the more pertinent since he makes many of the same assumptions as we do about the broader significance of voting, as well as reinforcing our inclination to see regionalism as an essentially political phenomenon.

According to Cox's model, deregionalization of voting patterns will occur where information exchanges are high, resistance to information is low, birth-death processes give a demographic advantage to those groups that set the national pattern, and population mobility is high. We would predict that the coincidence of these conditions would lead to a decline in the salience of regional divisions generally. But paradoxically, we would not be surprised to find these conditions accompanying continued regional cleavages. What is required is a reexamination of the assumptions made in using these four variables, along with a search for alternative or additional factors with greater predictive power.

Of the four variables, the consequences of information flow are most questionable. Cox's assumption is that the spread of information provides a milieu in which behaviour is more likely to be altered. But this same information can reinforce previously held views, as so many studies of the relation between personal contacts, the mass media, and partisanship have shown.[26] At a common-sense level, we expect understanding to be associated with acceptance: it was Madame de Stael's dictum that "to know all, is to forgive all." Yet it is too easy to generalize this to all human relations. Knowledge helps to dispel prejudice, but it as readily provides the rationale for prejudice.[27] In terms of regional cleavages, knowledge of conditions in other areas

---

25. See Clifford Geertz, "The Integrative Revolution," in C. Geertz, ed., *Old Societies and New States* (New York: Free Press, 1963), pp. 105-57.

26. Elihu Katz and Paul F. Lazarsfeld, *Personal Influence* (New York: Free Press, 1955).

27. Mildred A. Schwartz, *Trends in White Attitudes Toward Negroes* (Chicago: National Opinion Research Center, 1967), pp. 119-20.

and how they compare with those in one's own may be just what is needed to arouse a sense of regional identity. Parallel notions of class consciousness and relative deprivation also are premised on the importance of a cognitive dimension for contrast conceptions.

Resistance to information as a barrier to deregionalization rests on the premise that existing social ties, such as those of class or language, hinder the free exchange of information. To the extent that population groups are not evenly distributed throughout the society, but have greater concentration in some regions, these social ties reinforce regional divisions. Even though the unrestricted flow of information may not always have nationalizing consequences, its absence does not have the opposite effect. Restrictions on communication associated with the uneven dispersion of ethnic and class groups are a primary source of regional divisiveness.

The expectation that population subgroups will have differential birth and death rates leads to the prediction that party supporters in a given area have greater or less chance of reproducing themselves. From the perspective of deregionalizing voting patterns, Cox predicts that the process will be encouraged where localistic parties are depleted through an imbalance in net replacement rates. It is not difficult to extend this generalization to other subgroups, and to regions as a whole. That is, regional cleavages may be sustained through demographic tenacity, or lost through lack of it. The spectre of decline may in itself be a powerful stimulus to conflict. In Belgium, the population of what is now defined as Wallonia declined from 39 percent in 1910 to 33 percent in 1961, while that of Flanders increased from 47 to 51 percent in that same time span. This has accompanied exacerbated tensions between Walloons and Flemings, as the former see their dominant, though never majority, status threatened by loss of numbers as well as by the economic decline of their region.[28]

Shifting voting patterns will also follow from the relocation of voters. This may come about in several ways. The population could be redistributed with equal probabilities of partisanship or voting changes occurring in all regions. Mobility could result in conversion, so that migrants become like those they live amongst, exchanging their former statuses and behaviour patterns for new ones. This would result in deregionalization only if population exchanges among regions were not equal, and particularly if the most parochial regions suffered greatest net loss of population. Another alternative would be for out-migration to be greater for the most parochial, even if not accom-

28. Val Lorwin, "Belgium: Religion, Class, and Language in National Politics," in Robert A. Dahl, ed., *Political Oppositions in Western Democracies* (New Haven: Yale University Press, 1966), pp. 171-72.

panied by any conversion. The end result would still be the same as long as the migrants remained a minority in the host region, unable in the aggregate to affect election outcomes or similar group decisions. Mobility, however, can be associated with the reinforcement of regional cleavages. Movement can be temporary, it can be almost solely instrumental, done regretfully, under duress of economic necessity. The new place of residence may then be viewed with ambivalence. Where this occurs, population mobility may bring about some de-regionalization without the forging of nation-wide ties. But perhaps the greatest impact of mobility results from the differences between migrants and those who remain at home. Not the least of these is a different commitment to the area of origin. In other words, if those who stay behind have the strongest attachment to their region, then migration may actually reinforce regional cleavages.

From Cox's model we can derive one principal component by which to account for the relevance of territorial divisions. It is a demographic one, subsuming population composition, rate of natural increase, and geographic mobility. To the extent that there are discernible compositional differences among regions, and that these are reinforced both by natural increase and migration patterns, regionalism will continue to be an important social and political force. Where compositional differences are eroded by differential fertility and mortality and by the nature of migration flows, then we expect the significance of territorial divisions to decline as well.

Over sixty years ago, Frederick Jackson Turner predicted,

> that as the nation reaches a more stable equilibrium, a more settled state of society, with denser populations pressing upon the means of existence, with this population no longer migratory, the influence of the diverse physiographic provinces which make up the nation will become more marked. They will exercise sectionalizing influences, tending to mold society to their separate conditions, in spite of all the countervailing tendencies toward national uniformity. National action will be forced to recognize and adjust itself to these conflicting sectional interests.[29]

Turner, as we would expect from the exponent of the frontier theory of American development, gave primacy to the consequences of population movement in detracting from regional divisiveness. We have already suggested how such mobility, whether or not to a frontier, may not always contribute to this effect. But even more important than the possible consequences of mobility or the lack of it, is Turner's

---

29. Frederick J. Turner, "Is Sectionalism in America Dying Away?," *American Journal of Sociology,* 13 (March, 1908): 675.

recognition that regions have enduring qualities that set them apart from each other. In his language, "Geographical conditions and the stocks from which the people sprang are the most fundamental factors in shaping sectionalism. Of these the geographical influence is peculiarly important in forming a society like that of the United States, for it includes in its influence those factors of economic interests, as well as the environmental conditions that affect the psychology of a people."[30] Mobility could conceivably wash out the influences of particular population groups, at least insofar as they were able to operate from a territorial base. It would be possible, for example, for Canada to face problems of language rights for the English- and French-speaking without either group being concentrated in one or more provinces. But no matter how much population mixing occurred, and it is unlikely that it would ever be complete, this in itself would not detract from regional singularity stemming from geographic and economic conditions. It is these which assure the continuity of regionalism. Only when steps are taken to eradicate them, or to make the resulting inequalities less painful, can we be certain that territorial divisiveness will abate.

JUDGING THE SIGNIFICANCE OF REGION

It is possible to divide most nation-states into smaller territorial units. Having done so, are we merely left with geographic demarcations without much further relevance, or have we established a major source of continuing political tension? Writers in the field have provided some clues for recognizing importance, but their generalizations do not always apply to the broad range of situations where region may appear. What is needed is a systematic way of assessing the importance of regions at a given point in time and for predicting their future importance. In order to deal with these issues in Canada, we have formulated eight sets of conditions which, if satisfied, would contribute to the salience of region. They also have predictive power for determining the continued significance of regional divisions. While these are confined to Canada in their use as organizing themes in the following chapters, each set of conditions is of sufficient generality to apply across nations.

Economy

The first set of conditions relates to the economy. The economic base of an area, no matter how it is later elaborated, is initially tied to

---

30. Ibid., 662.

pre-existing resources. In the early stages of economic development, dependence on the resources at hand is almost absolute. Associated advantages and disadvantages tend to perpetuate themselves, though they are not irreversible. Change comes from technological advances in the development of new sources of energy, new products and industries, and the depletion of resources. The economic development of an area is also related to its general power, in the sense that it has control over the exploitation of its own resources. To compare regions, we need to evaluate the economy with respect to available resources and the ability to fully use them. In the modern world this means that the signs of a developed economy include heavy reliance on secondary industry.

The industrial composition of an economy bears on the makeup of its labour force. This is reflected not only in the occupations directly connected with existing industries, but also in supportive and service occupations. Again this gives us a measure of the relative modernity and level of industrialization of regions. Taken together, the industrial and occupational structures underlie the class system of an area. They also affect the nature of economic outputs, both for the industries and for the rewards obtained by individual workers. Industry, occupation, and workers' rewards do not always fit perfectly, and as we see in the following chapter, reveal regional differences that are otherwise inexplicable without the attribution of an independent effect from region itself.

People

What the land holds is primary; what is done with it depends on human resources. Hence the nature of the population is temporally second only to basic resources. The relations between man and his environment contribute to the overall economic structure, and with it, to the resulting class system. If the economic bases of regions vary, we can also expect variation in class structure. The coincidence of regional and class interests will enhance regional relevance.

Independently of class, the composition of regional population is significant for its contribution to particularistic cultural heritages. Where regional demarcations are associated with differences based on religion, national origin, or language, region as an important aspect of political existence becomes enhanced. Wherever origin and social class become interrelated within a territorial context, regional distinctiveness will be even further accentuated.

Quality of Life

The services and amenities available and the prevalent styles of life make up another set of conditions which may vary on a territorial axis. Important examples are the availability of health services, the quality of education, and the means for communicating. Related are such style-setting factors as the levels of education normally attained by the population, the likelihood of exposure to an urban environment, and population movements between parts of the country. Taken together, they contribute to the quality of life which either sets regions apart from each other or provides them with common experiences.

In some ways, urbanization operates as a causal force, creating the conditions making for better and more widely available health and educational services, and communication media. A better educated population also makes greater demands for the provision of health services and greater use of the means of communication. To the extent that urban areas generally have more advantages, they serve as magnets for a mobile population. Mobility in itself extends the networks of communication, ensuring that both stable and mobile groups will, in contact, be exposed to broader experiences.

However we choose to measure quality of life, it is apparent that it is made up of interrelated elements. But it is also related to characteristics of the economy and the population. For example, wealthier areas have more to spend on health services. But it is also true that people vary in the importance they attach to scientific medicine. This is partly a result of their level of education, but also of more general values about the nature of disease, suffering, and so forth. To illustrate such connections further, we know that the occupational structure is strongly linked with the educational system, the latter providinging the skills required for employment. But education has some independent effects, putting pressures on the occupational structure through the spread of new ideas, technologies, and skills. Where particular ethnic groups have differential access to education, either through some form of discrimination or because of values placed on formal training, the links between population characteristics, occupation, and education are strengthened, and with it the creation of an ethnically–tied class structure. As a final illustration, we note that migration rates are largely dependent on job opportunities, linking the industrial and occupational structure with the mobility of the population. At the same time, among the significant factors influencing movement, are values associated with the desirability of migration. These in turn may have roots in the cultural life of a group, either inhibiting or enhancing the likelihood of movement. From the perspective of regional divisions, what is crucial is how such movement affects the cultural homogeneity of territorial units.

These are only some examples of the possible interconnections between population, economy, and quality of life. They illustrate that even where each of the three associated sets of conditions operates independently as a source of regional differentiation, there are also likely to be important interactive effects. But whatever the processes, it is the end results which are of concern. At issue is the extent to which economy, population, and quality of life, either singly or in combination, produce regional differences. The greater the differences they cause, the greater the likelihood that region will be a significant dimension of political life. For Canada we deal with the three sets of conditions in Chapter 2.

Power

The political power that any region is able to mobilize may range from zero to some positive amount. Power will be virtually absent where there are no channels through which a single region can make known its demands or influence the outcome of political decisions. In some political systems, there may be no legitimate channels of influence, but power still exists and operates clandestinely, through passive resistance, organized or isolated acts of terror, or other such means. In other situations, regional interests are formally recognized. One characteristic means is through a federal system of government, in which national and local governments each have their sphere of influence. The existence of such formal channels and a comparison of the range of autonomy given to regional governments is one criterion of the ability of region to affect politics.

Another way of viewing power as a differentiated resource is through a comparison of the ways in which regions participate in the national government. A full rationale for this approach is given in Chapter 3, where we examine differences among Canadian regions in their share of the national power. Our thesis there is that popular support and representation in the crucial decision-making groups, with slightly more weight to be attributed to the latter, give a measure of regional power. The relationship is a direct one, with greater support and greater representation associated with greater power. Our assumption is that if there is a differential distribution of power, this will be experienced as an important part of regional existence. As such, this should be one of the causal forces in making and continuing regional divisions.

Power, as it is conceived here, is a distinct dimension of possible regional variation, independent from any others. Yet we should not overlook the possibility of overlaps and linkages. Most apparent is the tie between support and population. Other things being equal, more populous areas will give more support and be entitled to more representation. To some extent, influence will lie with those who have the most votes. But population density in itself may not be a major criterion in the formation of governments, for reasons we explore in

Chapter 3. Politics is not just a numbers game; the rewards go to those who know how to use whatever resources they have. These may, for example, be economic as much as demographic. We should at least be sensitive to such possible associations.

Party Systems

Parties can play a unique role in mobilizing and organizing the needs and demands of isolated individuals and groups, and in transforming these into authoritative and binding decisions. From our perspective, they have particular potency as vehicles for expressing demands of a regional character to the national government. While there is a current tendency to downgrade the importance of political parties as leadership agents, particularly as they operate in the United States (and it is probably true that politics in that country, in recurring cycles, reflects the negation of party rule), both the real and the potential political capacity of parties remains basically unchallenged.[31]

Throughout this volume, our interest in parties lies in their comparative ability to deal with the tensions between regional and national interests. Parties appear in our model twice; we are first concerned with the effects stemming from the nature of the party system, and later, with the impact of party actions and partisan behaviour. Here we ask whether the party system operates within each region so as to give voters the same kinds of choices. Specifically, the question is whether parties of the same number, type, and ultimately, of the same name, are evenly distributed across regions. If they are not, then to the extent that they are avenues for channelling public demands, residents of different regions will have differential access to these means of influence. The results are another form of regional cleavage. The manner in which this is manifested in Canada is described in Chapter 6.

It is apparent that regional differences in party systems will not suddenly emerge, without regard to prior conditions. One source of difference could be constitutional and legislative patterns that are regionally specific. But as we will see in the case of Canada, there may be no constitutional provisions for any kind of party system, while precedent would seem to presume a common experience. Where differences do exist, especially where these have emerged without constitutional provision, we may assume underlying differences in political traditions and in the social and political problems that parties are called upon to handle. Such assumptions, of course, need also to be tested.

---

31. Walter Dean Burnham, "The End of American Political Parties," *Trans action*, 7 (December, 1969): 12-22.

Perceptions

The foregoing conditions all deal with aspects of the social and political systems of regions. The remaining three more properly relate to characteristics of individuals that, collectively, become properties of regions. They do so only in the sense that they are representative of majorities, or at least numerically dominant groups, in each area.

The first set of relevant conditions linked to individuals concerns evaluations of self and others. To the extent that regions enjoy different advantages, their divisions are politically relevant. Our thesis here is that these circumstances may or may not be accurately perceived. Of the possible factors affecting the fit between reality and perceptions, two are especially pertinent. One is obviously the objective conditions themselves, which may be described as the reality factor. Second are the distorting factors, which could be either collective or idiosyncratic. Though the latter are undoubtedly important, they do not concern us here. Our interest is in group-related factors affecting perceptions. In the following discussion we explore the alternative relationships and the implications these are likely to have for continuing regional differences.

It is possible for an outside observer to describe regional differences based on economic, demographic, or political criteria without these being recognized or acknowledged by the respective residents. Such a levelling of distinctions could come about where there are strongly shared values supporting identities that cut across regional lines. These identities can be national in scope, in which case they are likely to be strongest during times of external or internal threat, when crises are present that affect almost everyone equally. On the other hand, where more particularistic identities are prominent, such as those related to social class or religion, these lack a territorial base. Whatever form these overriding or cross-cutting loyalties assume, we are also alerted to the nature of communication in such national settings, since it would apparently operate to prevent the spread of information about regional differences. The consequences of perceptual levelling would be a form of regional "false consciousness." Lack of recognition of regional inequalities would then be a major handicap in mobilizing the public to press for action on regionally defined interests.

Even though regional differences could be minor, it might generally be believed that they were extensive. This could come about if perceptions were attuned to objective conditions at some earlier time. Circumstances may have altered, but beliefs about them persist. Even without such historical precedent, strong regional consciousness can exist without the support of objective inequalities, but this is likely to be true only where there is some recognizable source of difference.

The most appropriate form would be linked to population character-istics, primarily those of origin, whereby those who bear them and are concentrated in one or more regions develop a minority group consciousness. In other words, regional consciousness would be an outgrowth of some other identity that had, more or less adventitiously, a territorial base. Under these circumstances, it is difficult to antici-pate the consequences of regional differentiation based almost solely on perceptions. If it were associated with minority status, it could have considerable impact. If it were the outgrowth of conditions that had existed at an earlier time, then at least the continuity of regionalism would be in question. W. I. Thomas laid down the sociological prin-ciple that "If men define situations to be real, they are real in their consequences." No doubt this has considerable truth behind it, but as a basis of prolonged social organization and action, it seems to be tenuous. We anticipate that perceptions without the support of reality will not have more than a passing impact, except when they become institutionalized.

Assuming that regional differences exist and that these are per-ceived, there are still three alternatives. One is a perfect mesh be-tween conditions and their evaluation. In this instance, no distortion is introduced through group ties. Differences could also be either under or overestimated. The significance of such "errors" depends on the objects that are being judged. If, for example, residents of a region evaluate their own situation as more favourable than it is, an opti-mistic perspective predominates that may hinder political concern with the need for change. This is especially likely where the over-estimate is accompanied by an undervaluing of the benefits of other regions. Self-centredness, in other words, can lead to the view that regional differentiation has taken an ideal form. An underestimation of one's own region is associated with a pessimistic outlook. Where residents feel particularly deprived in comparison with other areas, there is a precondition for political alienation. This in turn can lead to active efforts to bring about changes or to passive withdrawal in the face of apparently insurmountable obstacles. In either case, optimism or pessimism combines reality factors and some aspect of the regional environment affecting outlooks.

Chapters 4 and 5 in this volume are concerned with such percep-tions in Canada. Data for them were obtained from a national prob-ability sample of voters, interviewed after the 1965 federal election. The rationale for the study, the participants, and other pertinent de-tails are included in the preface to this volume. A description of the sample is given in Chapter 4, when we first make use of it.

Orientations

The ways in which citizens orient themselves to their political milieu is another possible dimension of regional differentiation. By this we mean that the questions people ask about their own political power and about the ways in which the government carries out its activities can be answered differently, depending on where one lives. Differences can arise from regional variations in the political system or from the unique attributes of individuals. The latter again will not be examined here. But even where there is a common political system, orientations to the polity can take on a regional hue as a result of either prevailing objective conditions, particularly with regard to the exercise of power and the party system, or of regionally-specific perceptions of these conditions. The likelihood of regional political orientations will be greater where both objective conditions and perceptions of them contributed to regional divisiveness.

The presence of such orientations makes its contribution to regionalism by providing a differentiated framework both for explaining political events and rationalizing political behaviour. Where explanations and rationales differ, the conduct of politics itself takes on distinctive manners. This does not mean, for example, that government personnel necessarily behave differently in different regions, but that residents behave differently *toward* them. Universalistic standards of government may be true initially; but once the chain begins, we can be sure that those who are subject to specific orientations also begin to alter their behaviour in conformity with expectations. The political orientations of Canadians have been gleaned from our 1966 survey. They are a major focus of this volume, covering Chapters 7 to 10.

Political Behaviour

We view political behaviour as, in a sense, the outcome of the preceding seven sets of conditions. Put in its simplest terms, if region matters politically, this will be revealed behaviourally. Relevant behaviour may be ascribed to a large number of actors: those who operate within the federal and provincial arenas, those who operate within government and outside it, and those who act or do not on the basis of a recognized and overt partisan affiliation. Given the scope of this volume, we will concentrate solely on the national arena, and deal only with partisans.

A large number of possible actions also reflect regionalism. Certain alternatives are proscribed by law, making them neither feasible nor legitimate. Yet illegitimate forms of behaviour are as relevant as legitimate ones, and with regard to regionalism, such activities as the organization of secessionist movements are primary examples of the tie between region and political behaviour. Within the realm of what is considered legitimate, actions may have either a direct or indirect impact on regional cleavages. We consider activities of government manifestly linked to the interests of one or more regions to exemplify direct actions. We treat voting as an example of indirect actions. This assumes voting to be a crucial indicator of both demands on the political system and the giving or withholding of support, resulting in a perspective on regional cleavages that emphasizes mass responses.

Out of the range of possible actions, our approach stresses the legitimate and indirect. A primary focus is on party behaviour as it is manifested through the beliefs and actions of supporters. In a few instances, party behaviour is viewed through the activities of party leaders. The behaviour of voters is considered independently as well, with respect to the way in which their support patterns influence regionalism.

Linking Conditions and Regionalism

Regionalism, as a manifestation of politically-mobilized territorial cleavages, occurs where the previously described eight sets of conditions are present. In accounting for the emergence and continuity of regionalism, we have progressed to a complex causal model. It attempts simultaneously to link demographic, social structural, and social psychological factors and processes, each with more or less important historical dimensions. This model developed from what was essentially an intuitive recognition of genuine linkages among the eight sets of conditions. Later, reading Stinchcombe's work on complex causal structures, a way of making visible the connections was suggested.[32] We show this in Chart 1–1. The chart is presented without the thought that it is necessarily fully compatible with Stinchcombe's thinking. It is simply a useful device for drawing together all

Chart 1–1   **The conditions for territorial cleavages.**

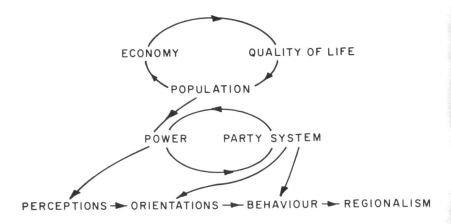

32. Arthur L. Stinchcombe, *Constructing Causal Theories* (New York: Harcourt, Brace and World, Inc., 1968), pp. 57-148.

the components, both to help visualize their interconnections and to emphasize our treatment of all of them at the same level of analysis.

Some links may seem to be more direct than the graph shows, but in fact the graph does not deny this; it is simply a means of demonstrating, in what should be an easily understood way, the dominant connections. The arrows linking variables are "operators," the conditions acting on one variable to translate it into another. In all instances, the operator in our conceptualization is regional differentiation. That is, where a variable is distinguished by regional differences, we expect it to have an impact on another set of conditions, and ultimately, on the existence of regionalism. Creation of the chart has required some simplification of the processes involved in the real world. While all arrows point in a single direction in our graph, this does not mean that there cannot be more reciprocal influences than those indicated. Yet, though such mutual influences may exist, they are subordinate to the principal direction of the effects shown. The greatest loss is the concept of time. The historical dimension, so important to our thinking, cannot be represented in any convenient fashion.

To speak of regionalism as the end result of eight sets of conditions still leaves undefined the relative importance of each of the components. In most discussions of causal relationships, it is common to ask whether component parts are necessary and/or sufficient conditions for a given outcome. For us, the question is whether all eight forms of regional differentiation need to be present in order to have regionalism. Alternatively, could some conditions be absent without affecting its existence? Or, in the absence of some conditions, is the result a weaker form of regionalism? As Blalock points out, one of the difficulties in using notions of necessary and sufficient relationships is that they imply a simple dichotomy of existence or non-existence. Yet in real life these extreme situations are rarely present. For this reason Blalock counsels the rejection of such either-or formulations and the consideration of conditions as continuous variables rather than dichotomous attributes.[33] This perspective is certainly compatible with the kinds of conditions we are talking about. But its adoption requires that we face up to some problems in our conceptualization of regionalism. For each set of conditions, our measure of relevance is the existence of regional differentiation. Since it is possible to have more or less differentiation, we are left to speak of more or less regionalism. Is this a reasonable formulation? Our judgment is that, at some times at least, it may be appropriate, though quite unnecessary at others.

The differentiated quality of regionalism can be grasped if we view

---

33. Hubert M. Blalock, Jr., *Causal Inferences in Nonexperimental Research* (Chapel Hill: University of North Carolina Press, 1964), pp. 30-32.

it as a principle of inequality. What this means is that whenever political actors (and obviously, the more critical their position in the social structure, the more impact they will have) use regionalism as a guide to decision-making, the differences will be preserved or strengthened. In other words, regionalism enters the political process as a means of continuing existing differences, either in the pre-existing conditions or in other areas of life.

In some areas, regional differences are clearly linked to inequalities. For example, the character of the economy, quality of life, and power can be ranked along a single dimension of advantage. For the individual, unless he is committed to some Thoreau-like concept of society, such conditions represent relative states of desirability. Regionalism will be strongest where such inequalities are most apparent, and where political actions do little to reduce them.

In other areas, the relationship between differences and inequalities is not so clear. It might be thought that ethnically homogeneous societies are more stable than poly-ethnic ones. Where multiple ethnic groups are present, political stress is less where groups are equally dispersed through all regions, rather than geographically concentrated. But from the perspective of the individual, especially one with a committed ethnic identity, a regional locus is the most satisfactory way of living his ethnic experience. While uneven concentrations of ethnic groups are not always felt to be undesirable, they are almost invariably a source of tension. One reason for this is that geographic concentration encourages cultural bonds that increase within-group communication to the detriment of that with outsiders. The probability of a regional group-consciousness then becomes enhanced, and with it, the likelihood of perceiving objective inequalities. Translating this back to regionalism, we predict that differences based on such population characteristics promote stronger regionalism, the more the areas differ from each other. In turn, regionalism operates where political decisions serve to further these differences.

The implications of these differences for other spheres of life are even less clear. That the number and kind of political parties varies by region, or that residents collectively differ in their views of the political process, is not in itself either good or bad, nor an unequivocal source of inequality. But the result is still important, since it creates the environment for regional group-consciousness and for the mobilization of political action on the basis of regional, as opposed to any overriding national, interests. In this sense too, greater differentiation should mean stronger regionalism. Political decisions that serve to protect and increase these differences are a manifestation of such regionalism.

Despite what might be interpreted as the pretentions of our chart, we have not yet arrived at a precise definition of regionalism or its preconditions. We see regionalism as an abstraction for subsuming a configuration of many coexisting elements. It is a combination of elements, linked in varying ways within territorial units, that region-alism achieves its emergent qualities. Just exactly what these are con-tinues to be elusive. At the least we know that regionalism is a property of a total society, deriving from a variation in the differences in its constituent parts. Regions can differ from each other to varying degrees, but the more they do, the more we can be sure that the overall consequence is a territorially-divided society.

The selection of conditions for the existence of regionalism was made, to some extent, with the thought of their appropriateness for a description of Canada. But we are convinced that they are in no way culturally-bound.

CHAPTER

$$2$$

Life in the provinces: as it is

Canada covers a vast land mass – 3,852,000 square miles. Within its boundaries are frozen wastes and temperate regions, suitable for all but tropical vegetation; flat prairies and soaring mountains; densely populated cities and great stretches of empty land; the poverty and the richness of nature.[1]

The physical aspects of diversity concern us here primarily insofar as they influence the social diversity of life in the provinces, and affect the activities and benefits dependent on a particular physical environment.

Regional diversity derives from three sources. The evolution of the physical characteristics now contained in the political state has resulted in a differential dispersion of resources and climatic conditions. The consequences are so obvious, we sometimes forget their implications. But the presence or absence of oil, gas, coal, minerals, particular soil conditions, rivers, and lakes, all condition to an important extent the potential wealth of a specific area, regardless of anything else. At a second level, diversity in life styles were established from the outset of settlement, when groups with distinctive characteristics made their homes in some areas rather than others. Finally varying conditions have emerged as a result of the differential process of urbanization and technological development. The time at which all of these began

---

1. The reader who requires empirical evidence should consult Donald F. Putnam, ed., *Canadian Regions,* 2nd ed. (Toronto: J. M. Dent & Sons, 1954); P. Camu, E. P. Weeks, Z. W. Sametz, *Economic Geography of Canada* (Toronto: Macmillan, 1964).

varies greatly. Moreover, the continuity of their significance is also variable. At least some factors, then, need to be treated historically, along a time dimension. The following discussion treats separately the three factors making up regional diversity: the economic structure, the people, and the quality of life.

THE ECONOMY

A full-fledged discussion and analysis of the regional basis of Canada's economic structure is the task of economists, and there is no plan here to trespass into others' fields. The reader must find other sources for a detailed exposition of this topic.[2] At a more superficial level, however, sufficient material is provided to demonstrate the nature of economic differences among regions. This includes discussion of available resources and industries, the occupational structure, and financial rewards.

Canada began as a resource-producing country. Its wealth has continued to come in large measure from staple products, the recognition of which fact has provided the basis for the reputation of some of its major economists. But Canada quite evidently is an industrialized society, and as such, has channelled increasingly more of its economic output into secondary and tertiary industries. For example, in 1941, 37 percent of the male labour force was engaged in primary industries. In 1961, it was 16 percent. But as in other aspects of life, the move to modernization has affected each region differently.

The Prairies derive the majority of their wealth from commodity-producing industries in primary resources.[3] These are first agriculture, and then mining and refining, the latter of major importance in Alberta. The Atlantic provinces are next in their dependence on resources, with fairly equal distribution among all the major primary industries. British Columbia ranks third in this respect, with an espe-

---

2. Three particularly useful sources are R. D. Howland, *Some Regional Aspects of Canada's Economic Development,* Royal Commission on Canada's Economic Prospects (Ottawa: Queen's Printer, 1958); George W. Wilson, Scott Gordon and Stanislaw Judek, *Canada: An Appraisal of its Needs and Resources* (New York and Toronto: Twentieth Century Fund and University of Toronto Press, 1965); T. N. Brewis, *Regional Economic Policies in Canada* (Toronto: Macmillan, 1969).

3. Data are for 1960, based on figures published in Canada, Dominion Bureau of Statistics, *Canada Year Book, 1962* (Ottawa: Queen's Printer, 1963), pp. 1068-73. We use these data since they provide the context for our 1966 survey. In addition, the relative position of regions, with respect to dependence on primary or secondary industry, remains the same.

cially large share of its wealth coming from forestry. The central provinces are quite similar, and together represent by far the most industrialized region of Canada. Moreover, approximately two-thirds of their wealth comes from manufacturing, with construction contributing about one-sixth to the output from secondary industries. In other less industrialized regions, construction adds about one-quarter to total output.

In each of six areas of commodity production—agriculture, forestries, mining, electric power, manufacturing, construction—Ontario and Quebec together contribute at least 40 percent of the total value. In the case of manufacturing industries, this is over 80 percent. The contrast with the Atlantic provinces is dramatic. While the home of about 10 percent of the Canadian population, the Atlantic region characteristically contributes proportionately much less to its share of the national wealth. Fisheries are the major exception, more than half of which are located in the eastern provinces. The area is, however, underdeveloped in electric power and highly deficient in secondary industry. The Prairies make their major contribution to agriculture, mining, and refining.[4] British Columbia follows the Atlantic provinces in fisheries and has a dominant role in the forestry industry. It has about 9 percent of the population, and hence its 11.6 percent share of electric power production slightly exceeds the minimal expected contribution, while it makes about what expected to manufacturing and perhaps a little more than anticipated to construction.

Rewards

Given these structural differences, it is not surprising that there are large and continuing differences in the economic rewards enjoyed in each region. Yet a full accounting of why these disparities persist has yet to be produced. In a recent study prepared for the Economic Council of Canada, Frank Denton reports, ". . . one cannot go far in accounting for basic differences in levels of earnings in terms of mere statistical differences in industrial and occupational distributions, age composition, hours and weeks of work, average levels of education,

---

4. Differences in occupational distribution within the three Prairie provinces have suggested that it is perhaps misleading to treat them as a unit. See Donald L. Mills, "The Occupational Composition of the Prairie Provinces: A Regional-National Comparison," *Transactions of the Royal Society of Canada,* vol. VI, series IV (June 1968): 229-43. A major difference is in the percent employed in agriculture. Yet since Mills reports, in Tables 1 and 10, that despite such within-group variation, there are significantly more engaged in agriculture than is true for the national norm, this objection need not influence our grouping procedure.

and rural-urban population distribution."[5] That is, while earnings are higher for better educated people, certain industries and occupations, and in cities, these factors in themselves account for but some of the regional variations in earnings, although areas differ to the extent that they have these more favoured characteristics. Economists, then, are far from satisfied that they know how to explain earning levels. What is unequivocal, however, is the differential in earned income. For example, in Table 2–1 we see that the Atlantic provinces represent only 66 percent of the average earned income per person between 1961 and 1964 for all of Canada. This contrasts with 113 percent for British Columbia and 118 percent for Ontario. Both the Prairies and Quebec are lower than these two provinces, but still considerably better off than the eastern provinces.

Despite these qualifications on the explanatory force of present analyses, we do have considerable data on the correlates of better or worse economic situations. Denton lists six characteristics related to the particularly unfavourable position of the Atlantic provinces.[6] These include a very high rate of unemployment. For example, between 1951 and 1955, when the national level of unemployment was only 3.3 percent of the labour force, in the Atlantic provinces it was 5.5 percent. In 1961, a period of some recession (the national unemployment rate was 7.2 percent), the Atlantic provinces suffered from a rate of 11.1 percent.[7] These provinces were also characterized by an

Table 2–1 **Earned Income per Person (1961-64 Averages)**

	Average Earned Income per Person	Regional Average as % of Canadian Average
CANADA	$1312	100.0%
Atlantic	863	65.8
Quebec	1139	86.8
Ontario	1543	117.6
Prairies	1302	99.2
British Columbia	1483	113.0

Source: Frank T. Denton, *An Analysis of Interregional Differences in Manpower Utilization and Earnings,* Staff Study no. 15, Economic Council of Canada (Ottawa: Queen's Printer, April 1966), p. 2.

5. Frank T. Denton, *An Analysis of Interregional Differences in Manpower Utilization and Earnings,* Staff Study no. 15, Economic Council of Canada (Ottawa: Queen's Printer, April 1966).

6. Ibid. The following discussion is based almost entirely on the Denton report.

7. Canada, Dominion Bureau of Statistics, *Unemployment in Canada,* Bulletin 71-503 (Ottawa: April 1962).

unfavourable age structure, having a greater proportion of their population in the non-productive ages under fifteen than any other region
in Canada. Moreover, the percentage of the adult population in the
labour force, whether employed or not, was lower than for any other
part of the country. The 1961-64 labour force participation rate was
47.4 for the Atlantic provinces, compared to 54.0 for the country as
a whole. While some of the difference was attributable to a particularly
low participation rate among women, men too were less likely to be
in the labour force. Seasonality of employment, a feature of life in
Canada that continues despite technological innovation, is especially
irksome in the eastern provinces. "It is estimated that the average
number of persons with jobs in the period 1961-1964 would have
been higher by some 280,000 or about 4½ percent had it not been
for seasonal declines. In the Atlantic Region, employment would have
been about 8½ percent higher, reflecting the impact of winter conditions on the primary industries which constitute a very important
part of the total economic activity in this region."[8] With respect to
education as well, the Atlantic region was at a disadvantage. At the
time of the 1961 census, 50 percent of all Canadian males fifteen years
of age and older and no longer at school had no more than an elementary school education. In the Atlantic provinces, it was 56 percent.
Four percent of this same population had university degrees in the
nation as a whole, but only 2 percent did so in the east. (See also Table
2–4, where reference is to both males and females, and the disadvantage of a low level of education in Quebec looms larger. However,
Quebec was clearly among the advantaged provinces with regard to
the proportion with university education.) Finally, an exceptionally
large proportion, 42 percent of the population, resided in rural, non-
farm areas, which typically have low income levels. Only 19 percent
of the total Canadian population lived in such population centres.
(Compare with Chart 2–2, which shows trends in levels of urbanization.)

All of the factors listed, which illustrate the disadvantaged economic
situation of the Atlantic provinces, were exactly reversed in Ontario.
Unemployment rates were low and labour force participation high.
Ontario had 32.6 percent of its women in the labour force at the time
of the census, the highest rate for the country. It had the largest share
of the population in the most productive ages of fifteen to sixty-four.
The province was the most highly urbanized, enjoyed a fairly high
education level, and was minimally subject to seasonal fluctuations.

British Columbia was also among the highly advantaged provinces.
It had, in fact, the highest basic earning rate in Canada. For the
period 1961-64, the average earned income per person employed was

8. Denton, *Analysis of Interregional Differences*, pp. 6-7.

$4,331, compared to $4,113 for Ontario. But because participation rates were lower, both for men and women, partly because of the highest proportion of any province having a population of sixty-five years of age and older, and unemployment rates higher (8.5 in 1961 compared to 5.5 in Ontario), earned income per person was lower than in Ontario.

Quebec was also affected by the factors plaguing the Atlantic region, but not nearly so severely. High unemployment, seasonality of work, and low levels of education all contributed to low average earnings. Denton implies that other factors were likely also involved, but does not yet have the kind of data which would account for these.

Except for seasonal fluctuations related to agriculture, the Prairies were very close to the Canadian average in most respects.

Denton concludes his analysis with a set of predictions, based on anticipated unemployment rates. His conclusions attest to the stability of economic differences among regions.

> In light of past experience, a relatively low level of unemployment for Canada as a whole would not of itself ensure correspondingly low unemployment levels in all parts of Canada, in particular the Atlantic Region and Quebec. The over-all disparity of income levels among the regions, and especially the gap between the Atlantic Region and the rest of Canada, have proved to be surprisingly stable over several decades in the face of marked changes in the fortunes of the national economy.[9]

The accompanying Chart 2–1 provides clear-cut evidence of the continuity of these regional differences since the 1920s. With the exception of the Prairies, the disparities have remained remarkably constant.[10] The Prairies have, at least in the past, had a more volatile economy affected most sharply by the depression and drought of the 1930s and by the postwar boom, especially the development of the oil and gas industries in Alberta.

PEOPLE

In the centuries of colonial expansion, what is now Canada was the arena for competition and open conflict between England and France. Unlike the British colonies in North America, New France received

---

9. Ibid., p. 15.

10. Such findings have not been unchallenged, as Brewis points out, since they are closely tied to the measures and techniques used. Brewis, *Regional Economic Policies,* pp. 24-28.

Chart 2–1   **Relative levels of per capita income, Canada and regions, 1926–1962**

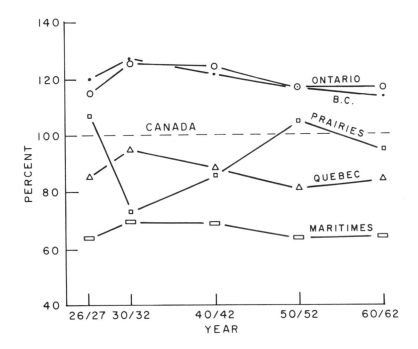

Source: R. Marvin McInnis, "The trend of regional income differentials in Canada," paper presented to the Canadian Political Science Association conference on statistics. (Ottawa: June 1967).

barely a trickle of migrants. The last census of the French regime was taken in 1754, and at that time New France had only one-tenth the population of the neighbouring British colonies. When the French colony was ceded in 1763, the British instituted guarantees of continued French, Catholic existence in the New World. Some of these guarantees were remarkable at that time for their tolerance. Even more remarkable, however, was the unanticipated demographic tenacity of the French.

Since the federation of the colonies in 1867, *the population of French origin has remained at every decennial census within the narrow range between twenty-eight and thirty-one percent of the total,* despite immigration, emigration, differential birth rates, and the addition of six new provinces to the original four. From the standpoint of numbers—and the very

> exactitude of the counting is a testimony to the distinctness of
> the fragments—the balance between the two cultures has
> been stable for the past century.[11]

Given this population stability, it is hardly necessary for us to consider regional variations over time. While these have been important,
at least for the last several decades, that of French origin groups has
remained stable. At the time of the 1961 census, 81 percent of the
population of Quebec was enumerated as having French origin. Moving westward, it was 10 percent in Ontario, 9 in Manitoba, 6 in
Saskatchewan and Alberta, and 4 in British Columbia. Outside of
Quebec, the only sizeable concentration of French origin was in New
Brunswick, where they comprised 39 percent of the total population.

Historically, there have been much greater variations in the proportion and distribution of those who are neither of British nor French
origin. At the first census after Confederation, these other origins
constituted 7 percent of the population: at the 1961 census, they were
26 percent. As the west opened to settlement, it became a home to
people from all parts of the world, including Americans and Canadians. But it was largely European peasants who flocked to the prairie
farmlands, and today, they and their children, along with settlers from
other parts of the world, make up one-half of the population of the
three Prairie provinces. Large-scale migration since World War II has
not affected this area as much as previous waves of immigrants. The
majority of these recent migrants have gone to Ontario, and about
one-quarter to Quebec and British Columbia. The results have been
an appreciable change in the ethnic composition only of Ontario and
British Columbia. In 1941, 18 percent of the Ontario population was
neither British nor French; in 1961 it was 30 percent. During the
same time span, British Columbia changed from 27 to 37 percent
other origins.

The Atlantic provinces were the most British, having 72 percent
claiming this origin. Quebec, as might be expected, had the least, with
11 percent. Of the remaining regions, the Prairies have 43 percent,
British Columbia 59 percent, and Ontario 60 percent. Groups of
greatest numerical importance in the prairies were Germans, Ukrain-
ians, Scandinavians, Dutch and Poles, in that order. In British Columbia, it was Germans, Scandinavians, and Dutch. Ontario has such a
diversity of groups, few are numerically dominant, but over three
percent of the population other than French or British was German,
Italian, or Dutch.

---

11. Kenneth D. McRae, "The Structure of Canadian History," in Louis
Hartz, *The Founding of New Societies* (New York: Harcourt, Brace & World,
1964), p. 220. Emphasis added. McRae's entire essay provides excellent background to the history of Canada, especially as it relates to this volume.

Related to the ethnic variation of Canada is its religious diversity. The single largest religious denomination is Roman Catholic, representing 46 percent of the population in 1961. The Catholic percentage ranged from 88 in Quebec, 52 in New Brunswick, to 22 in Alberta, and 17 in British Columbia. Conversely, the major Protestant denominations, United Church and Anglican, were not nearly so regionally skewed, except for their minor representation in Quebec. But there was some variation, and this was even more pronounced for the smaller denominations. For example, about 15 percent of the population of New Brunswick and Nova Scotia were Baptist and 9 percent of the Prairies, Lutheran. In the same way that the Prairies are distinctive in ethnic origin, they are distinctive in religious composition. More than three-quarters of all Canadians were either Catholic, Anglican, or United Church, but this was true of only two-thirds of the residents of the Prairie provinces.

The link between population and economic structure is provided by the class system, allocating individuals to a hierarchy of class relations. In industrial societies, class is often described through an examination of the occupational system, and this is also a useful approach for ascertaining whether the Canadian class structure varies by region.[12] Blishen's socio-economic index, constructed by combining an estimate of the prestige ranking of occupations with their associated income and educational levels, provides a short-hand perspective.[13] A summary of these measures for each province, based on 320 predominantly masculine occupations, is given in Table 2–2. Each index gives the average socio-economic status current in a province, allowing us to infer the nature of the class system. A ranking of the indices indicates that those in the Atlantic provinces, on the average, occupied the lowest rungs of the class hierarchy. This is simply an added confirmation of what we already know about the economic circumstances of that area. The same was true, with quite opposite results, for Ontario. In the remaining provinces, however, some additional information was gained in this way. Indices and ranks gave us another view of the uneven development of both Quebec and British Columbia,

---

12. For the importance of occupation as an indicator of the class system, see Peter M. Blau and Otis Dudley Duncan, *The American Occupational Structure* (New York: John Wiley & Sons, 1967), pp. 1-10.

13. Bernard R. Blishen, "A Socio-Economic Index for Occupations in Canada," *Canadian Review of Sociology and Anthropology,* 4 (February 1967): 41-53. Prestige rankings are derived from Peter C. Pineo and John Porter, "Occupational Prestige in Canada," *Canadian Review of Sociology and Anthropology,* 4 February 1967): 24-40. For a somewhat different index, based on the 1951 census, see Bernard R. Blishen, "The Construction and Use of an Occupational Class Scale," *Canadian Journal of Economics and Political Science,* 24 (November 1958): 521-31.

Table 2–2 **Index of Overall Class Position, By Province, 1961**

	Mean Socio-Economic Index of Labour Force Population	Rank in National Class Hierarchy
Newfoundland	35.58	10
Prince Edward Island	35.59	9
Nova Scotia	37.27	7
New Brunswick	36.76	8
Quebec	38.48	5
Ontario	39.61	1
Manitoba	38.78	3
Saskatchewan	38.15	6
Alberta	39.20	2
British Columbia	38.72	4

Source: Adapted from Bernard R. Blishen, "A Socio-Economic Index for Occupations in Canada," *Canadian Review of Sociology and Anthropology,* 4 (February 1967): 53.

where, despite their basic wealth, there were class structures with a relatively large share of low ranking occupations. We also see how grouping into a single region obscures the differences among the three Prairie provinces, not only of the less advantaged position of Saskatchewan but of the high average ranking of Manitoba.

From our perspective, the relation between social class, ethnicity, and region is one of the most interesting issues, but at this time information is quite meagre. We know of the generally high position enjoyed by those of British origin, presumably regardless of where they live. The main contrast was with the French-speaking in Quebec, who despite far-reaching changes in their class composition, were still seriously underrepresented in most high status occupations.[14] This alone has been a major source of discontent among those actively concerned with the revamping of Quebec society.

QUALITY OF LIFE

We have chosen to define quality of life through a number of measures of where and how people live. Primarily these deal with the extent of

14. John Porter, *The Vertical Mosaic,* (Toronto: University of Toronto Press, 1965), p. 94. See also Hubert Guindon, "The Social Evolution of Quebec Reconsidered," *Canadian Journal of Economics and Political Science,* 23 (February 1957): 58-66; Stanley Lieberson, *Language and Ethnic Relations in Canada,* (New York: John Wiley and Sons, 1970).

urbanization and the amenities that go along with this. Also included are facilities conducive to social welfare and the quality of educational opportunities. Education is frequently viewed as an input to the economic system, as one of the components shaping outputs. Our concern will be with variations in attributes of regional education systems themselves as much as with the distribution of persons at different educational levels. Our final indicator of the kind of life basic to a particular region derives from the types of contacts people have with each other. To this end we examine newspaper circulation, ownership of transportation and communication facilities, and interregional mobility. A scrutiny of these items permits us to characterize regions, and the degree of isolation and attractiveness allotted to their residents. Isolation means a limited exposure to experiences outside the confines of a narrow geographic area, and a consequent lack of these stimulations which encourage critical self-examination, adoption of new ways of doing things, and other types of social change. Attractiveness is a measure of the pull of a province, of its assessment as a good place to live. In a sense then, it tells us how the population generally perceive qualitative differences in regional life styles.

There are, no doubt, many other ways in which as elusive a notion as the quality of life could be viewed. The choices made here have been determined by a desire to find factors which differentiate regions according to access to those experiences which provide a richer, more varied, and more comfortable life. Certainly there is considerable personal judgement here. Not everyone would agree that the indicators used here are truly indicative of the better life: those dedicated to the more traditional, simpler forms of existence would argue exactly the opposite.

There is no easy answer to the critics of the approach taken here. We can only say that most of the elements selected pertain to those amenities which vast numbers of people in all countries assiduously seek to enjoy. The majority may be wrong, but in this context we argue that, wrong or not, they are by their behaviour defining what they personally feel is the better life, and we abide by this definition.

Urbanization

Canada is sharing in the world-wide movement towards increasing ubanization. Despite differences in defining the urban population, it is still possible to conclude that the move to urbanization has been even greater in Canada than in the United States. A forty-year comparison of trends in Canada, shown in Chart 2–2, points up several noteworthy findings. For one thing, Ontario remains the most urbanized, with its share of the population living in communities of 1,000 or more progressing evenly, as along a straight line. Quebec is second and British Columbia third. There is some unevenness in the pattern

Chart 2–2   **Percent of population urban, 1921–1961, Canada
and regions.**

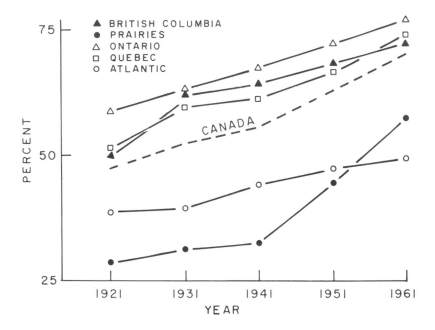

Source: Adapted from Leroy O. Stone, *Urban Development in Canada*
          (Ottawa: Dominion Bureau of Statistics, 1967), p. 29.
Note: "Urban" follows usage in the 1961 Census, as residence in communi-
          ties of 1,000 or larger. Canada excludes Newfoundland, Yukon, and
          Northwest Territories. Atlantic excludes Newfoundland.

of their urbanization, but more revealing is the continuity of the gap
among the three most highly urban provinces. The Prairies and Maritimes are much more distinctive. While the Prairies began, in the time
span we are dealing with, as the least urbanized, they changed dramatically after World War II, and by 1961, 8 percent more of their
population was urban than was that of the Maritimes. These changes
had been anticipated to some extent by data we examined on changes
in the industrial structure and changes in per capita income. The Maritimes too have been affected by these trends, but much less sharply.
(Newfoundland has been excluded from this analysis, but it is similar
to the Maritime provinces, with about half of its population rural.)

Life in a community of 1,000 is, after all, not terribly citified, and
some further evidence is required to substantiate our thesis of both
growing urbanization and accompanying regional differences. This is
provided by Table 2–3. The census takers in 1961 found fifteen communities with populations of 100,000 or more. These were metropoli-

Table 2–3 **Distribution of Urban Population in Cities 100,000 and over, 1961**

	Percent Urban Population[a] in Cities 100,000+	No. of Metropolitan[b] Areas 100,000+
CANADA	64.0	15
Atlantic	29.5	1
Quebec	67.8	2
Ontario	64.6	7
Prairies	65.2	3
British Columbia	75.6	2

Source: [a]*1961 Census of Canada,* vol. 7.1–2, pp. 2–10, 2–26–28
[b]Leroy O. Stone, *Urban Development in Canada* (Ottawa: Queen's Printer, 1967), p. 278.

tan areas, defined by the census as communities in close economic, geographic, and social relationship. Seven of these were in Ontario, and two each in British Columbia, Quebec and Alberta. Of the total urban population, three-quarters in British Columbia lived in these large cities. In the Atlantic provinces, less than one-third did so. In the remaining regions, about two-thirds of the urban population were found in cities of 100,000 population or more.

Social Welfare

Access to health services is one indicator of the quality of life. While having health services readily available is not in itself a guarantee that a population will be physically fit, it is, at the least, an indication of the responsiveness of a region's leadership structure to the health needs of its inhabitants. Among the ten provinces, there was considerable variation in the distribution of various health services personnel.[15] British Columbia ranked first in the per capita availability of physicians, dentists, pharmacists, and optometrists. Ontario generally ranked second, although Manitoba had a higher ratio of pharmacists to population. Collectively, the Prairie provinces were in about third place, although there was quite a bit of variation among them. Quebec ranked fourth on physicians and optometrists, sixth on dentists, and eighth on pharmacists. Last place was reserved for the Atlantic provinces. The magnitude of the difference between the eastern provinces and the remainder was often very large. The most extreme instance was Newfoundland, where the ratio of dentists to population was three

15. For full details, see Canada, *Royal Commission on Health Services* (Ottawa: Queen's Printer, vol. I, 1964; vol. II, 1965).

times less than the Canadian average, and that of optometrists six times less.

The availability of health services personnel was in all cases greater in urban than rural areas. To some extent, differences in levels of urbanization accounted for differences in health services, but only partially. Quebec, for example, although the second most urban province, ranked no higher than fourth on access to personnel. Saskatchewan, while among the two least urbanized provinces, was only moderately below the national average in the ratios of physicians, dentists, and optometrists, and somewhat above the average in that of pharmacists.

Education

As we have already pointed out, education can be viewed as an input to the social and economic systems. The educational level of a given population is a good predictor of the potential, if not the real, occupational structure. Given an industrialized society with adequate capital investment, a highly skilled and educated labour force contributes to high levels of per capita income and the production of wealth for the nation. In this connection, it is worth considering Table 2–4, to which we have already referred in our discussion of income differences.

Table 2–4 **Highest Level of Schooling Attained, Population 15 Years and Older not Attending School, Canada and Regions, 1961** (percent)

			Level of Schooling		
	None	Elementary	Secon-dary	Some University	University Degree
CANADA	1.6	45.2	47.1	3.1	3.0
Atlantic provinces	2.7	47.8	44.8	2.7	1.7
Quebec	1.0	54.2	39.2	2.6	3.0
Ontario	1.1	42.7	50.0	2.8	3.4
Prairies	2.5	41.0	50.0	3.6	2.6
British Columbia	1.5	32.1	58.0	5.1	3.3

Source: *1961 Census of Canada,* Bulletin 7.1–10, Table XIII.

Comparing regions on the basis of proportions with less than secondary schooling, Quebec ranked lowest.[16] British Columbia, in con-

---

16. However, if we were to consider provinces individually, then Newfoundland and New Brunswick would rank lower than Quebec, with 58.2 and 56.6 percent respectively of their populations having less than secondary education.

trast, had the fewest in this educational category. One of the sources of existing disadvantage to the province of Quebec was the inordinately large share of the population with a low level of educational attainment. While not quite so badly off, the Atlantic provinces too had slightly more than half their population with only elementary or no schooling. This helps to illustrate the sense in which education is both an input to and output from the economic system as it aids in perpetuating the economic disadvantages suffered by this region. British Columbia, while educationally best off according to this measure, was somewhat limited in this seeming advantage because of its reliance on primary-producing industries, which do not require large numbers of highly educated personnel.

A different perspective comes from looking at the population with university degrees. Now the three most industrialized and urbanized provinces emerge as having the largest proportion with degrees. There is currently not much difference among regions in the proportion of the labour force in professional, proprietorial and managerial occupations. However, there is some slight, though meaningful, difference in the population at least potentially able to fill highly skilled and demanding jobs. It is from this most educated group that the leaders in business, industry, science, politics, and the professions increasingly come. A population lacking in those with the requisite training is hence to be counted among the disadvantaged. In this respect, then, it is the Atlantic provinces which in our survey clearly manifested both an important source and consequence of a low level of economic development.

Conceiving of education as an output from the social and economic systems leads us to the notion of the relative quality of educational systems. One indication is the ability of the school system to retain its students. Table 2–5 gives two different indications of this retention ability: the proportion of the population attending school at age seventeen, which is beyond the legal school-leaving age; and the percentage rate of retention for students between grades two and eleven. Quebec had the lowest proportion in school at age seventeen, only one-quarter. This percentage rises as we move westward, reaching over one-half in British Columbia. Of the Atlantic provinces, Nova Scotia was best off in this respect (as it is generally in other ways which our analysis of regions has sometimes obscured), having had slightly more in school at this age than Ontario.

There is a close, though not perfect, association between population continuing in school at age seventeen and the retention of those between grades two and eleven. This measure of retention points up even more sharply than our previous index the unfavourable position of Quebec and the favourable one of British Columbia, and now also of Alberta. Considering the trends we have reviewed on industrial

Table 2–5 **Retention Level of Schools, by Province, Circa 1960**

	Percent of Population at School, Age 17[a]	Percent Retention Rate Grades 2 to 11[b]
Newfoundland	31.9	29
Prince Edward Island	31.8	35
Nova Scotia	41.0	40
New Brunswick	34.2	35
Quebec	25.5	20
Ontario	38.8	41
Manitoba	41.9	46
Saskatchewan	47.1	47
Alberta	48.9	60
British Columbia	53.1	68

Source: [a]Paul Nash, "Quality and Equality in Canadian Education," *Comparative Education Review,* 5 (Oct. 1961): 125.

[b]John E. Cheal, "Factors Related to Educational Output Differences Among the Canadian Provinces," *Comparative Education Review,* 6 (Oct. 1962): 121.

output, occupational structure, income, and urbanization, it would look as though Quebec might become economically even more disadvantaged, while British Columbia and possibly Alberta would increase their ascendency, and perhaps even outdo Ontario. Other indications suggest that the two westernmost provinces, and to some extent Saskatchewan, regard the investment in education as a major form of resource-development. While Ontario was not as well off in this regard, it still retained some important advantages at the level of university education. Quebec, however, ranked poorly for a modern, industrialized province, and changes in the educational system in that province are greatly needed, even if viewed reluctantly by some.[17]

Communication

The educational system is closely associated with the occupational structure and helps determine opportunities for economic advance-

17. A thorough scrutiny of all aspects of education in Quebec was undertaken by the Parent Royal Commission, along with recommendations for change. The latter have been the source of great controversy and purportedly contributed to the defeat of the Liberal government in 1966. Government of the Province of Quebec, *Report of the Royal Commission on Education in the Province of Education,* 5 vols. (Quebec City: 1963-66). For additional regional comparisons, see Canada, Dominion Bureau of Statistics, *Salaries and Qualifications of Teachers in Universities and Colleges* (Ottawa: Queen's Printer, 1963).

ment. These opportunities, in turn, are related to the likelihood that other facilities of the social system will be utilized to full advantage. Our thesis has been that not only the amount, but also the quality, of education will have a bearing on occupation, rewards obtained, and general style of life. While it was possible to point out interprovincial differences in both these measures of education, the consequences of quality differences are much more difficult to assess. Since our concern in this respect is with education as a "mind-opening" experience, it is perhaps preferable to look at other indications of access to or enjoyment of such broadening experiences. One of these is reading. We have no overall measure of the amount or kind of reading people do, but we have two slightly more oblique indicators. These are library holdings and newspaper circulation.

Data supplied in Table 2–6 give the ratio of library holdings to the population served in each province. The stock of books, periodicals and similar holdings in each province's libraries do not, of course, tell us much about readership. A relatively small number of books could be more widely read than a large number. Relatively small holdings could be offset by widespread private purchase of books. These are certainly possibilities, but the more likely pattern is for size of holdings to be associated with readership, and also with private book purchase.[18] Moreover, by looking at holdings, we get another measure

Table 2–6 **Ratio of Library Holdings to Population Served, by Province, 1962**

	Ratio of Library Holdings to Population Served
Newfoundland	.67
Prince Edward Island	1.06
Nova Scotia	.87
New Brunswick	.85
Quebec	.83
Ontario	1.28
Manitoba	.97
Saskatchewan	1.60
Alberta	1.50
British Columbia	1.39

Source: John Porter, *Canadian Social Structure, A Statistical Profile,* The Carleton Library no. 32 (Toronto: McClelland & Stewart Ltd., 1967), p. 126.

18. Philip H. Ennis, *Adult Book Reading in the United States: A Preliminary Report* (Chicago: NORC Report no. 105, September 1965), p. 52.

of life in the provinces themselves. That is, whether or not sizeable budgets are provided for public libraries is an indication of what decision-makers consider important, regardless of the reading behaviour of the mass of citizens. By this criterion, Saskatchewan and Alberta ranked as the provinces with the largest allocation of library resources for the population served. They are followed, in order, by British Columbia, Ontario, and Prince Edward Island. All others were below the Canadian average, with Quebec and Newfoundland especially so.

Newspaper circulation for each province is shown in Table 2–7. Circulation again does not in itself guarantee that people will read what they buy, but it is certainly reasonable to assume that readership is highly correlated with circulation. Differences among provinces in the number of daily newspapers available and their circulation were highly skewed. As of September, 1966, Ontario was reported to have forty-six daily newspapers. The two provinces next in number were British Columbia and Quebec, but they had only fourteen each. Alberta and Manitoba had seven each, followed by New Brunswick

Table 2–7 **Average Daily Newspaper Circulation for Six Month Period Ending September, 1966, Expressed as Rate per 1000 Population, by Region.**

	Average Circulation Rate Per 1000 Population
Newfoundland	63
Prince Edward Island	260
Nova Scotia	211
New Brunswick	172
Atlantic Provinces	165
Quebec	180
Ontario	268
Manitoba	229
Saskatchewan	132
Alberta	201
Prairie Provinces	189
British Columbia	265

Source: Circulation figures are based on publishers' statements to Audit Bureau of Circulation, published in *Canadian Advertising Rates and Data* (Toronto: MacLean-Hunter Publishing Co. Ltd., June, 1967), p. 37.

Rates are calculated from Dominion Bureau of Statistics population estimates for June, 1966.

with six, Nova Scotia with five, Saskatchewan with four, Newfoundland with three, and Prince Edward Island with two. Circulation, however, is fairly independent of the number of local newspapers available. It is true that Ontario, with the largest number of newspapers, also had the highest circulation rate. But Prince Edward Island, with the smallest number, had a circulation rate not far behind that of Ontario. We also estimated a circulation of at least 200 for every 1,000 population in British Columbia, Manitoba, Nova Scotia, and Alberta. But considering these data in terms of the five regions rather than individual provinces, only Ontario and British Columbia had rates of over 200.

It is clear that exposure to those varied experiences that are possible through reading were much less likely to be enjoyed in Newfoundland, New Brunswick, and Quebec than elsewhere in Canada. On the whole, the Atlantic provinces ranked lowest of the five regions in access to library holdings and newspaper circulation. However, the smallest province, Prince Edward Island, had not only greater exposure to printed communication than other Atlantic provinces, it also appeared in a more favourable position than some of the otherwise more advantaged Prairie provinces. Communication does not, however, stop with the printed word, and we have three additional ways of assessing the relative isolation of regions: ownership of television, telephone, and passenger automobiles, presented in Table 2–8.

Of all the indicators of regional differences in life style considered thus far, ownership of television sets was associated with the least amount of differentiation. On the basis of a survey of household facilities conducted in 1965, it was estimated that 93 per cent of all households in Canada owned a television. The range of variation for regions was from +3 to −7, and for individual provinces, with one exception, +3 to −10. The one exception was Newfoundland, where only 69 percent of the households reported television ownership. Despite the small amount of variation, regional differences were of the expected sort. That is, Ontario and Quebec had the highest percent of owners, followed by British Columbia, and then the Prairie and Atlantic provinces.

Telephones were not quite so common a possession, although even so, 89 percent of all households had a telephone at the time of the study. Ownership was greatest in Ontario, followed closely by British Columbia. Quebec ranked third, with its rate of ownership falling exactly at the national average. Manitoba also had the same percent ownership, but because of lower rates among the other two, the overall rate for the Prairies was 83 percent. Last were the Atantic provinces, three of which were under the national average by 10 percent, while a fourth, Newfoundland, fell 33 percentage points below.

Our final indicator of access to the outside world was ownership of

Table 2–8 **Households with Specified Possessions, Canada and Regions, May 1965**

	Percent Ownership			
	Tele-vision	Tele-phone	Auto-mobile	Total House-holds ('000s)[a]
Newfoundland	69	56	49	96
Prince Edward Island	83	79	75	24
Nova Scotia	92	79	69	180
New Brunswick	91	80	71	137
Atlantic provinces	86	74	65	437
Quebec	96	89	66	1,280
Ontario	96	95	81	1,766
Manitoba	87	89	74	246
Saskatchewan	83	78	79	248
Alberta	87	83	79	377
Prairie provinces	86	83	78	871
British Columbia	92	93	80	499
CANADA	93	89	75	4,853

[a]Estimate in thousands.

Source: Canada, Dominion Bureau of Statistics, Special Survey Division, *Household Facilities and Equipment*, May 1965 (Ottawa: Queen's Printer, November, 1965).

passenger automobiles. In a sense, this indicator may underestimate actual access, since farmers, for example, may typically own and make use of pickup trucks rather than passenger cars. It is not, however, likely that such trucks are used for extensive pleasure travel. Be that as it may, we are still constrained to use this indicator by the logic of our argument (*i.e.,* according to our definition of what constitutes access to mind-broadening experiences) and the availability of data. On this measure again, Ontario and British Columbia were most advantaged, with about 80 percent ownership. The Prairie provinces too were quite similar, although Manitoba was slightly below average, with 74 percent ownership. Quebec was low in car ownership, with only 66 percent in this category, a rate exceeded by three of the Atlantic provinces. Prince Edward Island, in fact, had a rate of 75 percent ownership, as high as that of the national average. Lowest was Newfoundland, where only 49 percent reported that they owned an automobile.

A review of the data presented here produces three unequivocal generalizations. On all measures of communication used, Ontario ranked in first place or close to it, British Columbia second or nearly so, and Newfoundland invariably last. A shorthand way of assessing each province's access to a variety of potentially stimulating experiences has been obtained by ranking the communication measures and then averaging the ranks. We obtain the following composite ranking, beginning with the province with the greatest potential for communication: Ontario, British Columbia, Alberta, Manitoba, Prince Edward Island, Quebec, Nova Scotia, Saskatchewan (the latter two tied), New Brunswick, Newfoundland. This confirms our earlier generalizations about the provinces at the extremes. It also enables us to locate the remaining provinces a little more easily. This way of ranking provinces further establishes the way in which the Prairie and Atlantic regions are each made up of similar units, with two exceptions: Prince Edward Island and Saskatchewan. On the average, then, residents of the Atlantic provinces lacked extensive contacts with each other and with the outside world, a condition shared to some extent with Quebeckers. Exactly the opposite was true for those in Ontario and British Columbia, while, in general, the Prairie provinces were in a middle position. We must also note, that in basing our interpretations on rankings, we may mislead the reader into thinking that absolute differences between regions were necessarily great. Large differences were consistently found only for Newfoundland; for the remainder, they were quite variable and often of minor proportions.

Mobility

Canadians are a highly mobile people, never completely losing the migrant status established by settlers born outside the country. Movements have occurred from the farms to the cities, which we have already documented. In addition, there continues to be great movement from one province to another. It is this interprovincial movement which concerns us here, presenting as it does further indications of relative exposure to new people, and possibly new ideas.[19] It is also, conversely, an indication of the relative isolation of some regions, which either lose population or at least do not gain through migration. Rates of migration for ten year periods are shown in graphic form for Canada and the five regions in Chart 2-3. Even before looking at details, the chart strikes us by the erratic shape of the trace lines. In the forty-year time span, the Atlantic provinces have continued to suffer from a net loss of population. While all other regions experienced the greatest dip in population gained through migration during the depression period covered in the 1931-40 interval, the Maritimes suffered relatively least loss then.[20] Where was there to go when the whole

---

19. Migration to and from Canada is not considered here.

20. The Prairies had an even greater loss at the following time interval.

Chart 2–3 **Rate of net migration per 1000 population, by region, 1921–1960**

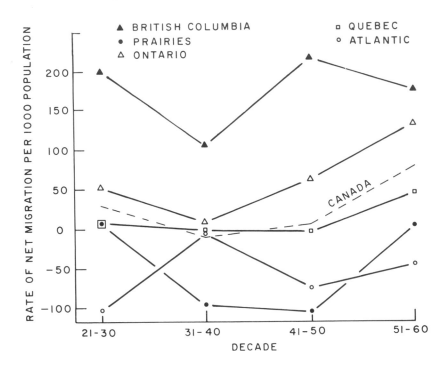

Source: Isabel B. Anderson, *Internal Migration in Canada, 1921-1961,* Staff Study no. 13 (Ottawa: Economic Council of Canada, March 1966), p. 22.

Note: Newfoundland has not been included in Atlantic until 1951.

country was mired in the depths of a depression? Certainly some movement took place, notably to British Columbia, but except in the particularly hard-hit Prairie provinces, Canadians were most inclined to stay home.[21] The ten year period beginning in 1931 was the one instance when the declining population of the Maritimes was almost halted. Of individual provinces, Prince Edward Island had the least pull for migrants, suffering a net loss of over 100 for every 1,000 population.

The shape of the migration trend line for the Prairies best resembles the letter U. In addition to the depression decade dip, there is also one

21. During this time, the United States, which normally forms the destination for those seeking richer opportunities, suffered from similar misfortunes. In 1925, over 100,000 Canadians (and Newfoundlanders) emigrated to the U.S; in 1935, the number was less than 8,000. U.S. Bureau of the Census, *Historical Statistics of the United States, Colonial Times to 1957* (Washington: G.P.O., 1960), p. 58.

for 1941-50. At the first time period noted, western settlement on the land was still sufficient to account for a net increase in migrant population. But the depression years were accompanied by drought, and vast numbers moved from the Prairies, especially from Saskatchewan. Even though the economic situation improved in Canada, the next decade saw continued out-migration, accentuated by the movement from farm to cities, often elsewhere in Canada. The upper arm of the U is affected mainly by Alberta in this past decade. Although both Saskatchewan and Manitoba lost less population than in the two preceding decades, it was now Alberta that showed a major gain. During the 1951-60 interval, Manitoba lost seven people for every 1000 population, Saskatchewan lost ninety-five, and Alberta gained 112. The latter change was accompanied by a movement to increased urbanization and enhanced attractiveness due to the wealth of the expanding oil and gas industries.

Quebec displayed the most moderate curve for net migration, coming out about even in terms of migrants in and out between 1931 and 1950 and gaining more than losing at the two end points in the time period.

Ontario had, during the forty-year period, always won more migrants than it had lost, despite the fall-off in the critical depression period. Since that time, the population increase through internal migration has been steadily upward.

British Columbia had the most appeal for migrants, and by the same token, for its native inhabitants. While still gaining 114 persons for every 1000 population during the 1931 decade, this represented a considerable dip from both previous and following time periods. Yet even this relative attractiveness is not constant, and the last period measured showed that the rate of net migration was 176, compared to 229 for the preceding ten years.

Based on the most recent data contained in Chart 2–3, British Columbia emerged as the most attractive region. Ontario was next, followed by Quebec, the Prairies, and the Atlantic provinces. The gap between each of the regions is considerable, ranging from a difference of thirty persons for every 1,000 population, to eighty-eight persons per 1,000. The lack of holding power for the Atlantic provinces was consistent, and particularly strong in Prince Edward Island, which had, between 1951 to 1960, a net rate of migration of −105.

REGIONAL PROFILES

Each region, and to some extent its constituent provinces, has been described in terms of population composition, economy, and quality of life. On some of the characteristics there were great differences between regions; on others, absolute differences were small. In almost every instance, however, it was possible to discern sufficient variation to conclude that each region was distinct from the others. But, since it is absolute differences which more clearly establish the uniqueness of a region, the construction of regional profiles which follows is based primarily on these. When judgements about the meaning of absolute differences were not self-evident, for example in access to communication media, then relative rankings were employed.

Atlantic Provinces

The Atlantic provinces are peopled mainly by those of British stock, largely unaffected by post-World War II immigration. Large pockets of French are concentrated in New Brunswick. Religious affiliation is diverse, with Protestants in the majority but Catholics the largest single denomination. The economy is imperfectly industrialized, having a low manufacturing capacity and a major strain toward resource production. Residents are poor, and have been so for decades; at least since the days of Confederation. The population live mainly in rural areas and small towns where they have poor access to health services personnel. The educational level is low and the quality of education suffers from meagre financing. With the exception of Prince Edward Island, where residents have a high rate of access to newspapers and libraries, the media of communication have relatively low potential usage. Out-migration has been high for decades and even commensurate numbers of immigrants from elsewhere in Canada have been difficult to attract.

Quebec

The population is predominantly of French origin and Catholic. While Quebec possesses a highly industrialized economy, the average income of residents is quite low, which is reflected in the socio-economic status of residents, especially of the French-speaking. The majority live in cities, but the urban character of the province is the result of concentration in a few large centres. Access to health services varies, being moderately good for physicians, but poor for others. Educational quality tends to be low and a large portion of the population have less than secondary schooling. However, this is offset to some extent by the numbers with university degrees. Access to formal communication is moderately low, especially with respect to libraries and automobiles. Population movement over the years has been relatively modest and, since World War II, internal migration has produced a net gain in population.

Ontario

Those of British stock continue to be in the majority, but both through internal and foreign migration, there is now also strong representation of other ethnic groups. While Catholics and the two major Protestant denominations represent the bulk of residents, other groups contribute to religious heterogeneity. Ontario is industrialized, wealthy, and thoroughly urbanized. Health services personnel are readily available, at least potentially. On the average, the population is moderately well educated. On the basis of the large numbers with university degrees and the particularly high quality of the educational system, the educational outlook is good. The communication of people and ideas is facilitated by the widespread distribution of such items as newspapers and automobiles. Since the depression years, Ontario has continued to attract increasingly large numbers of migrants.

Prairie Provinces

The ethnic base of the Prairie provinces is most diverse. Those of stock other than British or French are equal in number to the British "charter members." Religious variety is also a feature of these provinces, such that no single denomination is numerically dominant. Resource production remains the major characteristic of the economy, either through agriculture or mining and refining. Income levels are about average in relative terms, and absolute levels are analogous. These levels represent a very great improvement over the depression years of the 1930s. The Prairies are less urbanized than most regions in Canada but, since the census of 1941, there has been a large upsurge in the growth of cities. There is moderately good access to health services, although individual provinces vary in this respect. For example, Manitoba has a high ratio of physicians and pharmacists to the population, and Alberta of dentists and optometrists. Currently these provinces have only a small proportion who are university graduates, but the disadvantages of this situation may soon be overcome since there already exists a good educational distribution in general and a moderate to high quality educational system. Access to communication is also moderate to good. The Great Depression stimulated a population exodus that was not halted until after World War II, but even now, the population gains enjoyed by the Prairies as a whole are mainly the result of movement to Alberta.

British Columbia

Those of British origin predominate in the Columbia they named. There are very few French but a large number of other European origins. Compared to other regions, British Columbia is unusually Protestant. The majority are either United Church or Anglican, while other denominations are also well represented. The economy is mixed, partially industrialized but with a remaining heavy dependence on resource production. This has not, however, prevented its inhabitants from becoming wealthy. While the province must be described as mainly urban, the major portion is unusually concentrated in two centres. Health services are readily available. The means of communication are broadly distributed to a population both very well educated and possessing a high quality educational system. Though there has been some decline in population flows, British Columbia continues as the California of Canada, a magnet to migrants.

The connection between objective conditions and regional individuality is clear-cut both in generating and sustaining regionalism. But while we have described what are probably necessary generative conditions, these are not the sole requirements for the continuation of regionalism. What we still need to demonstrate are the existence of those behavioural and attitudinal differences which give regionalism its full strength in the political sphere. The manifestation of these objective conditions, however, will continue to be one of the prime motive forces in the perpetuation of regionalism.

CHAPTER

The distribution of power among provinces

SOURCES OF UNEQUAL POWER

The existence of a federal form of government in Canada is a structural guarantee of continuing regionalism. Since the essence of federalism is some autonomy for both central and provincial governments, each with an arena in which its authority is paramount, the essential conditions are present for perpetuating regional separateness at the government level.[1] For the most part, we take this consequence of federalism as given. Except for some concerns with voter perceptions and attachments, whenever our analysis touches on questions of government, it is confined to the central government. This means that we are not looking to one of the traditional sources of power differentials —the relations between federal and provincial governments. We do so because studies of federalism which focus on federal-provincial relations do not normally enable us to distinguish among provinces with respect to their share in the power bank of the central government. Exceptions to this limitation are commentaries on the quasi-

---

1. Kenneth Wheare, who has done much to clarify the meaning of federalism, uses a very similar definition. Because of the powers of reservation and disallowance, Wheare considers the Canadian constitution a quasi-federal one, yet he has no hesitation in terming Canada's government federal in practice. K. C. Wheare, *Federal Government,* 4th ed. (New York: Oxford University Press, Galaxy Books, 1964), pp. 10, 19 20.

colonial status of the western provinces early in their history[2] and the special claims of Quebec in the confederation arrangements.[3] But even such studies are concerned primarily with the relations between the central and provincial governments with respect to their relative bargaining power, rather than with the broader issue of power differentials generally.

Our approach is not as unorthodox as it may first appear. For one thing, we are not rejecting other conceptions of federalism, nor other sources of power. Motivated by a desire to find some way of comparing the major geographic components of the national government, we take into account some aspects of the federal structure that are often neglected. As Tarlton points out, "in studies of federalism the prevailing emphases avoid sufficient consideration of the diverse ways in which each member state in a federal system is able to relate to the system as a whole, the central authority, and each other member state."[4] What should perhaps carry most weight in evaluating our approach is its close relationship to how the Canadian political system actually works.

Wheare appears to have given some thought to the issue of differential power when he speaks of the relative size of the units making up the federal union. His concern, echoing that of John Stuart Mill, is that there be no unit so small that it will be overruled by the others or so large that it can overwhelm the remainder. The factors of size that are mentioned as important are wealth, area, and population. What is not clear is how these factors operate in affecting differences in power. One interpretation is that they influence the likelihood that a unit can have a viable and autonomous government which in turn can make claims on the central government.

> It is this divergence [in size] which leads the poorer or less populous states to desire federal rather than unitary government for in it they see a safeguard for their independence. It is an important factor in the making and maintenance of federal systems today. The agricultural states of Western America with their smaller populations find in the federal form of union their safeguard against the wealth and popula-

---

2. J. R. Mallory, "The Five Faces of Federalism," in P. A. Crapeau and C. B. Macpherson, eds., *The Future of Canadian Federalism* (Toronto: University of Toronto Press, 1965), pp. 3-15.

3. Pierre Elliot Trudeau, *Federalism and the French Canadians* (New York: St. Martin's Press, 1968); René Levesque, *et al., Option Québec* (Montréal: Les Editions de l'homme, 1968); Jacques Cotnam, *Faut-il inventer un nouveau Canada?* (Montréal: Fides, 1967).

4. Charles D. Tarlton, "Symmetry and Assymetry as Elements of Federalism: A Theoretical Speculation," *Journal of Politics,* 27 (1965): 861-74.

tion of the East and especially New York; the Canadian maritime provinces and the prairie provinces seek protection from
Ontario and Quebec; . . . .[5]

This suggests that what Wheare had in mind was the give and take
between the provincial and the central governments, rather than provincial interaction within the central government. It is to that latter
arena, however, that we must look in order to make a straightforward
comparison among provinces. Yet the factors of size that Wheare
mentions as having a bearing on provincial governments should also
be critical in establishing a ranking for provinces according to the role
they play in the central government.

What we need is some uniform way of comparing regions along a
power dimension that would be analogous to per capita income, dollar
output from manufacturing industries, or other such measures used in
Chapter 2. The notion of power as similar to a financial resource is
hardly new. It approximates Parson's conception of power as "a
general medium parallel to money."[6] We can think of the central government as a bank, into which the provinces make deposits and then
withdraw interest and capital. We may do this if we remember that
the central government is in a sense an abstraction. It is, at one level
of analysis at least, the sum of its constituent, provincial parts. Like a
bank, its capital derives in large part from the willingness of its de-
positors to entrust it with their resources. The bank then must convert
these raw resources into ones greater in magnitude and negotiability.
How the provinces, as parts of the central government, contribute to
it is one indication of their relative strength. By stressing the regional
composition of government, it becomes possible to develop several
related measures of power differences. These will relate to power as it
stems from support and representation. The support dimension will
be measured through popular vote and representation by seats in the
House of Commons and cabinet positions. Our approach does not,
obviously, exhaust the sources of a region's political power. For example, it leaves open the role played by arguments concerning Quebec's special status. But what it gives us is a simple standard of comparison, enabling us to deal with all regions simultaneously.

Popular Support

Even at first sight, it is not too difficult to understand why representation enters into a discussion of relative power. It is probably not so

---

5. Wheare, *Federal Government,* pp. 50-51.

6. Talcott Parsons, *Sociological Theory and Modern Society* (New York:
The Free Press, 1967), especially pp. 297-354.

clear why support should be considered an aspect of power. Possibly the strongest argument for doing so derives from Easton's discussion of the significance of support for the persistence of a political system.

> First, without support for some of the authorities, at least, demands could not be processed into outputs. Only the smallest, least differentiated system could handle its demands if each time a decision had to be made, a new set of rulers arose and if each output requiring implementation gave rise to a different set of administrators. Most systems require some relatively stable set of *authorities*.
>
> Second, without support it would be impossible to assure some kind of stability in the rules and structures through the use of which demands are converted into outputs, an aspect that will be designated as the *regime*. And third, support is vital in order to maintain minimal cohesion within a membership, an aspect of a system that I shall identify later as its *political community*.[7]

Easton points out that support may be manifested either through actions or attitudes, and the latter are discussed in the chapters on political orientations. Here we focus on one form of support, that of voting. Although, as Parsons has noted, there seems to be some contradiction in treating voting, in which all citizens may equally participate, as a social act which has repercussions on the creation of an unequal status hierarchy, this is indeed the case. It is Parson's view, to which we will also adhere, "that the franchise is directly a form of authority and that its exercise is a form of power. The link between franchise and hierarchy lies in the aggregation of votes to determine electoral victory—that is the difference between being in and out of office."[8] By looking at popular support for the governing party as it varies regionally, our underlying assumption is that those regions which give greater support to the government are equipped with greater potential power to take their places in the governing councils. By extension, we argue that residents in those regions who have, in the aggregate, given this greater support, also derive a greater share of the general power inherent in the central government.

Chart 3–1 presents trend lines on the percent of the popular vote that went to the governing party in fourteen general elections between

---

7. David Easton, *A Systems Analysis of Political Life* (New York: John Wiley & Sons, 1965), p. 157.

8. Talcott Parsons, "The Political Aspect of Social Structure and Process," in David Easton, ed., *Varieties of Political Theory* (Englewood Cliffs: Prentice-Hall, 1966), p. 85.

Chart 3–1 Regional trends in percent of popular vote won by governing party, 1921–1965.

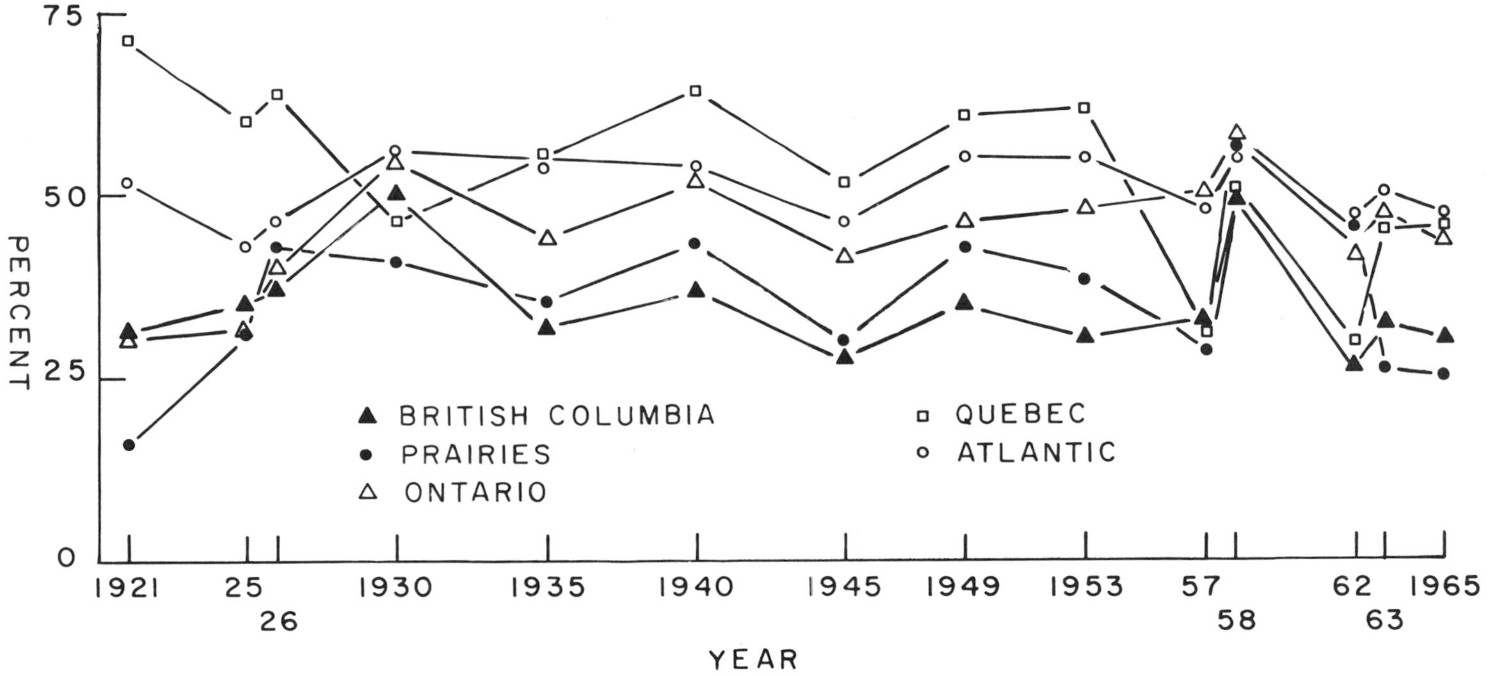

1921 and 1965.[9] The results of six of these elections were to return minority governments: those in 1921, 1925, 1963, and 1965 with the Liberals governing; and 1957 and 1962 with the Conservatives in office. In 1921 the Liberals were but one seat short of a majority, because of the strong showing of the Progressive party. But since the government was able to stay in office for four years, it appeared to have the stable character of a majority government. The election of 1925 is the most difficult to classify. Although the Conservatives won a larger number of seats than the Liberals, the latter, having formed the previous government, attempted to continue in office as was their constitutional right. The Liberals delayed calling parliament into session, and when they did they were able to stay undefeated for six months. At that time, having lost a vote of confidence, Prime Minister Mackenzie King called on Governor General Lord Byng for a dissolution of parliament. Byng chose instead to call on the Conservative leader, Arthur Meighen, to form a Cabinet. The Conservatives were not able to survive beyond three days, when they too fell to a vote of confidence. Another election was called, with Mackenzie King invoking the cry of constitutional crisis as a result of the Governor General's actions.[10] The propriety of these, including King's charges, need not concern us here except for one troublesome issue: which party really did win. Since we have selected as our criterion the governing party, rather than the one with the largest share of the popular vote or seats, we consider the Liberals to have been in this position after the 1925 election. This despite the fact that the Conservatives too, formed a government, but only for a few months, if we count the time between the fall of the government and the next election.

Of the remaining eight elections, the Liberals firmly took or retained office in 1926, 1935, 1940, 1945, 1949, and 1953. The Conservatives were in this position only after the elections of 1930 and 1958.

In Chart 3–1 we have the full distribution of popular vote in the time period under study. For purposes of analysis it is most useful to focus on those instances where the governing party won at least 50 percent of the popular vote. This is of course the point of division where majority rule begins. Yet voters themselves do not rule, and the concept itself is hedged with conflicting interpretations. Dahl, for

---

9. We begin at 1921 for several reasons: party lines were obscured in the preceding government, it was the first election using an almost contemporary franchise, and it heralded the new outlines of party politics that would operate in subsequent elections.

10. R. McGregor Dawson, *Constitutional Issues in Canada, 1900-31* (London: Oxford University Press, H. Milford, 1933), pp. 72-91; Eugene A. Forsey, *The Royal Power of Dissolution of Parliament in the British Commonwealth* (Toronto: Oxford University Press, 1943); H. V. Evatt, *The King and His Dominion Governors* (London: Oxford University Press, H. Milford, 1936).

example, uncovers the logical inconsistencies of theories of majority rule based on both Madisonian and populist views of democracy.[11] It has also been established that any attempt to base the "will of the majority" on the outcome of elections is bound to fail whenever there are more than two choices, a situation common in many Canadian constituencies.[12] It is not then any traditional concern with majorities that motivated our choice of a cutting point for analysing election results. Neither Easton nor Parsons, for example, discuss the significance of majorities in their emphasis on the necessity of support for the continuity of a political system. Easton explicitly avoids the issue by noting that support need not be evenly diffused through the population, but has its greatest impact when it stems from situationally specific, relevant groups.[13] Robert Dahl deals with this same problem in another way when he speaks of the intensity of preferences. That is, one of the ways of coping with the problems raised by majority rule theories would be to take into account the strength of preference for a number of alternatives, in order to choose, for instance, between the consequences of adopting the desired alternative of an apathetic majority versus an intense minority.[14] This would seem to compliment Easton's concerns about support from stategically placed groups. The position of contemporary theorists with respect to the place of majorities is hence paradoxically both clearcut and equivocal. On the one hand, there is major emphasis on the crucial role played by support as an input to the political system. At the same time, what kinds of support, in what amount, and from whom, remain problematic, or at best are relegated to determination by specific situations.

Why then the 50 percent plus cutting point? Aside from the fact that it provides some continuity with traditional approaches in political theory, its significance lies as an empirical indicator of more current concerns. At the simplest level, the nature of support is inherently of a more or less character, and our dividing line is a measure of this. Moreover, it is a point in the continuum of election results that matters, and not only to theorists. While it is possible for a government to achieve office with less than a majority because the Canadian electoral system requires only a simple plurality, such governments have had widely recognized weaknesses. The most usual is that the government has less than a majority of seats in the House. In the

11. Robert A. Dahl, *A Preface to Democratic Theory* (Chicago: University of Chicago Press, 1956).

12. James M. Buchanan and Gordon Tullock, *The Calculus of Consent* (Ann Arbor: University of Michigan Press, 1962), pp. 327-34, and the sources cited there.

13. Easton, *A Systems Analysis,* pp. 154, 222.

14. Dahl, *A Preface to Democratic Theory,* pp. 90-102.

time spanned by our analysis, this occurred following the elections of 1921, 1925, 1957, and the first three elections in the 1960s. But it can also happen that less than a majority of the popular vote will still result in a majority of the seats. Yet this is usually accompanied by some serious bias in the makeup of the government. For example, a Conservative government was elected in 1930 with 49 percent of the popular vote. This translated into 56 percent of the seats, but it still could not disguise the gross underrepresentation of Quebec on the governing side. Such patterns of uneven support are visible to the electorate, and perhaps even a source of concern, as they undoubtedly are to the government. Our use of aggregate electoral statistics gives us no way of either dealing with intensity or isolating significant groups of supporters. Yet insofar as we can quantify support, this quantity, though not necessarily the same as intensity, should have some implications for it. In other words, knowing that 70 percent of the voters supported the government in one area and 30 percent did so in another, we can speak of the differential strength of support without doing violence to the fact that the 30 percent minority may have been much more strongly committed than the 70 percent majority. By distinguishing between areas in the amount of support they give we cannot pretend to have discovered all the relevant supporters needed to give stability to a system, but at least the unevenness of support from regions is an important source of potential stress.

The best record of voters picking the winning side belongs to Quebec and the Atlantic provinces. British Columbia and the Prairies have generally lacked majority support for the government, while Ontario has tended in the direction of the west.

In nine out of fourteen elections, the government won more than 50 percent of the popular vote in Quebec. In one of these, the election of 1921, the Liberals, who were one seat short of a majority, obtained an unusually high proportion of the vote: 70 percent. This was the result of the bitter feelings aroused by conscription issues of 1917, closely identified with the Conservatives in the wartime Union government. Damage to the federal Conservatives in Quebec was almost irreparable. Of the five elections where the government received less than majority support in Quebec, those elected in 1930, 1957, and 1962 were ones where the Conservatives were the governing party. Even in 1958, another Conservative year but this time of more sweeping victory, support came from barely half—49.6 percent to be exact. In 1963 and 1965, when the Liberals formed minority governments, Quebec voters were among their strongest supporters, although third party strength kept this to a minority 45.6 percent. In total, however, of the more than four decades under consideration, over three of these have been spent under a government supported by a majority.

The Atlantic provinces follow closely behind Quebec in their leaning to the winning side. In half the elections between 1921 and 1965, over 50 percent of the vote went to the government and in one additional, it reached 49.9 percent. Because of the weakness of minor parties in this region, support for the governing party has never been less than 45 percent. During this time, approximately twenty-five years have been spent under the rule of a party supported by a majority.

The western provinces are at the opposite extreme. At no time during the forty-four year time span have those in British Columbia given majority support to the government. They came closest to doing so in 1930 and 1958, when over 49 percent voted Conservative, the two elections permitting the Conservatives to form a majority government. The election of 1958 was the only one when over half the voters in the Prairie provinces supported the governing party. Otherwise, they have remained apart from the dispositions of voters elsewhere.

Only in the elections of 1930, 1940, and 1958 did voters in Ontario give at least half their support to the governing party. Two of these cases occurred when the Conservatives were victorious, and the third when Canada had already entered World War II and appeals to national unity, including a stronger mandate for the party in power, were particularly effective. Yet altogether, if we interpret the trend lines in our chart to indicate the ebb and flow of voter support between and at elections, majority support for the government was confined to about six years.

Insofar as support is a criterion of power, it resides most often in Quebec and the Atlantic provinces and least in the Prairies and British Columbia.

Seats in the House of Commons

The sense in which representation is linked with power is expressed for us by Hanna Pitkin in her discussion of representative government.

> . . . we show a government to be representative not by demonstrating its control over its subjects but just the reverse, by demonstrating that its subjects have control over what it does. Every government's actions are attributed to its subjects formally, legally. But in a representative government this attribution has substantive content: the people really do act through their government, and are not merely passive recipients of its actions. A representative government must not merely be in control, not merely promote the public interest, but must also be responsive to the people.[15]

In other words, the agents of such a government are those who have been freely chosen by the public, which continues to exert some con-

---

15. Hanna Fenichel Pitkin, *The Concept of Representation* (Berkeley: University of California Press, 1967), p. 232.

trol over its agents, if only through the threat of defeat in the next election. Since our approach throughout this book avoids conceiving of a completely undifferentiated public, but considers at least the minimal divisions provided by regional boundaries, we might be led to question who the representative actually represents: the constituency, locality, or nation. As Pitkin argues persuasively, the question does not generate anything useful, and we are well advised to think of him as representing all three levels.[16]

To the extent that a member of Parliament in the Canadian House of Commons represents the region that elected him, his authority is greater if he belongs to the governing party. For a province to be represented by the party in office means that its members of Parliament are part of the governing caucus and it has direct channels for making known its special interests to the government. In some instances at least, this should lead to direct benefits to the province. On those occasions when no single party holds a majority of the seats, government by a single party is possible only so long as the opposition forces are not united. At such times, opposition members of Parliament, particularly from third parties, hold the balance of power, a role which increases their importance out of all proportion to their number. This is not likely to be of much benefit to a province with such third party representation, however, at least during the tenure of that government. In the subsequent election, the interests of that province may play a larger part in the platform of the majority party as it attempts to win over the voters. This approach was taken toward the Prairie provinces by the minority Liberal government during the 1925 election. But since campaign promises directed to special interests are a common feature of elections, though not always successful nor always kept, they are not really pertinent to the issue of representation. That is, our interests are in representation as it is, not as parties wish it to be. This means that the benefits that may accrue to provinces because of their third party representation cannot be readily evaluated, and we will not make the attempt.

Chart 3–2 describes regional trends in the percentage of seats in the House of Commons won by the governing party. Because of the imperfect fit between popular vote and the seats which derive from this, the fluctuation within regions and the span between regions is even more extreme than that shown in Chart 3–1.[17] Quebec and the Atlantic provinces again emerged as the regions most supportive of

16. Ibid., pp. 215-18. We also see no reason to consider such issues as the delegate vs. mandate controversies, which the Pitkin book treats with authority.

17. For a pertinent discussion on the relation between votes and seats, see J. Murray Beck, "The Democratic Process at Work in Canadian General Elections," in John C. Courtney, *Voting in Canada* (Scarborough: Prentice-Hall of Canada, 1967), pp. 21-27.

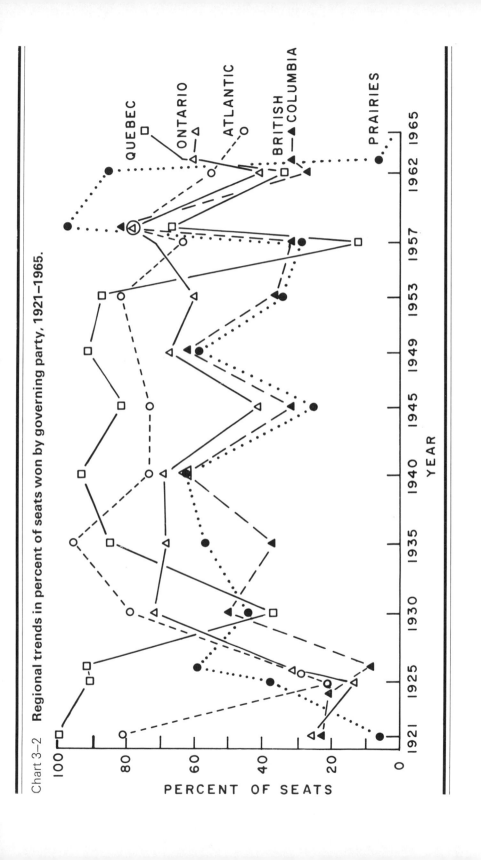

Chart 3–2 Regional trends in percent of seats won by governing party, 1921–1965.

the government, this time in returning a majority of members of Parliament from the ruling party in the largest number of elections: eleven out of fourteen. British Columbia and the Prairies, though least supportive of the government, returned some members of the ruling party in all elections, and they have on several occasions even had a majority of their sitting members from the governing party. Ontario was again in the middle position, but with respect to seats as compared to popular vote, emerged as closer to the eastern provinces.

The makeup of the House of Commons, much more so than the distribution of popular vote, has tended to be polarized along regional lines. Only in three elections, those of 1940, 1949, and 1958, have a majority of seats in all five regions been held by the government. Even then, the percentage range of seats held varied from 62 to 94, 59 to 93, and 67 to 98 respectively. During the times when there have been minority governments, their precarious stability has been accentuated by the regional skewness of seats. For example, in 1962, only two regions had given a majority to the governing Conservatives: 87 percent of the seats in the Prairies and 55 percent in the Atlantic provinces. But the Conservatives held only 41 percent in Ontario, 35 percent in Quebec, and 27 percent in British Columbia. Another example is the 1965 election, when the Liberals formed a minority government. Then Quebec and Ontario elected a majority of their representatives from the Liberals, but the Prairies returned only two percent of their seats to the government.

If we look at the *strength* of representative support for the government, we see an even sharper differentiation among regions. For example, not only did a majority of Quebec's seats go to the government in eleven out of fourteen elections, but in nine of them, majorities were 70 percent or more. In the three instances where Quebec voters withdrew their support from the government, one was a particularly isolating experience. This occurred in 1957, when only 12 percent of the seats were won by the Conservatives.

The Atlantic provinces too returned majorities in eleven of the elections between 1921 and 1965 inclusive. In seven of these, at least 70 percent of the seats went to the government. In one other, however, support declined to a low of 21 percent.

As we have already noted, in terms of seats, the trend in Ontario had been to give greater support to the government than we might anticipate on the basis of popular vote alone. Yet while nine of the fourteen elections resulted in the return of a majority of governing members of Parliament, in only three of these elections did this majority reach 70 percent. In the five elections where seats were more often filled by opposition parties, there were two where the government obtained fewer than 30 percent of the seats.

The Prairie provinces have a slightly better record of support than does British Columbia, both in terms of popular vote and seats. They are unique, however, in the sharp fluctuations of their patterns of support. A majority of seats went to the government in six elections. In one of these the government gained 98 percent of the seats, and in another, 87 percent. But in five other elections, the government was left with fewer than 30 percent of the seats. Some of this fluctuation was due to the amount of support given third parties, a fact that accounts to an even greater degree for the low proportion of the popular vote won by the government. Yet the greatest extremes occurred in more recent years, in the four elections between 1958 and 1965. In each of these instances, the outcomes were due to the unusual appeal of the Conservatives and the related weakness of the Liberals, rather than to the attractions of third parties.

British Columbia followed a trend line of least support, though slightly less given to extremes than the Prairies. Only once had the government captured over 70 percent of the seats, although on four occasions this proportion was lower than 30 percent. Here the battle was not between the major parties, even to the extent that we saw in the Prairies; instead third parties took over, inhibiting the possibility that any single party would achieve overwhelming support.

With respect to seats then, the relative ranking along our power dimension is the same as that which we found for popular vote. This measure of power differs, however, in accentuating the distance among regions, and locating Ontario in a relatively more powerful position.

Some skepticism may have been aroused by this analysis because of the way in which representation itself is allocated. Since each province's representation in the national government is roughly dependent on its population density, a measure of inequality is immediately introduced. If seats alone were at issue, then Ontario would always be more powerful since it has the largest number. From 1917 to 1965, the House of Commons consisted of 265 seats. Ontario was alloted eighty-two of these until 1949, when it received an increase of one, and then two more in the following election. From 1953 on, Quebec had seventy-five seats, the Prairies forty-eight, the Atlantic provinces thirty-three, and British Columbia twenty-two. (The Yukon and Northwest Territories had the remaining two.) But since our concern is with the support aspects of representation, we have chosen to set aside the issue of absolute numbers. Thus we have focused on the inequalities in a province's share of seats dependent on their relation to the governing party. Our simple assumption has been that seats held by the governing party are those with greatest bargaining potential. Yet we cannot completely ignore the effects of size. These effects will be treated indirectly in the following section on cabinet representation.

Cabinet Representation

Whatever the Fathers of Confederation may have thought about the possible "tyranny of the majority" they made no effort to avoid this, within the context of the federal government, by giving equal voting privileges to regions, regardless of size. Equal representation was adopted in the United States in its second chamber, but in Canada, while the second chamber too was assigned the task of protecting provincial rights, this was assumed to be possible through the over-representation of smaller areas.[18] In any event, the number of representatives in themselves did not contribute to the lack of efficacy of the Canadian Senate. It soon became clear that a structure made through appointments for life, or now close to it, by the central government was better adapted to furthering the interests of the federal governing party within the provinces, rather than the other way around. As a result, "Any province today would relinquish all its senators without the slightest compunction or regret if by so doing it would be allowed to double its representation within the Cabinet."[19] This is because, despite a monarchical form of government, the real executive power rests with the cabinet, a body of men who, through tradition shared with the British parliament, has become responsible to Parliament. This means that ministers must hold a seat in either the House of Commons or the Senate, although they need not have been initially appointed from them. The cabinet is of special interest to us because of the role it has assumed as the protector of provincial rights. Within the cabinet, "Each minister is constantly concerned with the widely scattered interests of his special province and he acts, and is supposed to act, as its spokesman, advocate, and (where necessary) dispenser of patronage. In Cabinet councils he will be expected to advise, not only on matters within his particular department, but also on any topic whenever it concerns his province; and his opinion, by virtue of superior knowledge of that locality, will merit exceptional consideration."[20]

Unlike our preceding measures of relative power, inclusion in the cabinet, though the most visible and unequivocal indicator of potency, is not completely satisfactory for differentiating among regions. One reason is simply that it is so widely recognized that cabinet posts are

---

18. According to Smiley, in joining in Confederation, "Undoubtedly the Maritimers believed that the over-representation of the region in the Upper House relative to Ontario and Quebec was of crucial importance in defending their interest in the new Dominion." Donald V. Smiley, *The Canadian Political Nationality* (Toronto and London: Methuen, 1967), p. 13.

19. R. McGregor Dawson, *The Government of Canada,* 4th ed., revised by Norman Ward (Toronto: University of Toronto Press, 1964), p. 194.

20. Ibid., p. 196.

important. As a consequence there have developed conventions with
almost constitutional authority for equitably dealing with problems
of representation. These include at least one minister for each province, and four or five each for Ontario and Quebec. Difficulties arise
in fulfilling these conventions only when the governing party is particularly weak in one or more provinces. Dawson gives us a lively
description of such a situation after the 1921 election, whose circumstances were repeated in 1935, 1957, and under the minority governments of the 1960s. In 1921, Mackenzie King was forming his first
cabinet.

> The Province of Alberta had by a singular oversight neglected
> to return even one Liberal to Parliament, and none of the
> twelve United Farmers of Alberta would betray his party for
> a portfolio or help King and advance the provincial interest
> by resigning in favour of a Liberal. The new Prime Minister,
> however, was not easily discouraged, and after some inquiry
> and negotiation found a solution: he appointed to the Cabinet
> Charles Stewart, a Liberal ex-Premier of Alberta, and then
> opened up a seat for him in the Province of Quebec."[21]

Such makeshift arrangements are one possible way of handling the
demands for provincial representation, though they are obviously
not nearly so satisfactory as when a minister is elected by the province
that considers him its spokesman.

The attachment of ministers to their province can be rather tenuous, since the Canadian electoral system does not require that candidates for the federal parliament be residents of the province in which
they run, let alone of their constituency. This has resulted in some
interesting switches, perhaps the most notorious of which concerned
Mackenzie King. Despite his apparent stature as leader of the Liberal
party and prime minister, his personal appeal as a vote-getter was
limited. In the period we are discussing, he represented in turn
Ontario, Saskatchewan, and again Ontario. The fact that a member
of parliament can, during the history of his tenure in office, switch
the regional locus of his seat, is hence one apparent weakness in our
discussion of cabinet representation. When a political notable such
as the late Robert Kennedy sought a Senate seat in a state other than
his native one, although he had earlier established residence in the
state of his political ambitions, this still aroused an outcry from those
who felt he was "carpet-bagging." In Canada, reactions are generally
quite the opposite. If a well-known political figure is advised to seek
election in a particular constituency, even though he had no previous
contact with it, this is frequently welcomed by party activists and

21. Ibid., p. 194.

supporters. Moreover, if such a man is appointed to a cabinet post, either before or after his election, this often serves to enhance his appeal to voters. They would then normally treat him as their special representative, regardless of his previous regional affiliation. This is not to say, of course, that such people are never rejected by the voters, for indeed they are, but they would not be regarded as "foreign" to the region after their successful election.[22]

Another problem in our analysis of representation is that the cabinet which serves during the life of a single parliament need not have a stable composition. That is, a province could begin with a given number of cabinet seats, but because of resignations and replacements, it may during the period between elections increase its normal number of ministers. Our procedure will be to treat all of these as provincial representatives. According to the general assumption we are working with, this would mean that such a province had unusually high access to power. Yet the circumstances of the added representation may reflect quite a different situation, and we will have to be alert to the range of possible explanations for such patterns of representation.

No attempt is made here to differentiate among cabinet posts according to their relative importance.[23] Even though, in fact, this is not a completely accurate conception of the authority of cabinet members, all are treated equally. This is true as well for those ministers who are members of the Senate although that body does not have the legislative authority of the House of Commons. Whatever effect the inclusion of senators might have is minimized, in any case, since prime ministers avoid appointing more than two to their cabinet.

Table 3–1 presents the regional distribution of cabinet ministers in the time we are covering. Liberal ministries were heavily weighted in favour of Quebec and Ontario. Conservative ministries gave more equitable representation to all regions, with a bias toward Ontario. Calculation of a Chi–square test to evaluate the comparability of the cabinets under either party indicates a significant difference between the two at the .10 level. In other words, a statistical test confirms what observation suggests, that Liberals and Conservatives form their

22. Some insights into these phenomena can be gained from a study of the riding of Toronto-Eglinton in 1962, when the incumbent Minister of Finance, Donald Fleming, ran against three other candidates, among them Mitchell Sharp, who was slated for a cabinet post if the Liberals were elected. Brian Land, *Eglinton: The Election Study of a Federal Constituency* (Toronto: Peter Martin Associates, 1966).

23. For some discussion of this point, as well as an independent assessment of the composition of cabinets, see Richard J. Van Loon and Michael S. Whittington, *The Canadian Political System* (Toronto: McGraw-Hill, 1971), pp. 346-55.

Table 3–1 **Regional Distribution of Cabinet Ministers,**
1921–1965

	Liberal Ministries %	Conservative Ministries %
Atlantic provinces	14	18
Quebec	33	19
Ontario	31	33
Prairie provinces	14	19
British Columbia	7	11
Total number of Ministers[a]	230	110
Total number of Parliaments[b]	10	5

$X^2 = 7.87$ $p < .10$ df 4

[a]Excludes those without seats in either the House or Senate. Includes those who have served at any time during a single Parliament, and hence gives multiple weight to those in more than one Parliament.

[b]Notations are based on the life of a Parliament, and not a Ministry. In the time covered, there were fourteen Parliaments, but one of those, the 15th, had two distinct Ministries.

Source: Canada. Privy Council. *Guide to Canadian Ministries Since Confederation* (Ottawa: Queen's Printer, 1957).

Parliamentary Guides, various years.

cabinets in different ways. Yet the significance level is not particularly high, and most of the difference can be attributed to contrasts in the frequency of choosing ministers from Quebec. Further probing is needed to uncover the particularities of cabinet formation as this reflects on the power of regions.

Our concern with the composition of cabinets comes from the importance attached to this by regions themselves. Since the cabinet itself is so crucial in the government of Canada, and serves as the most powerful instrument for protecting and furthering provincial interests within the federal government, it is natural that there be strong pressures for adequate provincial representation.[24] These pressures are both responded to and constrained by the conventions previously discussed for ensuring each region an equitable share of posts.

24. Pressures come from sources other than provinces. In addition, at least some provinces request that their population diversity be respected in cabinet choices. Paul Fox, "The Representative Nature of the Canadian Cabinet," in Paul Fox, ed., *Politics: Canada,* 2nd ed. (Toronto: McGraw-Hill, 1966), pp. 206-10.

Naturally, each province would like more than its share, but sometimes some may get even less because of inadequate support for the governing party. How demands for representation are reconciled, at least as these derive from regions, could be understood if we had complete information on the actual politics of cabinet formation.[25] Lacking this, it is useful to compare existing cabinets with five possible criteria underlying their composition.

The ten Liberal and five Conservative cabinets (the 1925 election is counted as producing two cabinets), serving governments elected between 1921 and 1965, were compared in their regional distribution to that of voters at each election. A second comparison was made with the distribution of seats allocated to each region. These two criteria take into account a factor that has been previously neglected in our analysis of power differentials: the effect of population density. We next considered the relation between cabinet composition and the distribution of popular votes and seats for the governing party. That is, by using as our percentage base the total number of votes or seats for the government, we could array regions according to their contribution to the total results. This differs from the procedures used in the previous sections of this chapter, where we were interested in the nature of support within regions. Finally, we constructed a model of what might be considered the ideal cabinet, in which 20 percent of the seats would be given to both the Atlantic provinces and the Prairies, 25 percent each to Quebec and Ontario, and the remaining 10 percent to British Columbia. No attempt was made to vary this composition over time. While the theoretical model is a rather personal assessment, it is derived from widely-held conceptions of what is ideal.

In each of the ten tables that follow, there is, in a modest form, the test of the five models of cabinet selection, examined separately for Conservative and Liberal cabinets. Some small departures from the five criteria would be expected by chance. The problem then is one of determining whether the observed departures from zero (in each column) are significant. Inspection of Tables 3–2 to 3–11 clearly shows that, with one exception, the departures are sizeable. With guidance from a standard analysis of variance (and the sacrifice of degrees of freedom to correct for the fact that differences add approximately to zero in each row), we conclude that the model specified by the title of each table can be rejected in nine out of ten cases. The one exception, shown in Table 3–7, indicates that Liberal cabinets have, over time, been formed to fit the distribution of votes for the governing party in each of the regions.

---

25. As an example, see Sir George Foster, "Getting into the Cabinet," in Fox, *Politics: Canada*, pp. 211-12.

Table 3–2 **Conservative Cabinet Representation Compared with Voters in Federal Elections**

		(% difference)			
Election	Atlantic	Quebec	Ontario	Prairies	BC
1925	6.6	−18.7	8.1	−3.4	7.5
1930	4.3	− 4.5	− .1	−2.2	2.5
1957	6.3	−13.5	−2.5	5.1	4.6
1958	5.7	.8	−9.4	1.0	2.1
1962	6.5	− 9.0	−3.1	5.6	0
ξ	29.4	−44.9	−7.0	6.1	16.7
N	5	5	5	5	5

H_o: rejected

It might be easier to follow our argument if we discussed each of the five comparisons separately, first for one party and then the other. But to do so would obscure the primary purpose of our analysis, the delineation of each region's share of cabinet strength. To do the latter, we may sacrifice some clarity, but it is for good reason.

Atlantic Provinces. An examination of actual cabinet compositions compared to either the Atlantic provinces' contribution to the total voting public or its share of seats in the House of Commons (Tables

Table 3–3 **Liberal Cabinet Representation Compared with Voters in Federal Elections**

		(% difference)			
Election	Atlantic	Quebec	Ontario	Prairies	BC
1921	5.0	6.6	− 4.3	−10.2	3.0
1925	− 6.3	17.5	−24.3	11.9	1.3
1926	− 4.6	11.7	−10.2	− .2	3.4
1935	5.1	1.8	− 8.4	2.6	− 1.0
1940	.3	16.9	−15.6	− 1.5	− .2
1945	9.0	− 3.0	− 2.6	− 3.3	− .2
1949	4.2	2.0	− 1.3	− .9	− 3.8
1953	0.0	7.4	− 3.6	− 4.1	− .3
1963	3.6	2.8	5.5	− 9.9	− 2.1
1965	.1	8.2	6.7	−13.2	− 1.9
ξ	16.4	71.9	−58.1	−28.8	− 1.8
N	10	10	10	10	10

H_o: rejected

Table 3–4 **Conservative Cabinet Representation Compared with Seats in the House of Commons** (% difference)

Election	Atlantic	Quebec	Ontario	Prairies	BC
1925	8.2	−19.8	13.2	−8.7	7.2
1930	5.6	− 4.8	1.3	−4.6	2.6
1957	5.7	−14.7	− .3	4.6	4.6
1958	5.4	.3	− 7.1	− .2	1.7
1962	5.7	−10.1	− .3	4.6	.1
ξ	30.6	−49.1	6.8	−4.3	16.2
N	5	5	5		5

H_o: rejected

3–2 to 3–5), indicates a slight excess over the comparison criteria, especially for Conservative cabinets. The fit is even closer if we use as our standard votes or seats for the governing party. That is, the share of cabinet posts given to the Atlantic provinces is quite similar proportionately to the percentage of the popular vote and seats won by the governing party.

The one notable source of difference occurs when we compare Liberal cabinets with the theoretical ideal. The Atlantic provinces almost always obtained less than the share of seats predicted by the model. In most instances, the discrepancy was minor, but not in two.

Table 3–5 **Liberal Cabinet Representation Compared with Seats in the House of Commons** (% difference)

Election	Atlantic	Quebec	Ontario	Prairies	BC
1921	6.8	4.3	− 2.9	−10.3	2.1
1925	− 4.7	16.4	−19.2	6.6	1.0
1926	− 2.7	9.9	− 6.2	− 3.8	3.0
1935	6.1	1.3	− 5.7	− .2	− 1.3
1940	.9	15.8	−14.3	− 3.2	.8
1945	9.4	− 2.5	− 1.5	− 6.4	1.1
1949	3.7	1.3	1.6	− 3.5	− 3.0
1953	.5	6.5	− 1.7	− 5.1	− .3
1963	2.3	1.3	8.6	−10.7	− 1.6
1965	− 1.0	6.3	10.2	−14.3	− 1.3
ξ	21.3	60.6	−31.1	−50.9	.5
N	10	10	10	10	10

H_o: rejected

Table 3–6 **Conservative Cabinet Representation Compared with Vote for the Governing Party** (% difference)

Election	Atlantic	Quebec	Ontario	Prairies	BC
1925	3.7	−11.7	− .7	1.6	7.2
1930	2.7	− 2.2	− 4.4	1.5	2.4
1957	3.4	− 8.1	−11.1	9.7	6.1
1958	5.5	2.9	−11.2	.2	2.8
1962	4.0	− 3.4	− 5.1	2.1	2.4
ξ	19.3	−22.5	−32.5	15.1	20.9
N	5	5	5	5	5

H_o: rejected

These were cabinets formed after the elections of 1925 and 1926. For other regions as well, these years were often related to some form of inequitable representation. They cover a period of volatile third party strength, especially in the Prairies, and governmental instability. The three Maritime provinces, however, gave strong support to the Conservatives. A dearth of Liberal members from which to select ministers meant that the requirements of the model, based on a principle of equity bound neither by popular support nor population density, could not be fulfilled.

Table 3–7 **Liberal Cabinet Representation Compared with Vote for the Governing Party** (% difference)

Election	Atlantic	Quebec	Ontario	Prairies	BC
1921	1.4	−11.8	− 5.4	.7	4.4
1925	− 7.2	5.2	−15.8	15.8	2.1
1926	− 4.4	3.0	− 4.4	1.4	4.5
1935	2.6	− 3.8	− 6.4	6.7	1.0
1940	.1	11.1	−15.2	1.9	2.0
1945	7.3	− 9.4	− 2.2	1.9	2.5
1949	2.7	− 4.0	1.4	1.8	− 1.7
1953	− 1.6	.5	− 2.1	− .2	3.4
1963	1.5	.3	1.6	− 3.4	0
1965	− 1.9	4.6	3.7	− 6.9	0.4
ξ	0.5	− 4.3	−34.0	19.7	18.6
N	10	10	10	10	10

H_o: not rejected

Table 3–8 **Conservative Cabinet Representation Compared with Seats for the Governing Party** (% difference)

Election	Atlantic	Quebec	Ontario	Prairies	BC
1925	.2	3.3	−11.9	4.7	4.0
1935	.6	4.2	− 8.3	.6	2.9
1957	− .6	5.6	−22.7	10.2	7.4
1958	5.9	4.6	− 7.2	− 4.7	1.6
1962	2.7	6.1	1.6	−13.5	3.1
ξ	8.8	23.8	−48.5	− 2.7	19.0
N	5	5	5	5	5

H_0: rejected

With this exception, the Atlantic provinces can be said to regularly gain their reasonable share of cabinet posts, regardless of our standard of comparison. We can make this judgement despite the fact that differences between actual representation and the comparison criteria usually are positive, and hence appear to accumulate in the Atlantic provinces' favour. It is more important, in our judgement, that the individual differences tend to be small, especially when compared to other regions.

Quebec. History has conspired with the short-sightedness of men to

Table 3–9 **Liberal Cabinet Representation Compared with Seats for the Governing Party** (% difference)

Election	Atlantic	Quebec	Ontario	Prairies	BC
1921	− 1.6	−24.0	13.9	6.3	5.4
1925	1.0	−16.7	3.2	8.4	4.1
1926	2.1	−10.5	7.0	− 6.8	8.3
1935	2.2	− 4.0	− 4.6	4.3	2.1
1940	1.0	8.6	−12.3	.4	2.2
1945	4.8	−18.4	4.8	4.8	4.0
1949	3.2	− 6.0	4.3	.6	− 2.0
1953	− 2.8	− 3.8	.6	3.1	2.9
1963	− .7	− 6.8	.4	5.1	2.0
1965	0.0	− 8.1	3.4	3.0	1.6
ξ	9.2	−89.7	20.7	29.2	30.6
N	10	10	10	10	10

H_0: rejected

Table 3–10 **Conservative Cabinet Representation Compared with "Theoretical" Cabinet** (% difference)

Election	Atlantic	Quebec	Ontario	Prairies	BC
1925	0	−18.2	21.7	−6.7	3.2
1930	−2.6	− 3.2	9.9	−2.6	−1.4
1957	−1.8	−11.3	6.9	2.7	3.5
1958	−2.1	3.7	0	−2.1	0.6
1962	−1.8	− 6.7	6.9	2.7	−1.0
ξ	−8.3	−35.7	45.5	−6.0	4.9
N	5	5	5	5	5

H_o: rejected

alienate the French-speaking from the Conservative party. Having been in office during the Riel Rebellion, the controversy over language rights in Manitoba schools, the Boer War, and World War I, the Conservatives faced difficult decisions. That they believed the decisions they made to be correct is probably true. Such high-minded purpose did not prevent these same actions from turning away generations of Quebeckers from the Conservative party.[26] As a result, we

Table 3–11 **Liberal Cabinet Representation Compared with "Theoretical" Cabinet** (% difference)

Election	Atlantic	Quebec	Ontario	Prairies	BC
1921	0.0	7.0	7.0	−12.0	− 2.0
1925	−12.9	17.9	−10.7	8.6	− 2.9
1926	−10.9	11.4	2.3	− 1.8	− .9
1935	− 3.3	2.8	2.8	2.2	− 4.4
1940	− 8.5	17.3	− 5.8	− .8	− 2.3
1945	0.0	− 1.0	7.0	− 4.0	− 2.0
1949	− 3.3	4.2	8.3	− 3.3	− 5.8
1953	− 7.0	9.8	5.4	− 7.0	− 1.3
1963	− 5.2	4.6	15.7	−12.6	− 2.6
1965	− 8.5	9.6	17.3	−16.2	− 2.3
ξ	−59.6	83.6	49.3	−46.9	−26.5
N	10	10	10	10	10

H_o: rejected

26. For a review of the historical details, see Mason Wade, *The French Canadians, 1760-1945* (Toronto: Macmillan, 1955).

would expect that Quebec would be underrepresented in those Cabinets in which the Conservatives held power. This is true for four of the five criteria we are using, most notably in 1925 and 1957. (The fifth criterion, seats for the government, actually shows a slight plus, a reflection of Conservatives' failure to capture more than a small number of seats.) In the earlier year, memories of the 1917 conscription crisis were still strong, and the Conservatives could count on only modest support. In 1957, voters in Quebec continued their habitual opposition to the Conservatives, despite the new appeal of that party elsewhere in Canada.[27] Of the remaining three elections when the Conservatives formed the government, Quebec was able to fully participate in cabinet power, at least so far as numbers were concerned.[28] On the basis of total seats alloted to Quebec, and to some extent share of voters, the 1962 election did show some discrepancy, however, with fewer cabinet appointments than expected.

Given the long periods of Canadian history when Quebec has been the bulwark of the national Liberals, it is hardly surprising that a large share of cabinet ministers have represented that province. But our evaluation of just how great this share has been depends on what we use as the standard of comparison. Over-representation is greatest when compared to the model of the ideal cabinet. It occurred after the elections of 1925 and 1926, times when the Liberals did especially poorly elsewhere in Canada. It was also the case in 1940, but this was owing to quite different circumstances. Canada was now at war and the bitter memories of previous wars were again evoked in Quebec. Prime Minister Mackenzie King too remembered and attempted then and later, as the issue of conscription recurred, to retain support from Quebec.[29] Those ministers who opposed the government's policies and resigned had to be promptly replaced. This had the result of inflating Quebec's total representation during the time when the government elected in 1940 was in office. Over-representation occurred again in 1953 and 1965, but only in comparison to the more modest

---

27. Meisel notes that the Conservatives, recognizing their weakness in Quebec, decided on a strategy of "reinforcing success not failure." John Meisel, *The Canadian General Election of 1957* (Toronto: University of Toronto Press, 1962), pp. 166-68.

28. Numbers alone, however, have not completely allayed complaints. The late André Laurendeau, commenting on Prime Minister Diefenbaker's first six appointments after the 1958 election, is quoted as saying, "Not since the days of R. B. Bennett have French-Canadians felt themselves so absent from the affairs of state, as under Mr. Diefenbaker." Peter C. Newman, *Renegade in Power* (Toronto: McClelland & Stewart, 1963), pp. 283-84.

29. Robert McGregor Dawson, *The Conscription Crisis of 1944* (Toronto: University of Toronto Press, 1962); André Laurendeau, *La Crise de la conscription* (Montréal: Editions du jour, 1962).

requirements of the model. At the earlier time, it reflected no clear-cut issues, but more probably the tendency of a prime minister from French Canada, Louis St. Laurent, to reward those closest to him in interests and outlook. In 1965, it was again related to the minority status of the government, and its weakness in the western provinces.

If we compare cabinet representation with the distribution of either voters or seats in the House of Commons, then Quebec could be considered to have a larger than equitable share of ministers only in 1925, 1926, and 1940, presumably for the reasons we have already indicated. Yet if we look at support for the governing party, Tables 3–7 and 3–9, we get an interesting reversal. Compared to what would be expected if seats won by the government were the primary criterion, Quebec was given *less* than its share of cabinet posts in 1921, 1925, 1926, 1945, and to some extent, in 1965. As an aftermath of the feelings provoked by the war and the actions of the Union government, the 1921 election returned Liberals to all of Quebec's seats in the federal House. This meant that 56 percent of the government's seats were concentrated in Quebec. Similar loyalty to the Liberal side was displayed in the two following elections. The election of 1945 was another occasion for focusing on wartime complaints. This time, however, there was important opposition to the Liberals from third parties, particularly Bloc Populaire Canadien. Nonetheless, 82 percent of the Quebec seats were won by the Liberals, representing 42 percent of all seats held by the governing party. Somewhat similar results were produced by the election of 1965, but at that time regional representation was even more skewed than in 1945. All of this means that the excessive support given to the Liberals through seats won passes without additional reward in the form of cabinet posts. While Quebec could obtain this form of reward vis à vis what would be anticipated from criteria based on a theoretical model or the distribution of voters and seats, there is an upper limit to the allocation of cabinet posts regardless of the number of seats in a region won by the government.

When we make our final comparison, with popular votes for the government, we find discrepancies with only two cabinets: those serving the Fourteenth and Nineteenth Parliaments elected in 1921 and 1940 respectively. As in the case of seats, the amount of voting support for the Liberals was not fully taken into account in alloting cabinet posts. The special circumstances of the government elected in 1940 were related, as we have indicated, to the deliberate strategy of involving Quebec in the cabinet, regardless of the amount of support from that province. This resulted in a form of over-representation that disregarded the usual constraints on cabinet formation.

Ontario. At times Ontario appears as the mirror-image of Quebec.

For example, in Conservative ministries, the under-representation of Quebec is countered with the over-representation of Ontario compared both to the theoretical model and the total distribution of seats. (Tables 3–4 and 3–10.) Compared to our theoretical model, large discrepancies existed after the elections of 1925, when the Conservatives attempted to govern, and to a lesser extent, in 1930. An excess of cabinet posts is also manifested after 1925 if we use the distribution of total seats as our standard of comparison. But as we saw in the case of Quebec, the effects of a high level of popular support are hampered by other conventions concerning the regional makeup of cabinets. Hence, although 59 percent of the Conservative seats following the 1925 election were concentrated in Ontario, the Meighen government could not allot this large a proportion of seats to Ontario in the cabinet. Less than a full measure of reward for support also followed the 1957 election, when the minority Conservative government avoided antagonizing other regions (though other motives were involved), by giving Ontario fewer cabinet posts than would have been commensurate with such criteria as votes for the Conservatives or seats won by them.

To some extent the mirror-image analogy continues under Liberal ministries. But Ontario, as the most populous province, and hence the one with the largest number of seats in the House of Commons, always has a natural advantage. Even when its residents do not give the bulk of their vote to a Liberal government, there are enough seats involved that Ontario is likely to get at least its fair share of cabinet posts. This means that our results are not quite so clear-cut as they were for Quebec. If they were, we would anticipate that, on the basis of formal characteristics—the theoretical model, percentage of voters, and seats,—Ontario would be under-represented in Liberal cabinets, but on the basis of support, it would be over-represented. In overall terms, this pattern is confirmed when our comparison criteria are total voters and seats for the governing party. (See Tables 3–3, 3–5, and 3–9.) Compared to the theoretical model, however, Ontario appears to have been over-represented. This was particularly evident following the elections of 1963 and 1965. A minority Liberal government existed on the basis of regionally uneven support patterns. The government had to rely largely on Ontario for its selection of ministers, as it had with Quebec. As a consequence, Ontario was over-represented, compared both to our model and its total share of seats during those years. When the model is used as a measuring standard, cabinet representation conforms to our expectations of under-representation in only two instances. It did so by a sizeable percentage in the Liberal cabinet of 1925. The Liberals fared poorly in Ontario in that election, but perhaps more important is that they struggled along with an unusually small and necessarily makeshift cabinet. Hence on every criterion except the percentage of seats won by the Liberals, Ontario appears to have been under-represented.

The full measure of advantage accruing to Ontario emerges when we compare cabinet composition to the share of seats won by the Liberals in Table 3–9. In all but two instances, Ontario received greater representation than it gave in support. Frequently the discrepancy was quite small, but it was sizeable in 1921. With a government faced by meagre support from the Prairies and overwhelming support from Quebec, these somewhat undeserved rewards to Ontario were one way of balancing regional inequities.

Of the two instances of under-representation compared to seats for the government, only one requires comment. This is the cabinet serving the government elected in 1940. By all our standards of comparison except the theoretical model, Ontario received less than its fair share of cabinet posts at that time. Yet this was not so much the result of lack of support, but rather the effect of the preponderance of cabinet representation from Quebec. It is true, however, that Ontario was deprived of at least one extra cabinet minister. This came about when, in two by-elections, voters in Ontario defeated A. G. L. McNaughton, Minister of Defense for nine months despite his lack of a seat. The efforts made to conciliate French Canada on conscription were not completely successful. These policies also aroused dissatisfaction in English Canada, although not for the same reasons. McNaughton's defeats were then likely signs of this discontent.[30] But on the basis of seats won in the 1940 election alone, Ontario would still have been expected to have a large share of cabinet posts.

In both Liberal and Conservative governments, Ontario is rewarded with an excess of cabinet positions compared to what would be considered equitable on the basis of our model. Aside from this, governments tend to keep in check what would otherwise be the numerical preponderance of Ontario. Conservatives tend to do this less by taking into account Ontario's total allotment of seats than by other criteria. Liberals, on the other hand, to some extent discount the percentage of seats they win in Ontario, so that Ontario enjoys some advantage regardless of its level of support.

Prairie Provinces. The Prairie provinces have been inclined to benefit when a Conservative government is in office. This is not too clear from our tables because of the effects of third party support in the early years of the period under study. Particularly in forming a cabinet after the defeat of the Liberals in a vote of confidence following the 1925 election, the Conservatives found few they could call on for ministerial

---

30. Robert McGregor Dawson, *The Government of Canada* (Toronto: University of Toronto Press, 1947), p. 385.

posts from the Prairies. Yet with this exception, the Prairie provinces
have been consistently allotted their fair share of cabinet ministers, or
at least close to it. We make this judgement on the basis of comparisons with the three formal criteria of representation, particularly the
distribution of total voters. (Tables 3–2, 3–4, and 3–10.)

The Prairies have tended to receive slightly more than their share if
we compare actual representation with popular vote. Such over-
representation vis à vis both support criteria was most apparent following the election of 1957. A revitalized Conservative party came
out of the west under the leadership of John Diefenbaker but in 1957
it was only the vanguard of what was to follow in the 1958 election.
Until that point, even though popular support was rather modest,
cabinet posts were quickly forthcoming to those who shared an identity with the Prairies. Those provinces then benefitted in their representation from factors other than clearly regional ones.[31]

Under Liberal regimes, the Prairies have fared poorly when we
take into account what their role would have been in cabinets formed
according to the model, or the distribution of voters or seats. Under-
representation was particularly marked in those cabinets serving governments elected in 1921, 1963, and 1965. Support for the Liberals
was low during these elections, going instead in the earliest one to
the Progressives, and in the other two, to the Conservatives. In one
sense then, the Prairies received the cabinet representation they deserved. In another, however, they did better than deserved. That is,
if we compare cabinets with patterns of support, the Prairies appear
to have been slightly over-represented. The Liberal governments,
then, accepted some pressure toward the equitable representation of
the Prairies despite the low level of support they received.

The 1925 Liberal Cabinet, on the basis of votes, either those for
the governing party or that part of the total body of electors, appears
to have over-represented the Prairies. Some desire to win over the
Progressives was involved, but there was also a distortion introduced

---

31. When dealing with as select a body as the cabinet, numbers are necessarily
small, a fact which may sometimes be obscured by our use of percentages. For
example, in the 1957 Cabinet we are referring to only five men, one of whom
was the prime minister and the other government leader in the Senate. Still
there is evidence that cabinet posts held during this period were often rewards
for personal loyalty to the prime minister. Of the three remaining Prairie
ministers, one was of a group of four who had supported Mr. Diefenbaker
since his first bid for the Conservative party leadership in 1942. The two others
were part of a body of six ministers who had been converted to the Diefenbaker
cause at the 1956 leadership convention. Even as latecomers, however, they
were considered more loyal than those, who while given cabinet posts during
some part of the Diefenbaker period, had never been Mr. Diefenbaker's active
supporters. Newman, *Renegade in Power,* pp. 94-95.

by the unusually small cabinet, the result of a poor electoral showing that would soon lead to the collapse of the government. The discrepancies that our comparisons reveal were only a temporary phenomenon, related to the unusual circumstances of that election.

British Columbia. However we choose to look at the composition of cabinets, representation for British Columbia is never deficient. It does not suffer despite a frequent tendency to give a low level of support to the government. Support is usually sufficient to allow British Columbia at least the one or two ministers that are its due. When Conservatives are in office, British Columbia does particularly well, as it generally gains some over-representation.

Regional Power. Our interest in cabinet representation centred on its potential for evaluating the relative power of regions. The review of both Liberal and Conservative cabinets between 1921 and 1965 was interesting, but not immediately understandable in terms of such power. To make this translation, we need to make some judgements, perhaps rather metaphoric in character, about the meaning of cabinet positions. These are "rewards" by the party in office for the support demonstrated by a region. Conversely, the lack of such positions are "punishments." These rewards and punishments operate within a set of constraints, namely the population density of the region and the conventions about how many seats it should have. Such constraints establish what we might call a system of "equity." A region that regularly receives its fair share of cabinet appointments is then equipped with a given amount of the power bank. Support is deposited and interest can be regularly anticipated. This is the case of the Atlantic provinces. But when a region regularly withholds its support from the government, considerations of equity may be set aside, and punishments will be manifested in less than a fair share of the federal power reserve. This occurs in Quebec when the Conservatives are in office, and in the Prairies, under the Liberals. Some regions, however, will receive more than they would have simply on the basis of equity. Such circumstances may be associated with strong support for the government, as is the case for Quebec under the Liberals and the Prairies under the Conservatives. We need to qualify our Quebec example, however, since we recall that cabinet rewards sometimes could not keep pace with the extent of support. This power bonus may be more than a reward for loyalty, as in the case of Ontario, and to some extent, British Columbia. If the Prairies and Quebec at times make large deposits in the power bank and are rewarded with a high rate of interest, the two other provinces make low deposits with the same result. It is as though, for whatever reasons, Ontario and British Columbia are able to invest their support resources more shrewdly.

THE RELATIVE STRENGTH OF REGIONS

The task we set ourselves—to evaluate the relative power of each region as a part of the national government—can now be completed. While the three indicators of power we have used are related, they also gave us three distinct ways of treating regional power. The distribution of popular vote is most clearly tied to the role of individual citizens, and permits us to judge the extent of support that citizens give the government. Our specific concern was with how regions varied along this support dimension.[32] The government's share of each region's seats in the House of Commons measures the potential for participating in the business of government. Finally, the regional allotment of cabinet positions, while furthest removed from the behaviour of voters and hence from support, is most closely tied with the actual exercise of power. Cabinet ministers, as the principal decision-makers in government and the principal representatives of regions, do most to affect regional fortunes.

In summing up, some simplification seems permissible, especially since our preceding analysis has been so detailed. In order to assign each region to a position of power, we would like to take into account the three aspects of power, trends over time, and where pertinent, differences associated with Liberal or Conservative governments. It is easiest to do this if we confine our approach to power along two dimensions: representation as measured by cabinet posts, and support measured by both votes and seats won by the governing party. A region's share of cabinet posts can then be treated as fairly determined (0), above an equitable proportion $(+)$, or below equity $(-)$. Support for the government could be conceptualized as high, medium, or low. If we then constructed a three by three table, it would have the following format.

	Cabinet Posts		
	$+$	0	$-$
Support:			
High	a	x	
Medium	y	b	
Low		z	c

If cabinet posts were perfectly correlated with support, then we would expect only those cells along the main diagonal (a, b, c) to be filled. An examination of correlation coefficients in Table 3–12 shows that

---

32. Viewed from the perspective of the party system, our results also confirm the continuing impact of regional factors on it. Compare Donald E. Blake, "The Measurement of Regionalism in Canadian Voting Patterns," *Canadian Journal of Political Science*, 5 (March 1972): 55-81.

Table 3–12 **Correlation Between Regional Composition of Federal Cabinets and Selected Characteristics, 1921–1965**

Correlation between Cabinet and:	Liberal Cabinets	Conservative Cabinets
Theoretical model	.77	.60
Total voters	.76	.75
Total seats in House	.80	.68
Votes for government	.88	.91
Seats for government	.90	.88

both measures of support do in fact show a strong association with cabinet composition. Support alone accounts for from 77 to 83 percent of the variance, an unusually strong relationship for social phenomena. But remaining factors, not in themselves of such crucial importance, nonetheless affect which cells in our 3 x 3 table are filled. The placement of symbols x and z represent the Atlantic provinces and British Columbia. Perhaps it is the result of a pressure toward equity, or perhaps the consequence of factors we have not considered, but for whatever reasons, the eastern and westernmost provinces are pushed away from cells a and c, respectively. This regression toward the mean does not, however, operate for the remaining regions. Ontario is not found in cell b, but in y. This advantageous position derives in part from the actual number of seats going to the government, rather than merely the percent. This means that Ontario is almost always treated as the keystone of a government, to some extent regardless of the dispositions of its voters.

Quebec and the Prairies interchange positions a and c. They do this according to the party in office. For Quebec, high support for the Liberals is associated with a large share of cabinet posts. Low support for the Conservatives tends to be followed by low cabinet representation. The opposite pattern operates for the Prairie provinces. As we have seen, some of the extremes of rewards and punishments for support are held in check by considerations of equity, based on the need for the party in office to govern the whole country and not just its supporters. Yet Table 3–12 indicates one place where the Conservatives are not always effective in offering equitable cabinet representation. This occurs where we use as our standard of judgement a theoretically ideal cabinet. The resulting correlation coefficient of .60 is not significantly different from that for the corresponding Liberal correlation.[33] While our statistic does not fully capture this, a

33. $Z = 1.34$, not significant at the .05 level.

possible source of stress is introduced when the Conservatives over-represent the Prairies and under-represent Quebec.

If we assign a numerical value to the cells in our 3 x 3 table, we can finally arrive at a ranking of relative power. Since a large share of cabinet posts is obviously the most valuable position for a region, we will give a value of one to cell *a* and 2 and 3 to the remainder in that column. Following this procedure, cell *c* is valued at 9. It then becomes a simple matter to give a power score to each region. For Quebec and the Prairies we took into account the total frequency of Liberal and Conservative regimes and averaged the results. We may also adjust for the over-representation of British Columbia in Conservative governments.[34] A high numerical score is associated with relatively less power within the national government. The rankings and scores are: Ontario, 2; Quebec, 3.7; Atlantic provinces, 4; British Columbia, 5; Prairies, 6.3.

---

34. Quebec P. S. $= \dfrac{(1 \times 10) + (9 \times 5)}{15} = 3.7$

Prairie P. S. $= \dfrac{(1 \times 5) + (9 \times 10)}{15} = 6.3$

CHAPTER

4

Life in the provinces: as it is seen

The objective measures used in Chapters 2 and 3 give a powerful description of how regions differ, and at the same time, explain how territorial considerations continue to permeate the political life of the country. One might even argue that no further analysis is necessary: the case for regionalism is proved. For those, however, willing to consider less precise kinds of measurement, additional depth and complexity can be added to our understanding of regionalism. This comes when we move into the more personal world of one who lives in Canada's regions, exploring how these differences affect him, and how their existence becomes manifested in his perceptions of reality.

It is only by directly approaching residents that we can discover whether regional differences are in fact acknowledged. When such acknowledgement is made, we have a precondition for the emergence of regional identity. In general, the development of group consciousness begins when members acquire an awareness of their uniqueness. It is an awareness that links together feelings about the self and the collectivity, feelings that arise from contrast with others. Regional consciousness is a form of group consciousness in which region becomes the salient identity. The acquisition of such awareness may be linked to what is broadly subsumed under the concept of reference group. "In the process of self-appraisal, from many possible groups available as framework for social comparison, individuals make their own particular selection, thus reflecting the true complexities of their social location but not necessarily the arbitrary social position to which the scientist may have assigned them."[1]

In the text that follows we provide evidence that Canadians in the 1960s had an awareness of differences closely tied to the content of their comparisons. Thus virtually everyone made distinctions about regions in which they would like to live, three-quarters recognized disparities in the economic well-being of regions, and somewhat more than half acknowledged differences in power.

Having residents know about differences is a minimal condition for the development of regional consciousness. More important is how these differences are evaluated. Are they accurately judged, or are there distortions in judgement leading to over or under estimations? In any case, we are concerned with the links between such evaluations and the sense of relative advantage or disadvantage prevalent in each region. It is just such feelings which either dampen or exacerbate the tensions originating from the sheer fact of regional differences.

SOURCE OF DATA

The data presented here were obtained from a sample survey of the Canadian electorate interviewed after the 1965 general election. Respondents were selected from official lists of voters, after first stratifying their constituencies. Stratification was based on province, urban-rural distribution within the constituency, and the constituency's past voting history. Twenty-nine constituencies out of a total of 263 were eliminated as being too remote and sparsely populated to make interviewing practicable. Randomizing procedures were then used to select constituencies, sampling units within them, and finally respondents themselves.[2]

In order to ensure adequate numbers of respondents in areas with low population density, the decision was made to oversample outside of Ontario and metropolitan Montreal. To then arrive at a sample

---

1. Herbert H. Hyman and Eleanor Singer, eds., *Readings in Reference Group Theory and Research* (New York: Free Press, 1968), p. 3. The entire volume is a useful compendium of material on processes of identity formation and social comparison.

2. A somewhat fuller description of the sample design and procedures is contained in John Meisel and Richard Van Loon, "Canadian Attitudes to Election Expenses 1965-6," in Committee on Election Expenses, *Studies in Canadian Party Finance* (Ottawa: Queen's Printer, 1966), pp. 32-41, 143-45. Due to the urgency of their report, some of the problems noted in the text were not then apparent. Because of the elimination of a few cases and some slight variations in weighting procedures, minor discrepancies in the total sample used will be found.

that was properly representative of the distribution of the electorate, it was necessary to introduce weighting procedures. Montreal and Toronto were each given a weight of 1, and the rest of Ontario 1.5. Remaining areas were then all to be weighted twice. Due to some misunderstanding, the sample in British Columbia was half of what it should have been, requiring us to weight that province four times. Individual interviews completed numbered 2610, of which a few were discarded. The remainder were weighted by area, and then re-weighted to bring our sample size back to its approximate real value. This is the basis for arriving at the 2727 respondents that form our working sample.

While weighting is sometimes a device to disguise an inadequate sample, this is not so in our case. Because it was the largest areas that were undersampled, we can feel quite secure in our assessments of population differences. Sample sizes were, however, too small to permit confident discussion of the individual provinces of Prince Edward Island and Newfoundland. Despite its less than optimum size, we consider the total for British Columbia reasonably reliable. Our confidence fades, however, when the British Columbia sample is divided into subgroups.

The design of the sample and the questionnaire were the responsibility of all five participants in the original planning of the study: Philip Converse, John Meisel, Maurice Pinard, Peter Regenstreif, and myself. Technical assistance in drawing the sample and the interviewing were both done by Canadian Facts Limited.[3]

THE ECONOMIC CONDITION OF REGIONS

Awareness of differences in the economic condition of regions was found for three-quarters of our sample, with little regional variation. Seventy-three percent in Quebec, 74 percent in Ontario and the Prairies, 79 percent in the Atlantic provinces, and 80 percent in British Columbia manifested this form of regional consciousness.

In order to probe more deeply into the evaluations associated with perceptions of economic well-being, several alternative approaches were examined. One was by using responses to a question about regions or provinces better off than others. Second was to use a question on regions or provinces worse off than others. A combination of these two, subtracting the worse from the better off, provided an index for a third alternative. A preliminary analysis was done using

---

3. Data are on deposit at the Inter-University Consortium for Political Research, University of Michigan, and the Survey Research Centre, York University.

the three approaches, but since they all provided similar information, only data on regions better off are presented. Data are summarized in Table 4–1. They are based on those respondents who recognized the existence of internal variation among regions.[4]

Data have been arranged in Table 4–1 to minimize the number of transpositions in the ranking of regions. Responses recorded in the main diagonal are the percentage of respondents in each region who selected their own area as better off. Even with our aggregating procedures, those in the Atlantic provinces were reluctant to choose their own region. No other part of Canada appeared so disadvantaged to its residents. Quebec, which ranked fourth in the frequency with which it was selected by residents, was separated from the Atlantic provinces by 35 percent. On this basis, Quebec can be located closer to the Prairies. The Prairies, in turn, approach the most favoured provinces of Ontario and British Columbia.

The relation between the perceptions of residents and non-residents emerges most clearly if we convert our findings into ranks:

1	2	3	4	5
2	1	3	4	5
3	2	1	4	5
1	3	4	2	5
1	3	4	2	5

The consistency of rankings can be measured by the coefficient of concordance, W, and the direction of inconsistencies, by the number

---

4. Since respondents were permitted to select either regions or individual provinces as better off, some adjustment had to be made for our aggregating procedures in the two collections of provinces. After inspecting all possible responses, it was decided to combine all mentions of the Atlantic provinces, either individual or collective. While this inflates choice of the Atlantic provinces slightly, it does not affect their relative ranking, nor does it alter the fact that few chose these provinces as better off. A similar procedure for dealing with the Prairies was abandoned since it seemed to distort the relative position of that region. All mentions combined would mean that 85 percent of those living in the Prairies felt that region was better off, a frequency greater than that found for any other area. But conversely, 17 percent of Prairie residents selected this conglomerate as worse off, considerably more than made this self-selection in any other region except the Atlantic provinces. On the basis of the combined index of well-being the Prairies rank behind British Columbia and Ontario. For this reason, it was decided to find some alternative procedure for handling the Prairies. This was done by using Alberta, the most favourably rated of the Prairies, as the surrogate for individual provinces and adding it to mentions of the whole region. (On provinces worst off, it was generally Saskatchewan that was chosen, followed by Manitoba.)

Table 4–1 **Regions Better Off, By Region of Residence (percent)**

Region of
Residence: Region Better Off[a]

	Ontario	British Columbia	Prairies[b]	Quebec	Atlantic[c]	N[d]
Ontario	79	36	23	17	1	(778)
British Columbia	60	84	38	11	2	(204)
Prairies	43	50	70	9	3	(293)
Quebec	75	30	13	44	3	(579)
Atlantic provinces	78	30	19	31	9	(180)

[a]Respondents could mention more than one province or region.

[b]Includes all mentions of the Prairies plus Alberta.

[c]Includes all mentions of the Atlantic region plus individual provinces.

[d]Base N is all those who, in a preceding question, answered that they felt some regions were better off than others.

of transpositions required to produce perfect consensus. Ranks on regional well-being produce a W of .64, which leads to rejection of the null hypothesis of random ordering at the .01 level. In other words, there is a considerable degree of consensus about the state of regions, regardless of the regional vantage point of raters. This is probably the result of a reality factor, consistent with some of the objective indicators of economic conditions outlined in Chapter 2.

Of eight transpositions, five are due to the diagonal cells. We see this as a form of ethnocentrism, in which residents felt their own region to be better off than did non-residents. The strength of this ethnocentrism varied, and was usually accompanied by a greater choice of one's own area over any other. Only Quebec and the Atlantic provinces deviated from this pattern. Ethnocentrism in the Atlantic provinces was weak, rarely overcoming the reality of a constricted economy. It was stronger in Quebec, but there too it was restrained by the belief that economic conditions were not so good as elsewhere in Canada, or more accurately, in Ontario.

The remaining three transpositions occurred in the Prairies and Atlantic provinces. They were the result of Atlantic residents ranking Quebec second in well-being and Prairie residents ranking British Columbia first. This suggests some influence from propinquity, where a neighbouring region is selected more frequently than a more distant one. A comparison of columns in Table 4–1, disregarding the diagonal cells, makes this even clearer. British Columbia received more choices from the Prairies, the Prairies from British Columbia and secondly from Ontario, and Quebec from the Atlantic provinces and secondly from Ontario. Propinquity does not explain perceptions of Ontario. It was chosen by 75 percent in Quebec, but by even slightly more in the Atlantic provinces, and by 60 percent in British Columbia. Only the Prairie provinces, with their westward orientation, were reluctant to give Ontario full recognition of its advantaged position. Responses for the individual provinces indicate that Alberta was considered more prosperous by the largest numbers, with British Columbia ranking second.

REGIONAL ATTRACTIVENESS

Some of the same procedural decisions that were made in order to compare the economic condition of regions were also necessary before dealing with their attractiveness. Again two questions were asked: "In which Canadian provinces do you think you might like to live?" and "In which Canadian provinces would you definitely never want to live?" An analysis based on the two questions separately and then combined in an index produced no differences. For the sake of simplicity we will concentrate on responses to preferred place of residence.[5]

Since respondents could mention more than one province as well as the one they lived in, grouping of provinces was a problem. Our choice was between combining all the Atlantic and Prairie provinces, or using one of each, New Brunswick and Alberta, as surrogates for the total. The combining technique enhanced the attractiveness of the grouped provinces to their residents, but it had little effect on the views of outsiders. Consequently we chose to follow the grouping procedure.

Looking first at the cells in the diagonal of Table 4–2, we see that at least three-quarters of the respondents preferred their own region, with the result that there is little differentiation among four of the regions. Only in the case of British Columbia was the frequency of self-selection greatly different from the others. There almost all residents said that they preferred their own province. Within the Atlantic provinces, choices were mainly confined to respondents' own province

---

5. Because there was a great deal of variability in the percentage mentioning each of the provinces as preferred, we decided to compute our percentages based on the total sample. We do so in order to keep the extent of preference in perspective, particularly as we compare residents with others, since virtually everyone made at least one choice.

Table 4–2 **Preferred Place of Residence, By Region (percent)**

Region of Residence:		Preferred Region[a]				
	Ontario	British Columbia	Prairies[b]	Atlantic[b]	Quebec	N
Ontario	76	42	19	7	6	(1054)
British Columbia	10	97	16	4	2	(256)
Prairies	14	49	80	5	1	(395)
Atlantic provinces	20	14	15	75	4	(229)
Quebec	18	13	4	3	77	(793)

[a]Respondents could mention more than one province.
[b]Combination of individual provinces.

and not to other parts of the region. In the Prairies, however, Alberta was an important third choice to residents of Saskatchewan and Manitoba. Albertans gave no sign of reciprocating these feelings.[6]

Again converting the frequencies into ranks, we obtain a W of .30. Since this is associated with less than an acceptable significance level, we cannot reject the null hypothesis of inconsistent ordering.

1	2	3	4	5
3	1	2	4	5
3	2	1	4	5
2	4	3	1	5
2	3	4	5	1

Of a total of thirteen transpositions, the maximum number of ten are due to the diagonal cells. We conclude that ethnocentrism on where it

6. Details of these and other findings on reactions of each of the Prairie provinces are contained in Mildred A. Schwartz, "Attachments to Province and Region in the Prairie Provinces," David K. Elton, ed., *One Prairie Province? Conference Proceedings and Selected Papers* (Lethbridge, Alberta: Lethbridge Herald, 1971), pp. 101-105. The salience of these survey findings was demonstrated when the Premier of Alberta, Harry Strom, delivered one of the keynote addresses to the Lethbridge conference. In his talk he rejected any interest in Prairie union but suggested instead that Alberta join with British Columbia. Ibid., pp. 29-34.

would be desirable to live is exceedingly high. Not only did residents select their own region with great frequency but they looked on no other with comparable favour.

One of the remaining transpositions occurred as a result of those in the Atlantic provinces preferring the Prairies to British Columbia, but since this is based on only one percent difference, it may not be terribly important. At the same time, it does indicate that Atlantic residents did not share in the consensus about the relative attractiveness of British Columbia.

The two remaining transpositions are even more relevant. They occurred in British Columbia and the Prairies, where the two areas were mutual second choices. In addition to the strong ethnocentrism of these provinces, in which the home territory was chosen more often than any other region, we have evidence of a leaning away from other population centres in Canada.

In Chapter 2 we ordered regions according to their net gain of population. The most popular province had been British Columbia, followed by Ontario, Quebec, the Prairies and the Atlantic provinces. It is apparent that this ranking bears little resemblance to where people said they would like to live. We have described Canadians as a highly mobile people, moving from Europe to Canada, from farms to cities, from Canada to the United States, and from one province to another. Yet we would hardly suspect the latter form of mobility from the evidence presented in Table 4–2. It suggests the attractiveness of British Columbia, but only in very selective ways. Of all Canadians represented in our sample, only those living in Ontario were even moderately willing to name other, desirable provinces.

Canada is not only a mobile society, but it requires this mobility in the interests of industrial efficiency.[7] The fact that most of our respondents did not evaluate other regions with favour does not, of course, mean that they or others like them would not move under the proper circumstances. Yet these opinions surely mean something, not least of which is the evidence they give of the strength of inward-looking ethnocentrism. Quebec is a special case in point. The overwhelming majority of Quebeckers felt that their own province was where they would like to live, and concomitantly, there was no other place in Canada that was even moderately appealing. Meanwhile, migration from the rest of the country was light, and the perceptions of other

---

7. An interesting comparison is provided by Yugoslavia, a polyethnic society with strong regional cultures. There is evidence that there, high level professional and political leaders are reluctant to leave their home region, a situation that encourages the continuity of regional differences despite the centralizing tendencies of the national regime. Jack C. Fisher, *Yugoslavia: A Multinational State* (San Francisco: Chandler Publishing Co., 1966), p. 54.

Canadians negative. Here we have evidence of one formidable barrier to national integration: the reluctance of Quebeckers to leave their province and of others to settle in Quebec. Similar comments could be made about the Atlantic provinces, and even to some extent the Prairies.

DIFFERENCES IN POWER

Shifting to more explicitly political considerations, respondents were asked, "Are any provincial governments more powerful than others?" Over half replied that there were, but now, unlike the question on economic conditions, regional variations emerge. Comparing four regions, only six percentage points separated those with the lowest and highest awareness of differences, the Atlantic and Prairie provinces. British Columbia, however, was distinctive, with 72 percent of its residents perceiving power differences. We have no immediate explanation for this excess of concern with power. Those who recognized power differences were asked to specify the more powerful provinces. Results are presented in Table 4–3. Since respondents mentioned specific provinces, these have been added together in the case of the Atlantic and Prairie provinces with what appears to be a minimal inflationary effect. Ontario was mentioned most frequently

Table 4–3 **Regions with More Power, By Region of Residence (percent)**

| Region of Residence: | Regions with More Power[a] | | | | | |
	Quebec	Ontario	British Columbia	Prairies[b]	Atlantic[b]	N[c]
Quebec	66	63	15	17	3	(474)
Ontario	60	71	24	14	3	(578)
British Columbia	60	31	60	23	8	(184)
Prairies	56	33	31	46	2	(236)
Atlantic provinces	53	38	18	18	43	(123)

[a]Respondents could mention more than one province.
[b]Individual provinces have been aggregated to form a single region.
[c]Base N is all respondents who answered, to a preceding question, that some provinces were more powerful than others.

by its residents as having more power. The order of frequency decreased for residents of Quebec, British Columbia, the Prairies, and Atlantic provinces. In ordering regions, however, Quebec ranked first on the basis of its average position in all five regions.

Converting attributions of power into ranks and testing their consistency with a coefficient of concordance produces a W of .56. This is associated with a significance level less than .05, leading us to conclude that perceptions of power are fairly consistent.

1	2	3	4	5
2	1	3	4	5
1.5	3	1.5	4	5
1	3	4	2	5
1	3	4.5	4.5	2

This consensus, however, is completely at odds with circumstances described in Chapter 3, where we concluded that Ontario and then Quebec were the most powerful provinces. On the basis of the three indicators employed there, the Atlantic provinces were ranked third. Despite the unevenness of its support for the federal government, fourth ranking British Columbia had been more successful than the Prairies in retaining adequate cabinet representation, and consequently we judged it to have more power than the Prairies, which were left in fifth place.

Despite the greater objective power of Ontario, only Quebec residents recognized its importance, and even they attributed it to be secondary to their own. Elsewhere it was Quebec that was presumed to have more power. In the three remaining regions, Ontario was always ranked third. The percentage fewer choices given to Ontario compared to Quebec was 29 in British Columbia, 23 in the Prairies, and 15 in the Atlantic provinces. It seems reasonable to assume that both the actual exercise of power by Quebec politicians and the publicity this had received in recent years contributed to the inordinate amount of power that province was perceived to have.[8]

Even living in the Atlantic provinces did not provide sufficient conviction to rank that area high among those having power. Else-

8. Lewis Brand, former member of Parliament from Saskatoon, is quoted, "Every time Mayor Drapeau (of Montreal) weeps, the federal government is there to dry his tears; whenever we ask for something, they ignore us completely." That this was purported to have been said in 1969 does not detract from its relevance both to the time of our survey and even earlier. Walter Stewart, "The Coming Showdown with the West," *Macleans,* 82 (July 1969), p. 37.

where it fared more poorly, with only negligible numbers affirming its potency. This is, to repeat, in the face of considerable power within national governments over the course of decades. Why perceptions should be so at variance is not immediately clear, but we can suggest several reasons. One is the admitted ambiguity of the question itself. We must concede that what is meant by relative power in this context is not self-evident. Hence there was a greater possibility of respondents making variant interpretations than was likely on the two preceding questions. At the same time, independent support for the general validity of our interpretations comes from a Canadian Institute of Public Opinion survey, in which the same question was repeated in 1948 and 1969. Respondents were asked, "Do you think any province has more to say in the running of Canada than it should have?" At both times, under half agreed that this was the case, somewhat fewer than attributed power differences in our survey. Such discrepancies are understandable with the use of different questions, but most persuasive is the fact that at both times, Quebec and Ontario were mentioned most frequently as having more say. An analysis comparable to our own is not possible, but from the reasons given for selecting these provinces we do get the impression that the nature of provincial power differences is fairly well understood. For example, the main reason given for thinking that Quebec had more to say in running Canada was the belief that Quebec demanded too much, and that Ottawa catered to its wishes more than it should. Those who named Ontario referred most frequently to the accepted fact that it had the greatest economic power, and the largest population, and therefore its voice was more effective than other provinces.[9]

While we do not wish to cast doubt on our own procedures, it is still possible that the indicators used in Chapter 3 did not effectively measure relative power, so that the Atlantic provinces may in fact have been lower in power than we were able to discern. Rather than reject the results of Chapter 3, a more likely possibility is the fact, noted there, that no major political advantage accrued to the Atlantic provinces despite their history of loyalty to the government of the day. This may result in a generally depressive effect on the tenor of political evaluations of that region, both inside and out. The low sense of potency may also have stemmed from non-political factors. That is, those conditions considered earlier, contributing to the depressed nature of the economy and the restrained outlook on personal and regional prospects, could have been sufficiently pervasive to encompass the political scene as well. Yet if we look only at rankings and not at frequencies, then the self-evaluations of the Atlantic

9. Gallup Report, Canadian Institute of Public Opinion (20 September, 1969).

provinces can be viewed differently. Like all other regions, its residents too placed it in the forefront of the powerful.

The diagonal cells resulted in seven out of a total of eight transpositions. By this measure, as well as the W's, we can say that ethnocentrism on power was midway between that for regions better off and preferred. At the same time, we see some reality check, as the Prairies and Atlantic provinces both gave their home region second place, reserving first place for Quebec. In the Prairies, perceptions of provincial potency were highly variable, with Alberta residents assigning their province first place, while those in the remaining two provinces ranked their territories only above the Atlantic provinces.

RELATIVE ETHNOCENTRISM

On all three items used to evaluate the condition of regions, we found evidence of ethnocentrism. We have used that concept to refer to a tendency for residents of an area to view it in more favourable terms than do outsiders, and, concomitantly, to see other parts of Canada in less favourable terms than their own area. These conditions were not always fulfilled, an indication that ethnocentrism was not uniformly distributed. In addition, even allowing for the existence of such ethnocentrism, respondents did not always agree on their evaluations of regions other than their own, although we might anticipate that such consensus would be easier to achieve.

In a five by five table, such as we have been using, perfect agreement among all rows (that is, for all regions of residence) would be signified by the same ranking of columns (that is, of all regions as preferred places for living). This would mean that Canadians, regardless of where they lived, assigned the same rank order to all regions, including their own. While the magnitude of the choices could still vary, such that regions as a matter of course would make all selections more or less frequently, we would have some evidence of a general consensus about the state of regions.

Another possibility would be agreement on the evaluation of all regions except when that involved one's home province. This would be represented by the diagonal cells being out of order, making up ten transpositions. Where these transpositions are the result of inflated self-evaluations, as they have often been in our tables, we have considered this to indicate the existence of ethnocentrism.

Between perfect consensus and perfect ethnocentrism there are many other possibilities, including quite independent evaluations of self and others within each region. As we already know from our preceding analysis, at least some ethnocentrism was the rule on all three items. Based on rankings, it was weakest in the evaluation of each region's well-being. There were a total of eight transpositions, five of which were caused by the diagonal cells. Ethnocentrism was modest in Quebec and virtually absent in the Atlantic provinces. The same number of transpositions occurred in ranking regions more powerful, but in this instance ethnocentrism was stronger, producing seven transpositions. Neither the Prairie nor Atlantic provinces ranked themselves in first position, thereby modifying the full intensity of ethnocentrism. Ethnocentrism was unequivocally strong everywhere in selecting a desirable place to live. On this item we had thirteen transpositions, of which the maximum ten were caused by the diagonal. That ethnocentrism should be so pervasive with respect to preferred region suggests an emotional strength of attachment to a home territory that historical migration trends do not penetrate.

We suggested that ethnocentrism was tempered by reality when respondents looked at their region's well-being and relative power. The nature of this reality was not the same for the two items, nor was it experienced in the same way by residents and non-residents. For example, if we use the frequencies with which residents selected their region as better off to establish ranks, the order begins with British Columbia and continues with Ontario, the Prairies, Quebec, and the Atlantic provinces. When residents are omitted, Ontario and British Columbia are reversed. Both orders resemble ones obtained in Chapter 2, depending on the indicators used. British Columbia ranked first on education, both with respect to inputs and outputs, and in attractiveness to migrants. Ontario, however, was more often in the forefront, particularly when judged by economic indicators.

Perceptions of regional power by both residents and non-residents were quite different from that inherent in the regional makeup of federal governments. As we see in Table 4–4, there are three distinct rank orders. Based on the frequencies with which residents selected their region, Ontario ranked first. In this instance reality promotes ethnocentrism. This same reality affected the judgements of outsiders,

Table 4–4 **Ranking of Regions According to Their Power**

| | Ranks Based on: | | |
	Perceptions of Residents	Perceptions of Others	Actual Power
Ontario	1	2	1
British Columbia	2	3	4
Quebec	3	1	2
Prairies	4	4	5
Atlantic provinces	5	5	3

but they gave first place to Quebec, suggesting a distortion probably based on hostility to Quebec rather than the nature of the political system. In contrast, Quebec residents selected their province with a frequency that converted into third place, indicating that they tended to underestimate the potency of their province. In other words, ethnocentrism was in a sense lower than might be anticipated from overall rankings. British Columbia also revealed some discrepancies in rankings, with residents displaying more ethnocentrism than the exercise of power would warrant, or than outsiders would acknowledge as accruing to it. This can be linked with a generally greater sense of power differentials in this province. We have already discussed the position of the Atlantic provinces, while the Prairies collectively show the best fit among the three forms of ranking.

If region is one of the conditions leading to evaluations of self, self-conceptions are in turn one of the elements out of which group identity emerges. The developmental process begins with a set of individuals experiencing common problems within a territorial context. Our assumption is that they must first understand the character of their own affairs before they can relate this to a group phenomenon.

It goes without saying that self-awareness is much more than the product of experience within a particular territorial milieu. Family experiences, peer group contacts, social status—in short, all of the factors that contribute to the determination of life chances become in some ways incorporated into the concept of self. In the sense that territory too affects life chances, then it is also bound into self-perceptions. We could presumably seek to isolate how and to what extent background factors, current status, and region impinge on judgements of self. But since we want to know about perceptions of region and not of self, there is not much to be gained by such procedures. It is enough to recognize what is involved in arriving at self-awareness.

The most pertinent aspect of our argument derives from the way we interpret our data, as an aggregation of individual responses about the conditions of life. The results are a form of ecological correlation, in which aggregate responses are used to develop a characteristic of a larger unit. Because of this focus on region, we are not concerned with the origins of individual perceptions, even though we could readily surmise these. It is not, we repeat, the origins of perceptions that are relevant here, but their consequences, For example, if a large number within a region share a pessimistic outlook, an outside observer can reason, as we do here, that there is a general climate of pessimism in that region. To the extent that perceptions are differentially distributed along regional lines, then one consequence is a differentiated state of satisfaction with the nation. Obviously this is but one aspect of regional consciousness, and not even the most important part. Yet we feel these data are worth presenting here since they give us some insight into those mechanisms at the individual level that provide one of the components of regional consciousness.

Respondents were presented with four questions concerning their own lives. We began by saying, "We are also interested in how people are getting along financially these days. As far as you and your family are concerned, would you say that you are pretty well satisfied, more or less satisfied, or not at all satisfied with the way you are getting along?" The next question on perceptions of respondents' own lives enquired about changes in the financial situation in the past few years. The focus was then slightly shifted to take into account only the employment situation. With this question, respondents were asked to evaluate changes in their current employment situation compared to what it was several years earlier. In asking about employment, we tapped respondents' assessments of such things as regularity of employment, conditions of work, as well as income and fringe benefits. The earlier question on the financial situation was broader in scope, implying total income, savings, and purchasing power. We reasoned that, with a steadily rising cost of living, it was possible, for example, that employment benefits would increase at a faster rate than overall financial benefits. In addition, in a country such as Canada, with extensive seasonal unemployment, the fact of employment itself could be a matter of concern. As our final indicator of personal circumstances, we asked about expectations for the financial situation in coming years.

Our findings have been summarized in Chart 4–1, where the percent optimistic on each question have been arrayed to focus on regional differences. Wherever this is appropriate, the discussion that follows makes use of the full distribution of responses to the four items.

Those in Ontario were generally most frequently satisfied, but when asked about their current financial situation, they were outranked by satisfied voters in British Columbia. In contrast, while those in the Atlantic provinces were least often satisfied, it was Quebeckers who had less positive comment to make about their employment situation. In general, while those most likely to be pleased about their lives were in Ontario and British Columbia, and those least likely to be so in the three remaining regions, finer differences in the regional ordering of optimistic responses on the four items is not random. That is, satisfaction with current circumstances was greater in British Columbia than in Ontario, and employment was a greater source of concern to those in Quebec than in the Atlantic provinces. We stress this for a

Chart 4–1   **Percent in each region optimistic about personal circumstances.**

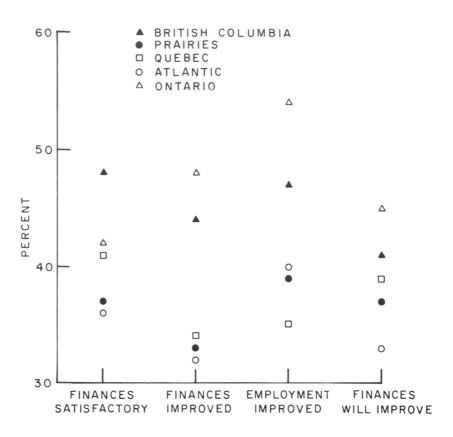

number of reasons. For one thing, we know that the rank ordering of regions is sufficiently different on each item to emerger as a statistically significant result on a Kruskal-Wallis one-way analysis of variance by ranks.[10] That this is substantively, as well as statistically, significant emerges from an examination of the total distribution of answers to these questions. For example, in British Columbia there were not only proportionately more who answered "pretty well satisfied' than in the next ranking province of Ontario, but there were also fewer who said that they were "not at all satisfied." Similarly, using a single response category in evaluating employment does not distort the relative position of regions. In most regions, there is a small minority of about 9 percent whose employment circumstances

10. H = 14.08 (corrected for ties), p < .01, df = 4.

had become worse. There were two exceptions, however. In Ontario, the outlook was particularly rosy: 54 percent reported some improvement and only 5 percent a decline. But in Quebec, there was both the smallest proportion reporting improvement, and the largest, 13 percent, who felt that there had been a worsening. In terms of the relative position of regions, then, we have both a general trend distinguishing the two most advantaged and the three least well off regions from the perspective of their residents, along with more varied evaluation of different aspects of economic conditions.

The range of difference in the level of satisfaction varied from a 12 percent spread on current finances and future prospects, to 16 percent on financial improvement, and 19 percent on employment improvement. Whether we consider these large amounts of difference is partly a matter of perspective. Compared to what we find on other items, these differences are not very large, but considered as indicators of group differentiation, they are considerable. In general, Ontario was most distinct, based on the predominant outlook of its residents. On all four items, it was approximately 10 percentage points removed from all other regions except British Columbia. Ontario and British Columbia were most alike in the amount of contentment displayed by their residents, and consequently the latter was also separated from the remaining regions, though to a lesser extent. The Prairie and Atlantic provinces were most alike, followed by the Prairies and Quebec. Quebec was separated from the Atlantic provinces by an average of more than four percentage points. This was due to less satisfaction in the easternmost region with the exception of greater concern about employment in Quebec.

A few cautionary words are still in order about the amount of difference between regions, obscured by our use of only one response category. On the first item, the current financial situation, the Prairie and Atlantic provinces appear to have been much closer in outlook than in fact they were. Although both had about the same proportion satisfied, outright dissatisfaction was much higher in the east. In the Atlantic provinces, 23 percent said that they were not at all satisfied, compared to 14 percent in the Prairies. The same was true for Ontario and Quebec, although not to the same extent. In Ontario 16 percent were dissatisfied, in Quebec this was 20 percent. In other words, while the ranking we have assigned the regions is correct, the gap between pairs is greater than it appears in the chart. To some extent this is also true for the question on economic prospects. While two percent more thought things would get better in Quebec compared to the Prairies, 3 percent more thought they would get worse in Quebec.

An examination of our two grouped regions indicates that they were not fully homogeneous, particularly on the issues of improved financial circumstances and prospects for the future. Because of the relatively few cases sampled in the smallest provinces, we cannot speak with full confidence about the evidence from the Atlantic provinces, but it at least suggests that respondents in Newfoundland and Nova Scotia felt more optimistic than our aggregate measure would otherwise suggest, while those in New Brunswick were uniformly pessimistic about their personal circumstances, regardless of the issue. In the Prairie provinces, the results were both more consistent and, because of the sampling, more credible. Those in Alberta were always more buoyant about their conditions than those in Manitoba and Saskatchewan. At times the distance between Alberta and the other two was considerable, placing that province close to Ontario and British Columbia.

Despite the differences noted, there is no reason to discard our grouping procedures since they are based on more than simply notions of total homogeneity. After all, we do not impose such restrictions on single provinces, and we can assume that they too are not free of internal variations. This additional analysis tells us the direction of difference within the two grouped regions, aiding our interpretation of the nature of regional perceptions.

RELATION TO REGIONAL CONDITIONS

It would be false to conclude from the subjective evaluations of individual's financial state a similar set of evaluations for regions. We looked at these judgements in order to see if they were differentiated along regional lines. Having found some differentiation, we could conclude that regions differed in the extent to which they were inhabited by relatively satisfied people. To now ask about the relationship between these subjective ratings and the objective conditions present in each of the regions might seem unwarranted. In other words, there is no necessary relation between thinking one's economic situation is good and living in an area enjoying economic advantage. But given the fact that such connections are not inevitable, it is even more worthwhile to examine them. As the basis for our judgements about objective conditions we use material presented in Chapter 2.

Generalizations about Ontario and British Columbia are simple enough. If one lives in a region notable for modernity and economic well-being, then the probability is high that one will also assess his personal economic circumstances with satisfaction. The aggregate effect of such personal assessments is to add another dimension by which that region is set apart. These conclusions applied best to Ontario. British Columbia was not as fully industrialized nor thoroughly urbanized, yet objective indicators of prosperity were apparent, and the sense of well-being enjoyed by its residents contributed to its distinctiveness. Within the Prairies, this assessment also applied to Alberta.

The remaining three regions are not quite so easy to deal with. On the basis of the objective indicators used in Chapter 2, we painted a consistently bleak picture only for the Atlantic provinces. Yet while, with the one exception already noted, the Atlantic provinces always displayed a lower level of satisfaction than the other regions, the amount of difference was often small. Why were residents in the Atlantic provinces not even less contented? Or perhaps more to the point, why did those in the Prairies and Quebec, who were, collectively, appreciably better off, not display more satisfaction? What were the specific sources of concern about employment in Quebec? We can offer no definitive answers to these questions, but we can offer some speculations based on our regional profiles.

The profiles suggest that, both in the Prairies and Quebec, the unevenness of industrialization and the subsequent distribution of rewards may have created relatively more tensions than is true in a system such as the Atlantic provinces. We may infer that, where contrast in conditions of life are not so marked, a sense of relative deprivation is not so likely to emerge. Even modest improvements may help generate hopeful feelings, as unreported data on Newfoundland and Nova Scotia suggest. Moreover, while in the Prairies the growth of urbanization and rising economic standards had been dramatic, these had not been evenly distributed nor had such improvements erased bitter memories of the Great Depression. Perhaps it is just such memories which dampened any widespread enthusiasm about personal conditions, especially outside Alberta. The easternmost region may then be expected to respond mainly in terms of economic conditions, without the radicalizing potential of contrasting conditions with the past or current strains from uneven economic development.

The limited sense of satisfaction that Quebec residents expressed in assessing improvements in their employment situation gave us particular pause. While unemployment rates in Quebec have always been above the Canadian average, these are regularly exceeded in the Atlantic provinces. To add to the confusion, they have also been above the national average in British Columbia, but particularly low in the Prairies.[11] This suggests that neither experience nor knowledge of unemployment in one's region is sufficient to create a climate of

---

11. Sylvia Ostry, *Unemployment in Canada* (Ottawa: Dominion Bureau of Statistics, 1968), pp. 26-32. For example, the year preceding our survey, 1965, was one when employment was high, but the characteristic regional differentiation persisted. The overall rate of unemployment was estimated at 3.9 percent. It was 7.4 percent in the Atlantic provinces, 5.4 in Quebec, 4.2 in British Columbia, and 2.5 in Ontario and the Prairie provinces. Ibid., p. 26.

opinion in which one's own employment situation is viewed with less than complete satisfaction. Instead, it is more likely related to a combination of factors disturbing the occupational structure.

In the case of Quebec, it is suggested that it was not unemployment itself that was so unsettling, but the changes brought about by rapid urbanization, industrialization, and an educational system that had not prepared displaced rural workers for their new industrial roles. As John Porter writes, "Nowhere has the old rural life been so completely broken as it had in Quebec."[12] Those of French origin in Quebec had, it is true, benefitted from the general expansiveness of the economy, but with respect to their distribution in the occupational class hierarchy, their overall position had actually declined. Porter attributes this decline partly to the migration of unskilled rural workers to the cities in Quebec, where they become part of an insecure, urban proletariat.[13] For those who leave the farm but remain in rural areas and small towns, vulnerability to seasonal as well as structural unemployment has been high.[14] It is experiences such as these which made Quebec residents more aware of the instability of employment and less satisfied with their own conditions. This combination occurred neither in the Atlantic provinces nor in British Columbia, both areas where we might otherwise have anticipated less satisfaction on changes in the employment situation.

Finally, Quebec and the Prairies differed from the Atlantic provinces by their ethnic makeup. Missing from the Atlantic provinces were either the French-speaking Catholic majority of Quebec or the other European origin groups of the Prairies, each a sizeable minority in the larger society. The existence of such minorities contributes to a sense of self-conscious identity for all groups. Such feelings of distinctiveness enhance the likelihood of finding other ways of being set apart, extending to a sense of economic exploitation perhaps even greater than warranted by existing conditions.[15]

Clearly, we have not exhausted the sources of personal satisfaction

---

12. John Porter, *The Vertical Mosaic* (Toronto: University of Toronto Press, 1965), p. 143.

13. Ibid., p. 144.

14. Marc-Adelard Tremblay et Gérald Fortin, *Les Compartements économiques de la famille salariés du Québec* (Québec: Les Presses de l'Université Laval, 1964); Maurice Pinard, *The Rise of a Third Party: A Study in Crisis Politics* (Englewood Cliffs, N.J.: Prentice-Hall, 1971).

15. What we are suggesting is analogous to what psychologists subsume under the concept of cognitive style. The most pertinent of its aspects includes a contrast between complex and simple modes of organizing stimuli. See for example, Riley W. Gardner, Douglas W. Jackson, and Samuel J. Messick, *Personality Organization in Cognitive Controls and Intellectual Abilities* (New York: International Universities Press, 1960).

or their implications. For the most part we can be sure that the views expressed by our respondents were the result of quite personal experiences related to home and job, often restricted in applicability to a time close to the interview. But beyond this, the coincidence of dominant views of personal circumstances and the state of regions in which these occurred is one link between life in a region and its consequences for a more general sense of regional consciousness.

REGIONAL BOUNDARIES AND REGIONAL CONSCIOUSNESS

In this chapter we have looked at perceptions pertaining to both personal and regional circumstances. We have given special emphasis to the latter, seeing in the judgements made of regional conditions a basis for the emergence of regional consciousness. Revealing the actual existence of such consciousness has been circumscribed by the measures available to us. It is obvious that we have not exhausted the ways in which regions could be differentiated, nor did we have available possibly more direct measures of regional identity. Yet despite these limitations we have uncovered at the least a potential for the emergence of regional consciousness. This in turn provides the potential for transforming the residents of a region into genuine groups, with a recognized identity of interest, a capacity to unite under acknowledged leaders, and an ability to act in concert. It is this transformation that makes the personal awareness of regional differences into a collective experience, and associated feelings of content or discontent into the motive forces behind a politics of regionalism.

In viewing levels of personal satisfaction we were concerned with their links to the resources of regions. We know that there need not be any relationship between personal satisfaction as experienced by the individual and the nature of his regional environment. But by treating levels of satisfaction in the aggregate, as characteristics of regions, we would have wondered about the validity of our inquiry if we had found no association with other regional characteristics. That satisfaction levels were closely associated with objective conditions meant, quite simply, that residents experienced their lives in ways bound by territorial confines. But it also meant that objective conditions and self-perceptions were linked in a mutually reinforcing network, operating to strengthen existing cleavages.

The socio-political significance of differences in the perception of regions is not so apparent. The solidarity of a nation depends to a degree on a competitive love of place. What occurs is a fusion between territory in its identity-conferring aspects and in its stature as a home, evoking primordial ties of loyalty. The fact that respondents ranked other provinces with considerable consistency, but rated their own in a fashion that reflects a sentimentality of outlook, is then a very human aspect of political reality. Our data do not clarify how much of such ethnocentrism would be ideal for national integration, but they do illustrate some of the range of possible reactions. We can exemplify by the Atlantic provinces and Quebec.

Like those elsewhere in Canada, residents of the Atlantic provinces displayed an in-group consciousness that inflated their region's position on all dimensions we have considered. Their ethnocentrism was most marked when rating preferred place of residence. Despite a recognition of their own and the region's disadvantages, they showed a consistent reluctance to even admit to the attractiveness of other provinces. Yet as we know from migration data, many of them do move on, especially the younger and more vigorous. So long as this movement takes place, no matter how reluctantly, the problems of the Atlantic provinces will remain unimpeded by the presence of a disgruntled majority capable of coming to grips with its problems. At the same time, without extensive pressure from within the region, those outside, no matter how willing they are to acknowledge its disadvantages, will hardly be willing to take on the responsibility for bringing about changes.

Ethnocentrism was high in Quebec, as we would anticipate in a province with the cultural and historical characteristics that lead to the development of a group consciousness even more readily than do common economic experiences. To outsiders, however, Quebec was unusually unattractive as a place to live and inordinately powerful vis à vis other provinces. We do not know to what extent Quebeckers were conscious of the ways they were viewed by other Canadians. Even if they were only dimly aware of these perceptions, feelings of a beleagured minority would be encouraged. Without having asked respondents directly what they thought of other provinces, it is still not too much to say that these findings, at variance as they are with objective conditions, suggest the hostility generated by the cultural separateness of Quebec.

It is patent that if ethnocentrism were so intense and pervasive as to erode concern for the well-being of other regions it would be disastrous for national solidarity. We have no inkling from our data that things have come to such a pass, but the echoes of hostility toward Quebec do give us pause. For the most part, however, the sober reality of the relative circumstances of regions other than one's own provides the baseline for invoking universalistic standards. The way in which these perceptions exist in the face of potentially cross-cutting pressures, that from national political parties, will be the theme of the following chapter.

CHAPTER

5

National party ties and regional outlooks

PARTY POLITICS AND REGIONALISM

Students of American politics, while recognizing the ubiquity of conflict, have usually been more attracted to those theories which
emphasize the consensual aspects of political life. It is Tocqueville
rather than Marx who has left the greater imprint.[1] Neither Tocqueville nor those who followed were blind to the existence of sharp
cleavages in American life. It is rather that their primary concern
was with how these divisions are kept in check. Within the more restricted context of political parties and regions, both themes are important to our study of Canada. Potentially consensus-building mechanisms can be viewed through the operation of national political
parties. At the same time parties are the vehicles of organized conflict.[2] Using data presented in the previous chapter, we will examine
the role of parties in the face of the primary cleavage of region.

According to Parsons, perhaps the most significant way in which
the potential disruption of cleavages is controlled is through the lack
of coincidence between political alignments and other social divisions.

---

1. S. M. Lipset, *Political Man* (Garden City, N.Y.: Doubleday, 1960), pp.
24-28.

2. For an earlier discussion with respect to Canada, see F. C. Engelmann
and M. A. Schwartz, *Political Parties and the Canadian Social Structure* (Scarborough: Prentice-Hall, 1967), especially pp. 222-24.

> . . . the tendency to political cleavage will tend to be checked
> by a set of mechanisms that operate *below* the level of party
> division as well as by the more general national consensus
> that operates above that level. The pressure of political
> cleavage—by activating ties of solidarity at the more differ-
> entiated structural levels that cut across the line of cleavage
> —tends automatically to bring countervailing forces into
> play. The point of view of the individual voter is likely to be,
> "My fellow union member (lodge member, co-religionist,
> office colleague, and so forth) who is intending to vote Re-
> publican (Democratic) is in general a pretty decent guy. I
> just can't see how all people who hold his views can be as
> bad as they're made out to be." Awareness that this type of
> sentiment will be activated may put a certain restraint on
> extremism in the campaign.[3]

The explanatory power of such cross-cutting loyalties is probably of
limited utility. Normally the essential countervailing forces do not
operate at the level of the individual voters. Moreover, even in the
United States, there is frequently a close relationship between particular social cleavages and partisanship. The conflicts that are generated among social groups may, in any case, take place outside the
political arena, or even within parties, as they do in the case of
internal conflicts in the Democratic and Republican parties. To the
extent that cross-cutting loyalties are important, they are so largely
because the American party system has continued to offer unusually
limited choices. In other countries, it has been customary for the
cleavage structure to be meshed with the party system. Certainly this
has meant serious strains, and even overt conflict; yet, in countries
such as the Netherlands,[4] Belgium,[5] and Austria,[6] the coincidence
between party and a network of social divisions has also been able
to continue without the breakdown of the state. In these countries
and others, mechanisms other than cross-cutting loyalties permit the
orderly conduct of government to coexist with deeply reinforced
political cleavages.

---

3. Talcott Parsons, *Sociological Theory and Modern Society* (New York:
The Free Press, 1967), p. 245. See also B. Berelson, P. F. Lazareld, Wm.
McPhee, *Voting* (Chicago: University of Chicago Press, 1954), pp. 319-20.

4. Arend Lijphart, *The Politics of Accommodation: Pluralism and Democracy in the Netherlands* (Berkeley: University of California Press, 1968).

5. Val Lorwin, "Belgium: Religion, Class, and Language in National Politics" in Robert A. Dahl, ed., *Political Oppositions in Western Democracies* (New
Haven: Yale University Press, 1966), pp. 147-87.

6. F. C. Engelmann, "Austria: The Pooling of Opposition" in Dahl, *Political
Oppositions,* pp. 260-83.

It appears that political cleavages are potentially most troublesome for the development of a viable nation-state when they are set apart by territorial boundaries. This is so because territory provides one of the primary foci of identity, not in the sense of any romanticized "territorial imperative," but simply because where one lives is a basic way of establishing a social as well as a physical location. As such, an identity rooted in locality is easily acquired, but disrupted with difficulty. People move about, yet the place where they originated is generally imbued with a special, emotional flavour. At the interpersonal level, the existence of boundaries also establishes the identity of a group, setting it apart from others, and increasing the likelihood of interaction among those within its confines. To the extent that communication is made easier—by the compactness of the area, the sharing of a language or culture, the existence of physical or psychological barriers to the outside—then the sense of apartness increases, and with it the recognition that the bounded group has interests distinct from, if not in opposition to, those in other territories. Insofar as this is accompanied by the means for political mobilization, we have the conditions for drastically interfering with the building of a unified nation.[7]

Political action based on territorial claims is frequently more uncompromising than that related to other cleavages. For example, sharp class conflicts can result in civil war, ultimately leading to the domination of one class over the others. But regional strife has a weapon not available to other groups—secession. It is in a real sense the ultimate threat, since if successful, it means the end of the existing state. Even without going to this extreme, the existence of territorial units within the state have an almost pervasive effect on the tenor of politics. In their seminal paper on the relation between cleavage structures and party politics, Lipset and Rokkan write, "Territorial-cultural conflicts do not just find political expression in secessionist and irredentist movements, however; they feed into the overall cleavage structure in the national community and help to condition the development not only of each nationwide party organization but even more of the entire system of party oppositions and alignments."[8] In such social systems, political parties can in turn be expected to feed back to the regional cleavages, either dampening, sustaining, or fostering them. Without prejudicing possible contradictory findings, we already have evidence of how national parties in Canada are related to the continuity of regional forces. In Chapter 3, we saw the

---

7. Seymour Martin Lipset and Stein Rokkan, "Cleavage Structures, Party Systems, and Voter Alignments: An Introduction" in Lipset and Rokkan, eds., *Party Systems and Voter Alignments* (New York: The Free Press, 1967), p. 13.

8. Ibid., p. 41

connection between party politics and differential regional representation, leading in turn to differences in regional power. Historical
circumstances have shaped the party system and the nature of individual parties in ways specific to each region, the implications of
which we examine in Chapter 6. In this chapter one other aspect of
the tie between regional units and party politics is examined—the
impact of parties on regional perspectives.

National political parties can promote regionalism by acting as the
spokesmen of regional interests through deliberate policies and programs. These may come about from regionally-oriented goals or
from the pressures of uneven regional support. Regionalism may
also be strengthened by parties assuming the role of opinion moulders
for their supporters.

The continuity of regionalism is aided when a party presents itself
as the advocate for one or more regions. This was exemplified by
Le Ralliement des Créditistes, the Quebec wing of the national
Social Credit party during its period of independence under Réal
Caouette. To some extent, it was also the role played by the Progressives. As the spokesmen of western farmers, the special problems of
that area were often as much at issue as those pertaining to an occupational or class group.

Regional advocacy would be prominent in a provincial rights party,
as it sought to further local interests against those of the national
government. We have no consistent example of such a party in
Canada, although the Liberals were inclined to play this role in the
early years following Confederation. In provincial legislatures and
under Laurier,

> the Liberals . . . stood for the rights of the provinces as
> against the dominance of the Dominion. This was confirmed
> by the numerous struggles between Liberal provincial Gov-
> ernments on the one hand and Conservative Dominion
> Governments on the other, and it was responsible in large
> measure for the Liberal victory in 1896, where the leading
> question was the Conservative Cabinet's coercion of Mani-
> toba on the separate school issue. From this time on, [but
> not after 1940] while both parties were careful to recognize
> the rights and powers of the provinces, the Liberals, partly
> as a result of their past history and partly because of their
> greater hold on Quebec, were the most solicitous for the
> maintenance of all provincial prerogatives. It was they, for
> example, who met the demands of the Maritime Rights
> movement, who returned the natural resources of the Prairie
> Provinces, and who later appointed the Rowell-Sirois Com-

mission in an endeavour to find a solution to the problem of Dominion-provincial relations.[9]

Support for the interests of particular regions may not be solely a matter of deliberate policy, but may emerge from factors related to support and organizational cohesion. For example, we would not be surprised if Social Credit members of the federal Parliament had tried to influence legislation favourable to the western provinces, since this was where their strength lay. If the Liberals pay more attention to Quebec than do the Conservatives, this is probably more marked when the Liberals are out of power, and hence more dependent than usual on their base of support in Quebec.

Parties may play their spokesman role somewhat unintentionally because of deficiencies in organizational cohesion. The demand for caucus solidarity in a parliamentary system of government sets severe limits on the extent of regional independence within a party. But not all issues are resolved through legislation needing a solidary vote, and this permits considerable scope for local activity, with each provincial party grouping acting as a kind of pressure group. The Progressive party, which was organizationally particularly loose, was dependent for its support on heeding the demands of local groups.[10] Yet even the older parties have not been immune from the pressures of regional interests, and at times these have come into open conflict with the need for caucus solidarity. For example, during World War II, opposition from Quebec members of Parliament to conscription for service overseas threatened to disrupt the Liberal party. Prime Minister Mackenzie King, recalling the strains on national unity that the same issue had created during World War I, delayed overseas conscription until nearly the end of the war, and while feelings were intense, the compromise adopted helped preserve both the party and the nation.[11]

Conservative opposition to the Official Languages Act in the Trudeau government also took shape along regional lines. Recognizing the issue as one critical to national unity, Conservative Leader Stanfield pledged his party's support to the bill. The bill in essence would permit government and ancillary services to be conducted in French

9. Robert MacGregor Dawson, *The Government of Canada* (Toronto: University of Toronto Press, 1947), p. 505.

10. W. L. Morton, *The Progressive Party in Canada* (Toronto: University of Toronto Press, 1967).

11. Robert MacGregor Dawson, *The Conscription Crisis of 1944* (Toronto: University of Toronto Press, 1961); J. L. Granatstein, *Conscription in the Second World War, 1939-1945* (Toronto: Ryerson Press, 1969); Mason Wade, *The French Canadians, 1760-1967*, rev. ed. (Toronto: Macmillan, 1968), pp. 916-1106.

wherever in Canada there was a 10 percent concentration of French-speaking people. Feeling it would impose an unnecessary and expensive hardship in western Canada, where other language groups are dominant, Conservatives from that area, under the leadership of former Prime Minister John Diefenbaker, refused to give their support.

These two illustrations are hardly examples of deliberate efforts by national parties to further regional interests. In the case both of conscription and language use, party leadership has been more concerned with broader interests. Yet as these interests come in conflict with local concerns, national parties may find themselves without the strength to subdue regionalism.

In general, the likelihood that parties will help shape the outlooks of their supporters is related to a number of factors.[12] These involve both active efforts to influence and more or less passive consequences from the influences of supporters. For example, parties differ in the extent to which rank and file members are involved in decision-making. In those parties where membership participation is relatively high, we would expect a greater uniformity of outlook. The same would be true of parties whose support was restricted to a single social class or region, since the latter would already have some common interests. Party influence would also be high where voters were attracted by an existing set of principles, in contrast to where partisanship was related to specific candidates or issues, or to the force of tradition. The likelihood that party supporters would hold to similar views is enhanced by a parliamentary system of government, in which both government and opposition are oriented to issues emphasized in election campaigns, and legislative members of the party are expected to present a united stand. These factors operate singly or in combination to increase the possibility of party influence on the views of their supporters.

Although we have no direct evidence for the homogeneity of their partisans' views, the conditions likely to promote this were especially strong in the United Farmers of Alberta (U.F.A.). The U.F.A. made use of study groups for propagating their principles, ensuring in this way that supporters would be more than casual voters at election time. Before the U.F.A.'s entry into party politics, it acted as, among other things, a pressure group on government.

> In this work the U.F.A. was concerned with practical matters
> of immediate need or desirability—freight rates, grain trade
> regulations, roads, and other things directly affecting their
> income and welfare.

12. Engelmann and Schwartz, *Political Parties,* pp. 204-206.

While the members of the U.F.A. were thus united by a common desire to better themselves and sometimes by a common resentment of the treatment of western farmers, no single social, economic, or political theory emerged.[13]

As the U.F.A. engaged in direct political action, it did develop a more consistent theory, among which was the belief in "constituency autonomy," which in effect so emphasized localism that the U.F.A. were unable to join with the Progressives in an enduring federal party coalition.[14] This recalcitrance helped the demise of the Progressives, but paradoxically, the sense of unity it produced in Alberta enabled the U.F.A. to capture, out of a possible sixteen, eleven and nine seats respectively in the 1926 and 1930 general elections. In all of the ways described here, the U.F.A. kept regional interests paramount.

Exactly the opposite set of characteristics is generally associated with the two older parties. These include a low level of membership participation in party activities, a broad base of support, and the absence of any consistent set of principles underlying their electoral appeal. As a result, these parties are not normally effective in providing their supporters with a unifying opinion framework. Compared to ties of party, region has often provided a greater focus for similarity in opinions.[15] The impact of parties on their supporters may then have consequences for sustaining regionalism either through their deliberate efforts to mould opinion, as in the case of the U.F.A., or through their failure to do so. Where parties are ineffective in playing an opinion-shaping role, the pull of region is unmitigated.

As Easton has pointed out, among sociologists the notion of cleavage is frequently opposed to consensus and hence associated with agreement or disagreement in opinions and attitudes. The study of such cleavages reveals the extent of diversity in a population, but not how these might be mobilized. It is political scientists who more often use cleavages to refer to divisions among groups as these are manifested in political actions. Diversity in outlooks and conflicts among groups are two interrelated aspects of cleavages, yet each may exist without the other. Hence the distinction is both analytically and empirically necessary.[16]

13. C. B. Macpherson, *Democracy in Alberta: Social Credit and the Party System* (Toronto: University of Toronto Press, 1953), p. 28.

14. Morton, *The Progressive Party,* pp. 170, 257.

15. Mildred A. Schwartz, *Public Opinion and Canadian Identity* (Berkeley: University of California Press, 1967), pp. 146-58.

16. David Easton, *A Systems Analysis of Political Life* (New York: John Wiley, 1965), pp. 234-36.

Yet despite our recognition of these two aspects of a cleavage such as that based on region, and our own admonition about the full range of ways in which parties may be related to regionalism, our task in this chapter is more restricted. Carrying on from the survey data discussed in the preceding chapter, we look at the ways in which national party support is associated with the outlooks prevalent in each region. That is, it is party as opinion-moulder (either active or passive) rather than as spokesman that concerns us here. While the spokesman role is important, it is difficult to document, let alone to treat systematically. Most students of political regionalism have concentrated on provincial politics, the major arena of regional controversy and of third party success. It is such third parties which have been the most obvious links with regional interests. But the whole thrust of our argument is that it is at least as important to look at the stresses for regional recognition within national politics. Moreover, given the relatively few examples we were able to assemble, it could be that party advocacy is perhaps not the best place to look for factors sustaining regionalism. It may well be that we will find the most persuasive evidence of support for regionalism in the consequences of party politics for voters.

REGIONAL CONDITIONS

Direction of Party Influence

In the previous chapter we demonstrated a relation between the assessment of regional conditions and the residence of respondents. Here we wish to go a step further and consider how parties, as measured by vote in the 1965 federal election, related to these evaluations. The assessment of regions is concerned with three questions—well-being, attractiveness, and power—solely from the perspective of each region's residents. We look only at those respondents who evaluated their own region in favourable terms. Results are presented in Tables 5–1 to 5–3.

No one party can be characterized as displaying strong regional ethnocentrism, regardless of the particular issue. The clearest results were obtained in response to perceptions of own region as better off. There the Liberals were inclined to see the advantageous situation of their region everywhere except in the Prairies, where they were exceeded in this assessment by Social Credit voters. In Ontario, they were tied with the NDP. The ordering of regions by Liberal supporters was identical to that for the whole country, beginning with British Columbia as the most advantaged, and followed by Ontario, the Prairies, Quebec, and the Atlantic provinces. The Conservatives and

Table 5–1 **Percent who see their own Region as Better Off, by Region and Past Vote**

Region	Liberal	Conservative	1965 Vote NDP	Social Credit	Total[a]
Atlantic[b]	13 (79)	6 (67)	0 (7)	—	9 (180)
Quebec	50 (259)	42 (72)	41 (63)	30 (46)	44 (579)
Ontario	81 (316)	75 (241)	81 (107)	—	79 (779)
Prairies[c]	69 (62)	60 (92)	54 (44)	81 (31)	70 (293)
British Columbia	94 (70)	78 (46)	81 (52)	80 (20)	84 (208)

[a]Row totals include other parties, don't knows, etc.
[b]Individual provinces as well as the collective region have been grouped together.
[c]Includes Alberta plus total region.

Figures in parentheses are base N's.

Table 5-2 **Percent who prefer to live in own Region, by Region and Past Vote**

Region	Liberal	Conservative	1965 Vote NDP[c]	Social Credit	Total[a]
Atlantic[b]	79	78	[43]	—	75
	(100)	(83)	(8)		(229)
Quebec	76	70	79	86	77
	(357)	(97)	(70)	(65)	(793)
Ontario	75	77	68	—	76
	(424)	(311)	(132)		(1,054)
Prairies[b]	64	90	73	84	80
	(89)	(125)	(56)	(37)	(395)
British Columbia	95	100	89	100	97
	(78)	(58)	(62)	(26)	(256)

[a]Row totals include other parties, don't knows, etc.
[b]Combines all mentions of individual provinces.
[c]Too few cases to percentage.
Figures in parentheses are base N's.

Table 5–3 **Percent Selecting own Region as more Powerful, by Region and Past Vote**

Region	Liberal	Conservative	1965 Vote NDP[c]	Social Credit	Total[a]
Atlantic[b]	56	40	[40]	—	43
	(50)	(53)	(5)		(123)
Quebec	75	61	64	36	66
	(212)	(62)	(44)	(39)	(474)
Ontario	62	71	67	—	71
	(272)	(169)	(77)		(578)
Prairies[b]	41	47	33	74	46
	(59)	(65)	(42)	(23)	(236)
British Columbia	60	54	68	[71][c]	60
	(60)	(48)	(44)	(13)	(184)

[a]Row totals include other parties, don't knows, etc.

[b]Combined selection of individual provinces.

[c]Too few cases to percentage.

Figures in parentheses are base N's.

NDP were quite similar in their evaluations. It is Social Credit that was most distinctive, as a result of the high evaluation voters gave to the Prairies. The Créditistes, in contrast, had the most negative view of their province compared to other voters in Quebec.

The attractiveness of one's own region is normally so strong that it is not possible to distinguish party perspectives outside of the Prairies. In that region, 90 percent of Conservative supporters selected the Prairies. Proportions declined in order from the Social Credit and NDP, to a low of 64 percent for the Liberals.

In the Atlantic provinces and Quebec, Liberal voters were more likely to attribute power to their province than the supporters of other parties. In Ontario and the Prairies they were outnumbered in such judgements by the Conservatives. It is actually Social Credit supporters in the Prairies who were most convinced of their region's power. In British Columbia, Social Credit and NDP voters made this assumption most often.

At first glance, these results seem somewhat erratic. They have a political meaning, however, one we will explore after first examining the extent to which party affects these views.

The Extent of Party Influence

A closer look at the relationship between party support and opinions can be done, but not without difficulty, because parties do not clearly operate as opinion moulders. That is, they are probably as much influenced by the views of their supporters as they actively influence supporters. Additionally, measurement of the effects we have in mind are troublesome when using qualitative data of the sort represented by opinions. It is generally also difficult reliably to demonstrate effects when distributions come close to 50–50 divisions. For instance, most measures of probability using sampled populations require larger samples to reduce the margin of sampling error as probabilities approach .5. With these problems in mind, we attempt to attach some quantitative level to the relation between regions, parties and opinions.

To assess the strength of these relations, we have employed a class of coefficients of association for nominal data suggested by Henri Theil,[17] and adapted for this purpose by James Wiley.[18] The concept of association that underlies these coefficients is based on the notion

---

17. Henri Theil, "On the Estimation of Relationships Involving Qualitative Variables," *American Journal of Sociology*, 76 (July 1970): 103-54. Theil's discussion includes a formal definition and analysis of uncertainty measures for cross-classifications.

18. The following discussion of entropy measures has been prepared by James Wiley, to whom special thanks are due for this advice and assistance.

of "entropy" or "uncertainty" in the distribution of responses. Maximum uncertainty occurs when respondents are evenly distributed among the possible response categories. Minimum uncertainty occurs when all respondents fall into a single response category. The coefficients developed by Theil compare the uncertainty of the distribution of responses, given additional information about the respondents (e.g. region of residence, party supported), with uncertainty when that additional information is absent. Association between two variables exists if knowledge of one reduces the uncertainty in the distribution of the other. The strength of the association between two nominal variables is measured by calculating the proportional reduction of entropy or uncertainty in the dependent variable which occurs when respondents are cross-classified by an independent variable.

In the analysis that follows, region and party are regarded as independent variables and opinion as the dependent variable. Three types of coefficients are shown: (1) coefficients of partial association between region and opinion, controlling on party; and between party and opinion, controlling on region, (2) coefficients of multiple association between party and region combined and opinion, (3) conditional coefficients, expressed as proportional entropy reductions, which measure the strength of association between party and opinion within each region. These coefficients have the properties of being bounded between zero and one, and not being symmetrical with respect to the specification of dependent and independent variables. They are indifferent to the actual direction of association between the variables, a property for which we have compensated by our previous discussion on the direction of party influence. The coefficients are analogous to correlation coefficients in the sense that their values may be interpreted as the "proportion of variance explained" in the dependent variable. For example, in Table 5–4, almost 18 percent of the variance is explained by knowing the region of respondents who see their own region as better off, while controlling for party support. In this portion of our analysis, we drop Social Credit.

We see in Table 5–4 the full force of regional influences. These are particularly acute in determining how respondents judge the well-being of their region. But even with respect to attractiveness and power, the partial associations for region outnumber the partials for party by a multiple of almost four. In no instance do the multiple associations, combining region and party, add significantly to the information about associations gained simply from knowing region.

Table 5–5 shows the proportion of entropy reduced when the influence of region is controlled. On the issue of regional well-being there is greatest entropy reduction, and hence greatest division of opinions, in the Atlantic provinces and British Columbia. Throughout, entropy measures are weighted to take into account the relative

Table 5–4 **Measures of Association for Region, Party, and Regional Conditions**

Views of own region:	Partial Association Region/party	Party/region	Multiple Association Region + Party
Better off	.179	.011	.182
More Attractive	.046	.018	.048
More Powerful	.040	.011	.041

Association measures are derived from entropy measures.

Table 5–5 **Proportional Entropy Reductions due to Parties Within Region, for Items on Regional Conditions**

Region:	Own Region: Better Off	More Attractive	More Powerful
Atlantic provinces	.035	.015	.019
Quebec	.005	.003	.014
Ontario	.005	.004	.007
Prairies	.010	.081	.008
British Columbia	.058	.102	.009

size of party groups. This serves to point up an important political phenomenon: entropy reductions are greatest where there is most contrast between large subsamples. That is, when differences are between supporters of the major parties, this will normally be reflected in larger proportional entropy reductions than when there is the same amount of difference between major and minor parties, or between a numerically dominant party and all others. Since results for the Atlantic provinces are related to a zero entry for the NDP, they are of little consequence to our analysis. In British Columbia, the size of the entropy reduction points up the contrast between the Liberals and Conservatives (as seen in Table 5-1), with the former most sanguine about their province.

Judgements of regional attractiveness produced larger proportional entropy reductions in the Prairies and British Columbia. In the Prairies, this was caused by differences of opinion between major party supporters, with the Conservatives most attracted by their region and Liberals least attracted. The range of difference in opinion distributions was considerably smaller in British Columbia, even though the entropy reduction is greater. This was affected by the attraction of British Columbia to the total sample of Conservatives, whose principal contrast were NDP voters. When we found similarly extreme results for the NDP in the Atlantic provinces, we chose to downgrade their significance, since the NDP were such a small share of our sample in that region, and more important, played a distinctly minor role in the political life of the Atlantic provinces. Now, however, we are discussing a major party, even if one that was not particularly successful in British Columbia in the 1965 election. Our inclination then is to take note of the large entropy reduction as an indication of some meaningful contrast between the supporters of different parties.

The issue of power differences produced least differentiation among parties within regions. Attributions of greater power were made more often by Liberals compared to Conservatives in the Atlantic provinces, Quebec, and British Columbia. Conservatives were more convinced of their region's power when contrasted to the NDP in the Prairies and to Liberals in Ontario.

Differences among the three parties were distinctly minor in Quebec and Ontario. On the items we have been considering, the position of Quebec itself was of sufficient dominance to override considerations of party. In the remaining regions, parties did serve to influence or attract voters with differing perspectives on the nature of their home territory. This presumably has some relation to the polarization associated with multiple parties in the western provinces. Yet we also have signs that neither the strong two-party tradition in the Atlantic provinces, nor the circumstances of provinces themselves, completely negate the likelihood that different points of view will be mobilized into different partisan channels.

Interaction Between Party and Region

While a national direction to party differences is not much in evidence, localized perspectives indicate that regional conditions interact with party situations to produce some noteworthy influences.

Selection of region better off resulted in the polarization of Liberal viewpoints, where from Ontario westward they revealed a high level of belief in the well-being of their own regions. In the case of Ontario and British Columbia, this was certainly in conformity with the objective conditions of those provinces. But why should it be Liberal voters who were most acutely aware of these conditions? Some of the answer may lie in the character of Liberal supporters, who reflected through the evaluations of their regions their own considerable personal privilege. (See Table 5–6.) We may also be seeing a correlate of the Liberal party's image as the party of prosperity and financial well-being.[19] To the extent that personal circumstances,

---

19. Schwartz, *Public Opinion and Canadian Identity,* p. 207.

Table 5–6 **Profile* of Party Supporters by Region**

Region	Liberal	Conservative	NDP	Social Credit
Atlantic Provinces	61% 40+; 7% URB 19% NIL 12% PO; 50% MAN $3,500	68% 40+; 13% URB 22% NIL 14% PO; 35% MAN $3,800	[57% 40+; 0% URB][a] [12% NIL] [25% PO; 38% MAN] $3,000	
Quebec	57% 40+; 47% URB 14% NIL 25% PO; 36% MAN $5,000	54% 40+; 37% URB 19% NIL 11% PO; 40% MAN $4,500	40% 40+; 65% URB 3% NIL 40% PO; 39% MAN $5,700	49% 40+; 25% URB 12% NIL 8% PO; 61% MAN $4,800
Ontario	53% 40+; 46% URB 10% NIL 20% PO; 45% MAN $6,700	58% 40+; 33% URB 15% NIL 22% PO; 28% MAN $5,500	55% 40+; 50% URB 5% NIL 13% PO; 60% MAN $5,500	
Prairie Provinces	49% 40+; 52% URB 16% NIL 19% PO; 31% MAN $5,700	66% 40+; 47% URB 19% NIL 14% PO; 26% MAN $5,000	66% 40+; 62% URB 14% NIL 18% PO; 36% MAN $5,400	49% 40+; 46% URB 11% NIL 13% PO; 41% MAN $5,200
British Columbia	67% 40+; 74% URB 18% NIL 28% PO; 18% MAN $6,100	90% 40+; 69% URB 38% NIL 24% PO; 17% MAN $4,900	63% 40+; 71% URB 13% NIL 16% PO; 32% MAN $5,500	62% 40+; 67% URB 8% NIL 23% PO; 52% MAN $6,200

*% 40 and older; % in cities 100,000+; (URB)
% household heads not in labour force; (NIL)
% professional, owner, manager (PO); % manual occupations (MAN)
Median family income

[a]based on only 8 cases.

regional conditions, and ties to a particular party work together, they serve to enhance the likelihood of a consistent group conscious-ness, in this case associated with judgements of regional well-being. This does not, however, account for the polarization of NDP opin-ions with regard to this same issue in Ontario. We suggest that the class consciousness and class-related appeals linked with the NDP made an important contribution to the ways in which reality was viewed. In the case of Ontario, the judgement was of a wealthy province, with opportunities for personal economic improvement (Table 5–9), but one where working-class status, both objectively (Table 5–6), and in terms of class consciousness (Table 5–13), may foster a sense of exclusion.

Greatest distinctiveness in assessing regional political power was displayed by Liberals in Quebec, Conservatives in Ontario, and NDP in the Prairies and British Columbia. While not part of our statistical analysis, Social Credit voters also were high in attributions of power in the west. We repeat these findings since, seen in this way, they suggest a pattern—one strongly influenced by the parties' position in provincial, and secondarily in federal politics. With the exception of the NDP in the Prairies, these assessments of power were greatest in those regions where the party of respondents had greatest strength, particularly at the provincial level. That this was not true for the NDP, with a history of government in Saskatchewan and their strength in Manitoba, may seem surprising, At the time of our sur-vey, the NDP were out of office in Saskatchewan and that might have had a depressive effect. The Liberals in the Prairies, whose party was then governing in Saskatchewan, also did not give much weight to the greater power of the entire region. We should recall that, objec-tively, the Prairies were low in power. In these terms, both the NDP and Liberals were most realistic in their assessments, choosing the Prairies even less often than the Atlantic provinces. We may consider the responses of the remainder then as out of line with reality, appar-ently inflated by the long period of provincial government enjoyed by the Social Credit party in Alberta and to a lesser extent, by the strong showing of the Conservatives in federal elections. That such local experiences have an inflationary effect seems confirmed by results from British Columbia, where third party supporters felt that province was especially powerful. It is in British Columbia that third party strength has been most consistently high both federally and provincially.

Given the extent of regional ethnocentrism with respect to the choice of a place to live, it is perhaps surprising to find as much party differentiation as we did. Unusually frequent choice of their own region by Conservatives in the Prairies and British Columbia suggest that we extend our argument on the importance of political power. For example, in the Prairies, 46 percent of the Conservatives chose Alberta, and 68 percent of Social Crediters, but 34 and 25 percent respectively of the Liberal and NDP supporters. The desirability of the Prairies, and particularly of Alberta, may then have been enhanced for those party supporters whose electoral choice had been successful, either federally or provincially. We cannot deny, however, that other, more personal, factors may have had greater bearing on the polarization of opinions.

Some comment needs to be made about the Créditistes. Although not a party with a national following, and hence not available to the kind of analysis and comparisons employed here, they played a special role within Quebec. There they attracted those most distressed by Quebec's economic situation in a way noticeably different from any other party. They also placed an unusually low evaluation on Quebec's power. Yet along with these opinions, and in company with characteristically inferior economic circumstances and a low level of personal satisfaction (which is discussed in the following section), Créditistes were undeterred in their preference for living in Quebec. This would suggest that Quebec was home to the Créditistes in a special sense. They were, of all party supporters in that province, most thoroughly French-speaking and Catholic, imbued with the ethos of small towns and rural areas, and of lower than the Quebec average in educational attainment.[20] None of their life experiences had prepared them to think of a move elsewhere in Canada as providing a means of greater personal opportunity.

PERSONAL CIRCUMSTANCES

The Direction of Party Influence

How does partisan support relate to economic satisfaction as a regional phenomenon? Our analysis relies on the same four questions used earlier: satisfaction with current circumstances, improvement of financial situation, improvement of employment situation, and optimism about future prospects. (See Tables 5–7 to 5–10.)

Collectively, Liberal voters were among the most satisfied. Their satisfaction was particularly great in the assessment of the current

20. Characteristics of Party Supporters in Quebec:

	Liberal	Conservative	NDP	Créditiste
% French-speaking	82	77	74	97
% Catholic	87	83	77	100
% in communities under 50,000	48	57	31	73
% grade 8 or less	45	54	21	69

Table 5–7 **Percent Pretty Well Satisfied with how They are Getting Along, by Region and Party**

| | 1965 Vote | | | | |
Region	Liberal	Conservative	NDP	Social Credit	Total[a]
Atlantic	42 (100)	35 (83)	— (8)	—	36 (229)
Quebec	45 (357)	24 (97)	53 (70)	26 (65)	41 (793)
Ontario	47 (424)	41 (311)	30 (132)	—	41 (1,054)
Prairies	43 (89)	41 (125)	36 (56)	38 (37)	37 (391)
British Columbia	54 (78)	48 (58)	45 (62)	38 (26)	48 (256)
Total	46 (1,048)	38 (674)	37 (328)	37 (67)[b]	40 (2,727)

[a]Row totals include other parties, don't knows, etc.
[b]The total for Social Credit includes 4 cases in the Atlantic provinces and Ontario. The Quebec Créditistes are not included.
Figures in parentheses are base N's.

Table 5–8 **Percent who Feel their Financial Situation has been Getting Better in the Past Few Years, by Region and Party**

Region	1965 Vote				Total[a]
	Liberal	Conservative	NDP[c]	Social Credit	
Atlantic	33	28	[25]	—	32
	(100)	(83)	(8)		(229)
Quebec	41	24	51	15	34
	(357)	(97)	(70)	(65)	(793)
Ontario	52	44	44	—	48
	(424)	(311)	(132)		(1,054)
Prairies	40	29	32	38	33
	(89)	(125)	(56)	(37)	(395)
British Columbia	59	38	36	46	44
	(78)	(58)	(62)	(26)	(256)
Total	46	36	41	37	40
	(1,043)	(674)	(328)	(67)[b]	(2,727)

[a]Row totals include other parties, don't knows, etc.

[b]The total for Social Credit includes 4 cases in the Atlantic provinces and Ontario. The Quebec Créditistes are not included.

[c]Too few cases to percentage.

Figures in parentheses are base N's.

Table 5–9 **Percent who Feel their Employment Situation is Better than it was a Few Years Ago, by Region and Party**

Region	1965 Vote Liberal	Conservative	NDP[c]	Social Credit	Total[a]
Atlantic	47 (100)	34 (83)	[50] (8)	—	40 (229)
Quebec	37 (357)	25 (97)	43 (70)	31 (65)	34 (793)
Ontario	59 (424)	44 (311)	62 (132)	—	54 (1,054)
Prairies	49 (89)	27 (125)	41 (56)	57 (37)	39 (395)
British Columbia	61 (78)	34 (58)	55 (62)	31 (26)	46 (256)
Total	50 (1,048)	36 (674)	53 (328)	47 (67)[b]	44 (2,727)

[a]Row totals include other parties, don't knows, etc.

[b]The total for Social Credit includes 4 cases in the Atlantic provinces and Ontario. The Quebec Créditistes are not included.

[c]Too few cases to percentage.

Figures in parentheses are base N's.

Table 5–10 **Percent Feeling their Financial Situation will Get Better in the Next Few Years, by Region and Party**

| | 1965 Vote | | | | |
Region	Liberal	Conservative	NDP[c]	Social Credit	Total[a]
Atlantic	32	34	[37]c	—	33
	(100)	(83)	(8)		(229)
Quebec	44	28	56	25	39
	(357)	(97)	(70)	(65)	(793)
Ontario	49	41	38	—	45
	(424)	(311)	(132)		(1,054)
Prairies	49	34	29	46	37
	(89)	(125)	(56)	(37)	(395)
British Columbia	54	35	35	54	41
	(78)	(58)	(62)	(26)	(256)
Total	46	36	40	47	40
	(1,048)	(674)	(328)	(67)b	(2,727)

aRow totals include other parties, don't knows, etc.

bThe total for Social Credit includes 4 cases in the Atlantic provinces and Ontario. The Quebec Créditistes are not included.

cToo few cases to percentage.

Figures in parentheses are base N's.

employment situation. Except for the question on current financial circumstances, there was also considerable internal differentiation according to place of residence. Normally, there was a characteristic regional ordering, with the amount of satisfaction decreasing as we move from British Columbia, to Ontario, Quebec, the Prairies, and then the Atlantic provinces. This order changed in response to employment, where there was a strong depressive effect from residence in Quebec.

Interestingly enough, Conservative voters were, in total, among the least satisfied with their personal circumstances. The most satisfied were generally in Ontario, followed by British Columbia, the Prairie and Atlantic provinces, and Quebec. Only on satisfaction with present conditions did Ontario lose first place to British Columbia, separated by 7 percent fewer satisfied than in the western province. Of special note is the consistently low level of satisfaction among that relatively small proportion of voters who marked their ballots for the Conservatives in Quebec in the 1965 election. In all instances, except the item on improvement in their financial situation, Quebec Conservatives expressed an even gloomier outlook than did the more explicitly, and hence expectedly, protest-oriented Créditistes.

It is more difficult to locate the NDP on a scale of personal satisfaction. In judging their current circumstances, improvement over the past, and expectations for the future NDP voters were similar to Conservatives. Within provinces, however, they revealed considerably less satisfaction than Conservatives with present circumstances, by 9 percent in Ontario and 13 percent in the Prairies. Improvement in the financial situation and the evaluation of future prospects produced very positive reactions from the NDP in Quebec. On the question about employment, judgements of improvement were made consistently more often by NDP voters compared to Conservatives, and even more frequently than Liberal supporters in Ontario and Quebec.

There is little to be said about Social Credit, since the Créditistes were not fully comparable, and not all regions were sufficiently represented to permit comparisons. We can, of course, see the consistently low level of satisfaction expressed by the Créditistes. In the Prairies and British Columbia, party response patterns shifted according to the particular question asked. These shifts may have had some meaning, but given the nature of our sample, we hesitate to interpret them.

Extent of Party Influence

Tables 5–11 and 5–12 give measures of association for party and region with regard to personal circumstances. Associations are small and in fact they are considerably less than those we obtained for questions about regional conditions. To some extent, however, the

Table 5–11 **Measures of Association for Region, Party, and Personal Satisfaction**

| Item: | Partial Associations | | Multiple Associations |
	Region/party	Party/region	Region + Party
Pretty well satisfied	.013	.015	.017
Financial situation improved	.019	.013	.025
Employment situation improved	.025	.019	.039
Finances will improve	.010	.013	.017

Association measures are derived from entropy measures.

smallness of the association is strongly related to the kinds of data we used, in which there was a low level of aggregation.[21] As a result, while in absolute terms we do not appear to demonstrate much in the way of associations, with respect to what can be expected from such data, the results are meaningful. They tell us that, in the aggregate, the party effect is almost as great as the regional effect on the four items in question. Modest though these results are, they do reveal that party plays some role in predicting the opinions of supporters. In addition, however, the combination of party and region increases predictability to a considerable extent only on the item of employment. There both party and region alone made relatively strong contributions to the views of respondents and together have an even greater influence on opinions.

The amount of entropy reduction associated with parties within regions is greatest on the issue of employment. (See Table 5–12.) This was particularly so in the west, where the contrast was between Liberals and Conservatives, as we noted in Table 5–9. The feeling that the financial situation will improve produced a strong contrast between Liberals and Conservatives in the same area. However, in this instance, NDP voters were more like Conservatives, while in the preceding question they resembled the more optimistic Liberals. Expectations for the future also polarized opinions in Quebec, with the NDP and Conservatives at opposite extremes. Similar alignments as well produced high inter-party differences in Quebec on the remaining items. Judgements of current improvement in financial cir-

21. Theil, "On the Estimation of Relationships," 133-34; Michael T. Hannan, *Problems of Aggregation and Disaggregation in Sociological Research* (Chapel Hill: Institute for Research in Social Science, University of North Carolina, 1970).

Table 5–12 **Proportional Entropy Reductions due to Parties within Region, for items on Personal Conditions**

| | | Optimistic Evaluation of: | | |
	Present Circumstances	Finances	Employment	Future Finances
Atlantic	.034	.003	.014	.001
Quebec	.026	.022	.012	.020
Ontario	.010	.005	.017	.006
Prairie Provinces	.002	.009	.032	.022
British Columbia	.004	.035	.037	.025

cumstances also led to sharp differences in British Columbia, where the contrast was between Liberals and all others.

We have found instances of party-linked opinion diversity in Quebec, British Columbia, and the Prairies. In all of these places, party differences were mainly related to the polarization of views in a major party, the Conservatives, as well as in a minor party, the NDP. We also found no clear-cut division of opinion associated with parties in either the Atlantic provinces or Ontario. In the east, the one exception has been primarily affected by the extreme distribution of the relatively few NDP voters in our sample. While statistically, the total absence of cases in one cell of a dichotomous classification is normally significant even when dealing with small samples, in this instance, the political significance is undoubtedly low. In total, then, we can conclude that the Atlantic provinces were characterized by considerable opinion homogeneity, regardless of party ties. This was related to a general level of discontent that cut across party lines. The opposite was not completely true in Ontario. That is, while satisfaction levels were generally high, there was also a fair amount of difference among parties, particularly the NDP, but in general this did not result in extreme splits. Particularly with regard to the major parties, in Ontario it was only slightly less likely that a satisfied voter would choose the Conservatives rather than the Liberals.

From what we have already presented in previous chapters, we might consider British Columbia the mirror image of the Atlantic provinces. In the east, economic conditions have been depressive, and residents had generally taken a consistently gloomy view. In the west, the economy has boomed and residents had been buoyed up in their optimism perhaps even more than the relative stability of the economy might have warranted. If one set of conditions had affected residents more or less uniformly, regardless of partisan ties, we could have anticipated the same to be true given the opposite combination of circumstances. In fact, such results might have seemed even more likely in British Columbia, with its lower level of political traditionalism and the greater volatility of party politics. Yet this does not emerge from our findings, suggesting that there was both greater population variability in British Columbia, and a political climate more attuned to the differing circumstances of voters. The latter is probably more likely to occur where there is a multi-party system, as in British Columbia, rather than a stable system of two, old line parties.

Interaction Between Party and Region

To the extent that political parties serve as rallying points for individuals and groups with varying economic interests and concerns, they perform these roles differently in each of the regions. For example, while the Liberals in the time studied attracted those with the greatest level of satisfaction with their own economic situation, they did this most effectively in British Columbia, and secondly in Ontario. All of the minor parties represented in our study have historically presented themselves as parties of protest, directly challenging the status quo and calling on the dispossessed for support. Yet from our results at least, we see evidence of a transformation. Neither the NDP in Quebec nor Social Credit in the Prairies attracted large numbers of already discontented voters. The Conservative party was most successful in attracting satisfied voters in Ontario, though not in so large a proportion as the Liberals. It is the evidence of the gloomy outlook of Conservative voters generally which merits most attention.

The dissatisfied who translate their perception of limited opportunities into political terms can follow several lines of action. Some of the most important of these, namely revolt and revolution, are not directly of concern to us here. We are more interested in the peaceful types of protest manifested by ballot behaviour. To say that some proportion of those voting Conservative were expressing such protest behaviour is not so strange as it may first appear. Consider the alternatives. Without engaging in any controversy over why voters vote the way they do, we do know that in a multi-party, as opposed to a one-party system, the voter can make a choice. In some variable percentage of instances, the voter chooses one party rather than another because of direct dissatisfaction with the policies, administration, candidates, or leadership of the unselected party, or because of some general dissatisfaction with his personal circumstances for which he finds an outlet in political action.[22] Some protest votes of this sort occur only occasionally; others become routinized. The latter are most likely to go to parties with the organization, program, and image that prepares them for the role of parties of protest. These are typically third parties in Canada, hence the low level of satisfaction among Créditistes in Quebec or NDP voters in the west seems perfectly understandable. Yet it is an obvious over-simplification to consider all votes for third parties as protest votes, or these parties themselves as foci of discontent. As we have already noted, neither the NDP in Quebec nor Social Credit in the west attracted relatively large proportions of economically dissatisfied voters. There are no doubt many reasons for such regional variations, but one source lies in the way these parties, in the areas in question, had become part of an alternative adaptation of the two-party system.[23]

But what about those situations where the alternative of viable

---

22. For an elaboration of the conditions related to "voting against" a party or candidate, see Murray L. Levin, *The Alienated Voter* (New York: Holt, Rinehart and Winston, 1962).

23. Maurice Pinard, *The Rise of a Third Party: A Study in Crisis Politics* (Englewood Cliffs, N.J.: Prentice-Hall, 1971), pp. 36-71.

third parties is not available, or where commitment to a traditional two party system is strong? It is there, we would argue, that choice of the Conservative party is important. On the federal scene, the Liberal party has been dominant since the turn of the century. Its defeat in 1957 was the first one in twenty-seven years. When third parties are unavailable or unacceptable, the Conservatives have come to assume the role of the party of the dispossessed and the dissatisfied, along with its continuing image as the spokesman of the prosperous farmer and businessman of British origin. Indeed, this image may be part of its appeal to those who feel not only cramped by economic conditions, but crowded by the prosperity and success of those of non-British origin. Admittedly, this is conjecture, and cannot easily be proved from our data.

Quite apart from the nature of political choices available through the party system, it should be possible to relate variations in the level of satisfaction to the character of supporters attracted to each party regionally. Table 5–6 summarizes what we believe to be the relevant characteristics. These are age, urban residence, whether the head of the household is in the labour force, the main thrust of the occupational distribution, and the median family income. While we treat each of these independently, they are in fact related. As potency declines with age, so does earning power, the ability to exert influence in occupational decisions, and even the likelihood of being employed. Under such circumstances, with the exception of the very rich, life is not likely to be unusually satisfying, nor will the future hold much promise. Similarly, despite the diatribes against life in the cities, it is there where individuals are most likely to enjoy the amenities of industrialized society, higher salaries, and more diversified job opportunities.

In a compressed form, the profiles capture the extent of which parties attract different kinds of supporters independently of the fact that regions themselves differ in their social composition. Since our main concern has been with the Conservatives, we again use those supporters as our standard of comparison. Only in the Atlantic provinces did Conservative voters have characteristics traditionally associated with that party. There they were older, more prosperous, and more heavily represented in higher status occupations. Yet they still had proportionately more voters the heads of whose households were not in the labour force. This was at least partially associated with the greater age of Conservative voters in general.

In Quebec again, Conservative supporters were more likely to live in households where the head was no longer employed. They were exceeded only by the Créditistes in the proportions living outside large, urban areas and employed in low status occupations. But they fell below even the Créditistes in reported median family income.

These characteristics are of course in contrast with Liberal supporters, but even more so with the NDP. The NDP voter was most likely to be young, resident in a large city (mainly Montreal), employed in a white collar occupation primarily of a professional nature and enjoying a high family income.

Conservative supporters had the same relative age and labour force characteristics in Ontario as elsewhere. They reported the same median income as NDP voters, but otherwise contrasted sharply with them on residence and occupation. NDP voters tended to be urban and mainly in manual occupations, but Conservatives were mainly resident in areas of less than 10,000 population, with relatively few in manual occupations. Though still a small share of the work force, Conservatives were more likely than those voting for other parties to be in farming occupations.

In the Prairies, NDP voters were again most urban and Social Credit voters lived more often in the blue collar households. Yet the main distinguishing feature of Conservative voters was their comparatively low median income. Conservatives were, like NDP voters, older than those voting Liberal or Social Credit.

Because of the nature of British Columbia society, all parties were inclined to attract relatively older voters, though none did so with the frequency of the Conservatives. Fully 38 percent were listed outside the labour force, hence it is hardly surprising that their median income should be low. The unusually high income of Social Credit supporters may reflect the actual social base of that party, but with a small sample, it is an estimate particularly subject to variability.

This resumé of regional profiles of party supporters does not, nor was it intended to, explain individual sources of greater or less satisfaction. That is, we are not saying that older voters, in rural areas, retired or in low status occupations, and with a low income were necessarily dissatisfied, although there is a high probability that this was the case.[24] Our concern is rather with using these characteristics at the aggregate level as a way of demonstrating a syndrome—the characteristics associated within a collectivity. As a rule, those groups which expressed a lower level of satisfaction also were characterized by greater numbers of economically depressed. This procedure was most effective in accounting for the rates of satisfaction of Liberals and Conservatives in all regions and of third party supporters in Quebec. It was much less helpful in explaining the views of third party voters in the west, where the characteristics of voters would have led us to anticipate greater satisfaction among NDP voters and less among Social Credit.

---

24. Norman Bradburn, *The Structure of Psychological Well-Being* (Chicago: Aldine Press, 1969).

Some further light on the distribution of regional and party variations comes from examining Table 5–13 on class consciousness. Respondents were asked, "If you had to pick one, which of the following five social classes would you say you were in—upper class, upper middle class, middle class, working class, or lower class?" The two categories selected most often were middle class, by 38 percent, and working class by 45 percent. In the table dealing only with working class identification, we find this to be highest in the Atlantic provinces and the Prairies, with modest internal differences among party supporters in these regions. Elsewhere, however, voters were sharply differentiated. In Quebec, where the divisions were strongest, there was a high frequency of working class identifications among Créditiste and Conservative voters and an unusually low one among those voting NDP. In other words, class consciousness was in line with objective class conditions, but again not in confirmation with what we might otherwise have expected to be the class characteristics of the Conservative and New Democratic parties. The way in which regional conditions have shaped the character of these parties is dramatized by contrast with Ontario. There Liberal and Conservative voters were almost identical, but NDP voters were set apart by the large proportion considering themselves working class, altogether more in line with expectations about the composition of these parties. In the Prairies, however, Conservatives were again less like Liberals and more like third party supporters. In British Columbia, finally, where class cleavages were strong, the two older parties were sharply separated from the third parties by approximately 30 percentage points. This is the one area where Conservative voters lacked, both objectively and in terms of class consciousness, the conditions of a proletarian image.

We could anticipate that, on questions with such an individualistic focus, individual characteristics and not group ones would be the primary determinants of opinions. Granting this, region and party do have some influence. In general, judgements of personal circumstances were almost equally affected by region and party. Of the two, region was preeminent in shaping opinions in the Atlantic provinces. Yet elsewhere regional effects were more pervasive than our results may at first suggest, since the major finding is the particular role that parties play *within* regions. In other words, the regional context is a prime determinant of the way parties will act as polarizing or balancing agents.

THE CONSEQUENCES OF PARTY TIES

The importance of national political parties in regionally-divided societies lies in their potential for setting in motion nationalizing

Table 5–13 **Percent Choosing Working Class Identification, by Region and Past Vote**

Region	*1965 Vote* Liberal		Conservative		NDP		Social Credit		Total[a]	
Atlantic	48	(100)	56	(83)	[37][c]	(8)	—		52	(229)
Quebec	37	(357)	52	(97)	20	(70)	59	(65)	40	(793)
Ontario	43	(424)	42	(311)	64	(132)	—		46	(1,054)
Prairies	44	(89)	52	(125)	52	(56)	57	(37)	51	(395)
British Columbia	28	(78)	21	(58)	55	(62)	61	(26)	39	(256)
Total	40	(1,048)	45	(674)	49	(328)	58	(67)[b]	45	(2,727)

[a] Column totals include other parties, don't knows, etc.
[b] The total for Social Credit includes 4 cases in the Atlantic provinces and Ontario. The Quebec Créditistes are not included.
[c] Too few cases to percentage
Figures in parentheses are base N's.

movements. One of the ways this occurs is through their recruitment of leaders and supporters from all regions. Two qualitatively different kinds of ties are established in this way. The first is through the establishment and consequent recognition of an identity of interest that cuts across regions. In the second, voters form attachments to some aspect of the party, but not to other party supporters. In either instance, large parties that are national in scope and wish to maximize their electoral appeal are constrained from making excessively particularistic approaches to voters, since what attracts one group may actively antagonize another. In this way, a party's desire to govern may propel it to discover larger, nationally-appealing issues and thereby push it away from narrow concerns with regionalism. This is not to say, however, that such actions result in the absence of conflict. We can be sure that conflict will still be present, since the very meaning of a regionally-divided society is one where local interests predominate and where many seek their continuity.

The achievement of shared loyalties built on ties with a party are difficult where regions provide formidable barriers. They do this by inhibiting the attraction of a relatively homogeneous social base nationally. It is just such a base that is required to build, for example, a competitive class-oriented party and traditional class voting.[25] In the case of all our parties, each attracted a somewhat different base of support in each region. Some of this is almost inevitable, given the uneven distribution of human and material resources in Canada. But some of it seems quite independent, as each party comes to be associated with different types of voters in any given region. For example, in Quebec the majority are French-speaking and Catholic and we would anticipate that any national party in that province would necessarily base its support on these majorities. At the same time, its composition may still differ from other parties in Quebec in ethnic composition,[26] and more important, as we noted in the profiles in Table 5–6, in the socio-economic characteristics of its supporters. The Conservatives, despite the nature of their leadership, their policies, and traditional concerns, attracted a relatively dissatisfied and disadvantaged body of voters, especially in some regions. In contrast, the NDP, with its principles firmly grounded in social democratic forms of socialism, was able in some parts of Canada to attract relatively satisfied, optimistic, and even privileged voters.

It is not sufficient then, as Parsons has suggested, to attract a diverse body of voters in order for a party to weaken or transcend the

25. Robert R. Alford, "The Social Bases of Political Cleavage in 1962," in John Meisel, ed., *Papers on the 1962 Election* (Toronto: University of Toronto Press, 1964), pp. 203-34.

26. See footnote 20.

cleavage structure. We have suggested that fairly homogeneous bases of support, where they cut across regions, may be even more important for the development of national themes. Our search for the part played by Canadian parties took us, in any case, from a concentration on the social characteristics of voters to their viewpoints. It was in the opinions of voters that we sought evidence of the influence of parties in building such nationally-spanning outlooks. Our understanding of influence has been deliberately imprecise, and is used to encompass both the deliberate efforts of parties to induce a partisan frame of mind and the more adventitious results of party workings, including the consequences of attracting particular kinds of supporters. In this chapter we have considered two kinds of issues, those pertaining to personal circumstances and those to regional conditions.

Opinions of the state of regions themselves are strongly affected by a form of ethnocentrism. This ethnocentrism is tempered to some degree (details of which were given in the preceding chapter) by a reality orientation that was affected by the actual conditions of the regions. In this chapter, we learned of an additional factor, that pertaining to the relative strength of the party, either in the nation as a whole or within the region. We also suggested that the local composition of party supporters had some bearing on outlooks, either enhancing a region's position, or depressing it. Finally, the ideology either implicit or explicit in the party also helped affect the views of those favouring the NDP, enhancing in some regions a pessimistic outlook that is probably compatible with the protest orientation of that party.

On issues dealing with respondents' own situation, party seemed to have more impact, but except for the Liberals, rarely of a sort consistent across all regions. Even for the Liberals, the absolute level of satisfaction varied considerably from one region to another.

The general theme of this chapter will be re-examined in Chapters 10 and 11. Here we confined our analysis to a series of issues whose overt focus was on the region. In this context, it is perhaps not surprising that parties were not able to exert much influence. Yet we should not forget that the outlooks of party supporters in particular regions were at least partially conditioned by the local character of that party. That is, national parties are not unimportant in the strain between regional and national interests; it is rather that their arena of influence is circumscribed by regional conditions.

CHAPTER

6

Party structure and voting behaviour

INTRODUCTION

The political sources of regionalism lie in mechanisms for making regional demands heard and for translating these into authoritative decisions. In our model of territorial cleavages, both of these concerns were represented by three sets of conditions and the interchanges among them. One, the power of provinces, has already been dealt with in Chapter 3. Little more will be said about it except in the conclusion of this chapter, when we emphasize its interconnections with the remaining two sets of conditions, the party system and the responses of voters. It is these latter which are our major concern here.

Without entering into the history of how it emerged, we will simply take the party structure as given. Each province, at both the provincial and federal levels of government, has a de facto system of one, two, or multiple parties. The lack of a single, national party structure has occurred without constitutional sanction, but with all the persistence that local conditions have demanded. The political behaviour of the electorate is necessarily responsive to the special circumstances present in each voter's place of residence. For the voter, the electoral choices he makes and the sense of partisan attachment he acquires are constrained by what the political structure offers as alternatives.

For each of the provinces, we wish to know whether citizens can choose from among one, two, or more parties. This may be interpreted as a concern with the extent of party opposition to the government. But as Robert Dahl has written in introducing a volume on political opposition, "Legal party opposition . . . is a recent unplanned invention that has been confined for the most part to a handful of countries in Western Europe and the English-speaking world. . . . of the 113 members of the United Nations in 1964, only about 30 had political systems in which full legal opposition among organized political parties had existed through the preceding decade."[1] The absence of opposition parties results, in many instances, from their prohibition by law. But such legal arrangements hardly account for all of the variations, since conversely, even in countries such as the United States, Britain, and Canada, where opposition parties exist, no constitutional provision was initially made for any parties, either governing or opposition. Without considering why there should be political parties of any kind, Dahl notes that constitutional arrangements are not sufficient to account for patterns of opposition, and goes on to suggest looking at the electoral system,[2] the extent and distribution of a common culture, the existence of subcultures associated with specific population groups, records of grievances against the government, and social and economic divisions in the country. All of these factors may be considered in terms of their conduciveness to the emergence of opposition parties.[3]

If we understand these factors to bring about differences among nations, we should also be alert to the possibility of variations in patterns of opposition within nations. At the same time we must also point out that we have set ourselves a task different from Dahl's. Our purpose in the following section on structural limits is to describe the operation of the party system. In so doing, we demonstrate how regions vary in the presence of opposition parties and in their number and strength. We do not, in an approach analogous to Dahl's, attempt to account for the sources of these regional differences. Differences in the nature of the party system within regions will help explain the continuation of regionalism generally. That the origin of these party differences themselves undoubtedly lies in the same conditions that gave rise to other forms of regional differentiation is quite clear. It is surely not accidental that most of the factors that Dahl describes as important for effecting the emergence and operation of opposition

---

1. Robert A. Dahl, ed., *Political Opposition in Western Democracies* (New Haven: Yale University Press, 1966), p. ix.

2. Douglas Rae, *The Political Consequences of Electoral Laws* (New Haven: Yale University Press, 1967), demonstrates how a comparative study of electoral systems helps account for some of the variation in the extent and nature of opposition.

3. Dahl, *Political Opposition,* pp. 348-86.

parties are also those, in both the preceding and following chapters, that we use to account for the emergence and continuation of regionalism.[4] We acknowledge then the importance of Dahl's focus on opposition parties and the sources for their emergence. By directing our attention instead to determining the extent of opposition in each region, and then searching for the effects of these different party systems, we hope to broaden the scope of Dahl's analysis to include the potential for understanding more about differentiation within a nation.

A second theme in this chapter, described in terms of psychological constraints, considers the ways in which voting choices are actually made. In a passage often cited, Ernest Renan wrote that the existence of a nation is a daily plebiscite.[5] By his presence and participation in the routines of life, the citizen affirms his support for the regime. "Voting with one's feet," however, leaves undefined the choices open to the citizen. Has he any alternative to staying within the confines of his state, and if he may leave, what cost must he pay? Does he have the option of different forms of participation, and again at what cost? Where there are no choices, Renan's plebiscite may be an empty one. It could be argued that the plebiscite remains real so long as there is no political resistance. In this sense, states with one-party systems still offer their citizens a choice in an election: to vote, and hence acquiese in the regime, or not to vote, and indicate their passive resistance. But since voting is usually compulsory in such systems, even this alternative is limited in scope.

A daily plebiscite in a literal sense is hardly possible. Yet its metaphoric qualities emphasize a theme crucial to understanding the varieties of political behaviour. Living in a nation does involve some sense of commitment to it, and voting does require the making of choices, at least partially on the basis of this commitment. At the same time, as we have indicated by the preceding questions, even the metaphoric plebiscite does not deal with the alternatives. To do so, one must take into account the nature of the political system within which the citizen operates. For example, if citizens in Country X always vote for one party, the sole one on their ballots, and citizens in country Y divide their votes between two parties, it is hardly fair to

---

4. One topic we do not discuss, though it is relevant to Dahl's theme, is the effects of federalism on the party system. See Leon Epstein, "A Comparative Study of Canadian Parties," *American Political Science Review,* 58 (March 1964): 46-57; and for further comments on the shaping of opposition, F. C. Engelmann and M. A. Schwartz, *Political Parties and the Canadian Social Structure* (Scarborough: Prentice-Hall of Canada, 1967).

5. "L'existence d'une nation est . . . un plébicite de tous les jours." Ernest Renan, *Discours et conferences,* 3rd ed. (Paris: C. Levy, 1887), p. 307.

characterize the citizens of X as less "democratic" than those of Y. Certainly it is true that every citizen contributes in some way to the kind of government by which he is ruled, but given a particular form of government, there is generally not much the ordinary citizen can readily do to change its nature. The individual's political behaviour hence needs to be evaluated in the context of the choices open to him.

This then is our task: to describe the nature of the competitive party structure within each region, and the ways in which choices are made from among the available parties. It should come as no surprise, to anticipate our findings slightly, that in general, each region consists of a unique configuration of party politics. Insofar as has been possible, our analysis employs a time dimension as a way of emphasizing the stability of political arrangements within regions. It will also enable us to fulfill an explanatory as well as a descriptive purpose —that is, to conclude that the party systems operate so as to help sustain the special character of each region.

STRUCTURAL LIMITS OF THE PARTY SYSTEM

From the beginning of Canadian nationhood until the end of World War I, Canadian politics were dominated by two parties, the Conservative and Liberal. There were, it is true, instances of third parties before this time, but never of sufficient appeal or durability to challenge the two-party system. Since then third parties have emerged to successfully restructure the party system, yet only in some provinces and at some times. It is not our intention here to review the history of party successes, nor to relate these to organizational strength and electoral appeal.[6] The characterization of parties which follows is, however, based on such an inventory, and illustrative details will be supplied wherever necessary. For the most part, our analysis relies on the work of Maurice Pinard and Jorgen Rasmussen.[7]

Pinard, in a masterly analysis of the rise of Social Credit in Quebec, contributes to our general sociological knowledge by his hypotheses on the emergence of third parties. In its simplest terms, his main theme is that whenever one party remains in office for a lengthy period, with the effect that the principal opposition party is not able

---

6. There is at present no comprehensive history of parties in Canada. For a brief comment on some of the events at issue here, see Engelmann and Schwartz, *Political Parties*, pp. 32-37.

7. Maurice Pinard, *The Rise of a Third Party: A Study in Crisis Politics* (Engelwood Cliffs, N.J.: Prentice-Hall, 1971), esp. Chapter 3; Jorgen Rasmussen, "A Research Note on Canadian Party Systems," *Canadian Journal of Economics and Political Science,* 33 (Feb. 1967), pp. 98-106.

to gain more than one-third of the popular vote, then that party loses its significance as a viable alternative. Consequently, when the pressure for opposition grows, it finds its outlet in a new, third party. In testing this hypothesis developed to account for the rise of Social Credit in Quebec, Pinard examined comparable situations in other provinces at both the federal and provincial levels of government from about 1900 to 1967. While his hypothesis is not central to our own discussion, the data on which it is based are readily transferable to it.

Rasmussen adapts the procedures suggested by Schlesinger to determine the competitiveness of a party system.[8] He uses as his data popular vote for the winning party in provincial and federal legislatures, covering the period between 1920 and 1964. Competitiveness is measured along two dimensions: the percentage of elections in which the leading party changed, and the percentage of elections where the dominant party won the greatest share of the popular vote. The five-fold distinctions made both by Schlesinger and Rasmussen on types of competitiveness are not particularly pertinent here beyond the delineation of one-party types. The criteria for determining competitiveness are somewhat arbitrary and different criteria would produce somewhat different results. Rasmussen's tabular results are useful for their conciseness, but inadequate for showing the interplay with third parties, a weakness which Pinard avoids. But again, his assemblage of data is a useful shortcut in preparing a classification of parties.

The classification of parties in Chart 6-1 is derived from the predominant adaptation of the party system made in each of the provinces. Political history since 1900 was taken into account in arriving at these distinctions. Whenever there had been major shifts in party types the chart contains the adaptation closest to the time of our survey. Needless to say, the classification does not refer to a constitutional or legal definition of party systems. It is quite simply a set of categories derived from the actual outcomes of the working of the party system in each province.

The three older members of the Atlantic provinces have maintained a stable two-party system from their formation. In two of these, New Brunswick and Prince Edward Island, Conservatives and Liberals have alternated fairly regularly in forming the provincial government. While third parties have emerged in the three provinces, they have been singularly unsuccessful. The CCF made strong overtures for electoral support in Nova Scotia, but whatever success it attained had

---

8. Joseph Schlesinger, "A Two-Dimensional Scheme for Classifying the States According to Degree of Inter-Party Competition," *American Political Science Review*, 49 (Dec. 1955): 1120-28.

Chart 6–1   **Predominant adaptation of the party system at the federal and provincial levels.**

	Party Systems	
	Federal	*Provincial*
Newfoundland	one	one
Prince Edward Island	two	two
Nova Scotia	two	two
New Brunswick	two	two
Atlantic Provinces	two	two
Quebec	one	two
Ontario	two	multi/one
Manitoba	multi	multi
Saskatchewan	multi	two (marginal)
Alberta	multi	one
Prairie Provinces	multi	multi/one
British Columbia	multi	multi

See text for elaboration

been mainly confined to Cape Breton Island. At the federal level as well, both major parties continue to command considerable support. The one exception to this picture of a strong two-party system in the Atlantic region is Newfoundland. It is a relative newcomer to Confederation, entering only in 1949, and throughout the period covered by this book it had been dominated by the Liberal Party at both levels of government. Despite these and other exceptions, however, it seems reasonable to characterize the Atlantic provinces as a unit in terms of the predominance of a two party system.

Rasmussen considers Quebec at the provincial level an example of a one-party cyclical type. In such types there is a single dominant party that wins more than 65 percent of the elections, yet the opposition is strong enough to pose a real threat and gain control of the government for short periods of time. Other examples that Rasmussen cites are New Brunswick and Prince Edward Island, both at the provincial level. We have already classified these two provinces as having a two-party system, choosing to emphasize, as does Pinard, the notion of a strong opposition, even if it is not one that regularly alternates in power.

We take this view as well with Quebec. There have been several important breakdowns in the traditional party structure, it is true. Most significant was the rise of Action Liberale Nationale in 1935, Union Nationale in 1936, Bloc Populaire Canadien in 1944, and Union des Electeurs in 1948. Pinard argues that the two early parties were associated with the weakness of the Conservative opposition and the dominance of the Liberals, perfect conditions for the rise of third parties. But Action Liberale soon disappeared, partly to be reabsorbed into the Liberal party of which it had been a dissident offshoot, and Union Nationale became the second major party, having replaced the Conservatives organizationally. Since then, it is the Liberals and Union Nationale which have alternated in office. Bloc Populaire did make some showing in 1944, winning 14 percent of the votes and four seats, but by the following election, the party had disappeared. Meanwhile Union des Electeurs appeared, running ninety-two candidates in the 1948 election, almost a full slate, not one of whom was successful. Since 1965, further third-party activities have taken place in Quebec, perhaps heralding major changes. But for the time span at issue, we feel confident in labelling the provincial politics of this province as primarily a two-party system.

At the federal level a quite different set of circumstances were operating. From 1896 to 1957, in sixteen general elections, voters in Quebec invariably gave the Liberals a majority. Only in 1958 was this pattern broken, and then only for that one election. One-party dominance has been associated with recurring challenges from third parties, notably Bloc Populaire in 1945 and Social Credit in 1962. The impact of both these parties was considerable: Bloc Populaire won 13 percent of the vote and Social Credit 26 percent. Yet Bloc Populaire's victories constituted only two seats and turned out to be ephemeral. After the 1963 election, a majority of those elected as Social Credit broke with the national party and were henceforth known as members of Le Ralliement des Créditistes, the body that originally joined with the national Social Credit organization. These organizational changes were not effective, however, in preventing a drop in popular favour. At the 1965 election the Créditistes obtained only 17 percent of the popular vote. None of these third parties had been able to effectively displace the Conservatives, nor to seriously challenge the Liberals. In federal elections, then, Quebec may be termed a one-party system.

Ontario has much more of a two-party structure federally than does Quebec, but not one that is totally consistent. Both the Liberal and Conservative parties continue to be strong, but with greater strength on the side of the Conservatives. For example, out of twenty elections between 1896 and 1965, Ontarians gave a plurality to the Liberals seven times, compared to the national average of thirteen. Moreover, third parties have played a significant role in Ontario's electoral history. The Progressives gained 28 percent of the vote in 1921, the Reconstruction party won 11 percent in 1935, and since 1945, the CCF and then NDP obtained at least 11 percent of the vote, reaching a high of 22 percent in 1965. Despite these inroads into the two-party system, its outlines still remain intact in Ontario.

Provincially, Ontario is much more difficult to describe. Rasmussen considers it an example of a one-party predominant case, in which one party wins more than 65 percent of the election, losing only because of some temporary weakness usually overcome by the following election. The second example of this type given by Rasmussen is Alberta, a province which we have no difficulty accepting as a one-party type. Our hesitancy in classifying Ontario comes from the relative strength of opposition parties. Pinard, in a personal communication, suggests that a good rule of thumb for determining the number of viable parties in the system is the requirement that each opposition party continue to obtain from 15 to 20 percent of the popular vote in every election. On this basis Ontario had a multi-party system, since not only did the Liberals gain about one-third of the votes over the years in question, but since 1943, when the CCF became the official opposition for one term with 32 percent of the vote, that party and its successor, the NDP, continued to win from 15 to 26 percent of the vote. At the same time Rasmussen's evidence is unequivocal: the Conservatives held uninterrupted power since 1943. Our compromise classification then is to term Ontario a multi-party system with one party dominant. Wilson and Hoffman, taking into account a longer time span, would seem to agree with this in their characterization of Ontario as a "three-party system in transition."[9]

The three Prairie provinces are all variants on the theme of the breakup of traditional party structures. The early strength of one of the old line parties (generally the Liberals), the local problems of new settlements dependent on agriculture and distant from industry and finance, the massive form that these problems took with the depression and drought of the 1930s, made this area a unique political setting. It is here that third parties have had their greatest success, although which parties had most appeal has varied by province.

In Alberta the United Farmers had a short-lived heyday, to pass into virtual oblivion when Social Credit came to power at the first election it contested. Federally, we see a multi-party system, with the

---

9. John Wilson and David Hoffman, "Ontario: A Three-Party System in Transition," in Martin Robin, ed., *Canadian Provincial Politics* (Scarborough: Prentice-Hall of Canada, 1972).

Conservatives dominant since 1958. Provincially, Social Credit has enjoyed overwhelming dominance since first attaining office, with only sporadic bursts of opposition strength. For our purposes, the 1971 victory of the Conservatives need not be evaluated.

The United Farmers and later the Progressives also had a period of strength in Manitoba and continued to enjoy modified electoral influence with the formation of the Liberal-Progressive party. A two-party system was further obscured with the emergence of the CCF and an almost totally reorganized Conservative party in 1958. Both federally and provincially, Manitoba can be classified as a multi-party system.

Federally, Saskatchewan too has several competing parties, mainly Liberal, Conservative, and CCF. But provincially, while the principal contenders altered, a two-party system remained, along with long stretches in which a single party stayed in power. Pinard, however, considers Saskatchewan a marginal case of a two-party system.

In total, the Prairie provinces exemplify a multi-party system at the federal level, dominated from 1958 to 1965 by the Conservatives. There is more variation provincially, but generally in the Prairies too, more than the usual two parties had success with some tradition toward one-party dominance.

Both federally and provincially, British Columbia has a multi-party system. Provincially, the two older parties have been especially weak, governing for the last time between 1941 and 1952 only through a coalition. Since 1941 the CCF/NDP, and since 1952 Social Credit, have had relatively greater success, the former as opposition and the latter as government from 1953 on. Federally the older parties seem to try harder, but first place is an evasive goal for all contenders.

PSYCHOLOGICAL LIMITS ON CHOICE

Our second avenue for discerning regional political differences is through voters' reports on the degree of stability of their partisan choice. We have chosen to term the effects of these patterns of behaviour "psychological limits," since we assume that their rationale lies primarily in the minds of the voters and not in some characteristic of the political system. This is not to say, of course, that the objective character of the political system is independent from what the voter perceives, but only that, for purposes of analysis and explanation, we need to examine the perceived world of the voter separately from the formal structure. We do so by considering a number of indicators of voters' attachment to the electoral system and to a specific political party. We know that regions vary in their political structure. Can we anticipate that they are also differentiated according to the habitual behaviour of voters?

Voting in Federal Elections

Table 6–1 reports the relation between vote in the 1965 election and always voting for the same party in federal elections. Marginals are not reported for regions, since to do so meant either excluding that part of the sample for which we did not have appropriate voting information, or averaging together incommensurate units of information.

The Liberals appeared to have the most loyal supporters, especially in the Atlantic provinces and Quebec. For the Conservatives, greatest loyalty was prevalent in the easternmost region and in Ontario. For both parties, voting patterns in the Atlantic provinces were indicative of the strength of the traditional two-party system in that region. Newfoundland was certainly an exception in this regard, but numerically it is not large enough to have much effect on our results, and historically the recency of its entry into Confederation makes its form of political behaviour a special case.

The Liberal party in Quebec and the Conservative party in Ontario benefitted from the solidity of tradition in those provinces, giving each the major nucleus of its continuing strength. Since the time of

Table 6–1 **Percent Saying They Always Vote for the Same Party in Federal Elections, by Region and Past Vote**

| Region | | *1965 Vote* | | |
	Liberal	Conservative	NDP	Social Credit
Atlantic	65	57	0	—
	(100)	(83)	(8)	
Quebec	60	43	13	9
	(357)	(97)	(70)	(65)
Ontario	48	52	29	—
	(424)	(311)	(132)	
Prairies	47	45	21	24
	(89)	(125)	(56)	(37)
British Columbia	43	34	29	31
	(78)	(58)	(62)	(26)
Total	53	48	24	25
	(1,048)	(674)	(328)	(67)[a]

[a]The total for Social Credit includes 4 cases in the Atlantic provinces and Ontario. The Quebec Créditistes are not included.

Figures in parentheses are base N's.

Laurier, electoral support for the Conservatives in Quebec has been whittled away. We may indeed be surprised at the amount of constancy our Quebec Conservatives express, unless we note their minority status and the importance of provincial Union Nationale assistance to the national Conservatives. In contrast, the Liberal party in Ontario, though 48 percent said that they always vote for that party, still got a relatively smaller share of loyal voters than the eastern provinces, reflecting both the greater appeal of the Conservative party in Ontario and the occasional attractiveness of third parties. The effects of third party appeal on the major parties were seen more clearly in the west, where as an extreme example, only one-third of Conservative voters in British Columbia always voted for that party.

Because of the uneven distribution of electoral support for third parties, there is not much more that can be said on the basis of Table 6–1. Perhaps it is worth mentioning that the low level of constancy of NDP voters in Quebec is indicative of the recency, not only of that party's formation, but also of its restricted appeal to a rapidly industrialized province.

Another indication of the force of habit is evident in Table 6–2 which presents the percentage of those who say they always voted in federal elections. Regions line up in an almost perfect progression from east to west. The Atlantic provinces had the highest proportion of regular voters, 66 percent, and the Prairies the lowest, with 45 percent. What is particularly interesting is the distribution of voting regularity by party within regions. Liberal voters everywhere were most regular in their voting practices, especially east of Ontario. In the east, 73 percent answered that they always voted in federal elections. Conservatives were next in regularity, with a high of 75 percent voting in the Atlantic provinces and a declining trend as we move westward, falling to 48 percent in British Columbia. NDP voters were slightly less regular in their habits than Conservatives. Moreover, they seemed to vote more often in those areas, Quebec and the Atlantic provinces, where they had been least successful in electing candidates. Social Credit voters reported a 53 percent rate of regularity, but it was only 38 percent in British Columbia, the lowest of any group. In all cases, while party attachment played some part in the likelihood of voting regularity, it is also clear that region of residence played an independent part in establishing a particular level of habitual participation. Hence, Créditiste voters in Quebec, while they might be expected to be fairly irregular in voting participation, because of the newness of their party and the evidence of their dissatisfaction with their previous political alternatives, reported the highest level of regular voting. Fully 82 percent of Créditiste voters said they always voted, exceeding even the above-average level of such behaviour in Quebec by 20 percentage points.

Table 6–2 **Percent Reporting They Always Vote in Federal Elections, by Region and Past Vote**

	1965 Vote				
Region	Liberal	Conservative	NDP	Social Credit	Total[a]
Atlantic	73	75	[63][c]	—	61
	(100)	(83)	(8)		(229)
Quebec	73	69	70	82	48
	(357)	(97)	(70)	(65)	(793)
Ontario	66	60	58	—	52
	(424)	(311)	(132)		(1,054)
Prairies	57	49	54	60	42
	(89)	(125)	(56)	(37)	(395)
British Columbia	59	48	45	38	44
	(78)	(58)	(62)	(26)	(256)
Total	68	60	58	53	49
	(1,048)	(674)	(328)	(67)[b]	(2,727)

[a]Row totals include other parties, don't knows, etc.

[b]The total for Social Credit includes 4 cases in the Atlantic provinces and Ontario. The Quebec Créditistes are not included.

[c]Too few cases to percentage.

Figures in parentheses are base N's.

The impact of these two kinds of behaviour—always voting for the same party and voting in all elections—is obviously not of the same order. Partisan loyalty affects the chances of a party's success: regularity of voting affects rates of turnout. We need to know the relation between these two variables, since those citizens who always vote and for the same party make a greater contribution to that party's likelihood of success than do either loyal irregular voters or regular voters who switch parties. Information for this assessment is contained in Table 6–3. As we might have already anticipated from Tables 6–1 and 6–2, voting regularity among party faithful was highest for the Liberals, especially in the Atlantic provinces and Quebec. In those provinces, 49 and 46 percent respectively said that they both voted for the same party in all federal elections and always voted. Such a large nucleus of loyal support was evident nowhere else, and for no other party except the Conservatives in the Atlantic provinces. In addition, as we move westward, the pattern was for a decrease in regular voting among partisans. While this was certainly indicated in the preceding two tables, the full extent of the impact of the two related trends—to always vote and for the same party—was not so clearly evident. For example, in British Columbia, the Conservative party could count on about one-third of those who voted Conservative in the 1965 election having done so in all preceding

Table 6–3 **Percent Reporting They Vote in All Federal Elections and Always for the Same Party, by Region and Past Vote**

		1965 Vote		
Region	Liberal	Conservative	NDP	Social Credit
Atlantic	49	46	0	—
	(100)	(83)	(8)	
Quebec	46	31	13	9
	(357)	(97)	(70)	(65)
Ontario	32	35	21	—
	(424)	(311)	(132)	
Prairies	29	22	16	14
	(89)	(125)	(56)	(37)
British Columbia	23	17	10	15
	(78)	(58)	(62)	(26)
Total	37	32	16	13
	(1,048)	(674)	(328)	(67)[a]

[a]The total for Social Credit includes 4 cases in the Atlantic provinces and Ontario. The Quebec Créditistes are not included.

Figures in parentheses are base N's.

ones. Of these same supporters in 1965, almost one-half reported
voting in all previous elections in which they were eligible. But only
17 percent said they always voted Conservative and in all federal
elections. While this may not be the best example, due to sampling
variability, the direction of the relationship is unequivocal. The farther
west we go, the weaker the attachment of voters to any single party.

Finally, in Table 6–4 we have those who voted for the same party
in 1963 and 1965. Predictably, the percentages are much higher than
in any of the previous tables for a number of reasons. With little
change in policies and programs between the two elections, little disadvantage to newer parties otherwise found when covering a longer
time span, and presumably, less memory distortion in the short period
covered, voter stability was high. Aside from these general effects,
several findings in the table need to be emphasized. Despite the expectations aroused by the preceding three tables on the greater voting
stability of Liberals, here it was the Conservatives who had more
support in the past two elections. This is mainly the result of a relatively larger number of Liberal voters in 1965 who probably had not
voted in 1963.[10] In that earlier election, in the Prairies, about 15

Table 6–4 **Percent Voting for Same Party in 1963 and 1965
Federal Elections, by Region and Past Vote**

Region	Liberal	*1965 Vote* Conservative	NDP	Social Credit
Atlantic	85	83	[25][b]	—
	(100)	(83)	(8)	
Quebec	80	74	33	69
	(357)	(97)	(70)	(65)
Ontario	71	82	61	—
	(424)	(311)	(132)	
Prairies	57	76	55	46
	(89)	(125)	(56)	(37)
British Columbia	72	76	77	38
	(78)	(58)	(62)	(26)
Total	74	79	56	40
	(1,048)	(674)	(328)	(67)[a]

[a]The total for Social Credit includes 4 cases in the Atlantic provinces
and Ontario. The Quebec Créditistes are not included.

[b]Too few cases to percentage.

Figures in parentheses are base N's.

10. This inference is based on the numbers who gave no answer or did not
remember how they had voted, as well as respondents who admitted not voting.

percent had voted Conservative and at least that many had probably not voted. Under half had not chosen the same party twice in the case of NDP supporters in the Atlantic provinces and Quebec, and Social Credit in the Prairies and British Columbia. In Quebec, the NDP picked up votes in 1965 from those who had previously voted Liberal (29 percent) or had not voted. During the 1965 election, Social Credit gained votes from those who had not cast a ballot in the 1963 election, but they also gained from other parties. In the Prairies, this was mainly from the Conservatives and in British Columbia, from the Liberals and to some extent the NDP.

In all other tables we have seen greater partisan and voting instability in the western provinces as compared to the east. We find this in Table 6–4 as well for the two older parties, but not for the minor ones. Particularly in the case of the NDP, the likelihood of voting for that party twice increased greatly as we move from east to west. We found, for instance, such two-time voters making up 10 percent of all NDP voters in Quebec, but 71 percent in British Columbia.[11] The distribution of Social Credit voters was quite unequal regionally, and hence regional comparisons are not possible, but on the basis of comparisons with other tables presented here, we find a significant difference. This is the high level of voting stability over those two elections found in the western provinces, despite quite different results from other measures of stability. Here we have reflected then, not so much the traditionalism of voting behaviour, but the effects of the immediate conditions in the 1963 and 1965 elections.

Dependence on a loyal electorate was most feasible, then, for the Liberals, and for them, in the Atlantic provinces and Quebec. To a lesser extent, although this depends partly on the measure being used, the Conservatives also had a dependable body of supporters, mainly in the Atlantic provinces and Ontario. With some individual variations, the western provinces were the seats of greatest political instability, in the sense that no party could depend on a large pool of regular and loyal voters.

Voting in Provincial Elections

As a further indication of the stability of the party system, we may look at voting behaviour in provincial elections. One thesis, widely publicized, has been that, not only is there considerable crossover among parties in provincial and federal elections, but that this is done

---

11. In two surveys of Vancouver-Burrard, prior to the 1963 and 1965 elections, Laponce found over 90 percent of the NDP supporters in the earlier election (i.e., in 1958 and 1963), planning to vote for the same party in the coming election. Jean Laponce, *People vs. Politics* (Toronto: University of Toronto Press, 1969), p. 141.

consciously, out of the desire to ensure that the governments in Ottawa and the provincial capitals differ so that they can actively oppose each other and thus ensure that the voter gets all he can from the system.[12] That such views have been propagated does little to help us understand why there is a cross-over, if indeed it occurs.[13] As a theory of motivation, it is difficult to support in the light of what is otherwise known about the level of reasoning normally employed in the electoral decision. An unresolved empirical question then, is to what extent voters choose the same party in both kinds of elections. For those who choose different ones, it will not be the purpose of this chapter to try to account for this phenomenon—the reasons, we feel, in any case lie mainly in the nature of Canadian politics and not in the motivation of voters. Table 6–5 gives the percentage reporting that they voted for the same party in both the last federal and provincial elections under consideration.

Greatest voting consistency was found in the Atlantic provinces, where 86 percent of the Liberals and 93 percent of the Conservatives voted the same way in both elections. This gave us further confirmation of the strength of the two-party system in that region, not only in terms of the party system itself, but also with respect to the responses of individual voters.

In Quebec, it was the Liberals who displayed greatest consistency, building on the stability of their partisanship at the federal level. The Conservatives no longer enter candidates in provincial elections, having been replaced organizationally by Union Nationale since the 1930s. The two are, however, not identical, with Union Nationale possessing a considerably larger base of support than the Quebec Conservative party in federal elections.[14] Nonetheless, there is good reason for us to note in Table 6–5 that 61 percent of those who voted Conservative in the 1965 federal election also voted for that party in the past provincial election. We do so because a majority of those

---

12. Frank H. Underhill, "Canadian Liberal Democracy in 1955," in G. F. Ferguson and F. H. Underhill, *Press and Party in Canada* (Toronto: Ryerson, 1955) pp. 27-46; Dennis H. Wrong, "The Pattern of Party Voting in Canada," *Public Opinion Quarterly,* 21 (Summer, 1957): 252-64.

13. From 1930 to 1957, there were 104 alternating federal and provincial elections. Of these, there were only 16 where the winning party in provincial elections was different than at federal. Compared to Australia and the United States, Canada has a low level of alternating elections. Howard A. Scarrow, "Federal-Provincial Voting Patterns in Canada," *Canadian Journal of Economics and Political Science,* 26 (1960): 289-98.

14. Herbert F. Quinn, *The Union Nationale* (Toronto: University of Toronto Press, 1963).

Table 6–5 **Percent Voting for Same Party in Last Provincial and Federal Election, by Region and Past Federal Vote**

	1965 Vote			
Region	Liberal	Conservative	NDP	Social Credit
Atlantic	86	93	[12][b]	—
	(100)	(83)	(8)	
Quebec	79	61	10	—
	(357)	(97)	(70)	
Ontario	53	82	46	—
	(424)	(311)	(132)	
Prairies	58	43	54	84
	(89)	(125)	(56)	(37)
British Columbia	38	28	71	92
	(78)	(58)	(62)	(26)
Total	64	68	44	82
	(1,048)	(674)	(328)	(67)[a]

[a]The total for Social Credit includes 4 cases in the Atlantic provinces and Ontario.

[b]Too few cases to percentage.

Figures in parentheses are base N's.

respondents recognized, in their answers to interviewers, the affinity between the two parties. For the remainder, we took the liberty of making this connection ourselves. Inheritance of the traditions of le parti bleu, incorporating a distinctly conservative political outlook, may not always be manifested electorally in support for either Union Nationale or the Conservative party, but it did so with sufficient frequency to permit us to make this extrapolation.[15] The extent of consistency was, however, noticeably lower than that for the Liberals. We noted again the weakness of consistent support for the NDP, a relative newcomer to the electoral scene in Quebec.

Greatest stability across the two kinds of elections was displayed by the Conservatives in Ontario. More than four-fifths of the Con-

15. For a discussion of conservatism in Quebec, see Léon Dion, "La Polarité des ideologies," in Fernand Dumont et Jean-Paul Montminy, eds., *Le Pouvoir dans la société canadienne française* (Québec: Les presses de l'université Laval, 1966), pp. 23-36. The conservatism of Union Nationale supporters is documented in Maurice Pinard, "Classes sociales et comportement électoral," in Vincent Lemieux, ed., *Quatre élections provinciales au Québec: 1956-1966* (Québec: Les presses de l'université Laval, 1969), pp. 153-56.

servatives voted the same way in the two elections, compared to about half of the Liberals and NDP.[16]

In the Prairie provinces, both older parties had their strengths and weaknesses, obscured in this instance by combining the three provinces. At the provincial level, the Conservatives had been strong in Manitoba, with the Liberals only moderately so. In Saskatchewan, the provincial Liberals remained strong despite two decades of CCF government, but the Conservatives were quite weak. In Alberta, neither party had been able to accomplish much at the provincial level, despite recent success of the Conservatives. Federally, however, Conservatives were able to attract considerable electoral support, something the Liberals failed to do since 1958. These variations are probably somewhat washed out by our presentation procedures, but some differences remain. For all parties except Social Credit there was considerable vote switching. Of the two older parties, the Liberals were in a stronger position with a proportionately larger body of loyal supporters (though not in absolute numbers). On the basis of information already examined, it appears that federally, Social Credit would not ordinarily have a pool of regular, constant voters. But an unusually high percentage of those who chose Social Credit in the 1965 federal election voted similarly in the most proximate provincial election. The bulk of these cross-election party loyalists were Alberta residents.

Provincial politics in British Columbia have witnessed the eclipse of the two major parties. Our results make clear, at least in recent years, how weakly voters were attached to the older parties. Knowing that 38 percent of those voting for the Liberal party and 28 percent for the Conservative party in the 1965 federal election also voted for the same parties in the last provincial election does not tell us much about cross-over patterns. But when we also see that 71 percent of the NDP voters and 92 percent of the Social Credit voters stayed with the same party in both kinds of elections, we can feel that we have touched on the true flavour of politics in that province.

In summary, then, the consistency of party support increased for the older parties as we move eastward, and for the minor parties, as we move westward.

A not dissimilar regional trend appears in Table 6–6, the percent

16. Survey data on the 1965 federal election and the 1967 provincial election in Ontario indicate similar trends. Fifty-three percent of the federal Liberal supporters voted Liberal in the provincial election. This compares with 71 percent consistent Conservative and 67 percent consistent NDP voters. This study also confirms that voters in federal elections in Ontario are less likely to exercise their franchise in provincial elections. John Wilson and David Hoffman, "The Liberal Party in Contemporary Ontario Politics," *Canadian Journal of Political Science*, 3 (June, 1970): p. 192.

Table 6–6 Percent Who Always Vote in Provincial Elections, By Region

	Percent Always Voting
Atlantic provinces	59
	(229)
Quebec	55
	(793)
Ontario	43
	(1,054)
Prairie provinces	36
	(395)
British Columbia	48
	(256)
Total	48
	(2,727)

distribution of those respondents who reported they had since eligibility, always voted in provincial elections. That is, voting regularity was more often found in the eastern part of the country, and tended to decline as we move westward. Additional data on regularity of voting and partisanship are not presented here, but they do support our earlier findings that regular supporters, provincially as well as federally, were more likely to be present in the major parties.

Party Identification

Our final measure of traditionalism and stability is self-reported partisan identification. This comes from answers to the following question: "Generally speaking, do you usually think of yourself as Conservative, Liberal, Social Credit, Créditiste, NDP, Union Nationale, or what?" Respondents with some identification were then asked if they were referring to national politics, provincial politics, or both. In this way it was possible to separate federal from provincial identifications. Results are reported in Table 6–7.

Identifying with a party is logically independent from voting for it. One may identify with a party because of its historic mission, its ideology, the character of its leadership, or for other similar reasons of either long or short range relevance. To vote for a party, however, the party must run a candidate in the voter's constituency, the candidate should be personally attractive, and the short run issues of the particular election should propel the voter in the direction of his existing partisan predispositions. When there is not a suitable match between electoral conditions and partisan identifications, then the latter may be temporarily suspended. While the voter may not recognize this, such suspensions often herald the permanent undermining

Table 6–7 **Percent With Same Partisan Identification Nationally and Provincially, by Region and National Party Identification**

National Party Identification

Region	Liberal	Conservative	NDP	Social Credit
Atlantic	96	99	[88]^b	—
	(96)	(87)	(8)	
Quebec	95	92	38	49
	(331)	(93)	(61)	(61)
Ontario	82	95	96	—
	(408)	(321)	(117)	
Prairies	77	66	92	100
	(102)	(136)	(49)	(43)
British Columbia	47	54	85	100
	(64)	(48)	(52)	(30)
Total	85	86	81	100
	(1,001)	(685)	(287)	(74)^a

^aThe total for Social Credit includes 4 cases in the Atlantic provinces and Ontario. The Quebec Créditistes are not included.

^bToo few cases to percentage.

Figures in parentheses are base N's.

of the identification. From our own data we find that, in general, voters tended to exceed identifiers. This occurred in eleven of the seventeen instances where comparisons were possible, suggesting that at least during the 1965 election, more voters were guided by immediate considerations—of party, candidates, issues, leadership—than by self-identifications as partisans.

Half of the exceptional cases, where identifiers outnumbered voters, were found in the Prairie provinces. The ratio of identifiers to voters was 1.1 for the Liberals and Conservatives and 1.2 for Social Credit. There is no obvious reason for these findings, but they do suggest that the special political climate of the Prairies, which as we know makes for an unusual amount of vote-switching, still permitted the continuity of partisan loyalties.

In contrast to the Prairies, British Columbia had the largest number of voters exceeding identifiers. Ratios of identifiers to voters were about .83 for the Liberals, Conservatives, and NDP. The volatile electoral situation of that province seemed to exist then without the stable underpinnings of extensive, long-term partisan identifications. The exception is Social Credit, even though the small sample should make us hesitant in drawing any conclusions. Still, despite the very real problems of sampling variability, it is worth noting that everywhere, including the Atlantic provinces and Ontario, Social Credit identifiers outnumbered voters. In some of these instances, respondents would not even have had the opportunity to find a Social Credit candidate on their ballot. Social Credit then seems to generate feelings of identification with its programs and ideology in ways neither of the major parties, with their weaker ideological stance, are able to do. It is even more interesting to compare Social Credit to the NDP, since along with its emphasis on principle, the latter too attracted more voters than identifiers.[17] (Ratios of identifiers to voters ranged from .89 in Ontario to .84 in British Columbia.) By failing to generate proportionately the same high degree of identification, the NDP was paradoxically able to win more votes, in much the same way as did the major parties.

A final word needs to be said about the Conservatives. In addition to their surplus of identifiers in the Prairies, they had a slight excess in the Atlantic provinces and Ontario. (Ratios are 1.05 and 1.03 respectively.) These were two regions where the Conservative party had a particularly solid base of support. At the same time, these areas were most responsive to changes in the political climate. Hence some proportion of the electorate is always ready to react to new circumstances. Even staunch Conservatives can be turned from their party when political events are in flux.

Examining Table 6–7 for information about the coincidence between federal and provincial party identifications, we find homologous identification to be very high, and always in excess of homologous voting. In addition, regional trends were similar to those for other questions. Homologous identifications were high in the easternmost part of the country for the major parties and declined as we move westward, while the opposite tended to be true for the minor parties. Three additional comments are in order. As we did with voting in the past federal and provincial elections in question, we equated identification with the Conservatives and Union Nationale in Quebec, since most respondents had already done so themselves. At the time of our survey, Créditiste voters did not have the choice of voting for that party in provincial elections, but we have recorded the percentage who, nonetheless, thought of themselves as Créditistes, regardless of level of government. In Ontario, identification at both levels of government with the NDP was particularly high, especially when we compare it to the stability and regularity of NDP voting in other tables. It is here, with respect to identification, that the full force of commitment to the principles for which the NDP stands first came through.

---

17. For a discussion of parties of principle and the ways in which they are exemplified by the NDP and Social Credit, see Engelmann and Schwartz, *Political Parties,* pp. 247-49.

CONSEQUENCES OF STRUCTURAL AND PSYCHOLOGICAL CONSTRAINTS

Each region is distinctive both in the nature of its functioning party system and in the responses of its voters. These distinctions have their roots, for the older settled parts of the country, from about the turn of the century, and for the new ones, since after World War I. The ways in which voters' attitudes and behaviour link together with structural conditions give the regions a special quality of politics. This is most apparent in those instances where voters display stable and consistent attachments to parties, and hence by their actions perpetuate the existing party system. But it is no less true that unstable and inconsistent voter attachments also contribute to the continuity of a party system, this time one subject to stress, change, and the development of new patterns of party politics.

Our thinking on this subject led to a search for more abstract formulations about the effects of different party systems. The results are three main propositions about the possible relationships between kinds of party systems and forms of partisanship. These include party systems where there are predominantly one, two, or more parties, and partisanship following stable or unstable patterns. We are limited in testing these relationships by the number of regions in Canada, but this may be offset by their more general applicability.

Data for testing the relationships are contained in Chart 6–1 and a selection of the behavioural and attitudinal materials from Tables 6–3, 6–4, 6–5, and 6–7. We treat Table 6–3 as indicative of hard core support and Table 6–4, of short-term support. Homologous partisan identification is derived from Table 6–7, short-term homologous voting from Table 6–5.

> Proposition 1:   In a stable two-party system, there will be
> voter attachments to both parties.

Only the Atlantic region had a predominantly two-party system both federally and provincially. It confirmed our prediction of highly stable attachments in terms of voting and identification across federal and provincial lines. Federally, Ontario was also classified as a two-party system, though one with significant weaknesses. We found Liberals and especially Conservatives similarly located in stable positions, although a noticeable distance from their counterparts in the Atlantic provinces, particularly with respect to homologous voting.

> Proposition 1a: In a stable two-party system, where there
> are third parties, these will have unstable
> voter attachments.

Although hardly of a number to be taken seriously, the NDP in the Atlantic provinces confirmed our expectation of instability. They were, however, unexpectedly high on identification. The NDP in Ontario tended to confirm our predictions by its location vis à vis the two older parties, but again the level of identification was high. The same tables also reveal the less stable attachment of the Liberals. Provincially, we recall the party system in Ontario was difficult to classify, and we compromised by labelling it a multiparty system with a strong tendency for one-party dominance. For this reason, as well as the confirmation provided by the data, we are better advised to use Ontario to test Propositions 2a or 3a.

> Proposition 2:   In a situation of one-party dominance, there will be stable voter attachments to that party.

One party dominance was found in Quebec federally, and to some extent in Ontario provincially. Other provinces where this occurred, Newfoundland and Alberta, cannot be considered because we have grouped our data into regions. In voting and identification, Liberals in Quebec were highly stable. A similar disposition appeared for Conservatives in Ontario, particularly on federal-provincial voting and identification.

> Proposition 2a: Where one party is dominant, there will be unstable attachments to other parties.

NDP supporters in Quebec were consistent in one characteristic: the lack of stable attachments to their party. This was also true of Créditiste voters, except that they displayed an unexpected amount of short-run stability. Interestingly enough, although they represented a minority of voters in that province, Conservative supporters had relatively stable party attachments.

Some comment has already been made about the case of Ontario. While we cannot characterize either the Liberals or the NDP as highly unstable, their attachments were somewhat weaker than the dominant Conservatives. The NDP again indicated an above-average level of identification compared to voting.

> Proposition 3:   Where there is a multiparty system, there will be unstable voter attachments in general.

> Proposition 3a: Where there is a multiparty system, there will be more stable attachments to the dominant or most successful party.

Multiparty arrangements were the norm in the Prairies and British Columbia. Ontario provincially could also be discussed in this context, although we have chosen to deal with it in terms of one-party dominance. Our expectations of generally unstable attachments in the

Prairies were only partially confirmed. Where the reference is solely to federal voting behaviour, respondents expressed somewhat firmer attachments to the two older parties. The Conservatives appeared out of phase, with more short-term voters than might be expected. The NDP and Social Credit more distinctly conformed to our proposition. The Conservatives displayed the pattern suggested by Proposition 3a in Table 6–4. The case of the Liberals suggested that factors other than the ones considered here had been operating to produce the extent of stable attachment found. Tables 6–5 and 6–7 reveal quite different patterns, indicating the greater pull of provincial politics on party alignments in the prairies. The most stable attachments were manifested by Social Crediters, sharing a level of attachment with the major parties in the Atlantic provinces, the Liberals in Quebec and the Conservatives in Ontario. The remainder displayed some short-run instability, with the Liberals and especially the NDP stable on identification. The Conservatives had the least stable attachments, indicating that despite their strength on the federal scene, the Conservative party had not been able to generate the same loyalties at the provincial level. We could anticipate that it was such Conservative voters who tended to be party switchers in provincial elections.

British Columbia repeated the same patterns, although the magnitude of the differences was somewhat different than in the Prairies. On hard-core federal support, the Liberals were relatively most stable, followed by the Conservatives, Social Credit and NDP. In absolute terms, however, with the possible exception of the Liberals, none of the parties manifested stable voter attachments. In this sense then, all parties in British Columbia supported both parts of Proposition 3, although we find considerable short-term attachment in Table 6–4. Federal-provincial homologous attachments also provide confirmation, at least for the older parties. Now, however, the Liberals lose the advantage that they otherwise have at federal elections. The two minor parties, and especially Social Credit, stood out by their high level of partisan identification, considerably in excess of what we might have expected even from Proposition 3a. Again we must add a caution about sample size in making generalizations about Social Credit.

Compared to what we found about other relationships, our data are most equivocal with respect to Proposition 3; that, where there is a multiparty system, there will be unstable voter attachments in general. The data revealed two unanticipated patterns which require further explanation. One was the relative strength of attachment to the Liberals, especially in the Prairie provinces. Because of the multiparty system, as well as the Liberals' weak showing federally between 1958 and 1965, and in all provincial elections except in Saskatchewan, we expected that whatever strong loyalties might have existed, would by now have been eroded. That this was not the case suggested the potential strength of the Liberal party, demonstrated in the election of 1968 when it was able to alter the pattern of minority government, even to the extent of breaking the Conservative's hold on the majority of voters in the Prairies.

Also unanticipated was the extent of attachment to the minor parties. Although we predicted in Proposition 3a that the most successful parties in a multiparty system—in this case the minor ones— would be associated with relatively strong voter attachments, these were unexpectedly high. Such attachments were not the case with respect to voting behaviour in federal elections, where the minor parties tended to support Proposition 3. It was on party identification, however, that divergences emerged. A high sense of identification, and one consistent across federal and provincial lines, was manifested for the NDP and Social Credit party. Somewhat separate from the actual choices made in the polling booth, self-identification with a party was high where minor parties had enjoyed success over some period of time. In the case of the Prairies in particular, and to some extent in British Columbia, this success, although missing in federal elections, had been prominent in provincial ones. It is provincial politics then that set the stage for the establishment of consistent partisan identifications. Data on identifications would be more supportive of Propositions 1 or 2, which describe the party situation of the western provinces provincially. Proposition 3 is, however, supported by our examples except to the extent that the provincial successes of the minor parties had established them as the equivalent of major parties.

Canadian settings of multiple parties suggest that the relation between a party system and voting behaviour is more complex than what is captured in Proposition 3. It is clear that multiple party systems foster intricate forms of political alignment. This becomes especially evident if we wish to take into account settings other than Canada. France, for example, with its history of multiple parties and political instability, might appear to illustrate Proposition 3. An examination of the French situation indicates, however, that at least Proposition 3a needs to consider the possibility of several dominant, and hence, stable parties. McRae's review of French politics between 1946 and 1958 indicates the simultaneous existence of highly stable voter attachments to several parties (Communists, Radicals, and Moderates), along with sudden surges for other parties (Gaullists and Poujadists), and equally sudden declines.[18] The *immobilisme* of the French political system may suggest a more general pattern, echoing Pinard's predictions. That is, where the existing party structure becomes stabilized to a degree where it loses the necessary flexibility to handle new problems and sources of dissatisfaction, opposition parties

18. Duncan MacRae, Jr., *Parliament, Parties, and Society in France 1946-1958 (New York: St. Martin's Press,* 1967), pp. 230-85.

will arise to cope with them. These may or may not be successful, but in either case, though most obviously in the latter, they may not generate strong feelings of attachment to them. Lack of stable attachment is especially likely where parties are associated with a limited number of issues or policy positions, or where they rely on the person of a charismatic leader whose message does not become translated into a strong organization.

VOTING BEHAVIOUR AND REGIONALISM

In keeping with the pivotal role we have attributed to political behaviour in the phenomenon of regionalism, the behaviour of voters is examined in a number of different contexts in this volume.[19] These stem from the view that responses of the electorate are a manifestation of two primary inputs to the political system, that of support and demands.[20] A review of our treatment of voting behaviour to this point should help in clarifying what these inputs involve.

In Chapter 3, electoral behaviour was viewed as an indicator of support for the federal government. This in turn was considered one, though a crucial, aspect of regional power. While relatively little was said about outputs from the federal government, these were assumed to lie in the forms and content of leadership and policy decisions responsive to regional demands.

The behaviour dealt with in Chapter 5 was tied to perceptions of regional conditions. There we were concerned with only two possible influences on the views of voters, those stemming from regional conditions and from partisanship. In this sense, voting was seen more as an indication of demand inputs rather than support. Perceptions, as used here, have little issue content beyond the way in which residents of a region see their interests, in either individual or collective terms. At first glance, this might suggest that perceptions are only weakly tied to demands. But to the extent that they are preconditions for the emergence of regional consciousness and the subsequent political mobilization of regional interests, they have distinct implications for the voicing of demands.

Again as in Chapter 3, voting behaviour is viewed here as a dimension of support. Support now becomes a more complex phe-

---

19. See Chap. 1, especially pp. 19-20.

20. Talcott Parsons, "On the Concept of Political Power," in Parsons, *Sociological Theory and Modern Society* (New York: Free Press, 1967), pp. 297-354; David Easton, *A Systems Analysis of Political Life* (New York: John Wiley and Sons, 1965).

nomenon as we consider the quality of voting. Specifically, we ask about the effects of loyalty and consistency, taking into account the full range of partisanship, rather than only support for the governing party. In this instance the interaction between behaviour and the party system is direct, if somewhat tautological: behaviour is constrained by the alternatives available, and the available alternatives are sustained by the patterning of behaviour.

In Chapter 3, the input of support was directly related to regional power, allowing areas to be aligned so as to reveal their relative power advantage. In this chapter, the linkages between the party system and behaviour are most obviously a way of perpetuating regional differences. That is, if regions differ politically, it is because social, economic, and political conditions specific to them have led to differing adaptations of the party system. These adaptations act as constraints on the choices open to voters. Electoral choices, either of a consistent nature (always voting for the same party) or not (lack of partisan identification, frequent vote switching), tend to become habitual, and these in turn produce further constraints. In other words, the conditions have been set for limits on the free play of party competition in ways that vary geographically. Party politics then continue to operate as one of the mechanisms for perpetuating the general distinctiveness of regions.

But more indirectly, and more basically, the ties between the party system and voting behaviour affect the power of regions. They do so by providing both the channels through which support and demands are mobilized, and leadership and decisions are provided. Parties play these roles, most effectively, but not exclusively, when they are able to govern. There is a familiar refrain from politicians: If those people (in Region X) want something (a response to regional problems), let them vote for us! Without wishing to justify the vulgarity of this argument, it appears to be descriptive of how the political system operates. Fortunately for the individual citizen, there are some restraints. The governing party will act as though it provides government for all residents often enough to prevent entire regions from becoming excluded from the political process. And the satisfaction of politically mobilized demands can come from sources other than the federal government.

CHAPTER

7

Political awareness

INTERPRETING THE POLITICAL ENVIRONMENT

In this and the following three chapters we examine interpretations by ordinary citizens of the political environment. At issue is how they orient themselves to political institutions, persons, and events. Our concern is with regional variations in these orientations, on the assumption that the way in which voters relate themselves to their political world will reflect the strength of regional forces and also provide an additional factor in the maintenance of these. Among the influences on orientations recognized by our model is the interaction between such features of the political system as regional power and the party system.

The cynic might ask whether such voters ever acquire any political orientations. And even assuming they do, what difference does this make? These points are raised, not as straw men to be easily demolished, but as frequently voiced, legitimate concerns about voters and their involvement in democratic government. For example, V. O. Key, whose own inclination led him to a different view of the electorate, sadly agreed that,

> by and large, the picture of the voter that emerges from a combination of the folklore of practical politics and the findings of the new electoral studies is not a pretty one. It is not a portrait of citizens moving to considered decision as they

play their solemn role of making and unmaking governments. The older tradition from practical politics may regard
the voter as an erratic and irrational fellow susceptible to
manipulation by skilled humbugs. One need not live through
many campaigns to observe politicians, even successful politicians, who act as though they regarded the people as man-
ageable fools. Nor does a heroic conception of the voter
emerge from the new analyses of electoral behavior. They
can be added up to a conception of voting not as a civic decision but as an almost purely deterministic act. Given
knowledge of certain characteristics of a voter—his occupation, his residence, his religion, his national origin, and
perhaps certain of his attitudes—one can predict with a
high probability the direction of his vote.[1]

Key, in the posthumous volume in which this appeared as well as in
other writings, was concerned with the excessively negative view of
voters that stemmed from studies of political behaviour, in which
purely political aspects were minimized if not completely ignored in
favour of social and psychological determinants. Rather than accept
such characterizations, Key sought to prove that "in the large the
electorate behaves about as rationally and responsibly as we should
expect, given the clarity of the alternatives presented to it and the
character of the information available to it."[2] To the extent that he
meant by rationality the operation of political considerations such as
responses to issues and political parties, he did in fact provide some
modest substantiation, although there seems to be no reason to treat
as categorically irrational voting along class or ethnic lines.[3] In any
event, the principal issue is whether voters have any conceptions of
the political milieu, quite independently of the need to take a position about democratic theory. A review of the literature, though it
might be considered as a digression, is intended to anticipate possible
reservations about the character and significance of political orientations.

The existence of well-developed ideologies is hardly common
among voters. For example, in the Survey Research Center's study
of the electorate in 1956, a distinction was made between ideology

1. V. O. Key, Jr., *The Responsible Electorate* (Cambridge: The Belknap
Press of Harvard University Press, 1966), pp. 4-5.

2. Ibid., p. 7

3. Maurice Pinard makes this point with particular clarity in his review of
the Key book, appearing in the *Canadian Journal of Economics and Political
Science* 33 (November 1967) 616. See also Arthur S. Goldberg, "Social Determinism and Rationality as Bases of Party Identification," *American Political
Science Review* 63 (November 1969): 5-25.

and near-ideology, with the first concept reserved for an integrated and extensive set of attitudes concerning politics. Near-ideology was used to describe beliefs without the full range of supportive attitudes or complex ideas associated with the true "ideologue." The authors of the study concluded that "despite our attempts at generous estimates, we find that with all of the ideologues and near-ideologues . . . cumulated we have only covered about 12 per cent of all subjects interviewed, and 15 per cent of our 1956 voters. In other words, about 85 per cent of the 1956 electorate brought simpler conceptual tools to bear on their issue concerns."[4] Results would probably be similar in Canada and other countries without traditional Marxist parties. Evidence of the low level of ideologues is not the same as saying, however, that citizens generally do not have simpler, though still fairly coherent attitudes toward political stimuli. The study just cited would certainly be compatible with such an interpretation. Robert Lane, while seemingly constrained by his scrutiny of only fifteen men in one community, was still able to view them as prototypes of the "American common man," and obtained confirmation that he possessed "a set of emotionally charged political beliefs, a critique of alternative proposals, and some modest program of reform. These beliefs embrace central values and institutions; they are rationalizations of interests (sometimes not his own); and they serve as moral justifications for daily acts and beliefs."[5] Our purpose is not, like Lane's, to search out core political beliefs and to explain their origins. But Lane's results are sufficiently convincing to indicate that it makes sense to speak of political orientations at the mass level.

The importance of such orientations lies in their ability to help the citizen make sense of his world, to guide him in interpreting the actions of others and in selecting appropriate responses himself. He has, in other words, the basis of a rationale for functioning as a political being.

Citizens' attitudes are also important from the perspective of the political system. They are a means for relating the individual to the political machinery, both cognitively and affectively. Moreover, they are an avenue through which citizens can express their support for the system. Without support it is doubtful that a political system could long persist. In Chapters 3 and 6 we treated voting as a form of overt support. Attitudes too are related to support, covertly it is true, but presumably able to be mobilized in either supportive or

---

4. Angus Campbell, Philip E. Converse, Warren E. Miller, Donald E. Stokes, *The American Voter* (New York: John Wiley & Sons, 1960), p. 234.

5. Robert Lane, *Political Ideology, Why the American Common Man Believes What He Does* (New York: Free Press, 1962), pp. 15-16.

hostile actions, should the need arise.[6] Attitudes are also an indication of the demands that may be placed on the political system, revealing both the sources of troublesome concern and the areas in which there is satisfaction.

The questions used for distinguishing among regions arise out of the commonalities of Canadian citizenship. Our survey format did not permit gathering separately for each region information on those political issues, beliefs, and concerns that were central to its residents. We have to use the same items for all, relying on the potentiality of differences in characteristics and experiences to affect the distribution of responses in ways distinct for each region.

DEFINITIONAL PROBLEMS

By orientation we mean those interpretations of the political environment that ordinary voters make either regularly, as they participate in the duties of citizenship, or more unusually, when they are called upon to overtly evaluate their political setting. In particular, we examine orientations with respect to the machinery and personnel of government and to the voter's place in the political system. This approach has similarities to that of David Easton, who urges dividing components of the political system into three: political community, regime, and authorities. "The regime is that part of the system which . . . represents relatively stable expectations, depending on the system and its state of change, with regard to the range of matters that can be handled politically, the rules or norms governing the way these matters can be processed, and the position of those through whom binding action may be taken on these matters."[7] Most of the issues dealt with in this and the following two chapters have some bearing on the structure of the regime, its norms, and authority structure.

The second major component, authorities, are those members of a system with the following attributes: "They must engage in the daily affairs of a political system; they must be recognized by most members of the system as having the responsibility for these matters; and their actions must be accepted as binding most of the time by most of the members as long as they act within the limits of their roles."[8] Several of our items also deal with actual authorities.

It is the concept of political community which is most difficult to

6. David Easton, *A Systems Analysis of Political Life* (New York: John & Sons, 1965), p. 160.

7. Easton, *Systems Analysis of Political Life,* p. 192.

8. Ibid., p. 212

handle. "This concept . . . will refer to that aspect of a political system that consists of its members seen as a group of persons bound together by a political division of labor. The existence of a political system must include a plurality of political relationships through which the individual members are linked to each other and through which the political objectives of the system are pursued, however limited they may be."[9] One difficulty is that empirical indicators of political community do not come readily to hand. Easton seems to intend the concept to refer to the ties that bind members of a polity to each other, even if their own sense of identification is not recognized as primarily political. For example, do those in Quebec feel closer to persons in their own province or to those elsewhere in Canada, or perhaps even in the United States? But this survey has no items that directly tap such feelings. Rather than abandon the concept altogether, we suggest that aspects of political community emerge when dealing with relations between the individual voter and his government, although obviously these also concern the regime.

This usage of political orientation has obvious affinities with what has been termed political culture. Indeed, Almond and Verba define political culture as "the specifically political orientations—attitudes toward the political system and its various parts, and attitudes toward the role of the self in the system. We speak of a political culture just as we speak of an economic culture or a religious culture. It is a set of orientations toward a special set of social objects and processes."[10] The first part of their definition is almost identical with our own, yet a number of considerations led us to abandon any inclination we may have had to conceptualize orientations as culture. Certainly an attraction of the concept lies in its potential for fragmentation: one can readily speak of regional political subcultures. But its drawbacks turn out to be greater than its advantages. If we speak of these mainly in terms of the Almond and Verba usage, this is not to say that it is their's alone which is at fault. Both before and after the publication of *The Civic Culture,* political culture had become a popular concept among students of political behaviour, and some of our comments will bear on other uses of the term.[11] But Almond and Verba's work is particularly pertinent here because of its elaboration of a theoretical concept using a number of empirical indicators obtained through sur-

9. Ibid., p. 177.

10. Gabriel Almond and Sidney Verba, *The Civic Culture* (Princeton: Princeton University Press, 1963), p. 13.

11. For a critical review, already somewhat dated, see Young C. Kim, "The Concept of Political Culture in Comparative Politics," *The Journal of Politics* 26 (1964), 313-36. Current uses are brought together by Lucian Pye, "Political Culture," *International Encyclopedia of the Social Sciences* (1968): 12:218-25.

vey research. In other words, if we direct our criticism mainly to their work, it is because it is mainly their work which is closest to our own.

Political culture to Almond and Verba consists of "specifically political orientations." But as the history of the concept of culture in anthropology attests, despite the diversity of definition found even in that discipline, to confine culture to orientations is uncharacteristically restrictive.[12] In borrowing across disciplines, it seems reasonable to expect some continuity of usage, if only to permit interdisciplinary communication. Almond and Verba, to be fair, derive their concept not directly from the anthropological literature but from the work of Talcott Parsons. Parsons does speak of culture at times as though it consisted almost entirely of value orientations,[13] yet at others he emphasizes that they are but one part of culture.[14] Culture as value orientations or political culture as political orientations is hence too narrow a definition.

Yet even if we were to ignore these conceptual difficulties, and concentrate, as we have done, on orientations,[15] we would still have some problems if we followed Almond and Verba's lead. According to them, an orientation

> refers to the internalized aspects of objects and relationships. It includes (1) "cognitive orientation," that is, knowledge of and belief about the political system, its roles and the incumbents of these roles, its inputs, and its outputs; (2) "affective orientation," or feelings about the political system, its roles, personnel, and performance; and (3) "evaluational orientation," the judgments and opinions about political objects that typically involve the combination of value standards and criteria with information and feelings.[16]

At one level, the above characterization of orientations holds true to the discussion of value orientations by both the sociologist Parsons and the anthropologist Kluckhohn. But what Kluckhohn at least makes perfectly clear is that the cognitive, cathectic, and conative aspects are, in some combination, always present in the manifestation of a value. Kluckhohn states that he is using the term value-orientation (as opposed to simply orientation) to call "explicit attention to

---

12. A. L. Kroeber and Clyde Kluckhohn, *Culture: A Critical Review of Concepts and Definitions* (New York: Vintage Books, 1963).

13. For example, Talcott Parsons and Edward A. Shils, eds., *Toward a General Theory of Action* (Cambridge: Harvard University Press, 1951), p. 21.

14. Ibid., p. 159 and following.

15. Young C. Kim, "Concept of Political Culture," p. 336.

16. Almond and Verba, *Civic Culture,* p. 15.

the union of normative with existential assumptions."[17] If we look
back at the passage from Almond and Verba, where they speak of
orientations and not *value*-orientations, it might be argued that by
avoiding the specifically judgemental and affective character of
values, they are also avoiding the relationship among aspects of
orientations. If this were true, we would again urge that another term
be used to prevent confusion. (For example, Kluckhohn refers to
orientations as mainly cognitive). But calling cognitive and cathectic
aspects separate orientations does not in itself solve the problem of
conceptual clarity or empirical relationship. Except for those items
which focus on the most narrow facets of political knowledge, every
question asked respondents in the five countries Almond and Verba
studied had, explicitly or implicity, some normative dimension. Hence
the division of questionnaire items into categories, no matter how
logical they may seem, has still resulted in arbitrary distinctions.

Our rejection of Almond and Verba's use of culture does not
affect our acknowledgement that they had indeed selected some of
the most crucial aspects of political orientations. We will often use
similar items to construct cues to the ways citizens interpret the
political environment. Most of these items, in turn, overtly or otherwise partake of both normative and existential elements.

POLITICAL INFORMATION

Attending to Politics

Almond and Verba have used a series of questions to determine
whether citizens pay attention to political and governmental affairs,
including political campaigns. These questions, they feel, can be used
to test

> the frequency of participant orientations . . . for they get at
> the dimension of attentiveness to political input. We may
> assume that if people follow political and governmental af-
> fairs, they are in some sense involved in the process by which
> decisions are made. To be sure, it is a minimal degree of in-
> volvement. The civic culture, as we use the term, includes a
> sense of obligation to participate in political input activities,
> as well as a sense of competence to participate. *Following
> governmental and political affairs and paying attention to*

---

17. Clyde Kluckhohn and others, "Values and Value-orientations in the
Theory of Action," in Parsons and Shils, *Toward a General Theory of Action,*
p. 411.

politics are limited civic commitments indeed, and yet there
would be no civic culture without them.[18]

The italicized sentence is the crucial one, justifying as it does attention to what otherwise might seem trivial questions. In this study,
the available questions differ from those used by Almond and Verba,
yet they tap the same general area.

As our basic indicator of awareness and interest, we asked: "How
much interest do you generally have in what is going on in politics—
a good deal, some, or not much?" For our total sample, 26 percent
answered "a good deal," 43 percent "some," and 30 percent, "not
much." Since we have no benchmark against which to judge this
particular question, we cannot say how much interest our findings
represent. Moreover, since the responses represent subjective assessments by respondents, it is patent that one man's "a good deal" may
be another man's "some." The latter problem is not as serious as
might be expected, since independent evidence reveals that answers
to this kind of question are good predictors of other forms of political
interest and involvement.[19] What is more serious is our inability to
assess the political meaning of the opinion distribution. We can only
speak of higher or lower levels of interest, without knowing what
significance to attach to these levels. Our concerns are dissipated,
however, since regional variations are almost negligible. For example,
the distribution of "good deal" responses ranged from 29 to 22 percent. In general, interest was highest in Ontario, the Prairies, and
British Columbia, and lowest in Quebec and the Atlantic provinces.

Knowledge

The level of interest we examined has implications for the operation
of the political system, but obviously it is only a minimal attribute
for intelligent citizen participation. Among the other attributes required is some degree of sensitivity to outcomes of electoral decisions.
We examined this through two questions about the identity of the
winning candidate in the respondents' ridings, one concerning his
name and the other his party affiliation. The results of both these
questions are reported in Table 7–1 for each region. Knowledge in
general was high, with three-quarters correctly naming the winner
and well over four-fifths identifying his party. This tendency for
significantly more voters to remember the party rather than the name
of the winning candidate is particularly interesting in view of voting
procedures then in force in Canada. Candidates were listed on the
ballot in alphabetical order, with no further identification except city
and occupation.

18. Almond and Verba, *Civic Culture,* p. 88.

19. For example, Campbell, *et al., The American Voter,* pp. 143-44.

Table 7–1 **Percent Correctly Naming Winning Candidate
and Party in Own Riding, by Region**

| | Correct Names for Winning: | | |
	Candidate	Party	N
Atlantic	89	90	(229)
Quebec	72	88	(793)
Ontario	78	86	(1,054)
Prairies	71	78	(395)
British Columbia	67	79	(256)
Total	76	85	(2,727)

In the Atlantic provinces, correct information on name and party was uniformly high. This was also true for Quebec and Ontario with respect to the proportion who knew the party label of the member of Parliament elected from their constituency in 1965. They were less likely to know their member's name, however, especially if they lived in Quebec. The two western areas revealed greater ignorance of party or name. For example, British Columbia was separated from the Atlantic region by 11 percent on the correct party and by 22 percent on the correct name.

The discrepancy between knowledge of the winning candidate's party and his name was greatest in Quebec and British Columbia. There are no obvious reasons for these outcomes at the aggregate level, although it is relatively easy to predict associations at the individual level. The outcome of the 1965 election may in part explain the disparity between knowledge of the winning candidate's party and his name. In Quebec, the Liberals were the major winner, outnumbering Conservatives by two to one in the popular vote and by seven to one in the seats won. This suggests that even if Quebec respondents were not able to recall the successful candidate's name, the chances were high that they could guess his party correctly. This same process may have operated elsewhere, but since electoral results were not so one-sided, we can make no predictions. Such an explanation may appear inadequate in accounting for responses in British Columbia, since in that province voting patterns and outcomes were particularly diffuse, spread among four parties. But what this may mean is that the likelihood of voting for a losing candidate is enhanced. Knowing that his candidate lost, the voter found it easier to recall the party that was successful, rather than its candidate.

Differentiating Among Leaders

Political leaders play their roles against many conceivable backdrops. They may represent one or two segments of a population, or they may at least strive to represent a diversity of interests and population groups. Where there is a mass electorate and a small number of political parties, we expect that the more successful leaders are those able to apppeal to and hence represent a large number of interests. In a country with the heterogeneity of Canada, the ways in which the national leadership copes with regionalism is of major concern. One approach has been to allocate representatives to regions in the federal cabinet.[20] From the perspective of the electorate, we might wonder how successful are such techniques in integrating the national polity.[21] Voters' evaluation of the various political means for binding together regions was not tackled directly in the survey used for this study, but indirectly there is some evidence from the way leaders are perceived. The items used to determine the regional identity of leaders are not, unlike the preceding ones, a direct measure of knowledge. But they can tell us whether voters attach a regional identification to party leaders, to the curtailment of their national stature.

To determine the existence of such perspectives on party leaders, respondents were asked: "Thinking now of the national leaders of the four (sic) main political parties, which part of the country do you think these men are closest to: the Maritimes, Quebec, Ontario, the Prairies, or British Columbia? Take Mr. Diefenbaker . . . Mr. Pearson . . . Mr. Douglas . . . Mr. Thompson . . . Mr. Caouette." Was this a meaningful question to respondents? The force of regionalism may be strong in Canada without it being perceived in terms of party leadership. Internal evidence from the question suggests that this is an unlikely possibility. One indication is the percent who answered "don't know" to the question about each of the leaders. Those who did not have an opinion varied for each of the leaders: it was 19 percent for Mr. Pearson, the Liberal leader; 15 percent for Mr. Diefenbaker, the Conservative leader; 34 percent for Mr. Douglas, the NDP leader; 46 percent for Mr. Thompson, the Social Credit leader; and 22 percent for Mr. Caouette, the Créditiste leader. Two of the three minor party leaders then were not readily identified in regional terms, but otherwise the question seemed to tap a relevant theme for the majority. The rate of "don't know" responses was generally higher than for other questions in our survey, but it still compares favourably with surveys of this kind.

While we might have some reservations about our question because of the level of no opinions, these are allayed by the distribution of responses. Each leader was seen as closer to one or two specific regions by at least half the total sample, or in two instances, that share of the sample that expressed an opinion. The individual with

20. See Chap. 3.

21. F. C. Engelmann and M. A. Schwartz, *Political Parties and the Canadian Social Structure* (Scarborough: Prentice-Hall of Canada, 1967), pp. 234-36.

the most clear-cut identity was Réal Caouette, whom three-quarters of the sample saw as closest to Quebec. Mr. Diefenbaker was next, with almost two-thirds believing he was closest to the Prairie provinces. Over half saw Mr. Pearson as attached to Ontario, and another one-quarter to Quebec. The Prairies were described as the regional focus of the less well known Messrs. Douglas and Thompson by about one-third, and additionally, less than one-fifth associated Mr. Douglas with British Columbia.

In addition to this evidence of the regional identity of leaders we are of course interested in the effect of region on the perceptions of these identities. Table 7–2 presents these data for each of the five leaders. Responses by region conform in general to our overall description of the identity of leaders with one exception. We see in Part C that residents of British Columbia were more likely to identify Mr. Douglas with British Columbia rather than the Prairies, although the reverse was true in all other regions. The British Columbia response was no doubt the result of Mr. Douglas having had his seat in that province since becoming the federal leader of the NDP. Since otherwise our results were quite consistent nationally, we can proceed with our analysis in a more summary way.

To begin with, we note the variations among regions in their likelihood of perceiving leaders in regional terms. One indication of this is the difference in levels of no opinions. This ranges from an average of 32 percent in the Atlantic provinces and Quebec, 28 percent in Ontario, 19 percent in British Columbia, and a low of 15 percent in the Prairies. The propensity for those in the Prairies to think of national leaders in terms of a regional locus was so marked, that not only did fully 85 percent identify such regionally-specific leaders as Diefenbaker and Caouette, one with the Prairies and the other with Quebec, but 63 percent even attached a regional identity to Thompson, who was otherwise barely known to the rest of the country. Of course, it could be argued that the origin of two of the three minor party leaders in the Prairies enhanced their likelihood of being known as native sons, as it were, but this argument is weakened by the nature of their responses to the third leader, Caouette. Moreover, while Pearson did not have the clear-cut regional identity of Diefenbaker, the Prairies again were more likely than those elsewhere to specify such an attachment.

Another way of looking at these responses is to consider the average amount of difference between regions in the single most frequently mentioned region assigned to each leader. This again confirmed the sharp contrast between the Prairies and the rest of Canada. The Prairies were most distant from Quebec, separated by an average of 25 percentage points, and then from the Atlantic provinces, by 22 percent. While they were closest to British Columbia,

Table 7–2 **Regional Identity of Party Leaders, by Region of Residence**

A. *Pearson Identified With:*

Region of Residence:	Atlantic	Quebec	Ontario	Prairies	British Columbia	All Equal	Don't Know
Atlantic	4	24	51	1	0	11	19
Quebec	3	21	42	5	3	14	25
Ontario	3	25	55	1	1	13	17
Prairies	6	40	65	2	*	6	11
British Columbia	4	33	49	4	5	9	12
Total	4	26	52	3	2	12	19

B. *Diefenbaker Identified With:*

	Atlantic	Quebec	Ontario	Prairies	British Columbia	All Equal	Don't Know
Atlantic	8	2	9	59	4	9	16
Quebec	11	1	11	49	10	4	22
Ontario	7	1	7	66	3	8	13
Prairies	3	1	2	85	3	3	8
British Columbia	9	5	9	69	3	4	16
Total	8	2	8	63	5	6	15

Some respondents gave more than one answer.

*indicates less than 1 percent

Table 7-2 (cont.) **Regional Identity of Party Leaders, by Region of Residence**

C. *Douglas Identified With:*

Region of Residence:	Atlantic	Quebec	Ontario	Prairies	British Columbia	All Equal	Don't Know
Atlantic	2	2	4	37	13	8	40
Quebec	3	2	6	27	14	7	43
Ontario	2	2	9	33	15	11	35
Prairies	2	1	6	47	31	10	17
British Columbia	2	2	7	36	46	11	17
Total	2	2	7	34	18	9	34

D. *Thompson Identified With:*

	Atlantic	Quebec	Ontario	Prairies	British Columbia	All Equal	Don't Know
Atlantic	0	3	7	26	9	7	52
Quebec	2	2	6	30	9	4	49
Ontario	2	5	7	23	8	6	52
Prairies	*	1	1	63	12	5	25
British Columbia	1	7	5	37	13	5	36
Total	2	3	6	32	9	5	46

Table 7–2 (cont.) **Regional Identity of Party Leaders, by Region of Residence**

E. *Caouette Identified With:*

Region of Residence:	Atlantic	Quebec	Ontario	Prairies	British Columbia	All Equal	Don't Know
Atlantic	*	64	0	0	*	*	34
Quebec	*	74	*	1	*	2	21
Ontario	1	74	*	*	*	1	23
Prairies	2	85	1	0	*	*	13
British Columbia	*	82	*	*	*	*	16
Total	1	75	*	*	*	1	22

they still averaged 16 percent difference. At the other extreme, Ontario and the Atlantic provinces emerged as most alike in outlook.
Quebec resembled them as well, but was differentiated by a tendency
of its residents to be less prone to attach a regional identity to the two
major party leaders. Based on the frequency of mentioning a particular region that was everywhere thought to be closest to a leader, those
in British Columbia were most similar to Ontario, and then the
Atlantic provinces and Quebec. They were separated, however, by
their inclination to identify Mr. Douglas with their own province.

   Why should residents of the Prairies have had a more highly segmentalized view of the national political leadership? Why did those
in the Atlantic provinces and Quebec, whom we know to have felt
more discontent than other Canadians, not feel that the national
leadership was more distant from them and closer to other regions?
Since three of the five leaders came from the Prairies and were seen
as closest to that region, this may have enhanced a particularistic attitude toward leadership there. Sectionalism in the Prairies, an outgrowth of a particular combination of economic and social strains,
had created a political setting that accentuated contrast conceptions,
as illustrated by party politics. This had apparently extended to perceptions of national leadership. Lack of similar outlooks in the east
require other explanations. We may be seeing the effects of the greater
political power of the east, acting to restrain politically divisive perceptions. Despite other forms of dissatisfaction in these areas, the
national stature of leadership may be enhanced by feelings of satisfaction with the quality and extent of political representation, which
had been greater, as we noted, than in the west. But without further
speculation, it is clear enough that there were marked regional divisions in attaching a regional identity to national leaders.

REGIONAL DIFFERENCES

We may interpret knowledge of winning candidates and parties as
indicating awareness of local political conditions. A high degree of
knowledge can be presumed desirable for the political system since it
is associated with the democratic ideal of an informed body of citizens. Conversely, lack of knowledge creates a form of system stress.
An uninformed and uninterested electorate are less likely to play an
active role in political events, a situation satisfactory in an authoritarian regime. But the essence of democratic government is a responsible leadership, and as evidenced by the oligarchic tendencies of
leaders, even the most benevolent leadership becomes no more than
benevolent despotism when citizens are unwilling or unable to exert
the influence necessary to keep their leaders responsible to them.

We suggested earlier that successful national leaders would be those who played down their regional identification. Yet it is apparent that office can be attained by leaders with the narrowest identity because of the fragmented nature of Canadian society. We would still argue that associating leaders with specific regions has a divisive thrust, undermining the integrative role that is normally an element of national leadership. Attaching leaders to regions could have some positive consequences for the total polity where this served to compensate for regional ethnocentrism. For example, some of the strain stemming from the way in which Prairie residents view national leaders is probably mitigated by their tendency to associate three of the five leaders with their own region. Similarly, those living in British Columbia, who identified the NDP leader with their own province to a greater degree than did others, were in a sense compensating for their segmentalized view of leaders. In total, however, there was not much evidence of such ethnocentrism.

To aid in our analysis of these two forms of possible stress we repeat our findings in graphic form. For the five items on leadership we have averaged the percent who gave leaders some regional identity. The two indicators of knowledge have been retained in their original form. Chart 7–1 allows us to look at the rankings of regions on the three items and the distances among them.

Our first observation is that there is an inverse relation between knowledge of candidates and the propensity to give leaders regional labels. This relationship holds most clearly for those areas which rank at the extremes. They also happen to be the geographic extremes. Except for one instance where Quebec is in a sense out of rank order, Ontario ranks in the middle on all three items. The association between relatively less knowledge of local conditions and a tendency to think in terms of a segmentalized national leadership may not be true at the individual level. But even if it does hold, it is not of concern to us here. What is pertinent are those features of regional social systems that encourage high knowledge about local conditions but depress the likelihood of recognizing the segmentalized nature of national party leadership. These are features that serve to lessen the two possible sources of stress isolated here. Without research directed to this topic, it is not immediately evident which elements of the social structure act to suppress or encourage stress, but one that is likely is the responsiveness of the political environment. The relationship is deceptively simple, and hinges on voters' chances of being on the winning side in any political contest.

The question on knowledge of candidates produced the greatest range of difference among regions, 22 percent. There were two main gaps between regions, one separating the Atlantic provinces and essentially the rest of Canada, and the other Ontario and the Atlantic provinces from Quebec and the west. The average regional identity

Chart 7–1   **Regional political awareness.**

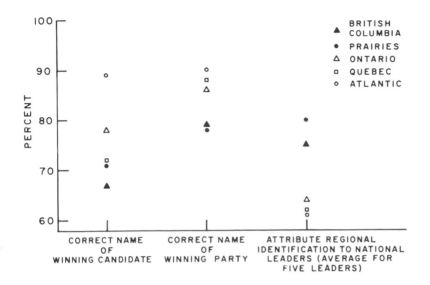

for the five leaders had a range of 19 percent, with the largest gap dividing east and west. Knowledge of the winning candidate differentiated among regions least well, with a total range of 12 percent. Even so there was one sizeable gap again separating east and west.

The items used to measure awareness tap only one aspect of political orientations, and that one not at the heart of the relation between voters and the political system. Yet these findings do suggest ways in which the regional context flavours reactions to politics. They include a basic east-west cleavage that is disturbed only by the difficulty of Quebec voters to correctly name the candidates winning in their constituencies. The important question concerns the implications of these findings. It is our contention that they tap two kinds of possible stress, one stemming from lack of knowledge about local conditions and the other from a tendency to see leadership in regionally specific terms. Both potentialities to stress were greatest in western Canada. They were least in the east and in the middle range in Ontario. Actual stress, in contrast to location in what are only relatively stressful situations, is probably minimized to the extent that knowledge is high in absolute terms. At the same time, stress deriving from the regional identification of leaders is more likely maximized, since such identifications are made by the majority of respondents in all regions.

CHAPTER

8

Parties and the exercise of authority

ISSUES OF LEGITIMACY

In this chapter political orientations are considered in terms of attitudes toward specific aspects of the machinery of government: the
party system, members of Parliament, and the ways in which they
exercise authority. Particular items were selected for their evident
political relevance. We expect, especially in a democratic regime, that
the reactions here explored have a bearing on the functioning of
government. This leads us to see the attitudes examined as touching
on issues of legitimacy.

According to Easton:

> The inculcation of a sense of legitimacy is probably the single
> most effective device for regulating the flow of diffuse support
> in favor of both the authorities and the regime. A member
> may be willing to obey the authorities and conform to the
> requirements of the regime for many different reasons. But
> the most stable support will derive from the conviction on
> the part of the member that it is right and proper for him
> to accept and obey the authorities and to abide by the re-
> quirements of the regime. It reflects the fact that in some
> vague or explicit way he sees these objects as conforming to
> his own moral principles, his own sense of what is right and
> proper in the political sphere.[1]

---

1. David Easton, *A Systems Analysis of Political Life* (New York: John
Wiley & Sons, 1965), p. 278.

An equally persuasive stress on the importance of legitimacy is made by Parsons, but he differs in differentiating legitimacy from support.[2] He does so by treating legitimacy as an input from the system of pattern maintenance to the political system, and support as an input from the integrative system.[3] This distinction adds little to our own analysis of legitimacy, but it has been interjected in anticipation of a later usage of the Parsonian schema.[4] At this moment it is sufficient to point out that in the Easton usage, one approach to an understanding of legitimacy is through the objects to which it is directed. These may be either the regime, the authorities, or both, and legitimacy may stem from ideological or structural sources, or from the personal qualities of the objects.[5] Most of our items concern attitudes toward authority, although our discussion of the party system is directed to the nature of the regime.

THE PARTY SYSTEM

Wherever they exist, parties are that part of the political system with the closest ties to voters. This is so because they have the primary task of translating political, including governmental, issues into the language of the voter. They also give the voter an avenue for making known his opposition or support for these issues, and more generally, his political needs and demands. Stated more abstractly, the party system is one aspect of the norms and structures through which the nature of the regime is manifested.[6]

In the course of our survey, two problems concerning the party system were explored. They involve an evaluation of the functioning of the party system under the conditions current at the time of the survey, and the perception of differences among federal parties. The results show how regions vary in judging the vitality of the party system according to their degree of satisfaction with it and their differentiation among parties. To the extent that both of these are high, we can begin to evaluate the ways in which the public confers legitimacy on the party system.

2. Talcott Parsons, *Sociological Theory and Modern Society* (New York: Free Press, 1967), pp. 285-86.

3. Ibid., pp. 347-54.

4. See below, Chap. 11. See also Mildred A. Schwartz, "Political Parties in Regionally Divided Societies," paper presented to the Eighth World Congress of the International Political Science Association, Munich, 4 September, 1970.

5. Easton, *A Systems Analysis,* p. 287.

6. Ibid., pp. 190-211.

Majority Government

Between 1962 and the election of 1968, no party had a clear-cut majority in the House of Commons. This was a situation bemoaned by politicians and other interested commentators, who through their criticisms, made evident their feeling that an effective government was a majority government. Despite this, the elections of 1963 and 1965 did not appreciably alter the circumstances. This makes the relation between these electoral outcomes and the outlook of voters especially pertinent to what we conceive of as issues of legitimacy.

Eight issues were presented to our respondents, selected as examples of partisan dissension during the 1965 election campaign. Respondents were asked to evaluate each of these in terms of their importance in effecting their voting decision. Using as our measure the proportion who answered that the issue was very important to their personal decision, we obtained the following ranking, beginning with the matter mentioned most frequently: strong leadership in Ottawa, majority government, Canadian unity, economic issues (such as government planning, unemployment, and foreign trade), social welfare, corruption in government, French-English relations, and the Canadian flag. By this measure at least, majority government appeared to have been a critical concern to most of the voters. Those in the Atlantic provinces mentioned it most often and those in Quebec least, the regions separated by a difference of 14 percentage points. The remaining regions ranged in between, with Ontario next to the Atlantic provinces, followed by the Prairies and then British Columbia. (See Table 8-1.)

The interview schedule followed the eight issues with a reminder to respondents that the party forming the national government had, in recent elections, lacked a majority of seats in Parliament. Attention was directed away from personal concern with the 1965 election to a more general perspective on the workings of government, as respondents were asked about the amount of difference it made whether the party forming the government had a majority. The percent who felt it made a great deal of difference was slightly larger than in the preceding question, with those in Ontario, the Atlantic provinces, and British Columbia most likely to share this view. Quebec again had the lowest proportion concerned about majority government, but in this instance was separated from Ontario, the most concerned, by only 8 percent. In other words, regional differences on this item were quite small.

When asked to assume that a party for which they did not normally vote stood a good chance of forming a majority government, respondents assessed the probability of voting for that party. The largest proportion, over two-fifths, said that it was not at all likely they would

Table 8–1 **The Importance of Majority Government, by Region** (Percent)

	Atlantic	Quebec	Ontario	Prairies	British Columbia	Total
Issue of majority government very important in voting decision	64	50	63	57	54	57
Makes a great deal of difference whether governing party has majority	63	56	64	58	62	61
Very likely to switch vote in order to have majority government	24	22	26	21	21	23
N	(229)	(793)	(1054)	(395)	(256)	(2727)

do so. Less than one-quarter predicted that it was very probable they would vote for such a majority-prone party. In the aggregate, there is not much difference among regions in the frequency with which a "very likely" answer was given, though Ontarians were somewhat more inclined to do so than others.

Reviewing results in Table 8–1, several conclusions can be drawn. One is the closeness of outlook in Ontario and the Atlantic provinces, where voters displayed most concern about majority government. These two regions differed as well from the remainder in some pertinent characteristics. Although Ontario did have strong representation from the NDP, and from the CCF before it, and despite some experimentation with third parties at the provincial level, it was a province with a strong two-party orientation federally. Moreover, the two parties in question were the traditional major parties. Nationally, with every administration, it is Ontario that sends the largest share of the crucial decision-makers to Ottawa. And it is possibly of some added significance that the seat of the national capital is in Ontario. For at least these reasons, then, residents of Ontario exhibited a slightly greater responsiveness to the problems supposedly occasioned by the lack of majority government. While the Atlantic provinces did not share all these characteristics with Ontario, they were noteworthy among all regions in their historical avoidance of strong support for third parties. Their view of majority government was probably somewhat conditioned, then, by their own electoral responses, in which one of the two major parties invariably achieves majority status.

A similar line of reasoning might be appropriate in accounting for the response of those in the west. There differences between the Prairies and British Columbia were slight, and there was somewhat less significance attached to majority government. In both areas the traditional two-party system had long been superceded by multiple parties, coalition governments, and the dominance of single parties. From such experiences it would appear that arguments for the maintenance of customary governing arrangements would have little appeal. Yet it was Quebec, and not the western provinces, where there was least conviction that majority government makes a difference. Certainly in Quebec as well there had been major adaptations of the two-party system inherited from Britain, and possibly these had been sufficient to affect political beliefs.

What meaning can we attach to the reluctance to shift parties? Put in its simplest terms, and ignoring now the evidence of regional variation, what we have is a recognition that the lack of majority government was troublesome to the political well-being of Canada, but without a concomitant willingness on the part of the ordinary citizen to do anything about it. Of course, when a single respondent ponders the usefulness of switching his vote, he may well feel that his decision will have no impact on the results. Yet, as we know, combining the behaviour of single voters is what brings about alterations in political alignments. We have then two possibilities, which may even be related. One is that voters, while expressing concern, do not really believe that the issue is of critical importance. Another possibility is that voters are so attached to their party, only a minority would be willing to change their voting pattern. The party shift of this minority would clearly be sufficient to change the party distribution and bring about majority government, but that is a fact outside the purview of this discussion. Of the two possibilities suggested, our hunch is that unwillingness to switch is mainly due to entrenched partisanship, for which we can look to the following discussion for some evidence. If this is the case, then theories of cognitive consistency would suggest that partisanship should lead voters to downgrade the significance of majority government, a theme that can be better explored in Chapter 10.

Party Differentiation

We began our analysis with the thought that perceptions of a differentiated party structure would be most compatible with a democratic regime, where parties are conceived as providing true alternatives. We were then prepared to argue that lack of differentiation was associated with voters according a low level of legitimacy to party politics, in much the same way as they did when expressing a lack of concern with majority government. But we have also suggested that the latter can be a concomitant of partisanship, in other words, of a situation where party attachments, and presumably party differentiation, are highly salient. It soon became clear that our model of regime norms was too simple. The appropriateness of the alternative approach we finally adopted should become evident after we review the results of our survey.

When our respondents were asked how much difference it made which party runs the country, 44 percent answered a great deal, 34 replied some, 17 said it made no difference, and the remainder had no opinion. Table 8–2 indicates regional differences in the frequency with which respondents felt it made a great deal of difference. Ontario and British Columbia displayed the highest frequency and Quebec the lowest. The Atlantic provinces were closest to the Prairies, in a middle range of differentiation, while Quebec was set apart from others by the relatively low frequency with which party differences were acknowledged.

Another approach to the issue of party differentiation was made with the question, "Considering everything the parties stand for, would you say that there is a good deal of difference between the parties, some difference, or not much difference?" To ensure some

Table 8–2 **Perception of Federal Party Differences, by Region** (Percent)

	Atlantic	Quebec	Ontario	Prairies	British Columbia	Total
Makes a great deal of difference which party forms government	42	37	50	44	49	44
There is at least some difference between political parties	52	58	61	63	63	60
There is some party least likely to be voted for	72	80	81	87	85	81
N	(229)	(793)	(1054)	(395)	(256)	(2727)

consistency to their frame of reference, respondents were directed
to think about federal parties. A good deal of difference was seen by
24 percent, 36 percent saw some, 35 percent said there was not much
difference, and the rest were not able to give an opinion. On this
question, perception of at least some difference increased from east
to west. The geographic extremes, which are also the opinion extremes, are separated by 11 percentage points. The remainder are
fairly similar, and most sharply distinguished from the Atlantic
provinces.

The final relevant question asked was, "Which of the federal
parties today would you least want to vote for?" Our major concern
was whether there was some party that the voter excluded from his
range of possible choices. Four-fifths of the respondents indicated
that this was the case, and they were especially prominent in the
Prairies and British Columbia. The most pronounced regional difference was due to the lower frequency with which those in the Atlantic
provinces excluded some party. Ontario and Quebec could be classified in the middle rank of excluders. In total, the party most often
selected as unappealing was Le Ralliement des Créditistes. No other
party seemed so unattractive, although Social Credit and NDP were
excluded by a sizeable body of voters.

We can obtain some insights into the meaning of party differentiation from additional questions. One was on parties most similar, and
there we found that a majority saw the Liberals and Conservatives as
most alike. No other pairs of parties were mentioned with anywhere
near the same frequency. Parties unlike each other, however, were
not so clearly perceived, and there were no sizeable concentrations of
any pairs. This may mean, that for the bulk of the electorate, it would
make a great deal of difference which party was in office if the party
were one *other* than the Liberal or Conservative. This interpretation
seems even more plausible when we consider those parties chosen
as unlikely voting choices. They were predominantly the minor parties
rather than the two older ones. In addition, when respondents were
asked to reflect on their choice of a second party, should they have
the opportunity to make another selection, the Liberal and Conservative parties were most frequently selected, regardless of the current
party supported by respondents.

The three items about parties do not differentiate among regions
in the same way. If we can be satisfied with a crude division, it is
possible to see an east-west cleavage, with Ontario aligned with the
western provinces. That the Prairies and British Columbia should be
concerned with party differences was partly the result of experiences
with the more distinctive third parties. In addition, there was some
association with the earlier noted tendency to differentiate among
national party leaders with respect to a regional identity. In Ontario

as well, third parties in provincial politics had probably helped condition a greater sensitivity to party differences. But moderately high political awareness and a concern with majority government also indicated a generally more differentiating political consciousness, reflected in the views of parties.

Voters in the Atlantic provinces were relatively less concerned about party differences. Their views were presumably affected by the firm establishment of the two older parties. The tweedledum-tweedledee image that the Liberal and Conservative parties had to some may be especially pronounced where, as in the Atlantic provinces, these parties consisted of almost the sole political avenues both for support and protest. In Chapter 3 we suggested that this strong two-party system did not have much pay-off for the Atlantic provinces, and our questions may have been tapping a recognition of this fact. In the preceding chapter, the Atlantic provinces were, in the aggregate, low in assigning a regional identity to party leaders. This might suggest as well an unwillingness to make sharp distinctions either about parties or leaders.

Quebeckers were also relatively low in discerning party differences, especially on the party forming the government. They also displayed a high degree of knowledge about local conditions, a low frequency of labelling party leaders in regional terms, and a low level of concern about majority government. These characteristics raised a suspicion that Quebec voters had more localistic political orientations.

These data led us to question our original hypothesis on the connection between party differentiation and regime norms in a democracy. It was not clear from these findings which set of attitudes toward party differences was most appropriate in a democratic regime, or even which we could infer to be legitimate within the Canadian context. Since our survey provided little guidance, we looked to comparative materials for possible enlightenment.

In a cross-national survey conducted in 1948, there were two distinct alignments in response to the question "Do you think it will make a great deal of difference whether one party or another is in power?" At the low end of concern were the United States, Canada, and France; and at the high end, Sweden, Denmark, Norway, and Great Britain.[7] Trends for Canada itself have fluctuated since that time, when 47 percent gave an affirmative answer. In 1953 it was 63 percent, 57 percent in 1958, and 44 percent in 1961, the same as in our 1966 survey.[8] Since the peaks are not readily explainable, we

7. Cited in Duncan MacRae, Jr., *Parliament, Parties, and Society in France 1946-1958* (New York: St. Martin's Press, 1967), p. 261.

8. Cited in Mildred A. Schwartz, *Public Opinion and Canadian Identity* (Berkeley: University of California Press, 1967), p. 208.

emphasize the continuities, which suggest that the Canadian level of attaching importance to party differences is generally characteristic of less than half the population.

Further comparisons in which Canada is included are not available, but in pursuing our exploration of the meaning of these opinions, we take what is often the dangerous step of using another country as a surrogate. This surrogate country is the United States, which, though differing in political institutions and traditions, manifested one important similarity to Canada, a relatively low degree of salience attributed to the party of the government. In the five nation study by Almond and Verba, in which the United States was compared to Great Britain, West Germany, Italy, and Mexico, Americans displayed markedly less negative attitudes toward the supporters of opposing parties,[9] almost complete indifference to marriage across party lines,[10] and expressed much less fear that when a political party were in office, it would do something harmful to the country.[11] Since democratic norms are at least as dominant in the United States as in any of the other countries with which it was compared, we cannot say that the low salience of party differentiation suggests low legitimacy to important regime norms. In the United States, with its tradition of two strong parties, government is to a large extent an alternation between "ins and outs."[12] As the ill-fated Goldwater campaign indicated, most Americans preferred an echo to a choice.[13] Whichever party is in office can be expected to do its job, without changing the rules of the game. We would suggest that this view of party government has been abetted by the absence of a strong class basis to politics, such that the election of one party does not appear to seriously threaten the interests of a whole class of people. In any event, these data suggest that regime norms in the United States do not place a high value on party differentiation.

These comparative data, especially from the United States, suggest some additional interpretations of the Canadian situation. To begin

---

9. Gabriel Almond and Sidney Verba, *The Civic Culture* (Princeton: Princeton University Press, 1963), pp. 124-32.

10. Ibid., pp. 132-43.

11. Inter-University Consortium for Political Research, *The Five Nation Study* (Ann Arbor, 1968), pp. 67-70.

12. V. O. Key, Jr., *Politics, Parties, and Pressure Groups,* 4th ed. (New York: Thomas Y. Crowell Co., 1958) p. 231; Frank J. Sorauf, *Political Parties in the American System* (Boston: Little, Brown and Co., 1964), pp. 27-32.

13. Philip E. Converse, Aage Clausen, Warren E. Miller, "Electoral Myth and Reality: the 1964 Election," *American Political Science Review* 59 (June 1965): 321-36.

with, since we have presented evaluations of majority government and party differences as indicators of the content and legitimacy of regime norms, the relationship between the two is particularly important. Our regional analysis reveals that there is no single set of regime norms, or if there is, there is sufficient alternative to raise questions about the level of legitimacy accorded these norms. There are four patterns in Canada, reflecting what we have designated as four national-types, although we do not suggest these as the origins. The typology is premised on the assumption that a multi-party system would downgrade the importance of a single, majority government. It also presumes that party differentiation will be more important where there is a strong emphasis on internal solidarity.

In Ontario there was a relatively high value placed on party differences and majority government. We would consider this a British response-type, based on the existence of two major parties in Britain characterized by fairly cohesive parliamentary responses.[14] We earlier predicted that this would be the primary model of attitudes in a democratic regime.

A high value on party differences but a low one on majority government was found in western Canada. This is similar to a Scandinavian type of political system, in which there are distinctive and multiple parties.[15] In this case, having one's party share in governing power would be more important than perhaps the impossible achievement of majority status.

Residents of the Atlantic provinces placed a high value on majority government but attached relatively less significance to party differences. From our discussion of the United States, this leads us to term this pattern an American one.

Finally, in Quebec, there was both low value on party differences and majority government. If indeed the opposite pattern is the legitimate one, this indicates that Quebec voters accorded low legitimacy to these particular regime norms. As a general pattern, we would style it a French one, where parties appear as ineffectual organs for representing interests or conducting government.[16]

---

14. Leon P. Epstein, *Political Parties in Western Democracies* (New York: Frederick A. Praeger, 1967, pp. 318-27.

15. ibid., pp. 338-39; Dankwart A. Rustow, *The Politics of Compromise* (Princeton: Princeton University Press, 1955).

16. Henry W. Ehrmann, "Direct Democracy in France," in R. C. Macridis, ed., *Political Parties, Contemporary Trends and Ideas* (New York: Harper Torchbooks, 1967) pp. 149-83; MacRae, *Parliament, Parties, and Society*, pp. 230-32; Stanley Hoffman, "Paradoxes of the French Political Community," in Stanley Hoffman, *et al., In Search of France* (New York: Harper Torchbooks, 1963), p. 51.

POLITICAL ROLES

Canadian politicians and commentators frequently act as though the views of the party system predominating in Ontario were the most legitimate ones. We are not prepared to make this generalization. But the existence of four regional response patterns indicates a situation that is in a sense more appropriate to four separate states than to the regions of a single state. The seriousness of these citizen orientations is obviously limited by the fact that our questions on the party system tap only one aspect of regime norms. Attitudes toward authorities are much less equivocal. We may not know the particular sources of satisfaction or dissatisfaction with political actors, but we have less doubt about the meaning or consequences of the views expressed.

MP's Doing a Good Job

The formal and informal roles of a member of the House of Commons are sufficiently varied to suggest that citizens could fasten on any number of them in making an evaluation. We attempted to control for some of the possible variation by directing respondents to think of the whole class of members of Parliament for a given party, rather than specific individuals, and to evaluate the job they had done in the past few years. To begin with, it is useful to consider the distribution of opinions for the country as a whole. No more than 35 percent of the respondents said that the MPs of any party were doing a pretty good job, and that these were Liberal members. Conservatives were rated this favourably by slightly fewer, and more felt they had been doing a poor job. A preponderance of clearly negative views was apparent only for Créditistes, about whom 36 percent said they had been doing a poor job. Unfavourable views were expressed about Social Credit by 24 percent, compared to about 15 percent who thought that NDP and Conservative members were not doing a good job. The minor parties were also noteworthy for the relatively large proportion of respondents (one-quarter to one-third) who had no opinion of them.

There is an undoubted tendency for people to evaluate the elected members of their own party in more favourable terms than those of opposing parties. As a consequence of the unequal distribution of party supporters regionally, regions can be expected to differ in the way they rate members of Parliament for this reason alone. In Chapter 10 we consider some of the effects of the interaction between region and party, but at this time, even though we recognize the causal connections, our concern is solely with the end result of how regions differ in their support for authoritative figures. These are documented in Table 8–3 on the basis of the most favourable rating available in our structured question: "a pretty good job."

Table 8–3 **Percent Rating Members of Parliament as Doing a Pretty Good Job, by Region**

Party MPs	Atlantic	Quebec	Ontario	Prairies	British Columbia	Total
Liberal	41	23	44	31	30	35
Conservative	39	13	33	38	25	28
NDP	23	20	35	33	32	29
Social Credit	13	6	14	29	25	14
Créditiste	7	17	4	7	9	9
N	(229)	(793)	(1054)	(395)	(256)	(2727)

If we use the frequency with which members of Parliament were rated favourably as a means for assigning ranks, then Liberal members were given the highest rank in the east, second in British Columbia, and third in the Prairies. The range with which Liberal MPs were chosen extends over 21 percentage points. Some of this separation between regions was obscured by our use of rankings, since even though Quebeckers ranked the Liberals first, they also rated them as doing a good job relatively infrequently. Quebec is separated from the Prairies, where the Liberals ranked third, by 7 percent. We can hence discern three groups of evaluators: Ontario and the Atlantic provinces, where the Liberals were most highly rated; the Prairies and British Columbia, where they were moderately well perceived; and Quebec, where relative ratings internal to Quebec were high, but low compared to other regions.

Ranking of Conservative party MPs was unusually varied. They ranked first in the Prairies, second in the Atlantic provinces, third in Ontario and British Columbia, and fourth in Quebec. The total percent separating regions was also greater than for any other parties' MPs: 26 percent. On the basis of the proportion giving these MPs the highest possible rating, the Prairie and Atlantic provinces were most alike, while Ontario was separated from them by about 5 percent. British Columbia stood apart from these three regions, as it did from Quebec, where Conservative MPs were most poorly evaluated. In this instance the tendency for Quebeckers to avoid high ratings for any party still did not compensate for their low opinion of the Conservatives. In evaluating Conservatives as well as Liberals, the five regions fell into at least three groups, but not quite of the same makeup.

Although they were a small number in the House of Commons, NDP members of Parliament did manage to impress a sizeable minority of voters with the calibre of their performance. They ranked first in British Columbia, second in the Prairies, Ontario, and Quebec, and third in the Atlantic provinces. There was more consensus about the NDP than the two older parties, with a range of 15 percent. Using the frequency of favourable ratings, rather than ranks, regions may be divided along an east-west dimension if Ontario is included in the west. More favourable views occurred with higher frequency in the west.

Social Credit MPs normally ranked in fourth position, except in Quebec, where they ranked fifth. Consensus was not high, however, if we look at the actual proportions giving these MPs a favourable evaluation. There was a total range separating regions of 23 percent. The Prairies and British Columbia were quite similar in outlook, and both agreed that, relatively speaking, Social Credit MPs were to be commended. The Atlantic provinces and Ontario were much less laudatory, separated from the west by over 10 percent. Such ratings came most grudgingly from Quebec.

Over one-third of the sample said that they were unable to rate Créditiste MPs, and less than 10 percent gave them a favourable rating. There was considerable consensus everywhere except Quebec that the Créditistes did not deserve much praise. In Quebec, however, Créditiste MPs ranked third, separated from the top ranking Liberals by only 6 percent.

At times we have been hesitant in interpreting the overall survey findings because we usually lack a comparative framework, a handicap that does not exist when discussing regions. On this question, however, there is no reason to avoid generalizations. It is clear that voters everywhere were reluctant to give unqualified praise to members of Parliament, regardless of party label. In no instance did a majority of the respondents admit that the MPs were doing a good job. When we attribute high ratings to MPs, we do so solely in relative terms.

From our previous discussion of party differences, where it appeared that these were considered important mainly with respect to the minor parties, it might be anticipated that the rating of MPs too would follow a major-minor division. In other words, since it was the major parties that were preferred, we could expect that the legislative members of these parties would be most highly regarded. Yet it was only in the Atlantic provinces, the safest haven for two-party government based on the traditional parties, that this division was clear. Aside from this region, it was in the Prairies alone that the Conservative party found relatively strong support. Instead, it was a third party, the NDP, which more often made a favourable impression through its performance in the House of Commons. This is of particular credit to the NDP, since we know that party operated with a small number of parliamentary members.

At this point in our data analysis we do not know how the evaluation of MPs was affected by respondents' partisanship, although we would suspect a strong relationship. Still it can be seen that ratings were at least somewhat independent of representation. For example, the more highly rated NDP had fewer representatives elected in Ontario than did the less praised but more numerous Conservatives. Yet those regions which had strongest representation from specific parties were also more likely to assign them a favourable rating. This includes the Conservatives in the Prairies, Social Credit in the west, and Créditistes in Quebec.

As the preceding indicates, the party affiliation of MPs usually resulted in regionally-specific ratings. This means that regions were aligned differently, depending on which party's MPs were being rated. At the same time there was one persistent cleavage, that between Quebec and the remainder of the country. This cleavage reflected a disposition to rank the Conservatives, Créditistes, and Social Credit in an order different from that which was more usual in other regions. But even where rankings were similar, as in the case of Liberal and NDP MPs, Quebec remained set apart by the particularly low evaluation its residents placed on the performance of all MPs, regardless of party.[17]

Criticism of Authorities

We have no direct information on why respondents were not especially approving of members of Parliament. We suggested that favourable views were partly affected by a region's electoral history. Without presenting any detailed evidence, we reasoned that the party preferences of respondents would affect their outlooks, so that regions with greater representation from one or more parties would also display more favourable evaluations of them. The implication was also that in those regions where a party received a sizeable share of electoral support over time, opponents as well as supporters would be inclined to give its elected members a good rating. This would be in confirmation of the thesis that the political system requires, and normally obtains, generally supportive attitudes toward authorities, regardless of party affiliation.

Some possible sources of concern about political authorities, but without attaching these to any political party, were tapped by two additional questions. As such, they cannot be directly related to our previous discussion, but they should give us some clues about what disturbed voters.

Table 8–4 gives the percentage of those who agreed that candidates elected to parliament soon lose touch with the people. More than half the sample agreed with this statement, and Quebec represented the region manifesting most criticism. With 69 percent of those in Quebec believing that MPs soon lose contact with their electors, we can be sure that we have discerned one aspect of political discontent in that province. No other region displayed this much agreement, although British Columbia came closest, separated by 9 percent. Slightly more than a majority in the Atlantic provinces complained

17. More recently than our survey, the Canadian Gallup Poll asked respondents to rate the job being done by their own members of Parliament. No regional breakdowns were included in the published release, but distributions of responses were given by mother tongue, as well as by a number of other variables. These indicate that those of French mother tongue, most but not all of whom would be living in Quebec, were the group most critical of their own representatives. (Canadian Institute of Public Opinion, Gallup Poll of Canada, 5 November 1969.) The local orientation of the French-speaking is further substantiated by the high rating given to provincial, compared to federal, legislators.

Table 8–4 **Percent Agreeing with Statements Critical of Authorities, by Region**

	Atlantic	Quebec	Ontario	Prairies	British Columbia	Total
Those elected to parliament soon lose touch with the people	52	69	48	46	60	55
Intellectuals take up too large a position in our government	44	42	30	32	36	36
N	(229)	(793)	(1054)	(395)	(256)	(2727)

about the distance between elected representatives and the people. The Prairies and Ontario were most alike, with fewer than half criticizing MPs.

To ask, as we did, whether intellectuals take up too large a position in government, is to evoke the anti-intellectualism prevalent among certain segments of the American electorate. Sneering attacks on "eggheads" in government were the hallmark of Joseph McCarthy, but the refrain had not been his alone.[18] This form of anti-intellectualism is thought by some sociologists not to be prevalent in Canada. Compared to Americans, Canadians are often described as more deferential to authority, less prone to challenge established structures, and more accepting of inequalities.[19] According to S. D. Clark, this setting does not provide the tolerance of dissent necessary for the emergence of McCarthyism.

> In Canada it would be hard to conceive of a state of political freedom great enough to permit the kind of attacks upon responsible leaders of the government which have been carried out in the United States. More careful examination of the American community in general, and perhaps of the academic community in particular, would probably reveal that, in spite of the witch hunts in that country, the people of the United States enjoy in fact a much greater degree of freedom than do the people of Canada.[20]

On the basis of these impressions we would expect Canadians to be reluctant to criticize governmental personnel because they were excessively intellectual. But appeals to the electorate on these grounds have not been absent from Canada, and Clark provides examples from politics in Alberta, Quebec, and the national campaign of John Diefenbaker.[21]

As we have implied, expectations about anti-intellectualism are not firmly based on empirical evidence, and hence our results could not really be anticipated, particularly since we do not have the benchmark of comparative data. Table 8–4 indicates that only a minority found the position of intellectuals troublesome. Yet it was a sizeable

---

18. Richard Hofstadter, *Anti-Intellectualism in American Life* (New York: Vintage Books, 1963).

19. For example, John Porter, "Canadian Character in the Twentieth Century," *The Annals of the American Academy of Political and Social Sciences* 370 (March 1967): 48-56.

20. S. D. Clark, *The Developing Canadian Community,* 2nd ed. (Toronto: University of Toronto Press, 1968), p. 216.

21. Ibid., p. 216.

minority, and could assume political importance depending on its distribution through the social structure.

Greatest concern about the role of intellectuals was manifested in the east, in what have been the two most traditional areas of Canada. It is in just such areas that greater deference to elites, including intellectual elites, would be expected. Yet Quebec at least can no longer be described as a traditional society. More than any other part of Canada, it has been going through a process of change, particularly in the past decade, that may be unparalleled in modern, industrial societies. In this situation, the intellectuals have acted in many different, and even contradictory, roles. They have been the vanguard of change in a host of social and political movements, providing leadership and ideologies for parochialism, nationalism, separatism, and other interests. As both advisors and participants, they have been active in the Liberal governments of Lesage in Quebec and St. Laurent and Pearson (and, after our survey, Trudeau) in Ottawa.[22] In some sense, these intellectuals disrupted the orderly life of substantial segments of the population. Their effects were frequently viewed with displeasure by respondents in Quebec.

Circumstances in the Atlantic provinces did not provide a similar context for viewing intellectuals in government. But since that region contrasted most sharply with Ontario and the Prairies, separated by 14 and 12 percent respectively, this suggests that the region with the greatest problems also felt greatest dissatisfaction with those, defined as intellectuals, who should be finding solutions. In Ontario in particular, problems were neither of the same scope nor were governmental personnel subject to the same criticism. We would guess that in those regions where criticism was less frequent, intellectuals were associated with technical experts and pragmatic problem-solvers; where they were looked on with less favour, as abstract thinkers, making and executing plans without regard for those they serve. This is conjecture, of course, and nothing more in our survey can aid our interpretations.

Of the two items with negative content, the one on elected officials losing touch with their constituents is most clear cut. The fact that a majority of Canadians expressed this complaint can be taken at face value. This item clarified for us one of the ways in which dissatisfaction with authorities, documented in the preceding questions on the rating of members of Parliament, arises. By a growing remoteness

---

22. Hubert Guindon, "Social Unrest, Social Class, and Quebec's Bureaucratic Revolution," *Queen's Quarterly* 71 (Summer 1964) 150-62; Gérald Fortin, "Transformation des structures du pouvoir," in Fernand Dumont et Jean-Paul Montminy, eds.; *Le Pouvoir dans la société canadienne-française* (Québec: Les presses de l'Université Laval, 1966), pp. 87-99.

from their electors, or at least by actions that lead to perceptions of such remoteness, legislators have helped generate discontent. They seem to have done so most often in Quebec, the province most critical of the job done by party representatives and also relatively concerned by the role of intellectuals in government.

British Columbia was also a centre of discontent with political authorities. Voters there were less likely to evaluate MPs in favourable terms than were all other regions except Quebec. In particular, the province ranked fourth in its assessment of the dominant Liberals and Conservatives. Less than two-thirds thought that MPs soon lose touch with their constituents, suggesting that this was a source of their low evaluations. British Columbia lay midway between the extremes on intellectuals, though it was slightly closer to the less critical regions.

Compared to other regions, the place of intellectuals was a particularly sore spot in the Atlantic provinces. In general, however, dissatisfaction in that area was not translated into inordinate criticism of authorities. On all items, Ontario and the Prairies were the least critical, although in absolute terms, we would still have to say that political authorities were subject to considerable disapproval.

Political Roles as Objects of Legitimacy

Each criterion we use indicates that support for authorities was low at the time of our survey. Within the country, there were also fairly consistent regional differences. At one end we find Quebec set apart by the low level of support expressed by its residents. At the opposite pole are Ontario and the Prairies, where at least relative to the Canadian context, there was a high level of support. British Columbia ranked next to Quebec in the amount of criticism its voters expressed, followed by the Atlantic provinces. Even without further confirmation, we can still be certain that we have uncovered an important area of stress. Just how serious its consequences could be requires that continuing assays of the population be made. For one thing, we require trend data to assess the rise and decline of support; it is not inconceivable that the Canadian political system has often operated with only modest support for authorities. We also need to know more about those who are most disgruntled with the performance of political actors, since their placement in the social structure has a major bearing on whether their feelings will have political consequences. We know already, however, that dissatisfaction is a regional phenomenon and this alone should give us pause.

What Easton says about leaders in situations of major change is also relevant to more stable times.

> The experience of mass societies confirms that at least large
> aggregates of members do not usually respond to ideas and

ideologies in and of themselves. To collect and focus the support of large numbers of members and to link their feelings to other objects requires some way of concretizing their attachments. Typically, this has been achieved in part by the emergence of vigorous and trusted leaders who, the members and followers are led to believe, in some way embody the ideals and stand for the promise of their fulfillment. They are the personal bridges acting as ties to the new norms and structures of authority.[23]

As objects of legitimacy, authority figures may receive support either because of their personal qualities, the structured aspects of their relationships, or their ties with some legitimating ideology.[24] We cannot determine from our survey just which of these sources of legitimacy were most in question. Making the simplest assumptions, premised on the directness of our questions and the low level of abstractness involved, we could argue that respondents were responding solely to the personal qualities of those authorities about whom they knew something. If this is in fact the case, then questions about the legitimacy of political figures are not seriously invoked, since none of the systemic bases for their positions are at stake. Yet it does not take much imagination to see that, should low levels of support continue as a regional phenomenon, we have one of the conditions for eroding support along more basic dimensions of the political system.

POLITICAL CYNICISM

Legitimacy and Trust

Trust is an essential ingredient of social interaction. Many situations occur where it is absent, and when they involve prolonged relationships, then greater reliance must be placed on coercive measures.[25] Within a political system, trust among participants is equally important. And there too compliance and control through the use of coercion is a measure of stress within the system, and even of failure. This is so because lack of trust indicates that members of society do not accord the moral right to govern to those in positions of authority, who must then use external means of control for imposing their will.

---

23. Easton, *The Political System*, pp. 304-305. Easton concurs, pp. 306-307.

24. Ibid., pp. 289-310.

25. Peter M. Blau, *Exchange and Power in Social Life* (New York: John Wiley and Co., 1964).

In this sense, trust is another way of conceptualizing the legitimacy of components of the political system.[26]

We will consider the issue of trust from the negative side, viewing it as political cynicism. As a topic of considerable interest, it has been explored using different measures than our own.[27] Also related are interests in normlessness as a form of alienation.

> Following Durkheim's use of "anomie," which denotes a devitalization of social norms regulating individual behavior, "perceived political normlessness" is defined as the individual's perception that the norms or rules intended to govern political relations have broken down, and that departures from the prescribed behavior are common. A belief that officials violate legal procedures in dealing with the public or in arriving at policy decisions exemplifies this mode of alienation.[28]

In all cases, emphasis is on the incidence and nature of lack of trust as a source of strain within a political system.

Measures of Cynicism

The five items used to measure cynicism here were previously used by the Survey Research Center. Published results from American studies do not provide us with more than tangential materials, since these are concerned with social psychological aspects of cynicism.[29] Our emphasis is on levels of cynicism as properties of political systems. Our neglect of factors other than region and party preference (in Chapter 10) turns out, in any case, to be justifiable on grounds other than the theoretical interests of this volume. Empirically, it is

---

26. "Legitimation is . . . in power systems, the factor which is parallel to confidence in mutual acceptability and stability of the monetary unit in monetary systems." Talcott Parsons, "On the Concept of Power," in Parsons, *Sociological Theory and Modern Society* (New York: Free Press, 1967), p. 309.

27. Edgar Litt, "Political Cynicism and Political Futility," *The Journal of Politics* 25 (1963): 312-23; and Robert E. Agger, Marshall N. Goldstein, Stanley A. Pearl, "Political Cynicism: Measurement and Meaning," *The Journal of Politics* 23 (1961): 477-506.

28. Ada W. Finifter, "Dimensions of Political Alienation," *American Political Science Review* 64 (June 1970): 390-91.

29. Donald E. Stokes, "Popular Evaluations of Government: An Empirical Assessment," in Harland Cleveland and Harold D. Lasswell, eds., *Ethics and Bigness: Scientific, Academic, Religious, Political and Military* (New York: Harper and Bros., 1962), pp. 61-72; Joel D. Aberbach, "Alienation and Political Behavior," *American Political Science Review* 63 (March 1969): 86-99.

region and party that are the principal differentiators of levels of cynicism, rather than more conventional social characteristics.[30]

The cynicism measures were designed to form a single scale, but personal preference led us to an item by item analysis. Methodologically this is also preferable since the items do not fully scale in the Canadian context.[31] Moreover, they do not fit together with complete consistency. A linkage analysis finds two clusters of items: concerns with crookedness and waste form one cluster, and those with trustworthiness, competence, and fairness another.[32] Each of the five items evoked different frequencies of cynicism from regions, so that there is no regionally consistent response pattern. For example, if regions are ranked according to the frequency with which they responded to a particular item, a test of consistency using the coefficient of concordance results in a W of .21. The probability level associated with it is less than .05, indicating that on each item regions are not ordered in the same way. Our analysis takes these variations into account.

Three of the five cynicism items presented respondents with a choice from three alternatives while the remainder gave only two. We have chosen to present our data in Tables 8–5 and 8–6 based on the most negative alternative. If we had instead concentrated on political trust, and used the most positive responses, the five items would have remained in a similar relationship to each other.

Comparative Results

The severest indictment of the federal government was delivered for its differential treatment of voters. About three-quarters thought that at least some of those in the highest level of government pay more attention to big interests, rather than to the ordinary voter. This item produced a high degree of consensus, with a negligible amount of regional variation. The 1964 Survey Research Center study of the American electorate did not ask quite the same question. While this may have had a bearing on the distribution of responses, it is still noteworthy that just over one-quarter in the United States answered that the government was being run for a few big interests.

The second aspect of government about which more than a majority chose the critical, and hence, cynical, category, affirmed that quite a few of the people running the government do not know what they

30. This is evident from unpublished tabulations as well as from Andrew Rojecki, "Political Powerlessness and Attitudes Toward Government: The Canadian Context," unpublished Master's thesis, Department of Sociology, University of Illinois at Chicago Circle, 1970.

31. Ibid., p. 10.

32. Ibid., pp. 11-13.

Table 8–5 **Comparison of Political Cynicism in the United States and Canada**

	Canada	United States
Some of the people high in government pay more attention to what the big interests want	75	
Quite a few of the people running the government don't seem to know what they are doing	52	27
The government (in Ottawa) can be trusted to do what is right only some of the time	36	22
People in the government waste a lot of the money we pay in taxes	36	47
(Government is pretty much run by a few big interests looking out for themselves)		28
Quite a few of the people running the government are crooked	24	29
N	(2,727)	(1,450)

Source: Data for the United States are from an unpublished 1964 survey by the Survey Research Center, supplied by Philip E. Converse and Linda A. Wilcox.

are doing. This again brought agreement from only about one-quarter of the sample in the United States. In Canada, the range of variability was fairly large—15 percent. Regions fell into three categories: the most highly cynical in British Columbia; a moderately cynical group exemplified by the Atlantic provinces; and the remainder least cynical. Even in this last category, however, approximately half took the critical view of government personnel.

While over one-third mentioned that a lot of money collected in taxes is wasted, we would still conclude that, comparatively speaking, the manner in which the government handles money does not seem to be a matter of serious public concern in Canada. In the United States the largest number said a great deal was wasted, making it the item distinguishing the most cynical. A total range of 12 percent separated Canadian regions into two, with those more often concerned with waste in the Prairies and Atlantic provinces.

Over one-third again said that the government can be trusted to do what is right only some of the time. Americans chose this response category 14 percent less frequently. Within Canada, all regions expressed less trust than in the neighbouring country. By this criterion we would say that the more cynical were in Quebec, set off from the most similar Atlantic provinces by 7 percent.

Table 8-6 **Percent Agreeing with Statements Measuring Political Cynicism, by Region**

	Atlantic	Quebec	Ontario	Prairies	British Columbia
At least some government officials pay more atten- tion to big shots	74	76	73	75	79
Quite a few people running the government don't seem to know what they are doing	58	49	51	52	64
The government can be trusted only some of the time to do what is right	37	44	31	36	34
People in government waste a lot of money collected in taxes	41	31	35	43	34
Quite a few of the people running the government are a little crooked	37	28	20	22	19
N	(229)	(793)	(1054)	(395)	(256)

Finally, neither Canadians nor Americans in extensive numbers were convinced of large-scale corruption in their respective governments. While we cannot be certain of the issues in the United States, in Canada the period preceding the 1965 election was one in which there were scandals uncovered within government circles. The most serious charges involved bribery to obtain bail for Lucien Rivard, a Montreal hoodlum with organized crime connections wanted for extradiction to the United States.[33] Evidence of criminal intent was found for several government officials, but of even more serious political consequences were charges of poor judgement directed against the minister of Justice and even the Prime Minister. In the 1965 election campaign, the Conservatives, and especially Mr. Diefenbaker, made wide use of the theme of immorality in government. Because many of the people involved were French-speaking, the Conservative campaign is thought to have encouraged anti-French feeling elsewhere in the country.[34] But whatever effects the issue of corruption may have had, these were not great by the time of our survey. Asked to evaluate the importance of political corruption in affecting their voting decision, just over 40 percent said that it was very important. Of the eight issues rated this way, corruption ranked sixth in importance. The question about crookedness as part of our cynicism measure did, it is true, result in the largest range of difference separating regions: 18 percent. On the basis of the percent taking the most negative view, regions could be divided into three, with the Atlantic provinces at the most cynical extreme, Quebec midway, and the remainder least negative. These results, however, cannot be readily related to the actual corruption issues that were current at about the time of the election.

Compared to the United States, it would seem that cynicism was more widespread in Canada. There were three main complaints about government: too much attention to big interests, lack of intelligent action, and low trustworthiness.

Within Canada, overall consistency among the cynicism items was low but regionally-specific patterns could be discerned. In some instances these had a clear association with previous findings. The most straightforward example was Ontario. Residents of that province were least cynical, both in terms of the average frequency with which they selected critical responses and in the consistency of their ranking on each item. This fitted well with evidence already accumulated about the character of Ontario: its objective well-being, widespread appreciation of its advantaged position, and the prevalence of generally supportive attitudes toward the regime and authorities.

---

33. Peter C. Newman, *A Nation Divided, Canada and the Coming of Pierre Trudeau* (New York: Alfred A. Knopf, 1969), pp. 264-87.

34. Ibid., pp. 353-55.

In addition, voters in that province exhibited highly conventional views of the political system with respect to the desirability of majority government and the existence of significant differences among political parties.

The Prairie provinces were mixed in their political orientations. While voters were only moderately concerned about majority government, they were highly differentiating among parties. They displayed no appreciable criticism of political authorities, yet they were moderately high on cynicism, especially in their concern with waste.

Voters in British Columbia were similar to those in the Prairies with respect to views of majority government and party differences. Yet in contrast they displayed considerable dissatisfaction with authorities. Compared to other regions, they were moderately high on cynicism, expressing relatively greatest concern about the lack of knowledge and understanding shown by government personnel. In total, we found British Columbia nursing feelings appropriate to political outsiders, although we cannot say that these were dangerously subversive.[35]

In general, the Atlantic provinces displayed most cynicism. While not altogether surprising, given that region's grievances, this finding does have some unexpected qualities. Voters tended to conventional views about the need for majority government. We were somewhat puzzled by their lack of sharp party differentiation, which we related to their experiences with the two major parties. That these views did not disguise dissatisfaction tended to be confirmed by their relatively positive rating of members of Parliament from the major parties. Beyond the concern about intellectuals in government, we had not previously detected any serious amount of criticism of political authorities. Moreover, the Atlantic provinces have remained heirs to a political system that has operated for generations without any strong challenges to the status quo. To the extent that our cynicism items do differentiate among Canadians in meaningful ways, we appear to have uncovered a reservoir of political disaffection to go along with those other forms of dissatisfaction previously noted.[36]

---

35. "Regional and class divisions have both contributed to the persistence of a negative community in British Columbia. The British Columbia community exists only in the negative conviction shared by many that coast society is somehow different from the larger Canadian society. Otherwise there are few effective bonds tying estranged and conflicting groups into greater communion." Martin Robin, "British Columbia: The Politics of Class Conflict," in Martin Robin, *Canadian Provincial Politics* (Scarborough: Prentice-Hall of Canada, 1972), p. 37. Robin also documents the extent of political immorality in that province.

36. This is not to say, of course, that grievances are not openly and frequently expressed in other ways. One need only read, for example, a randomly selected issue of that iconoclastic journal, *the mysterious east*.

Voters in Quebec were not particularly concerned about majority government nor did they differentiate much among political parties. Their failure to attach a great deal of significance to these aspects of parliamentary government suggested a more general lack of commitment to some principal values of the political system. This interpretation was reinforced both by the low evaluation given members of Parliament and the extent of specific criticisms of governmental personnel. We do not wish to read more into our data than in fact exists, but some commentators have gone even further in suggesting that the French-speaking majority in Quebec has failed to accept the basic values of democracy. This is attributed to their experiences as a conquered people. As a result they have been prone to exploitation by their own leadership, playing on the legitimate fears of exploitation from English-speaking Canada. Prime Minister Trudeau wrote before his entry into politics, "No amount of inter-group back-slapping or political *bonne-ententisme* will change the fact that democracy will continue to be thwarted in Canada so long as one-third of the people hardly believe in it—and that because to no small extent the remaining two-thirds provide them with ample grounds for distrusting it."[37] In recent years, outcries against political immorality, particularly in provincial government, had become strident.[38] Commenting on this in 1958, Trudeau was not optimistic about the possible outcome of such moralizing. "Political behaviour in Quebec can be described as immoral, objectively speaking; but subjectively the people are not conscious of wrongdoing, and consequently they see no reason to change that behaviour.[39] But changes have occurred, and there is evidence that Quebec voters are no longer as willing as they were once reputed to be to accept corrupt practices.[40] For example, a survey of Quebec voters taken before the 1960 provincial election revealed that over 80 percent did not feel it was normal practice to "passer les télégraphes" (the same individuals voting in more than one polling station), nor was it necessary for a party to foster this practice in order to get elected, nor to bribe voters. Under 70 percent felt that it was possible to maintain the secrecy of the ballot. Yet while illegal practices were deplored, the existence of political corruption was viewed as endemic. Of the 80 percent of the sample

37. Pierre Elliott Trudeau, *Federalism and the French Canadians* (Toronto: Macmillan of Canada, 1968), p. 103.

38. Gérard Dion and Louis O'Neill, *Political Immorality in the Province of Quebec* (Montreal: Civic Action League, 1956); and Dion and O'Neill, *Le Chrétien et les élections* (Montreal: Editions de l'homme, 1960).

39. Trudeau, *Federalism*, p. 123.

40. Herbert F. Quinn, *The Union Nationale* (Toronto: University of Toronto Press, 1963), especially pp. 131-51.

willing to express an opinion, 40 percent said corruption was inevitable regardless of the party in office, 47 percent gave a qualified response, admitting some corruption; and in a following question, 53 percent felt that corruption was bound to increase the longer a party remained in office.[41]

Both the survey findings and much of the commentary made about Quebec have dealt with politics at the provincial level. Our questions tapping cynicism referred only to the federal government and we cannot be sure how closely the two are connected in the minds of voters. On the basis of our measures, cynicism was high in Quebec, as it was elsewhere in Canada, but in overall terms, Quebec fell in a middle position. Given the regional differences we continue to find, and the circumstances of Quebec's existence, we could have expected to find even more cynicism. Yet there is evidence that on two aspects, Quebec voters were relatively more disillusioned than other Canadians. These items, one on trusting the government to do what is right, and the other on the relative honesty of people in government, deal with instances of outright corruption. The three remaining items consider stupidity, wastefulness, and lack of interest in the ordinary voter, but comparatively speaking, do not involve such obvious culpability. Hence while cynicism may not seem unusually high compared to the rest of Canada, crucial failures in public morality were certainly more frequently considered.

REGIONAL DIVISIONS

The polarization of regions takes different forms, depending on the issues examined. Views of the party system produced four distinct patterns, in which affinities were shown only between British Columbia and the Prairies. Assessments of members of Parliament divided Quebec from the remainder of Canada. This was true as well in criticizing authorities, but on these items an intermediate grouping was also discernible, that of the Atlantic provinces and British Columbia. Finally, regions divided into three on a cynicism, with the Atlantic provinces most cynical and Ontario at the opposite extreme.

We considered all the items included in this chapter as examples of issues of legitimacy. This should mean that their significance to the political system is great, but more specifically, it is difficult to trace through the direct implications. It is possible, for example, to draw at least two conclusions from regional views of the party system.

---

41. Le Groupe de recherches sociales, *Les Electeurs Québécois* (Montréal: multi., 1960), pp. 112-21.

One is that there is no single set of legitimate norms with respect to the party system. Another, using the Ontario responses as the legitimate ones, is to conclude that the level of support for these is low. Our own inclination is to take the first position and argue that regional experiences have shaped the party system in such ways as to inhibit the emergence of any single set of guiding norms. This is at least partly conjectural, but it does imply that, from the perspective of the citizens, there are a number of alternative ways in which to orient themselves to the political system.

Interpretations of views of authorities might appear less equivocal, but even here we are not fully certain of the implications. In general, support was low, and this was most crucially the case for Quebec. The operation of the political system at the federal level aroused low levels of trust, and this was especially noticeable for residents of the Atlantic provinces. These views surely indicate some areas of stress in the legitimacy of the political system. How far this stress has gone to undermine the system is a topic, however, to which our survey gives no further guidance.

CHAPTER

9

Relations between government and voter

As we have defined them, political orientations encompass a wide range of attitudes and beliefs, relating the citizen to his polity. In this chapter we look most directly at the perceived interactions between government and voters. For positive orientations toward government to exist, citizens should be confident that political activities have some value. This means that the individual citizen should feel that he can have an impact on political processes, and that governmental organs in turn affect him. The possible effect of the citizen on government is what is commonly termed a sense of political efficacy, and is discussed in the second part of this chapter. To begin with, we consider how Canadians view the impact of government on the country and on the individual.

THE IMPACT OF GOVERNMENT

Federal-Provincial Orientations

In a multi-levelled system of government, we would expect voters to distinguish among the respective tiers, evoking what has been termed "a salience map arranged according to geopolitical units."[1] In the Canadian context, three questions are of particular relevance. Is it

---

1. M. Kent Jennings and Harmon Ziegler, "The Salience of American State Politics," *American Political Science Review* 64 (June 1970): p. 523.

the federal, provincial, or even local government that is perceived as having greatest impact? Is there some distinction made concerning kinds of impact? And most important of all, do regions of the country vary in their perception of impact?

The sampled population was asked, "Thinking now of the most important problems facing Canada today, which government would you say handles most of these, the federal government in Ottawa or the provincial governments?" The largest proportion, almost one-half, selected the federal government, about two and a half times as many as chose the provincial governments. Another quarter answered that both were equally important. As we see from Table 9–1, regional variations were marked, particularly between Quebec and the rest of the country. In Quebec, the largest group of respondents, 37 percent, would not distinguish between the importance of the two levels of government, while about 25 percent each chose either the federal or provincial. Everywhere else more than half the respondents saw the federal government as having greatest significance. Even so, some degree of difference exists for the remaining regions. The Atlantic provinces, for example, were rather less convinced that the federal government alone was most prominent in handling problems facing the nation, while British Columbia followed Quebec in the proportion selecting the provincial government alone. At the same time, the largest numbers of those agreeing to the importance of the federal government were in the western provinces.

Quite a different distribution of responses resulted when the focus was shifted to personal concerns. Faced with the question, "As far as you are concerned personally, which government is more important in affecting how you and your family get on? The one in Ottawa or the one in this province?", provincial governments were mentioned most frequently. In this instance it was westerners rather than those in Quebec who saw the provincial government as most influential. Certainly the largest category of responses in Quebec was "provincial," but again the Quebec sample was more inclined than those elsewhere to say that both levels have equal impact. Ontario is distinctive in that the largest share of its residents, 39 percent, answered that it was the federal government which had most effect on respondents and their families. (See Table 9–2.)

The foregoing items indicate that Canadians differentiate between levels of government according to the nature of the government's impact and also in terms of their region of residence. One way of summarizing the pertinent data is to focus on views of the federal government, as we have done in Chart 9–1. It shows the percent differences between those who saw the federal government as most important in handling problems facing the country and most important in affecting themselves. We use this as a measure of discrepancy

Table 9–1 **Government Handling Most Important Problems Facing Canada, by Region** (Percent)

Residence:	Federal	Provincial	Most Important: Both Equal	Neither	Don't Know	N
Atlantic	52	11	27	1	9	(229)
Quebec	24	25	37	7	7	(793)
Ontario	56	15	17	*	12	(1054)
Prairies	63	12	19	1	5	(395)
British Columbia	59	20	13	2	6	(256)
Total	47	18	24	3	8	(2727)

Table 9–2 **Government Most Important in Affecting Respondent, by Region** (Percent)

Residence:	Federal	Provincial	Most Important: Both Equal	Neither	Don't Know	N
Atlantic	31	40	18	5	5	(229)
Quebec	20	40	25	12	3	(793)
Ontario	39	35	19	1	6	(1054)
Prairies	28	46	20	1	5	(395)
British Columbia	23	58	16	1	3	(256)
Total	30	40	21	5	4	(2727)

Chart 9-1   **Percent difference between national and self-orientation to federal government, by region.**

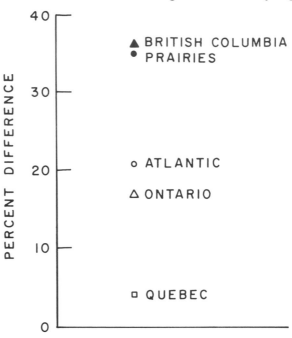

in the assessment of the federal government's role.[2] All the percent differences are positive, which simply means that more people credited the federal government with national rather than personal significance.

In the sense that we are using it here, it was westerners who displayed the greatest amount of discrepancy. While a good-sized majority indicated that they believed that it is the federal government which must cope with the critical problems of the day, they were also attached to the view that it is the provincial government which most significantly touches on their daily lives. Although the amount of difference was considerably smaller than shown in the west, the Atlantic provinces and Ontario too displayed the same pattern of inconsistency. Finally, Quebec residents, with the most lukewarm assessment of the federal government, at least as measured by these questions, turned out to be the most consistent in their response patterns. That is, similar proportions mentioned the federal level as

2. The following discussion relies heavily on a previously unpublished paper by this writer, "The Political Outlook of Canadian Voters in the November, 1965 Election," presented to the 39th Annual Meeting, Canadian Political Science Association, Ottawa, June, 1967.

important in dealing with national problems and in affecting themselves.

These results draw attention to some obvious features of Canadian political life, which, at the time of the survey more than ever, presented the voter with a set of dilemmas. These are dilemmas compounded of a federal system, where all levels of government, but particularly the national, impinge on more and more areas of the social and economic life of the country. At the same time, leadership provided by the federal government had appeared increasingly weaker and less decisive, reflected for one thing by the inability of any single political party in the three elections between 1962 and 1965 to achieve a clear-cut majority.[3] In the provinces, however, government had never seemed so strong, nor leadership so vigorous. Whatever explanation the political analyst may give to these phenomena, they must have been a puzzle to the voter, assuming of course he ever thought of them. But thinking about them or not, they were part of his world, and when called upon, as in the case of this survey, he did respond in the best way he could. If the responses, in turn, reflect a schizoid perspective, this is probably a consequence of the political realities.

But why should it be westerners who were so acutely aware of the dilemmas of their political existence? It is as though they experienced most directly the pull between province and nation. One area of such experience is the political sphere, pertinent details of which have been outlined in Chapters 3 and 6. Politics in these provinces were particularly lively and effective, aided everywhere except Alberta by the existence of a strong opposition party. At the federal level, however, representatives from these provinces had in recent years filled the ranks of the opposition. In the 1965 election, the Liberals won only eight out of seventy seats from the four western provinces. This contrast between effective politics at home and absence from the seats of power in Ottawa may well have had a bearing on voters' perspectives.[4] The conditions we outlined in Chapter 2 also affected the formation and expression of political orientations. Prosperity had come late to the region, and it had not erased memories of the depression and the seemingly exploitive policies of eastern business interests, aided by existing political alignments. The good times came from the richness of the land: from wheat, cattle, oil, gas, lumber. But if each

---

3. On the question of which of eight specific issues had an important effect on respondents' voting decision, the one mentioned most frequently as very important was political leadership, by 63 percent. It was cited by 68 percent in the Prairies and 71 percent in British Columbia.

4. Compare here our findings and interpretations on perceptions of provincial power in Chap. 4.

of the western provinces spewed forth its native richness, as it were, it is the federal government which controlled, cajoled, guided, and suggested how these resources might be converted into cash. The consequences may well have been an ambivalent attitude to the role of the federal government. Finally, we should not overlook the possibility that, while prosperity was helping to break the cocoon of western parochialism, the sentiment remained strong.[5] In these terms, the government in Ottawa was included among outside interests.

Quebec residents were, in the aggregate, much more consistent in their responses to the federal government. This hardly means that Quebeckers had a large-scale commitment to the scope of federal government activities—quite the contrary. Only about one-fifth of the respondents in that province selected the federal government in the two questions under discussion. But this does not reflect the existence of an overwhelming recognition of the importance of the provincial government. Instead, it seems that residents of this province believed that they had a solution to current problems. This did not lie in "going it alone." Rather, it was in some form of partnership between the two levels of government. Thus Quebeckers responded most frequently, especially compared to those in other regions, that they saw federal and provincial governments to be equally important. Whether or not this is realistic is beside the point: we are not enquiring from our sample how they, assuming they even were experts, would manage political affairs. Our concern here is solely with how they perceived the world around them. For Quebeckers, the partnership between governmental levels thus appeared to serve the function of overcoming or avoiding the split view of the political world prominent elsewhere in Canada, especially in the west. This perspective may indeed have been reinforced in Quebec by the experience of both strong provincial government and inclusion in the elected governmental machinery at the national level.

Not much more need be said about Ontario or the Atlantic provinces. As we have noted, they displayed the characteristic split perspective, though in much less exaggerated form than in the west. That Ontario, in particular, with its firm hold on the exercise of national political power, should still reveal a conviction that the daily lives of its residents were more influenced by the operation of the provincial government, is indicative of the strength of the schizoid view of politics current throughout Canada. But that this outlook was less prominent than elsewhere is also indicative of the greater orientation to the federal government present in Ontario.

Respondents were asked to consider the possibility that it was not always possible to vote in all elections. If it were necessary to make

---

5. We recall evidence of western ethnocentrism in Chap. 4.

a choice, would they consider local, national, or provincial elections more important? The answers are shown in Table 9–3. Essentially, responses were polarized in two ways, accounting for about two-thirds of the answers. One-third opted for the importance of national elections. The other refused to choose among the levels of government, answering spontaneously that all three kinds of elections are equally important for voting participation. But it is still noteworthy that federal elections were chosen twice as frequently as provincial ones, and about five times as frequently as local elections. A small percentage of the sample chose combinations of types of elections.

As we might anticipate from the preceding questions, each region again displayed some unique aspects, with Quebec most distinctive. While national elections were not selected by a majority in any of the regions, outside of Quebec they made up the largest category of responses. In Quebec, however, the largest group, 46 percent, said that all elections are equally important. Provincial elections were mentioned next in frequency, but only 18 percent chose national ones.

Ontario was barely edged out by British Columbia for first place in the percent selecting national elections. Yet Ontarians were less likely than those in British Columbia to feel provincial elections were most important: 13 compared to 16 percent. Residents of Ontario were almost as likely to choose local elections as they were provincial ones.

The Prairie provinces ranked third in the percent assigning priority to national elections. Those living in that region gave relatively more significance to provincial elections than their neighbours to either the east or west.

Less than one-third in the Atlantic provinces signified that federal elections were most important. One-quarter chose provincial elections alone, the largest proportion in any region.

These results extend our understanding of the relation between national and individual orientations to the federal government. That is, patterns of response are such to confirm our analysis that a federal system of government contributed to a schizoid view of the world, particularly for those in the west. In the Atlantic provinces, Quebec, and Ontario, similar proportions selected the federal government as crucial in affecting themselves and as the arena for the most critical elections. There is an 11 point difference between these two items in the Prairie provinces and a 22 point discrepancy in British Columbia. If we use as our standard of comparison the percent choosing the federal government as handling the most important problems, then the amount of discrepancy is greater for all regions. Most extreme were the Atlantic provinces, with 21 percent difference, and the Prairies, with 24 percent difference. In other words, at least three of the regions had comparable views of the significance of federal

Table 9–3 **Most Important Kind of Election, by Region** (Percent)

Residence:	Most Important:					Can't
	National	Provincial	Local	All Equal	Other	Choose
Atlantic	31	25	7	21	12	4
Quebec	18	21	4	46	7	3
Ontario	44	13	11	24	5	3
Prairies	39	23	6	24	7	3
British Columbia	45	16	5	27	6	1
Total	34	18	7	31	6	4

elections and the personal impact of the federal government. The westernmost provinces, however, remained most divided in their orientations to the different levels of government. Quebec, in contrast, had consistently the least positive orientation to the federal level.

POLITICAL EFFICACY

Comparative Findings

Kenneth Prewitt has presented a definition of political efficacy that summarizes current uses, including our own.

> The concept of political efficacy is used by students of political behavior to identify a citizen's feelings about the effects of his action on political events. It refers to the person's belief that political and social change can be affected or retarded and that his efforts, alone or in concert with others, can produce desired behavior on the part of political authorities. Efficacy has its origins in social psychology and is closely related to "ego strength," "subjective competence," "self-confidence," and "personal effectiveness." The concept has particular relevance for assessing behavior in democratic systems, where a premium is placed on citizen participation and where there are accessible channels for expressing political needs.[6]

This is also very close to the concept of "political powerlessness," used to describe one form of alienation.[7] We emphasize efficacy here because the measures employed consist of items most commonly used for this purpose, those developed by the Survey Research Center at the University of Michigan. This gives us the advantage of comparability and a standard for evaluating the level of efficacy in Canada. The items do have some shortcomings, however. For one thing, they fail to differentiate between levels of government, a serious handicap when dealing with a federal system of government.[8] Since items required only a simple agree or disagree response, and low efficacy was associated with agreement, we also have the possibility

6. Kenneth Prewitt, "Political Efficacy," *International Encyclopedia of the Social Sciences,* vol. 12 (New York: The Free Press, 1968), p. 225.

7. Ada W. Finifter, "Dimensions of Alienation," *American Political Science Review* 64 (June 1970): 390.

8. For an example of the importance of taking into account the political milieu in assessing efficacy, see Edgar Litt, "Political Cynicism and Political Futility," *The Journal of Politics* 25 (1963): 312-23.

that results were affected by a response set. Yet whatever difficulties these conditions create, they still do not detract from the value of having standard measures of efficacy.[9]

The item producing greatest consensus in the United States and Canada concerned the importance of voting. (See Table 9–4.) Seventy-five percent in Canada and 73 percent in the United States agreed that "Voting is the only way that people like me can have any say about how the government runs things." But what does this actually mean? Is it a sign of potency or lack of it to be able to influence the government through voting? Certainly voting can be a crucial means of influencing the political process, but the rub here is when it is perceived as the only one. "Only," then, is the significant word. The statement in which it is included is designed to measure the extent to which citizens see themselves confined to one source of influence. To do so, however, it relies almost totally on the significance which respondents attached to the word "only." If they did not attribute sufficient importance to it, then agreeing with the statement could well be a measure of efficaciousness rather than the contrary. But for whatever reason, the issue of voting turned out to be

Table 9–4 **Percent Agreeing with Statements Measuring Political Efficacy in Canada and the United States**

	Canada	United States
Voting is the only way that people like me can have any say about how the government runs things.	75	73
Sometimes politics and government seem so complicated that a person like me can't really understand what's going on.	69	66
People like me don't have any say about what the government does.	49	29
I don't think that the government cares much what people like me think.	46	36

Source: American data are from an unpublished survey conducted by the Survey Research Center prior to the 1964 Presidential election. Data were supplied by Philip E. Converse and Linda A. Wilcox.

9. As has been our custom, we employ an item by item analysis, rather than a summary index or scale, in order to distinguish the particular sources of each region's discontent. In the Canadian situation, the items did not form a Guttman scale, although a linkage analysis indicates that they are inter-correlated. Andrew Rojecki, "Political Powerlessness and Attitudes Toward Government: The Canadian Context," unpublished Master's Thesis, Department of Sociology, University of Illinois at Chicago Circle, 1970, pp. 10-11.

the poorest indicator of regional differences. (See Table 9–5.) The maximum range of variation was 5 percent.

Majorities of 69 percent in Canada and 66 percent in the United States also agreed that "Sometimes politics and government seem so complicated that a person like me can't really understand what's going on." There is little question that, with this issue, we have plumbed an area where the grasp of power is very low. Regions were separated by a range of 18 percent, with the Atlantic provinces set apart by the large number who reported a lack of understanding. Quebec is found at the other extreme, with less than two-thirds complaining about the complexity of government. The remaining regions form a middle group.

The statement that ranked third in frequency of agreement was that "People like me don't have any say about what the government does." In Canada 49 percent agreed; in the United States it was 29 percent. This is the first clear evidence of a lower sense of efficacy in Canada. That it should emerge with regard to influencing the government is of great importance. We see it as the negative face of other differences between the two countries. The political values of each country help buttress a host of social institutions, and from that perspective can be seen as performing positive functions for both. For example, the more restrained democracy in Canada helps perpetuate a more law-abiding public generally, and, up until recently at least, greater civility in the conduct of government.[10] But despite such positive effects, or more precisely because people do not normally see the connection between values and social structure, Canadian voters feel they are constrained from having their demands produce an impact on the political leadership.

The Atlantic provinces were sharply differentiated from the rest of the country by the high frequency with which residents thought that ordinary voters have little influence on government. They were separated by 17 percent from second ranking Quebec and by 25 percent from fifth ranking British Columbia.

The preceding item ranked third in Canada but fourth in the United States. In the neighbouring country, voters were more concerned that "the government does not care much what people like me think." Thirty-six percent agreed with this view, but it was still 10 percent fewer than in Canada. Canadians then felt less efficacious due to the perceived indifference of government. On this item Quebeckers had most complaint, with 62 percent agreeing. It produced a particularly large range of difference, with regions divided into three. Quebec was at the most dissatisfied extreme. It was followed,

---

10. Seymour Martin Lipset, "Canada and the United States: A Comparative View," *The Canadian Review of Sociology and Anthropology* 1 (November 1964): 176-77.

Table 9–5 **Percent Agreeing with Statements Measuring Political Efficacy, by Region**

	Atlantic	Quebec	Ontario	Prairies	British Columbia
Voting is the only way	79	77	74	74	76
Politics and government seem so complicated	81	63	69	73	69
People like me don't have any say	67	50	46	48	42
Government doesn't care	54	62	38	38	32
N	(229)	(793)	(1054)	(395)	(256)

but in a category by itself, by the Atlantic provinces, where a majority
supported the statement. In a third group were Ontario and the
western provinces, where about one-third complained about their
lack of influence.

In so far as the Michigan items are reasonable measures of effic-
cacy, we can conclude that Canadians ranked low in the perception
of their ability to influence political processes. There are only two
instances where regions were below the low efficacy totals for the
United States. Three percent fewer in Quebec agreed that govern-
mnt is too complicated and 4 percent fewer in British Columbia saw
the government as indifferent. Comparing only regions, there was
some variation in the relative frequency with which individual items
evoked agreement, but not sufficient to destroy an underlying similarity. If regions are ranked according to the proportions selecting the
least efficacious response, a coefficient of concordance indicates a
basic consistency in the outlooks. W is equal to .57, which is associated with a probability level of .05. The sum of the rankings also
permit us to locate regions with respect to each other. The lowest
sense of power was found in the Atlantic provinces, followed by
Quebec, and then the Prairie provinces. Ontario and British Columbia
possessed the greatest sense of efficacy, and in terms of rankings, were
almost identical.

Efficacy and Education

Previous studies of political efficacy provide clear evidence of a
strong association between it and education.[11] Most relevant are the
Survey Research Center studies using measures identical to our own,
in which education appeared as the principal determinant of a sense
of efficacy.[12] In our survey as well, education was the prime characteristic associated with efficacy.[13] These findings suggest that the
differences found for regions might be accounted for by regional disparities in the educational distribution of residents. The plausibility of
such an argument is supported by aggregate findings, in which
regions can be ranked according to the educational attainment of the
sampled population in ways almost identical to their ranking on
efficacy. In the case of efficacy, this can be done by summing the

---

11. For example, education was "by far the single most important predictor
of powerlessness" in Finifter's study, "Dimensions of Political Alienation,"
p. 399.

12. Angus Campbell, Gerald Gurin, and Warren E. Miller, *The Voter
Decides* (Evanston: Row, Peterson and Co., 1954) pp. 190-92; Angus Camp-
bell, Philip E. Converse, Warren E. Miller, Donald E. Stokes, *The American
Voter* (New York: John Wiley, 1960), pp. 516-20.

13. Rojecki, "Political Powerlessness and Attitudes Toward Government,"
pp. 16-17.

ranks for the four items. The ranking, beginning with the most efficacious region, was British Columbia, Ontario, the Prairies, Quebec,
and the Atlantic provinces. When ranked by the educational achievement of respondents, only the Atlantic provinces and Quebec reversed their order.[14] Yet these kinds of ecological correlations may
be misleading, by obscuring the nature of the association between
educational achievement and a sense of efficacy which exists at the
individual level.

Up to this point in our analysis, we have studiously avoided looking at relations between opinions and the attributes of opinion holders.
Analyses that examine associations between individual attributes
have an underlying model linking the characteristics in question to
the opinion. For example, where the better educated are found to be
more politically efficacious, this is related to the consequences of the
educational experience. On the average, increased education leads
to greater access to information, verbal facility, greater belief in one's
ability to control events, and so on. That higher education is generally
associated with higher income and more desirable occupations is also
important, guaranteeing in this way entry into higher social class
positions. All of these combine to give the educated person a sense of
his political potency. If we do not search for these kinds of associations and the explanations that stem from them, it is because the
problems they handle are not ours. The antecedent conditions of
opinions are interesting to us only in so far as they reflect on regionalism. Opinions, in the sense of their distribution, become for us
characteristics of regions, and not just of the individuals who hold
them. But because analyses of individual responses are so customary,
and these are supported at the aggregate level by our own study, the
need for a closer look at the association between education, region,
and efficacy seemed pressing.

If education is the prime determinant of feelings of efficacy, then
in all regions we should find the same linear effects. The tendency
toward a linear association appears for all items and in all regions,
but with some important discrepancies.[15] (See Chart 9–2.) Depar-

---

14. The ranking derived from the education of our respondents is identical
to that from a much larger labour force survey in 1966. Economic Council of
Canada, *Sixth Annual Review: Perspective 1975* (Ottawa: Queen's Printer,
1969), p. 130.

15. Years of schooling have been divided into three categories. The low
includes those with from none to eight years of schooling. The medium
category encompasses those with from nine to thirteen years of education. In
some provinces, this would include persons with up to two years of college,
while in Ontario it signifies the completion of high school. Such overlapping
of categories is inevitable in Canada, where educational standards are set by
each province. Those with fourteen or more years of schooling, which everywhere would mean at least some college, are placed in the high category. Most
important, using finer educational categories does not affect our results.

Chart 9–2   **Relation between education and political efficacy, by region. (percent agreeing)**

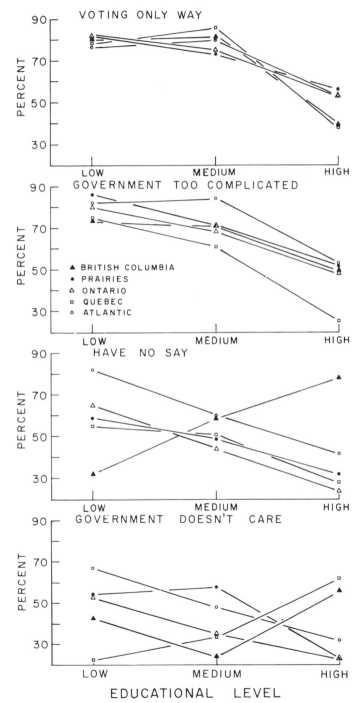

EDUCATIONAL   LEVEL

tures from linearity occurred everywhere except in Ontario, taking on most unique forms in Quebec and British Columbia.

Non-linearity is present for three of the four efficacy items in British Columbia. The importance attached to voting was identical for those we have categorized as belonging to low and medium educational groups. But as we can see for all regions, the spread between these two educational groups was minor everywhere, not exceeding eight percent. For this item, which we are in any case somewhat reluctant to interpret, the division between educational groups does not occur until at least the point of some college education. Comparing responses for those with or without college education does not reveal any departures from the expected pattern.

The most striking aspect of responses in British Columbia was the reversal in the percentages who believed they had no say in what the government does. In this instance it is the best educated who expressed the least sense of power. In contrast to our sample elsewhere in Canada, those with least schooling had least complaint.

The best educated again revealed greatest dissatisfaction with the interest shown by government in what they think. Here, however, we have a curvilinear relationship, with the medium educational category containing the most satisfied.

On the basis of these two items, we have evidence of the greater sense of alienation through powerlessness experienced by the best educated in British Columbia. How much importance we attach to these findings must be partially conditioned by the sample used. There were only eighteen unweighted cases of respondents with fourteen or more years of schooling, and this alone urges caution in our interpretation. Yet if only on the basis of their more usual response pattern to the issue of the complexity of government, we can assume that, though few in number, the better educated are not completely atypical. Their dissatisfaction was perhaps a reflection, as Martin Robin suggests, of the disdain of those in higher class positions, and among them especially the well-educated, for the methods and manners of the then reigning provincial Social Credit government.[16]

Quebec displayed two discrepant patterns, one of which relates to the importance of voting. But as we suggested earlier, differences between low and medium educational groups are not great, nor is it completely clear how respondents understood this issue. More important, and of more striking proportions, were the feelings that the government was indifferent to the views of ordinary voters, a form

---

16. Martin Robin, "British Columbia: The Politics of Class Conflict," in Martin Robin, ed., *Canadian Provincial Politics* (Scarborough: Prentice-Hall of Canada, 1972), pp. 27-68.

of powerlessness which increased with education. We assume that at issue was the perceived unresponsiveness of government by those very people whose education and training had led them to expect most. With the likelihood of high expectations, there was also the likelihood of high disappointment. Whatever the reasons, we found a significant point of similarity in the views of the best educated in both British Columbia and Quebec.

The remaining reversals in the orderly progression of increased education and efficacy occurred in the Atlantic provinces and the Prairies. In the easternmost region, medium education was associated with more concern about voting. More interesting was the finding that the complexity of government was unusually troublesome to all education groups, with the medium education category as much disturbed by this as the low category. In the Prairies, the apparent indifference of government affected the two less educated groups about equally, such that their views were in sharp contrast with those of the college trained.

The review of all these aberrant cases was made to illustrate one of the ways in which education is limited as a predictor of political efficacy in the context of Canadian regionalism. While the educational effect was certainly strong, it did not wipe out the significance of the regional setting in which voters acted. Further evidence comes from the regional differences in the ways in which educational groups were polarized, and in the items producing the greatest amount of polarization. If we compare the education group most in agreement with that least in agreement (usually, but not always the least and best educated), we found polarization greatest in Quebec, followed by British Columbia, the Atlantic provinces, Ontario, and the Prairies. The items producing greatest division were voting and the lack of influence in British Columbia. Lack of influence on government was also highly polarizing in Ontario and the Atlantic provinces, but in exactly the opposite way from British Columbia. In Quebec, meanwhile, the complexity of government was the source of greatest cleavage.

For the most part, we have demonstrated Canadian conformity with research in other countries, linking low levels of education and feelings of inefficacy. The political consequences of this association are manifested in the lack of interest and participation in political processes by the poorly educated. At the same time, there are undeniable independent effects of factors other than education on efficacy, factors which in combination create each regional milieu and serve to differentiate regional political orientations. Of particular concern are those intimations of tension in British Columbia and Quebec, where the best educated expressed grave impotency. The poorly educated may reveal their impotency through apathy and withdrawal. The best educated are much less likely to do the same. Their impotency can become a goad to seeking means, even radical ones, to overcome their lack of impact on the political system.[17]

Efficacy and Regional Power

We now have three ways of looking at power: the level of efficacy found in regions, the perceived power of regions (Chapter 4), and the actual power of regions (Chapter 3). The first of these is a characteristic of citizens within regions, actual power is a property of regional political systems, while perceptions of this is a characteristic both of citizens and the system.

In Chapter 4 we presented a simple causal chain linking actual and perceived power. It was our contention that objective conditions would affect respondents' evaluations of their region. We found this association to be strong only for the two most powerful provinces, Ontario and Quebec. For the remainder it was necessary to suggest that other factors intervened between conditions as we described them and their perception. These included specific aspects of the political system, such as the modest benefits won by the Atlantic provinces despite their loyalty to the federal government and the strength of provincial politics in the western provinces. We also suggested that some non-political conditions might have had a bearing on the perception of residents, for example, the depressed situation of the Atlantic provinces and the expansive economy of British Columbia.

Comparing perceptions of regional power with that of personal power raises some new issues. It is clear that there is no necessary connection between the way an individual sees himself and the way he views his political environment. At least three relationships are possible. These are described mainly in terms of the individual voter, and while our analysis is directed to regional units, the following discussion should help provide explanations for the ways opinions are generated and become interrelated.

The first possible association between the two kinds of perception would arise from an underlying disposition to see the world and oneself similarly with respect to power, such that either everyone possesses some power or no one does. That is, to the extent that power is a salient characteristic, it will be attributed both to oneself and to others. This disposition could be a psychological characteristic; it could as well be a consequence of the nature of the social system in which the individual operates.

The preceding relationship would appear unusual, if not im-

---

17. Our reasoning is analogous to that in Finifter's paradigm on the relation between alienation and behaviour. Finifter, "Dimensions of Political Alienation," p. 407.

possible, to those who conceive of power as a "zero-sum" phenomenon. According to this view, power is a limited quantity, and what A possesses necessarily deprives B. This conception is not normally used in speaking of the relation between individuals and the state, but there is no reason not to. If we consider power in this light, two possible relationships emerge. In the first, individuals are powerful but the political system is not. This is conceivable if we restrict ourself to the organs of government. Then the slogan of present-day radicals, "all power to the people," makes sense. It has been a refrain of other political ideologies, most notably that of populism. A strong body of citizens but a weak government was to be ensured by such mechanisms as initiative, referendum, and recall.

The opposite set of circumstances—a strong government and a weak citizenry—is typical of authoritarian forms of rule. There the population is subservient and ineffectual, but it may feel itself as much protected as controlled by the all-powerful state.

Finally, the way in which power is viewed in one context may have a halo effect for other contexts. Thus the power attributed to one's region may pervade the assessment of one's own position, or alternatively, the power attributed to oneself may spill over to the evaluation of the home region. Lucian Pye, for example, in discussing the emergence of a personal and a national identity, sees them as linked in an interactive process. "The search for individual identity hinges on the existence of a national identity, and the latter calls for a coherent and consensus-bound political process; but people cannot fundamentally respect their political spokesmen when they are not sure that they can respect themselves, and so back to the issue of personal integrity and identity."[18]

Making the simplest comparisons between regional and personal perceptions of power, that is, by treating them as components of a four-fold table, we obtained the full range of possibilities in Canada. In the first case, the region was perceived as powerful and citizens felt powerful. This was the situation of Ontario. The centrality of Ontario, its prominence in the national government, and its economic achievements led residents to recognize its power. That they also saw themselves in this light suggests that potency is pervasive through the social system.

The mirror image of Ontario was the Atlantic provinces. There the region was perceived as low in power and residents had similar perceptions of their own efficacy. These are views befitting a subject people, overwhelmed by their poor economic prospects and ineffective

---

18. Lucian W. Pye, *Politics, Personality, and Nation Building: Burma's Search for Identity* (New Haven: Yale University Press, 1962), p. 4.

political means for overcoming their problems. The primary feeling here is one of impotence.

We suggested that where citizens perceive their political system as powerful but see themselves as low in efficacy we have the outlook appropriate to an authoritarian regime. To the extent that we can speak of a region in terms of a political system, it is just this combination of attitudes that we found in Quebec. It provides the psychological milieu compatible with the growth of fascistic movements which have plagued Quebec at various times in its history. That these have generally been exponents of ultra–nationalism does not eliminate their essentially totalitarian view of the state.[19] In recent years these same propensities have been described as motivating Pierre Trudeau's entry into politics as a Liberal.

> Discerning in the new extreme nationalism a threat of neofascism, he saw, in 1964, the clear possibility that the new anti-clericalism in Quebec could mean merely the substitution of "national sectarianism" for "religious sectarianism."[20] Having helped to prepare his province for its release from the Duplessis bondage, Trudeau was appalled to see the direction being taken by a steadily growing number of his compatriots —a direction which he felt compelled to dub a "counterrevolution."[21] It was to stem the now common habit of looking upon and treating Ottawa as a foreign power that this brilliant and essentially non-political sophisticate plunged into the icy waters of federal politics in Quebec.[22]

But fascism in whatever form has not been a major threat in Quebec. Perhaps even more relevant are views of government, including the provincial government, as an external force whose behaviour is not entirely within the same world as the voters. For example, "Government expenditures made in the ordinary course of administration for such things as public works or social services have usually been looked upon, not as a right of the citizen, but as a special favour or privilege granted by the government. The party in power has a particular advantage as its expenditure of government money, partic-

---

19. For some examples see Mason Wade, *The French Canadians, 1760-1967,* rev. ed. (Toronto: Macmillan, 1968), pp. 906-10.

20. Pierre Elliott Trudeau, "Quebec Neo-Fascism?", *Canadian Forum* 44 (July, 1964).

21. Pierre Elliott Trudeau, "Separatist Counter-Revolutionaries," in *Federalism and the French Canadians* (Toronto: Macmillan, 1968), pp. 204-12.

22. Kenneth McNaught, "The National Outlook of English-Speaking Canadians," in Peter Russell, ed., *Nationalism in Canada* (Toronto: McGraw-Hill Co. of Canada 1966), p. 70.

ularly at election time, enables it to pose as a benefactor whose generosity should be rewarded by voting it back into office."[23] Without pushing our own bits of evidence too far, it is noteworthy that they are compatible with observations made at other times and by observers from different perspectives.

Our final case is the opposite of Quebec, where regions were perceived as low in power but personal efficacy as high. In the Prairies, perceptions of regional power were low and self-perceptions of efficacy moderate. In British Columbia, perceptions of that province's power were moderate and self efficacy high. It is again in conformity with our theoretical discussion of the zero-sum conception of power that this particular association of attitudes should have been present in the western provinces. It is there that populism, with its emphasis on participatory democracy, had been strongest. These views have been most closely associated with the CCF, the United Farmers, and the Progressives. In all of these political movements, a politically-educated, activist population was conceived as the ideal check on traditional parties and the remoteness of government. For example, Morton describes one of the themes underlying the emergence of the Progressives as a belief that "The people was in its nature good, all power belonged to the electorate, but existing government was bad and the will of the electorate was thwarted."[24] This same distrust of traditional government, although without an emphasis on participation by the electorate, also characterized Social Credit. Macpherson calls the approach advocated in Alberta "plebiscitarian democracy," in which voters were enjoined to give their support to Social Credit. At this point a Rousseau-like notion of the General Will would take over, and leaders could be trusted to act in the best interests of the population, unhampered by restrictions on what policies to follow. Along with this abandonment of more usual conceptions of democracy, Social Credit continued to foster a suspicion of the older parties and the forms of government they practiced.[25] Comparing the Prairies and British Columbia, we would assume that the greater sense of personal efficacy in the latter was related both to greater affluence and to the stronger militancy of working class movements.[26]

---

23. Herbert F. Quinn, *The Union Nationale* (Toronto: University of Toronto Press, 1963), p. 19.

24. W. L. Morton, *The Progressive Party in Canada* (Toronto: University of Toronto Press, 1967), p. 16.

25. C. B. Macpherson, *Democracy in Alberta: Social Credit and the Party System,* 2nd ed. (Toronto: University of Toronto Press, 1962).

26. Martin Robin, "The Social Basis of Party Politics in British Columbia," *Queen's Quarterly* 72 (Winter 1966): 675-90.

EFFICACY AND THE IMPACT OF THE FEDERAL GOVERNMENT

The underlying rationale for examining the relation between government and voter is one basic to democratic theory: that voters perceive governmental actions as affecting them and, in turn, feel that they can affect the government. Relating this to the measures used in this chapter, we would anticipate a strong correlation between high political efficacy and orientation to the federal government. Wherever this association occurs it indicates that citizens feel confident in their roles and free to participate in the government of the whole of Canada. That is, despite the importance of provincial governments, an orientation to the federal level recognizes that, at least since World War II, the federal government has taken on increasingly more pervasive activities, particularly in the fields of social welfare and economic control. Comparatively excessive concern with other levels of government, regardless of their actual importance, is a form of parochialism that detracts from the psychological capability to cope with political realities.[27]

Table 9–6 presents the overall rankings for political efficacy and orientation to the federal government. Although a measure of association is not quite statistically significant (the Spearman rank correlation coefficient is .725), we can discern an east-west cleavage, in which Ontario is similar to the western provinces. In the west there is a stronger orientation to the federal government and a greater sense of political efficacy.

It would be deceptive to conclude in such a straightforward fashion,

Table 9–6 **Regional Rankings on Political Efficacy and Orientation to Federal Government**

	Efficacy	Federal Orientation
British Columbia	1	2.5
Ontario	2	1
Prairies	3	2.5
Quebec	4	5
Atlantic provinces	5	4

Source: Rankings are derived from the sum of ranks for the 4 efficacy items and the 3 federal orientation items.

---

27. For example, Jennings and Zeigler found that those Americans who attributed greatest salience to state politics were also low on interpersonal trust. Jennings and Zeigler, "Salience of American State Politics," p. 528.

since our findings are hardly this consistent. As we recall, views of the federal government were quite unstable, depending on the issue in question. For example, regions were not ordered consistently in ranking the three items on levels of government. [28] One of our most striking findings was what we earlier termed a schizoid view of government, especially prominent in the west. Yet it is in that area that efficacy was particularly high. There seems to be no simple way to connect these two phenomena. It is not as though westerners displayed a strong and consistent orientation to the provincial level of government, such that their efficacy was associated with high governmental output from that source. Our reason for terming the perspective "schizoid" was exactly because respondents did not assume one or other level was always most significant. To some extent, of course, this is the reality of a federal system of government where there is a division of powers, but it was not anticipated that respondents recognized this in their answers to our quite unspecific questions. We are, in any case, not looking at the relation among comments made by individual respondents, which may of course be quite different from the pattern for entire regions. Based on this aggregate level of interpretation, we conclude that the western provinces displayed a high level of efficacy *despite* their inconsistent orientation to the federal government. We can only assume that those factors we described earlier which promote participatory democracy, as well as strong provincial governments, compensate for the lack of firm attachment to the federal structure.

The best illustrations of our hypothesis on the relation between efficacy and the impact of the federal government are provided by Ontario and the Atlantic provinces. In the case of Ontario, the relationship was a positive one. It is true that there was some attitudinal inconsistency in Ontario as well, but compared to all regions except Quebec, the schizoid perspective there was lowest. The Atlantic provinces demonstrated the inverse relationship, in which orientation to the federal government was comparatively low, as was efficacy.

Quebec was unique not only for the consistency of opinions found there, but also for the special quality of its attitudes toward government. Residents did not emphasize the provincial level, as we might have expected, but shared the responsibility for the impact of government between the federal and provincial levels. Again we would have to say that there is some truth in this characterization, but this did not provide much benefit to Quebec residents. We are not concerned with

---

28. The coefficient of concordance for the three items was .60. The sum of squares associated with it is not significant at the .05 level. With $m = 3$ and $n = 5$, $p = .117$. Even so, we used the sum of ranks to assign overall ranks for regions, as in Table 9–6.

the accuracy of perceptions, but rather with those attitudes which we can expect to be linked with a sense of personal potency. These are primarily ones that emphasize the federal level, not only because of the reality of its power and impact, but also because identification with it would help overcome the parochialism of region as it involved the citizen in the government of Canada, and not just that of his own province. But even an identification with the provincial level could contribute to a sense of efficacy—witness the western provinces. The fact that both were lacking in Quebec makes evidence of low efficacy particularly critical. It means, for one thing, that Quebec did not share in even the modicum of consensus about the impact of government that we could attribute to other Canadians. It means as well that the Quebec citizen felt peculiarly isolated. He was neither influenced by government in the way that most other citizens understand, nor could he influence government himself.

STRAINS IN POLITICAL ORIENTATIONS

The analysis undertaken in these last three chapters reveal that there was no single set of political orientations that could be said to characterize Canadian society. Each region, and possibly even finer divisions within regions, had its own perspective on the political process. Earlier, in developing our concept of regionalism, we stated that such differences were "not in themselves either good or bad, nor unequivocal sources of inequality. But their results are still of importance, since they create the environment for regional group-consciousness and for the mobilization of political action on the basis of regional interests, defined independently of any overriding national interests. In this sense, too, greater differentiation should mean stronger regionalism." While we continue to surmise that regionally-specified political orientations can be one of the sources of regional group consciousness and regionally–directed group action, we also believe these differences suggest additional consequences. In particular, the character of the regional orientations are associated with a number of strains in the political fabric of Canada. Looking at the orientations in terms of our categories of analysis, we have isolated six sources of strain. These in turn affect regions differentially.

One source of strain results from a cognitive dimension of political awareness, in which political knowledge is relatively low and a localistic view of party leaders is high. The Prairie provinces and British Columbia manifested this pattern most clearly. Stress can also be expected where the machinery of government, in the sense of differentiated political parties and majority rule, are not highly valued. Here we had to qualify our conclusions, since it was apparent that only Ontario possessed the full complement of traditional values. Yet the absense of regard for these customary political arrangements did suggest some strain elsewhere, most acutely in Quebec.

We experienced less uncertainty in interpreting the remaining orientations. For example, a highly critical attitude toward political authorities could readily be presumed to lead to questions of their legitimacy. Such critical views were most prominent in Quebec, and to a slightly lesser extent, British Columbia. In the same manner, a lack of trust in political authorities and the machinery of government could also undermine their legitimacy. The manifestation of such sentiments in high levels of political cynicism was strongest in the Atlantic provinces followed by British Columbia.

What the appropriate orientations to the various levels of government should be may be open to question. But there need be little doubt that discordant orientations, as we found between self interest and the interests of the nation, will be troublesome. Such discordance was most prominently displayed in the Prairie provinces and British Columbia. In addition, the situation of Quebec was also presumed to be stressful due to the unique pattern of orientations displayed by voters there.

Finally, the absence of widespread feelings of political efficacy can be associated with incipient strain, occurring in our study most often in the Atlantic provinces and Quebec. The Quebec case was a special cause for concern because of evidence of a sense of powerlessness among the best educated.

Not only then was each region characterized by different orientations, but everywhere except Ontario there were sources of tension in the relations between citizens and the total polity. Of the six themes we have discussed, we have interpreted stress in two instances in the Atlantic and Prairie provinces, and in four instances in Quebec and British Columbia. It is these latter two provinces which stand out because of their potential for conflict within the Canadian political system.

CHAPTER

Regional political orientations

THE PARTISAN CONTEXT

Running through our argument on the extent and implications of
regional differentiation has been a recurring concern with the party
system and with partisan behaviour. In Chapter 3, for example, we
looked at patterns of support from the perspective of the voting
public, and representation from the perspective of the governing
party. Chapter 6 tackled the structure of the party system, emphasizing the kinds of party choices available, and the attachments of voters
to these choices. Chapter 5 considered the relation between parties
and views of voters, taking the influence of parties to be either the
direct result of actively shaping opinions, or indirectly, through the
attraction of those with particular viewpoints into a partisan fold.
In all instances, whether treating structural characteristics, the
behaviour of voters or that of parties, political parties have been
viewed as a major channel for the expression of regional interests.

In the preceding three chapters we have put aside this interest
in parties to consider the ways in which the residents of Canada's
five regions describe the political world in which they operate. The
dominant responses found set each region apart, if not in gross terms,
at least with sufficient clarity to permit speaking of regional political
orientations. We see these as contributing to a milieu in which the
recognition of common interests and concerns can emerge into a
group consciousness, one with potential for political mobilization. In

the conclusion to the previous chapter, however, we went even further and made more specific judgements on the content of the orientations. That is, we interpreted the existence of particular constellations of opinions to be indicative of strains in the political fabric. At this point we can return to our concern with political parties and assess their relation to orientations, particularly to implications of political strain.

The relation between parties and orientations can best be understood in the context of two extreme situations, neither presented as an accurate description of reality, but as benchmarks for assessing reality. In the first case, the evidence of strain is accompanied by widespread consensus, such that parties are undifferentiated on these issues. In the second, strain is associated with strong partisanship.

To speak of an association between parties and orientations is not to say that parties are necessarily bound by the views of their supporters, or absolutely constrained in the policies they present. But it has been our contention, spelled out in detail in Chapter 5, that there is *some* tie between parties and voters, otherwise the interaction between the need for support and the expression of support, and the expression of demands and the response to demands, becomes virtually meaningless. Our concern in that chapter, repeated here, was with only one possible link between parties and voters, that relating party influence to voters' opinions. We feel no need to repeat the qualifications presented in Chapter 5, except to say that "influence" is broadly conceived, to refer to a channelling of viewpoints into partisan lines.

This brings us back to the first situation of widespread consensus. An absence of difference among party supporters is not the same, of course, as a lack of party differences. The issues examined may have little political content; voters may be out of step with the positions of their parties; or the questions may tap such general concerns that they strike a responsive chord in everyone. To the extent that the issues we have examined in the last three chapters are political ones, then we have every reason to expect that they will have partisan content. We have no way of testing the official positions of parties on these, and certainly it is possible that they are of widespread concern. The only means available to us for detecting party positions is through the views of voters. In situations where supporters do not vary along party lines, we must conclude, that for *voters,* parties are not differentiated channels for the expression of their concerns. When this occurs, to the degree that their concerns are serious ones, we have a gap, either structural or psychological, in the legitimate avenues for expressing demands and dissatisfactions. One might argue that issues of general interest will simply find their way into the programs of all parties. That may be so, but just as everyone may say he is for flag and country, for peace and motherhood, and not truly say anything, this is also the case for parties that share a unified rhetoric. In those areas where there are no differences between parties, they are failing to perform their crucial role as providers of political alternatives.[1]

What about the opposite extreme, where orientations representing political strain are *always* associated with different parties? If the previous situation implies lack of choice for voters, this suggests excessively clearcut choice. If the previous situation indicates a lack of partisan direction for what are clearly political issues, the current one indicates an excessive concern to politicize everything. Here the premium on partisan differentiation is associated with population polarization.

The extent to which each region resembles one or other of these extremes is examined using the full twenty-five orientation items. (This still recognizes their limitations in covering the range of issues with relevance both to regions and parties.) The association between parties and orientations is based on a review of the distribution of responses within regions, augmented with measures of association introduced in Chapter 5. Proportional entropy measures are used to evaluate the degree of association between parties and each orientation item. To keep the amount of data presented here within reasonable limits, only those items which highlight our analysis will be presented in tabular form. In general, these are items which show both considerable percentage difference among party supporters, and high entropy measures, indicating an association between party and opinion. Our conclusions are always based, however, on a full review of the data.

THE ATLANTIC PROVINCES

In the Atlantic provinces there were no major differences in orientations to the political process. This degree of relative opinion homogeneity is a characteristic of some durability and one that emerged with respect to quite different political issues, as we have demonstrated in earlier research.[2] At that time our argument was that similar conditions of life, encompassing limited economic opportunities, high out-migration, and little stimulation from immigrants, led to similarities in outlook. Here, with fresh data, we can better examine

---

1. Georges Lavau, "Partis et systèmes politiques: interactions et fonctions," *Canadian Journal of Political Science* II (March 1969): 38-39.

2. Mildred A. Schwartz, *Public Opinion and Canadian Identity* (Berkeley: University of California Press, 1967), p. 146ff.

the political meaning of the low level of association between parties and orientations.

Concern in this area with party differentiation was relatively low, and this is associated with some differences among parties. Party differences have been measured by three items, displayed in Table 10–1. Not much can be said about NDP supporters, yet their inclinations to be more differentiating than others appeared to be consistent with what we would expect for generally more distinctive third parties. The remaining response patterns were not totally consistent. While Conservatives were much more rejecting of all other parties, including the Liberals, and more inclined than the Liberals to feel that it makes a difference which party forms the government, they were less likely to see some difference between federal parties. In the latter instance, the proportional entropy measure is negligible, indicating that the findings are too close to an equal division to be statistically reliable. The remaining items, however, provide evidence that politics in this area had produced considerable animosity among supporters of the Conservatives. Unlike other regions, those who voted for one major party excluded the other from their realm of choices proportionately more often than they excluded the minor parties.

We recall from Chapter 8 that political cynicism was the rule in the Atlantic provinces, exceeding that of any other region. Yet we see in Table 10–2 that these cynical sentiments did not pervade the supporters of different parties to the same extent. Conservatives and the few NDP in our sample were considerably more likely than Liberals to believe that the government can be trusted to do what is right only some of the time. While this is the only aspect of cynicism in which party supporters were so different, Liberals and Conservatives were contrasted on two other items. There was less chance of finding the former among those agreeing that the people running the government are a little crooked and do not seem to know what they are doing. Only on the issue of attention to big interests were Liberals as cynical as Conservatives.

The most clearcut results of our study, many of which have been long familiar, concern the economic disabilities of the Atlantic provinces. These existed along with residents' sharp recognition of their relative, as well as their absolute, deprivation. In these chapters we have found evidence of political grievances as well. As yet, however, no effective channels for the political expression of these grievances had been developed. There had been no rejection of the traditional components of the regime as it is structured in Canada. Federalism and majority government remained the norms for voters here. While the similarity in outlook among the supporters of the major parties attested to the pervasiveness of the problems and values existing in

Table 10–1 **Party Differentiation by Past Vote: Atlantic** (percent)

	1965 Vote			Proportional Entropy Reduction
	Liberal	Conservative	NDP	
There is a difference which party governs	40	46	(80)	.028
Differences between parties	53	45	(63)	.001
Would not vote for some party	66	86	(75)	.044
N	(100)	(83)	(8)	

Table 10–2 **Percent Agreeing with Statements Measuring Political Cynicism, by Past Vote: Atlantic**

	1965 Vote			Proportional Entropy Reduction
	Liberal	Conservative	NDP	
At least some government officials pay more attention to big shots	75	76	(86)	.003
Quite a few people running the govt. don't seem to know what they are doing	54	61	(88)	.017
Govt. can be trusted only some of the time to do what is right	28	48	(50)	.030
People in govt. waste a lot of money collected in taxes	37	42	(63)	.008
Quite a few of the people running the govt. are a little crooked	32	46	(50)	.016
N	(100)	(83)	(8)	

the east, the lack of differentiation also reflected the absence of viable political alternatives.

Voters here were not lacking in political insight.[3] They were highly knowledgeable of local conditions, if we can generalize from the two items on candidate knowledge. They recognized the restricted nature of national leaders' regional identity, though not to the extent of voters elsewhere in Canada, yet they saw themselves as shut off even from the compensation of having a political figure most attached to them.

It is difficult to capture from survey data of these sort the personal dimensions of politics, but they do communicate some sense of the futility which voters must feel. Of the two major parties, the Conservatives probably had a greater potential for capitalizing on the mood of voters, simply because they were more disaffected, but the critical question of course was whether the Conservative party, either in Ottawa or the provinces, had the resources and discipline to speak to the problems of the economically and politically disinherited. This would seem to be a much more acceptable role to the NDP, and one even more compatible with the views of its supporters. Yet traditionally weak support from voters in this area makes it difficult, though not inconceivable, that the NDP adopt a major role in offering solutions to the problems endemic to the Atlantic provinces.

QUEBEC

Party supporters in Quebec were not sharply polarized in their political orientations. This conclusion is partly the result of excluding Créditistes from our statistical analysis. On the basis of comparisons among three parties, Quebec ranked next to the Atlantic provinces in the extent of association between party and the orientation items. The character of the differences found here, however, highlighted some of the political uniqueness of this province.

Awareness

Questions tapping political awareness revealed two kinds of differences, one important and the other much less so. When asked about winning candidates' name and party, the less knowledgeable NDP were separated from the remainder. In the case of party, the difference among those correctly naming the party of the winning candidate may have been trivial, even though it produced a large proportional

---

3. Compare Market Facts of Canada Limited, *The Maritimes and Maritime Union: An Opinion Study* (Fredericton: Maritime Union Study, 1970), pp. 33-44.

entropy reduction, since large majorities in all parties could correctly answer this question. But in knowing the winner's name, even though we were still dealing with majorities, NDP voters did indeed seem to be surprisingly ill-informed, considering their high level of education and general enthusiasm.

Of special importance in Table 10–3 is the regional identity of party leaders. While we find only Créditistes who attached their leader to Quebec, as we would expect, this is in fact not the source of the party associations recorded by the entropy measures. It is instead the result of comparisons among the other three parties. Almost one-quarter of the Liberal supporters identified Mr. Pearson with their province. We must conclude that this was a consequence of the centrality of Quebeckers in the Liberal party rather than an attribute of Mr. Pearson himself, since through all his years of government and diplomatic service, he was barely able to deliver a speech in French. Though our comparisons are based on small numbers, even the Scottish-born, Saskatchewan-based Tommy Douglas evoked more sense of attachment with Quebec than did Mr. Diefenbaker. As we noted in Chapter 3, during Mr. Diefenbaker's tenure as prime minister, French-speaking Quebeckers felt themselves particularly alienated from him and his party.

Party Differentiation

In general, perception of differences among parties tended to be low in Quebec, somewhat similar to the situation in the Atlantic provinces. The most interesting party differences in Table 10–4 are those evoked by feelings that there was at least some difference between federal parties. NDP voters were most divided from others in the extent of their perception of differences. This same pattern appeared with respect to some party that would not be among possible voting choices. It is quite consistent with the values of the NDP and its position as a minor party that its supporters should manifest most differentiating capacity. What is not so evident is why Créditistes, in essentially the same position, did not share this capacity. We might surmise, as we did earlier in Chapter 8, that voters in Quebec, by not being much concerned about party differentiation (or about majority government), were revealing their lack of commitment to some traditional values of the political system. In this regard, it should not be surprising then that the more protest-oriented Créditistes manifested this by undervaluing party differences.

Authorities

Members of Parliament received their poorest rating in Quebec. The province-wide norms for MPs doing a pretty good job were 23 percent for the Liberals, 13 for the Conservatives, 20 for the NDP, and

Table 10–3 **Political Awareness by Past Vote: Quebec** (percent)

	Liberal	1965 Vote Conservative	NDP	Créditiste	Proportional Entropy Reduction*
Know candidate's name	77	83	67	80	.009
Know candidate's party	94	89	83	91	.035
Identify own leader with region	24	2	7	77	.080
N	(357)	(97)	(70)	(65)	

*Créditistes are excluded

Table 10–4 **Party Differentiation by Past Vote: Quebec** (percent)

	Liberal	1965 Vote Conservative	NDP	Créditiste	Proportional Entropy Reduction*
There is a difference which party governs	40	32	41	43	.003
Would not vote for some party	84	87	94	85	.016
Differences between parties	58	59	79	57	.015
N	(357)	(97)	(70)	(65)	

*Créditistes are excluded

17 for the Créditistes. In Table 10–5, this rating from their own supporters was 35 percent Liberal, 33 Conservative, 64 NDP, and 59
Créditistes. Here we have an instance of sharp division between
major and minor parties, in which the latter came out much more
favourably. Direct criticisms of political authorities did not, however,
follow these alignments. Instead we found the ruling Liberals to be
less inclined to offer criticisms. In Quebec the NDP did not have a
primarily working class social base at the time of the 1965 election, a
fact reflected in the low level of criticism directed at excessive
numbers of intellectuals by that party's supporters.

Cynicism

Relative to other Canadians, feelings of cynicism were at a moderate
level in Quebec. It now appears, from Table 10–6, that these marginals disguised considerable internal differentiation along party
lines. Only the issue of lack of understanding revealed a general
consensus. Otherwise, we see a distinct cleavage between Liberals
and other party supporters, with the former much less likely to give
cynical responses. In contrast, Conservatives and the Créditistes were
among the most cynical groups in the country. The NDP were
inclined to be less cynical, but still considerably more so than the
Liberals.

Federalism

We found Quebec to be unique in its lack of federal-provincial discordance, but this was related to an unusually low orientation to the
federal government. These opinions pervaded the Quebec climate,
minimizing party differences. One exception to cross-party consensus
emerged in choice of the provincial government as having greater
impact on the voter. This was the response of 50 percent of the NDP,
43 percent of the Liberals, 41 percent of the Créditistes, and 29
percent of the Conservatives. The proportional entropy reduction is
only a modest .012, reflecting the numeric dominance of the Liberals,
augmented by the similarly-oriented NDP. Since NDP voters also,
like the Liberals, were more inclined to see the importance of the
federal level for handling problems and in choosing elections, this
resulted in their having the most schizoid perspective in the province.
If the NDP voters overselected the provincial government in a sense,
then in the same sense, the Conservatives underchose it. That is,
unlike other party supporters, Conservatives did not compensate for
their low federal orientation by a high orientation to the provincial
government. Instead, in all three items pertaining to federalism, they
most often adhered to the position that both levels of government
were equal in importance. This viewpoint, while partially descriptive

Table 10–5 **Opinions of Political Authorities by Past Vote: Quebec** (percent)

	Liberal	1965 Vote Conservative	NDP	Créditiste	Proportional Entropy Reduction*
Own party MPs doing pretty good job	35	33	64	59	.032
MPs soon lose touch	63	76	79	71	.016
Too many intellectuals in government	39	57	26	62	.015
N	(357)	(97)	(70)	(65)	

*Créditistes are excluded.

Table 10–6 **Percent Agreeing with Statements Measuring Political Cynicism, by Past Vote: Quebec**

	Liberal	1965 Vote Conservative	NDP	Créditiste	Proportional Entropy Reduction*
At least some government officials pay more attention to big shots	72	89	80	83	.024
Quite a few people running the govt. don't seem to know what they are doing	51	51	59	49	.002
Govt. can be trusted only some of the time to do what is right	33	59	56	66	.042
People in govt. waste a lot of money collected in taxes	23	44	40	45	.033
Quite a few of the people running the govt. are a little crooked	21	36	40	35	.026
N	(357)	(97)	(70)	(65)	

*Créditistes are excluded.

of reality, represented at the same time a measure of the separateness of those who voiced it. It had this separating capacity by virtue of its rarity elsewhere in Canada. We see now that it was not even evenly distributed throughout Quebec.

Party Differences

Liberal supporters appeared most satisfied with those issues tapped by our questions. They failed, however, to overcome the malaise of Quebec politics in evaluating their members of Parliament. The major focus for disaffection lay in the Conservative and Créditiste parties. In some sense, the position of Conservative supporters was most critical. Despite Créditistes' feelings of inefficacy, cynicism, and lack of attachment to conventional political arrangements, a bond to the political system was maintained through their party. Thus a large majority identified their national leader with their own province and a smaller one commended the performance of their members of Parliament.

The Créditistes symbolized a uniquely Quebec phenomenon: a provincially based, ethnically homogeneous party, totally inward-looking despite experiences in the national parliament. While the party provided psychological support for those disaffected who gave it their votes, it was hardly likely to bring about social changes that were national in scope. At the level of the province, its potential was almost as limited. As a national party, it might appear that the Conservatives had a much better opportunity for translating local concerns into national issues. But the picture appears quite hopeless, given not only the electoral weakness of the Conservatives in Quebec and the inability of the national party to adopt policies that would win over French-speaking Canadians, but also the grievances implicit in the political orientations of their Quebec supporters. Nevertheless, despite the limitations of both the Conservative party and Le Ralliement des Créditistes as direct carriers of political change, their existence as foci of protest must have an impact on the political milieu. Other parties cannot exist in smug disregard of the very real problems at issue, even when their own supporters do not share the orientations of the more overtly dissatisfied.

ONTARIO

Residents of Ontario had the most positive political orientations. Their views were channelled into partisan directions with a high degree of consistency, such that satisfaction with political arrangements was normally greatest for Liberals, less for Conservatives, and least for the NDP. The association between parties and orientations, measured by proportional entropy reductions, were of a magnitude to place Ontario third, after the Atlantic provinces and Quebec. If the high proportional entropy reduction associated with the identity of one's own leader is removed, however, then Ontario could be considered to have manifested least party division of all regions. The significance of finding consistent party alignments in political orientations is tempered then by the fact that most contrasts were between Liberals and the less numerous NDP, rather than between the major parties.

Awareness

Sharpest party differences occurred in response to the question of the regional identity of leaders. Mr. Pearson, then the Liberal leader, was thought to be closely identified with Ontario by most respondents, a view held mainly by his party's supporters. Neither Conservatives nor the NDP shared with Liberals the belief that their leaders were close to them in this regional sense. Yet the NDP did see their leader, Mr. Douglas, as close to their region more often than did the Conservatives with Mr. Diefenbaker. If we consider this question to be an indication of positive feelings to one's party leader, then the ranking of Conservatives in last place is suggestive of an aura of dissatisfaction which surrounded the party in this province.

Table 10–7 shows that the remaining two indicators of political awareness were associated with few party differences. Those that did occur were between the more knowledgeable major party supporters and the NDP, a sign perhaps of the latter's lesser electoral success.

Majority Government

Of all Canadians, those in Ontario were most consistently troubled by the absence of majority government. For all three items, Liberals were most often concerned by the lack of a clear-cut majority for the government. (See Table 10–8.) That NDP suporters shared this view least often is probably not surprising, given their minor party status. In a parliamentary system, such parties have greatest scope for exercising power when there is a minority government dependent for tenure on support actively sought from them. It is less obvious why Conservatives too were less concerned with the existence of a majority. This was particularly the case in response to the importance of major government to respondents' voting decision. It is true that on two of the three occasions in past years in which the Conservatives formed the government, they held less than a majority of seats in the House of Commons. This might suggest, that in order to govern, Conservatives are more willing to accept the limitations of minority

Table 10–7 **Political Awareness by Past Vote: Ontario** (percent)

	Liberal	1965 Vote Conservative	NDP	Proportional Entropy Reduction
Know candidate's name	85	86	75	.011
Know candidate's party	90	93	88	.008
Identify own leader with region	65	6	15	.293
N	(424)	(311)	(132)	

Table 10–8 **Opinions of Majority Government by Past Vote: Ontario** (percent)

	Liberal	1965 Vote Conservative	NDP	Proportional Entropy Reduction
Majority govt. important to vote decision	74	55	47	.040
Majority govt. makes difference	73	63	54	.017
Would shift usual vote to ensure majority	29	23	18	.008
N	(424)	(311)	(132)	

status. Yet considering the short duration of both these governments, and the difficulties they faced in producing governmental output, it is difficult to believe that voters found this a desirable state of affairs. It is more likely that what we see here reflects the lesser commitment of Conservative supporters to traditional forms of governance. Outrageous as this may at first appear, especially in view of the Conservatives' alleged adherence to British traditions and to the Mother Parliament, it is not too farfetched to say that lack of experience as an initial supporter of the governing party had produced lesser commitment to fusty traditions. Such traditions may simply be perceived as ways of keeping their party from taking its rightful place in Parliament. This was perfectly illustrated by the election of 1925, when the Conservatives actually won more seats than the Liberals, but were even less able to govern. We do not, of course, suggest that the 1925 election was a stimulus to even a few of our respondents. But it takes only a modest amount of knowledge about political events to recognize that majority governments are much more likely to be non-Conservative governments.[4]

Differentiated Parties

Recognizing a differentiated party system can be interpreted as part of conventional orientations to the regime. Such outlooks were prominent in Ontario, as were related opinions on majority government (and federalism). Party differences in these views were generally not large. Yet the extent of belief that it is important which party is in office did give further evidence that Conservative supporters showed some lack of conviction about traditional aspects of the regime. Only 43 percent of the Conservatives felt it made a great deal of difference which party formed the government, compared to 52 percent for the NDP and 60 percent for the Liberals.

Authorities

In Chapter 8 we noted that members of Parliament received some of their highest ratings in Ontario. These favourable ratings were accompanied by relatively infrequent criticism of government personnel. Voters were not particularly upset by elected officials losing touch with their constitutents, nor did they feel that there were too

---

4. This suggests an interesting analogy with the United States, where the Republicans have been more often out of office than the Democrats. Since the 1950s, when a Republican President has been elected, he has usually had to contend with a Democratic Congress. If the reasoning we applied to the Canadian situation is correct, we would expect that Republican voters would appear less convinced than Democratic voters that it was very important to have a President and Congress of the same party.

many intellectuals in government. The experience of politics in Ontario was not, however, uniform for all party supporters. All three items are associated with some differences among parties, indicated in Table 10–9 by proportional entropy reductions of modest size. The ratings of members of Parliament for respondents' own party showed a division between the NDP and Liberals on the one hand and the Conservatives on the other, with the former much more likely to praise their representatives. It is not immediately evident why Conservatives were so reluctant to give a favourable rating to their MPs, but whatever the reason, the result was undoubtedly important. From their provincial stronghold in Ontario, Conservatives viewed their representatives in the federal parliament with less than widespread enthusiasm.

Criticism was also least evident among Liberal supporters. On these issues, Conservatives were more critical than Liberals, but less so than NDP voters. The most extreme critics were the NDP voters, despite the appreciation they showed toward the efforts of their own representatives. This is consistent with their other, more negative, orientations. In addition, their views of intellectuals confirmed a tendency noticed in other contexts. Although the NDP, and the CCF before it, has given a welcome place to intellectuals, their presence has at times been a source of tension, especially with working class, trade union members.[5]

Federalism

Ontario was highly oriented to the federal level. For example, only in this province did a larger percentage feel that the federal rather than the provincial government had greatest effect on themselves. Yet the dominance of this set of opinions did not completely obviate differences associated with adherence to particular parties. This was particularly the case in evaluating types of elections.

Normally, Liberals had the greatest federal orientation and NDP supporters the least. (See Table 10–10). However, on the question of which elections are most important, where there was greatest party contrast, the response patterns of Liberals and NDP adherents were almost identical. This means, for one thing, that by being less committed to the federal level on this question, Conservatives were less schizoid in their total perspective. The opposite was true for NDP

---

5. Horowitz gives examples of tensions where intellectuals were concerned with socialist ideology and pragmatic trade unionists with "bread and butter" issues. Gad Horowitz, *Canadian Labour in Politics* (Toronto: University of Toronto Press, 1968). Such difficulties have often appeared in other working class parties, as Michels documented for pre-World War I Europe. Robert Michels, *Political Parties* (New York: Collier Books, 1962), pp. 293-304.

Table 10–9 **Opinions of Political Authorities by Past Vote: Ontario** (percent)

| | 1965 Vote | | | Proportional |
	Liberal	Conservative	NDP	Entropy Reduction
Own party MPs doing pretty good job	61	46	64	.015
MPs soon lose touch	41	48	60	.013
Too many intellectuals in government	25	30	40	.011
N	(424)	(311)	(132)	

Table 10–10 **Federal Orientation by Past Vote: Ontario** (percent)

| | 1965 Vote | | | Proportional |
	Liberal	Conservative	NDP	Entropy Reduction
Federal government handles important problems	63	55	50	.007
Provincial government affects self and family	32	39	41	.003
National elections most important	53	31	53	.031
N	(424)	(311)	(132)	

supporters. They were less likely than other partisans to select the federal level as handling important problems or affecting themselves, and hence answers to the question on elections is a prime source of inconsistency. The views of Conservatives had probably been influenced by the greater power of their party at the provincial level. This may have led them to conceive of the political process as more provincial in nature, almost as a pressure toward cognitive consistency. The reasonableness of this argument is confirmed by the responses of Liberals, who had had greatest success in the national sphere. The NDP position was more paradoxical. Having once served as the official opposition in Ontario, their prospects for dislodging the Liberals, if not the Conservatives, in the provincial government, should appear quite plausible. In addition, by operating in a highly industrialized province, the potential for a working class party should be unusually good compared to other parts of Canada. It is these factors which may contribute to NDP supporters' relatively modest federal orientation. Yet it is in the national arena that critical decisions are made, and grudgingly perhaps, NDP supporters acknowledged this in evaluating the importance of elections.

Efficacy

Efficacy again measures the extent of relative political well-being in Ontario, with respondents in that province reporting the greatest sense of political potency. According to our entropy measures, efficacy items have only a very modest association with party. Table 10–11 indicates that the greatest contrast among parties is with reference to the government not caring about voters' opinions. Parties are ordered in the expected way in this and the remaining items, that is, L>C>N. A lower sense of efficacy was most prominent among NDP supporters in response to the government not caring and the complexity of government. In these two instances they were separated from the Conservatives, whom they resembled most, by 12 and 10 percent respectively. But on the lack of say in what the government does, Conservatives felt similarly lacking in potency.

Party Variability

Liberal voters in Ontario could easily be characterized as satisfied, loyal, committed to the status quo, and supportive of the regime and authorities. In most instances, NDP voters were at the opposite pole. Their one source of positive attachment to the political system, to the extent that we have analysed the matter, came from their supportive attitudes toward their own parliamentary leadership. It is the stance of Conservative voters that was particularly interesting by its very complexity. Reviewing the totality of their response patterns, one

Table 10–11 **Percent Agreeing with Statements Measuring Political Efficacy, by Past Vote: Ontario**

	Liberal	1965 Vote Conservative	NDP	Proportional Entropy Reduction
Voting is only way that people like me can have any say about how govt. runs things	73	73	78	.002
Sometimes politics and govt. seem so complicated that a person like me can't really understand what's going on	65	68	78	.008
People like me don't have any say about what the govt. does	40	50	52	.009
I don't think that the govt. cares much what people like me think	30	39	51	.017
N	(424)	(311)	(132)	

must locate them closer to those dissatisfied with the authorities and the regime and with their place in the political community.

Everything we know about the privileged situation of Ontario would lead us to anticipate that political orientations would be shaped by a sense of satisfaction and potency. At the same time, Ontario has been able to achieve its position through internal diversification associated with an industrialized society that is also highly variegated in the composition of its population. Orientations then should not be completely similar across population groups, since needs and demands are likely to be diverse. These of course could be expressed in many ways, but that some of them were captured by the boundaries of party support suggests that political parties were aligned in ways that coincided with critical differences in population. Our findings also suggest, to the extent that the national face of the NDP was one dissatisfied with existing political arrangements, and hence out of step with dominant views in the province, that the NDP remained confined in its third party role.

THE PRAIRIE PROVINCES

The pattern of political orientations in the Prairie provinces were sometimes similar to those in British Columbia and sometimes to Ontario. The former resemblances usually pertained to the regime, the latter to authorities. Party differentiation was often sharp, and the Prairies ranked fourth in the extent of their internal diversity, even when excluding Social Credit.

Awareness

In Table 10–12 we see the effect of party ties on the regional identification of leaders, an instance where partisan viewpoints are strongly associated with measures of political awareness. Liberals failed almost totally to identify Mr. Pearson with their region. In part, this was a crucial indication of the nature of Liberal weakness in the Prairies. This is especially pertinent since each of the three other leaders had their major source of identification in this region. The contrast must have been particularly isolating for Prairie Liberals. There was also a noticeable tendency for Liberals to be less knowledgeable of candidates, reflecting perhaps as much competitive weakness as indicating less clearly defined citizen roles.

NDP supporters were much less likely than Conservatives or Social Crediters to identify their leader with the Prairies. Normally we have viewed such lack of identification, from the perspective of the region, as a barrier to its full integration. From the perspective of the nation

Table 10–12 **Political Awareness by Past Vote: Prairies** (percent)

| | 1965 Vote | | | | Proportional |
	Liberal	Conservative	NDP	Social Credit	Entropy Reduction*
Know candidate's name	76	86	86	78	.017
Know candidate's party	72	84	80	70	.016
Identify own leader with region	2	89	59	89	.510
N	(89)	(125)	(56)	(37)	

*Social Credit is excluded.

as a whole, however, it may have just the opposite effects. We would be inclined to pursue the latter interpretation in the case of the NDP for two reasons. One was the greater likelihood of NDP voters saying that Mr. Douglas was equally close to all regions. Another was the tendency of those in British Columbia to feel close to him. Even in Ontario and Quebec, he was more likely to be seen as associated with those provinces than was Mr. Diefenbaker. This suggests that, in general, Mr. Douglas enjoyed a more universalistic image.

Majority Government

There was only moderate concern with majority government in this region, but the extent of this concern varied along party lines. More precisely, party differences were associated with a division between Liberal voters and others. Liberals, as they were in all regions, were most oriented to majority government. The extent of these differences were particularly strong on two issues: the importance of majority government in affecting the 1965 voting decision and the likelihood of switching parties. (See Table 10–13.) Conservatives were aligned with minor party supporters on these two items. They responded more like Liberals, however, in the importance they attached to having a majority in the federal government.

Party Differentiation

Residents of the Prairies attributed considerable distinctiveness to parties. This was accompanied by large partisan differences in the case of those who felt it makes a great deal of difference which party forms the government. (See Table 10–14.) It was the Liberals who held this view to a significantly greater extent than did the supporters of other parties, particularly the NDP and Conservatives. Other questions concerned with this topic revealed minimal percentage differences but they at least suggest that party alignments were similar. That is, it was Liberal and Social Credit voters who were more perceptive of differences.

Authorities

Prairie residents gave members of Parliament a relatively high rating on performance, especially when they represented parties other than the Liberal. Looking only at the evaluations of respondents' own party in Table 10–15, we found large differences among supporters, due to the propensity of NDP voters to give their own MPs a high rating. It is in the Prairies, the home of their predecessors the CCF, that NDP members of Parliament found most favour among their supporters.

Complaints about political authorities did not shed further light

Table 10–13 **Opinions of Majority Government by Past Vote: Prairies** (percent)

| | 1965 Vote | | | | Proportional |
	Liberal	Conservative	NDP	Social Credit	Entropy Reduction*
Majority govt. important to vote decision	76	54	56	54	.032
Majority govt. makes difference	66	60	54	46	.007
Would shift usual vote to ensure majority	35	15	16	27	.044
N	(89)	(125)	(56)	(37)	

*Social Credit is excluded.

Table 10–14 **Party Differentiation by Past Vote: Prairies** (percent)

| | 1965 Vote | | | | Proportional |
	Liberal	Conservative	NDP	Social Credit	Entropy Reduction*
There is a difference which party governs	63	39	33	47	.044
Differences between parties	63	63	59	75	.000
Would not vote for some party	94	86	91	95	.026
N	(89)	(125)	(56)	(37)	

*Social Credit is excluded.

Table 10–15 **Opinions of Political Authorities by Past Vote: Prairies** (percent)

	1965 Vote				
	Liberal	Conservative	NDP	Social Credit	Proportional Entropy Reduction*
Own party MPs doing pretty good job	52	54	77	54	.029
MPs soon lose touch	40	54	50	43	.011
Too many intellectuals in government	28	32	25	38	.003
N	(89)	(125)	(56)	(37)	

*Social Credit is excluded.

on sources of dissatisfaction. For example, while Conservative MPs received their highest ratings in the Prairies, their supporters were still inclined to be more concerned than others that MPs lose touch with the electorate and that intellectuals had an excessive share in government. Liberals, despite the relatively low rating of their MPs, were otherwise not excessively critical, nor were NDP supporters unusually low in criticisms, except in their evaluation of intellectuals. These data then do not give us firm enough findings to explain the basis of MP ratings.

Cynicism

Only in the belief that people in government waste a lot of money collected in taxes did Prairie residents appear in the forefront of the cynical. Otherwise, cynicism was comparatively moderate in this region. Major differences among party supporters were present for two of the items, the trustworthiness of government and excessive attention to big interests. In both instances, these party cleavages were the result of the greater frequency with which NDP supporters selected the cynical response. On these and other items, Liberals appeared least cynical. (Table 10–16.)

Efficacy

The sense of efficacy in this region was, by Canadian standards, relatively high. On two items, the importance of voting and the complexity of government, differences among party supporters were minor. (See Table 10–17.) But belief that the government does not care about public opinion or that the ordinary voter had no say in government did separate voters, particularly the Liberals and Conservatives. It is the Conservatives who were at the low efficacy extreme. Neither the experience of having been on the side of the government, nor unusual success at the polls in the Prairies, had given Conservatives the personal confidence that characterized Liberals.

Party Differences

The existence of multiple parties, and the very real differences among them in policies and platforms, helps to promote partisan diversity in political orientations. Only on attitudes toward federalism was the Prairie climate of such a character as to overwhelm party contrasts. With respect to recognition of party differentiation, attachment to majority government, and feelings of cynicism and efficacy, Liberal supporters tended to take the same position as Liberals elsewhere. Compared to other Liberals, as well as to others in their region, they were low on political awareness and on evaluations of their own members of Parliament. In general, however, NDP and Conservative supporters alternated in having the most negative orientations.

Table 10–16 **Percent Agreeing with Statements Measuring Political Cynicism, by Past Vote: Prairies**

| | 1965 Vote | | | | Proportional |
	Liberal	Conservative	NDP	Social Credit	Entropy Reduction*
At least some government officials pay more attention to big shots	70	75	89	78	.028
Quite a few people running the govt. don't seem to know what they are doing	52	48	55	57	.002
Govt. can be trusted only some of the time to do what is right	27	33	54	38	.031
People in govt. waste a lot of money collected in taxes	36	49	55	38	.016
Quite a few of the people running the govt. are a little crooked	13	24	23	16	.015
N	(89)	(125)	(56)	(37)	

*Social Credit is excluded.

Table 10–17 **Percent Agreeing with Statements Measuring Political Efficacy, by Past Vote: Prairies**

| | 1965 Vote | | | | Proportional |
	Liberal	Conservative	NDP	Social Credit	Entropy Reduction*
Voting is only way that people like me can have any say about how govt. runs things	74	80	84	68	.008
Sometimes politics and govt. seem so complicated that a person like me can't really understand what's going on	71	75	70	76	.003
People like me don't have any say about what the govt. does	38	56	45	43	.018
I don't think that the govt. cares much what people like me think	25	46	38	35	.030
N	(89)	(125)	(56)	(37)	

*Social Credit is excluded.

BRITISH COLUMBIA

British Columbia was the scene of an intriguing complex of attitudes. Like Ontario, its residents felt themselves politically potent; like the Atlantic provinces, they were critical of authorities; and like Quebec, they tended to reject those aspects of the regime relating to the structure of government. The amount of party differentiation associated with these views puts British Columbia in fifth place. In other words, voters reflected a highly differentiated political milieu.

Awareness

In Table 10–18 we see that voters in British Columbia were most divided on the identity of their own party's leader. Only Mr. Douglas of the NDP was seen as close to British Columbia. Though his original base of operation had been in the Prairies, NDP voters in this province were almost as likely as those in the Prairies to associate Mr. Douglas with themselves. Since his assumption of the national leadership, Mr. Douglas had run as a candidate in British Columbia. The views of voters may also have been partially a measure of the success of the NDP in British Columbia, where its leader could inspire a sense of closeness. To the extent that such self-leader identifications are beneficial for the integration of national party supporters, the major parties were particularly deficient in this regard. Such identification was totally absent for Mr. Diefenbaker and, in the case of Mr. Pearson, present for 5 percent of the Liberal voters.

A second item on which party supporters were distinctive was the name of the winning candidate. Here Liberals were least knowledgeable, with Social Crediters rather similar. NDP supporters were most aware of the candidates' names. Altogether then, NDP supporters displayed more of the characteristics of the informed, involved citizen.

Majority Government

The issue of majority government evoked a modest level of concern. At the same time, it did distinguish among party supporters as an issue affecting the 1965 voting decision and the likelihood of switching parties, as summarized by our entropy measures in Table 10–19. If we add the question on whether it makes a great deal of difference if the party forming the government has a majority of seats, then it is clear that Liberals felt a greater concern for this issue and NDP voters the least. This is not, however, associated with an expected major-minor party division. Those voting for Social Credit were more like the Liberals, while Conservative voters were more akin to the NDP. We have here an indication of the uniqueness of political responses in British Columbia. Majority government was *not* a pressing concern, nor did it affect party supporters in the same way. Moreover, this

Table 10–18 **Political Awareness by Past Vote: British Columbia** (percent)

| | 1965 Vote | | | | Proportional |
	Liberal	Conservative	NDP	Social Credit	Entropy Reduction*
Know candidate's name	59	72	81	62	.033
Know candidate's party	77	76	84	85	.007
Identify own leader with region	5	0	52	15	.374
N	(78)	(58)	(62)	(26)	

*Social Credit is excluded.

Table 10–19 **Opinions of Majority Government by Past Vote: British Columbia** (percent)

| | 1965 Vote | | | | Proportional |
	Liberal	Conservative	NDP	Social Credit	Entropy Reduction*
Majority govt. important to vote decision	67	48	40	69	.042
Majority govt. makes difference	69	62	58	61	.007
Would shift usual vote to ensure majority	36	17	10	23	.072
N	(78)	(58)	(62)	(26)	

*Social Credit is excluded.

issue isolated the Conservatives from what would otherwise be anticipated to be their political counterparts with respect to support for the same rules of the game.

Authorities

British Columbia voters were quite broadly convinced that those elected to Parliament soon lose touch with the people. They were second only to Quebec in the extent of their criticism. This was primarily a complaint of major party supporters, and in particular, of the Conservative voters. As we see in Table 10–20, NDP, and to a lesser extent Social Credit, voters were much less often disturbed by this possibility. Our second measure of criticism, that pertaining to the position of intellectuals, was both much less a source of concern and less a source of party division. Yet Conservatives remained as the most critical.

The other side of these complaints against authorities were the positive ratings assigned to members of Parliament. Compared to ratings elsewhere, MPs received a relatively poor evaluation in British Columbia. A comparison of the way in which party supporters viewed their own representatives shows that Conservatives achieved the lowest level of support. Social Crediters were most satisfied with the performance of their representatives. Over half the Liberals shared this view, as did less than half the NDP. Both positive and negative views of authorities supported each other: Conservatives were most disappointed in political authorities while Social Credit voters had most supportive views.

Cynicism

Relative to the Canadian experience, cynicism was moderately high in British Columbia, especially in the belief that quite a few of the people running the government did not seem to know what they are doing. This item was also associated with considerable party differentiation, as we see in Table 10–21. It separated the more cynical major party supporters from the less cynical minor party supporters, and in particular the Conservatives from the NDP. A second indicator of this concept, the trustworthiness of government personnel, permitted Conservatives to retain their most cynical outlook. But this time the least cynical were Liberals, with the NDP more like the Conservatives, and Social Credit resembling the Liberals. In this case, the high entropy measures accent the contrast between the two major parties. To the extent that we are willing to describe any consistency to response patterns for all five items, we can only be certain of the greater cynicism of the Conservatives. The remainder vacillated with the issues under consideration, although it is probably true that the NDP were second to the Conservatives.

Table 10–20 **Opinions of Political Authorities by Past Vote: British Columbia** (percent)

	1965 Vote				
	Liberal	Conservative	NDP	Social Credit	Proportional Entropy Reduction*
Own party MPs doing pretty good job	54	34	48	69	.019
MPs soon lose touch	62	76	45	54	.045
Too many intellectuals in government	28	41	35	31	.010
N	(78)	(58)	(62)	(26)	

*Social Credit is excluded.

Table 10–21 **Percent Agreeing with Statements Measuring Political Cynicism, by Past Vote: British Columbia**

| | 1965 Vote | | | | Proportional |
	Liberal	Conservative	NDP	Social Credit	Entropy Reduction*
At least some government officials pay more attention to big shots	80	76	87	69	.014
Quite a few people running the govt. don't seem to know what they are doing	69	76	48	54	.043
Govt. can be trusted only some of the time to do what is right	21	52	39	23	.058
People in govt. waste a lot of money collected in taxes	23	38	39	46	.021
Quite a few of the people running the govt. are a little crooked	18	21	23	15	.002
N	(78)	(58)	(62)	(26)	

*Social Credit is excluded.

Federalism

British Columbia shared with the Prairies a highly schizoid perspective on the operation of the federal government. While the federal
level was seen as crucial for problems of the country, and even as the
arena for the exercise of the franchise, it lagged behind the provincial
government in its impact on individuals. These contrasts were
especially sharp in British Columbia, where at the same time, federal
elections were seen as most important by a greater proportion than
in any other region in Canada.

Distinct party differences appeared only in responses to the provincial government having most impact on self. The major contrast
was between the Liberals, 46 percent of whom chose the provincial
government, and the Conservatives and NDP, with 65 and 61 percent
respectively. The resulting proportional entropy reduction is .036,
indicating relatively strong party effect. The weakly represented Social
Credit also were sharply differentiated from other parties, with 85
percent choosing the provincial level.

On the basis of these responses and those pertaining to elections,
we would conclude that an orientation to the federal government
was most prominent among Liberal supporters, who were also lowest
in the split view of the federal structure. The remaining parties were
more inconsistent and consequently highly schizoid in perspective.
It is only the Liberals, then, who were even modestly able to break
through the framework imposed by life in British Columbia to
identify, with any consistency, with the powers of the federal government.

Efficacy

Except for the question of whether voting is the only way for ordinary
citizens to influence government, all other measures of efficacy were
associated with clear party divisions. The strength of the associations
is summarized by measures of proportional entropy reduction in
Table 10–22. The sharpest division emerged in response to the statement that the government does not care about the views of the
ordinary citizen. Over one-half the Conservatives agreed with this
view, compared to less than one-quarter of the Liberals and NDP.
Social Credit supporters were midway between these extremes. More
than half the Conservatives and Social Crediters also shared the view
that people like themselves do not have any say in what the government does. Complaints about the complexity of government were
more frequently voiced by everyone, and in this instance it was Social
Credit voters who most often felt this way. They were joined
by about three-quarters of the NDP and Conservative supporters,
and over one-half of the Liberals. On the basis of these three items,

Table 10–22 **Percent Agreeing with Statements Measuring Political Efficacy, by Past Vote: British Columbia**

	Liberal	1965 Vote Conservative	NDP	Social Credit	Proportional Entropy Reduction*
Voting is only way that people like me can have any say about how govt. runs things	74	72	81	92	.006
Sometimes politics and govt. seem so complicated that a person like me can't really understand what's going on	56	72	74	85	.024
People like me don't have any say about what the govt. does	36	55	32	54	.028
I don't think that the govt. cares much what people like me think	23	52	23	38	.062
N	(78)	(58)	(62)	(26)	

*Social Credit is excluded.

we can attribute least efficacy to the Conservatives, followed by Social
Credit, NDP, and then Liberal supporters.

Party Differences

The experience of life in British Columbia interacts with the political
system to produce internally diverse political orientations. Party
viewpoints of the kind we described in Ontario and Quebec were
sometimes present, but often took unique forms. For example,
Liberal voters shared with their counterparts elsewhere feelings of
greater efficacy, belief in the importance of majority government, and
a federal orientation. Yet they did not have the positive feelings
toward authorities that the minor parties did, nor the extent of political awareness found among NDP voters. Both minor parties displayed
some satisfaction with the political process, and if they were not
especially committed to traditional aspects of the regime, nonetheless
they did not have nearly the negative orientations of Conservative
supporters. Despite very different political circumstances, the latter
shared with their counterparts in Quebec a low sense of efficacy,
cynical attitudes toward government personnel, a low commitment to
majority government, and critical views of political authorities.

At the same time that we recognize the ways in which dissatisfaction is related to particular parties, we must also recall that it was
fairly widespread throughout British Columbia. The juncture of personal potency, political diversity, and dissatisfaction appear to be a
volatile combination. Potential volatility could be kept in check by the
conditions outlined in Chapters 2 and 4, and to some extent, 3. That
is, the buoyant economy, the perceptions of life, and the political
potency of the province all contributed to a degree of satisfaction
that political grievances may not have penetrated. But at the same
time, deterioration in the conditions of life are not implausible. Given
the province's uneven development, reliance on primary resources,
and mobile, detached population, a more radical approach to the
political process is not out of the realm of possibility. The existence
of four viable parties, none with very strong ties to a central organization, and with voters only imperfectly sharing in a national consensus, means that channels of protest could be readily mobilized.

CONSEQUENCES OF PARTY OUTLOOKS

The polarities of a total lack of association between parties and
orientations, and a total dominance of party-linked opinions, have
led us to build a case for the existence of a politicized environment.
But can we truly say that one degree of politicization, as reflected

solely in orientations, is necessarily better or worse than another? To what extent do judgements on the undesirable effects of either extreme really hold?

There is always the temptation to move beyond any particular set of data in interpreting their consequences. In this connection, we have been acutely aware of the dangers in the attribution of strains in a social system when based upon data about individuals. Yet data of the sort we have employed rarely speak for themselves. If we want to make statements about how the social system operates, we have no alternative but to gather all our empirical forces and then move on to at least some slightly higher order of abstraction. Our arguments do not rest on any single orientation item, nor do we understand politicization to consist only of patterns of orientation. We treat the orientation items as useful mechanisms for evaluating the state of each region with respect to party channels for expressing voter demands. The focus here is on the party system in its interaction with voters. No attempt is made to test direct responses to voter demands through actions either by individual parties or by the central authorities.

No region displayed a total absence of ties between partisanship and orientations to the political process. The Atlantic provinces did come close to approximating this extreme, with their residents showing little association between the parties they supported and the views they held. This could be interpreted as evidence of lack of political consciousness among the voters in this region. Yet this position is difficult to support for a number of reasons. We recall that the Atlantic provinces were the possessors of a strong and stable two-party system, which means in this instance that they almost always have had viable alternatives open to them. We saw as well that voters showed considerable commitment to the parties of their choice, and a regularity of voting practices that was not found elsewhere in Canada.[6] Is this mere traditionalism? To some extent, it is true, we have argued for the strength of tradition in this area, but we can hardly equate this with an unsophisticated lack of politicization. From all we know of voting behaviour cross-nationally, we understand that participation in itself is an important indicator of involvement, and commitment is even moreso.[7] On these bases it is appropriate to argue that the traditionalism found was not associated with lack of political consciousness, but with a situation in which special needs and concerns remained channelled in traditional outlets. That

6. For comparative data on turnout, see F. C. Engelmann and M. A. Schwartz, *Political Parties and the Canadian Social Structure* (Scarborough: Prentice-Hall of Canada, 1967), pp. 40-41.

7. Lester Milbrath, *Political Participation* (Chicago: Rand McNally, 1965).

is, our lack of ability to differentiate among party supporters with respect to their political orientations (and these include, we recall, statements of genuine grievances), reflected the absence of apparent alternatives for voters. Many had similar concerns and interests, yet few had differentiated avenues for expressing them.

In reviewing the findings for Quebec we made no judgements about the conditions of political stability or unrest in that province. We observed that the amount of party differentiation was not associated with strong links between parties and opinions, according to our statistical measure. The reasons for this are of particular importance. They reflect the fact that the available alternatives on the federal scene, with the exception of the Liberal party, all have some fundamental weakness. In the case of the NDP, they have a base of support found almost exclusively in Montreal and leaving untouched the bulk of the working class. The Conservatives are associated with the negative image of a party that has, for generations, been suspect as a spokesman for Quebec interests. Créditistes provide an outlet in yet another of those third party movements that generally have had brief histories and weak political impact. At the same time, the dominance of the Liberals federally in a sense polarizes what there is of an opposition.

We have suggested that the Liberals in Quebec must take account of the very real concerns that the supporters of other parties manifest, but since they are not critical rivals, they do not have to consider them too seriously. To some extent, this structural characteristic stems from the facts of French ethnic existence, where varied perspectives, and with them, extensive partisan differentiation, have been suppressed in the interests or survival. The arguments for solidarity in the fact of the English-speaking majority have become less persuasive in the past decade, as Quebec society becomes more highly differentiated internally. Out of these conditions, new contenders for power have arisen. Breton describes the sociological meaning of even terrorist separatist groups in this context, viewing them as desperate, but virtually excluded, competitors.[8] The tensions reflected in the volatility of provincial politics in recent years do not have adequate counterpart in the federal scene in two, even contradictory senses. Politics federally, despite the participation of such men as Pelletier, Trudeau, and Marchand in the 1960s, still has a traditional air, lacking the lively competition between nearly equal contenders. In addition, the more radical elements of Quebec politics do not have much of a legitimate stage for operating, however we may care to evaluate the efforts of the Créditistes. In Quebec, we are left

---

8. Raymond Breton, "The Socio-Political Dynamics of the October Events," *Canadian Review of Sociology and Anthropology* 9 (February 1972): 33-56.

with sources of strain in orientation patterns (summarized in Chapter 9), as well as from many other sources, with only modestly effective alternative channels for partisan expression.[9]

Is the situation of Ontario to be interpreted as close to an ideal, with just the right amount of party differentiation? Obviously we are in no position to make such a judgement. Our findings show that the most disgruntled find their home in a third party. The question is to what extent this third party is able to muster sufficient forces to take its message into the national arena and affect the course of politics. If the NDP cannot play this role, then voters in this province are left with limited avenues for expressing variations in needs and interests.

The situation of the Prairie provinces is even more ambiguous than that of Ontario. There are political strains inherent in the way residents view their political environment, and there is considerable association between parties and orientations. Some of the consequences of this degree of diversity is exaggerated by our procedures of analysis, in which we have grouped together three provinces. But this point aside, we do find in the Prairies not only strong third party movements with some scope federally, but also that the two older parties, and especially the Conservatives, have undergone a degree of transformation that allows them to capture some of the concerns endemic to the prairies. This is not to discount the strains that exist here, or the mood of discouragement that at times afflicts Manitoba and Saskatchewan, but only to suggest that at the same time, the political environment permits the expression of many of these themes.

British Columbia is closest to the extreme of total politicization. Its political volatility has been evident through every measure we have used. If some of the apparent potential for unrest has gone unnoticed, this has been aided by the checks imposed by both structural conditions and a psychological mood that emphasizes the positive. Underneath, however, a smoldering level of discontent eats at the fuse of high politicization.

The kinds of political strains considered here have been of a qualitatively different sort than those enumerated in the conclusion to the preceding chapter, where we looked at particular patterns of orientation. It is worth at least passing mention that only one of these patterns, dealing with orientations to federalism, was marked by the relative absence of association with parties. This was particularly

9. Breton, for example, isolates five broad sets of factors related to profound social changes. These include changes in opportunities for entry into elite positions, alterations in the role of the Catholic Church, new self-conceptions producing pressures to participate in decision-making, opposition to bureaucratic expansion, and demographic changes. Ibid., 42-43.

evident in the three areas, Quebec, the Prairies, and British Columbia, where views of federalism were most distinctive. This one pattern of orientations apparently tapped issues that evoked rather profound regional feelings, feelings that cut across more usual partisan outlooks. But the scope of parties as they interact with regional concerns is obviously of more diffuse impact than that indicated through voters responses, and it is the more comprehensive concern with the interaction between parties and regional interests that will be dealt with in the following chapter.

CHAPTER

11

Political parties in a regionally divided society

NATIONAL AND REGIONAL INTERESTS

In Whose Interests Should the Government be Run? The answer to this question is a principal reason for the existence of political parties, linking as they do interests and government. The interests represented are most apparent in class or confessional parties. That broad-based parties are typically aggregative in approach, that is, that they "seek to form the largest possible interest group coalitions by offering acceptable choices of political personnel and public policy,"[1] does not detract from the selectivity of their representation. As long as there are contending parties, no single one will be entirely successful in attracting the full spectrum of interests present in a society. Governing is also the business of political parties. While some political systems ensure a greater measure of "party government," it is difficult to conceive of the operation of democratic government without an important place for parties.[2] Though the scope and method vary greatly, political

---

1. Gabriel A. Almond, "Interest Groups and the Political Process," in Roy C. Macridis and Bernard E. Brown, eds., *Comparative Politics,* 3rd ed. (Homewood: Dorsey Press, 1968), p. 229.

2. "To begin with, parties are inevitable. No large free country has been without them. No one has shown how representative government could be worked without them." James Bryce, *Modern Democracies,* vol. I (New York: Macmillan, 1921), p. 119.

parties in western countries seek to translate their advocacy of specific interests into authoritative and binding decisions.[3]

The concern of this volume is restricted to the representation of territorial interests by parties. Are the interests of one or more regions emphasized in the national government? Or does the government seek to maximize the satisfaction of more broadly conceived national issues? Whether they wish to or not, political parties in regionally-divided societies assume a position on this national-local dimension of interest.

In Canada, national and provincial interests were separated in the British North America Act setting forth the Confederation agreement. We know that the division of powers between the two jurisdictions has not been without controversy or differences of interpretation. Yet an overview of the enumerated responsibilities should help us distinguish between what is national and what is local. Section 91 of the Act begins with the statement that the national Parliament has exclusive authority to make laws for "the peace, order, and good government of Canada." Specific areas of concern encompass monetary policy, including the "raising of money by any mode or system of taxation" and the organization of facilities for its exercise and control; defence; postal service; criminal law; and trade and commerce. In other words, the federal government is empowered to protect Canadian interests in relations with other countries,[4] while internally it regulates the means for allocating goods and services and the relations between groups. Provincial powers are spelled out in Section 92, and despite past interpretations by the Judicial Committee of the Privy Council, it quite obviously was intended to give the provinces a relatively modest share of power, commensurate with what were then viewed as purely local concerns. These deal with such matters as the maintenance of government at the provincial level, control over municipalities, administration of justice within the province, property and civil rights, and education. While probably unanticipated, the allotment of these responsibilities has resulted in the provinces being the major arena for contention over ethnic, religious, and linguistic rights.

It is not our intention to enter the morass of federal-provincial responsibilities.[5] The relevant sections of the British North America

---

3. Leon D. Epstein, *Political Parties in Western Democracies* (New York: Frederick A. Praeger, 1967), pp. 315-50.

4. Even these prerogatives have not been undisputed. A particularly touchy example has been the direct links between the governments of France and Quebec.

5. For a useful overview, see Robert MacGregor Dawson, *The Government of Canada,* revised by Norman Ward, 5th ed. (Toronto: University of Toronto Press, 1970), pp. 76-98.

Act are introduced here only to provide a link between the constitutional divisions and what we see as the socio-political bases of Canadian existence. Whatever perspective we take, there are two discernible realms of interest in Canadian life, the national and the local-provincial. The constitution recognizes these and provides for their perpetuation. The dynamic quality of the tension between nation and region cannot, however, be captured by any formal document. It is here that we look to the operation of political parties to illustrate how tensions are manifested.

PARTY AND TERRITORY

The relationship between political parties and the demands of territorial interests pose issues that extend beyond the confines of any single nation. For example, when Rokkan looks at the ties between social cleavages and party development in Norway, he begins with a description that suggests some similarities with Canada. "The original lines of cleavage in the Norwegian system were territorial and cultural."[6] Conflicts between rural and urban ways of life and between the peripheries and the centre were inherent in the beginnings of political parties. But with social changes accompanying industrialization and the rise of urban working and middle classes, the more critical lines of conflict became functional-economic ones. This resulted in either the emergence of new or transformation of existing parties into those with a strong class orientation. Forces for territorial defence have not disappeared, nor the parties that represent them, but they have become much less important in the face of nationalizing pressures.

Parallels between Norway and Canada are suggestive, but there are also some important divergences. Canada clearly has a national industrial society as developed as that in Norway, yet the force of region remains stronger. Ignoring for the moment the ways in which the political system has reinforced regional cleavages, there are at least two other important distinctions. The links between territory and cultural differences are much stronger in Canada, most strikingly, but not exclusively, because of the existence of Quebec. In addition, regional economic cleavages not only cross-cut regions, as they do in Norway, but add another dimension to regional distinctiveness. As a consequence, we would expect that Canadian political parties would

6. Stein Rokkan, "Electoral Mobilization, Party Competition, and National Integration," in Joseph LaPalombara and Myron Weiner, eds., *Political Parties and Political Development* (Princeton: Princeton University Press, 1966), p. 253.

be continually subject to pressures from regional as well as national interests, whether or not we define these latter as solely functional-economic in nature.

The generality of the issues raised by Rokkan is made explicit in an article co-authored with Lipset.[7] Lipset and Rokkan use Parsons' schema for classifying functional problems of any social system as a means of relating cleavage structures and party systems. Parsons' basic system problems are adaptation, integration, goal-attainment, and pattern maintenance (AGIL). While each system may evolve different institutional arrangements for their solutions, and variations in the interchanges between subsystems, the problems themselves remain endemic to an ongoing social system.[8] Within the context of their concerns, Lipset and Rokkan illustrate the AGIL relationships by asking which cleavages are important at different developmental stages, how they are expressed politically, the relation between the dominant cleavages and party support, and their reflection in the electoral system and its outcomes.

Use of the Parsonian scheme is not without difficulty, partly stemming from the generality of the theory. For one thing, system problems occur within regional confines as much as in the nation as a whole. Hence the notion of interchange between functional problems becomes confusing, since we can conceive of this occurring within the nation, within individual regions, between regions, or between nation and region. Parsons suggests that institutions and related organizations will more or less specialize in one of the four system problems. At the same time, the problems themselves occur within each institutional area. To some extent, Lipset and Rokkan overcame the diffuseness of the Parsons' conceptualization by focusing primarily on political parties, yet even this is not without difficulties. For example, they now speak of the territorial dimension of the national cleavage structure as manifested along a line linking *l* (pattern maintenance and tension management) with *g* (goal attainment).[9] At the *l* end of the axis they suggest local oppositions to national elites as an example of the basis for party formation. At the *g* end would be found conflicts over the goals and policies of the system as a whole.

---

7. S. M. Lipset and Stein Rokkan, "Cleavage Structures, Party Systems, and Voter Alignments: An Introduction," in Seymour Martin Lipset and Stein Rokkan, eds., *Party Systems and Voter Alignments* (New York: Free Press, 1967), pp. 1-64.

8. Talcott Parsons, R. Freed Bales, Edward A. Shils, *Working Papers in the Theory of Action* (Glencoe, Ill.: Free Press, 1953).

9. Lipset and Rokkan, "Cleavage Structures," in Lipset and Rokkan, *Party Systems,* p. 10. We follow the convention of using capital letters for problems of the total social system and lower case letters for subsystem problems.

But goal-attainment is as much a rationale for regionally-oriented parties as it is for nationally-oriented ones; it is only that the goals differ. In the same way, pattern maintenance can be of a nationalist character, downgrading the significance of particular ethnic or linguistic groups in the interests of more broadly conceived cultural patterns.

Similar objections can be made to the conception of adaptation and integration as pertaining only to the functional dimension, and hence cutting across territorial units. For example, economic problems may be quite local in nature, associated with particular resources, vulnerability to disasters, or the composition of the population. As long as they are confined to one or two areas they may never become a part of the national concern. Even when they do, their relation to other problems of adaptation, and the priorities assigned to their solution, will likely be quite different when viewed from a national as opposed to a local perspective. Local interests do not simply disappear. They may, of course, be transformed, and one way this can happen is through the initiative of the national government. In a sense, then, the thrust of our objection to Lipset and Rokkan's application of Parsons relates to the creation of local-national dichotomies where these are not appropriate. The kind of system problems they abstract from Parsons are as much a part of the operation of territorial units within nations as they are of the nation as a whole. We can then anticipate that the way specific problems arise and are faced in one realm will have implications for those in the other realm. The interchanges that are most pertinent in viewing the operation of political parties on the national scene are those that take into account the consequences of regional diversity.

CHOICE OF INTERESTS

Just as parties emerge in response to different felt needs in the same society, so they may vary in their continuing responsiveness to them. Since needs always have some dynamic quality, this alone can be a source of tension. In other words, a party that begins by responding to a particular set of interests may, over time, lose sight of the way these interests have changed. Parties may make a deliberate choice, and ignore the claims generated by either the national or regional interests. Whatever they do, and whether or not it is intended, we can expect parties in regionally divided societies to make some contribution to the inevitable strains between national and regional interests. The strains occur since both realms require the satisfaction of system problems, some of which are complimentary and others, in conflict.

Some of the most drastic instances of parties associated with either an exclusively national or regional perspective come out of Africa. In those countries with a colonial history, modern nation-building was inimical to the colonial power. "The essential doctrine of the colonial ruling elite was that the meaningful social entity remained the tribe (and, by extension, the region). By upholding the traditional definition of the situation, they hoped to maintain their power by control via their clients, the chiefs.[10]

Nationalist movements, the precursors of nationalist parties, used the colonial power as their unifying enemy, since regional-ethnic interests were viewed as highly divisive. Freedom from the old rulers has often led, however, to the reassertion of the old loyalties. The single-minded drive toward a unitary national integration has been illustrated by the policies of Sékou Touré, leader of the Parti Démocratique de Guinée (PDG), and president of Guinea.

> One of Touré's major preoccupations has been to break down the tribal divisions which had plagued Guinea's political life until he took firm charge of the PDG in the early 1950's. The immediate postwar years had seen a mushrooming of political groups in Guinea as elsewhere in French Africa, but they had for the most part been limited to particular ethnic communities. Touré regarded this situation as intolerable, and with an explicit aim of achieving national integration he moved to smash the hold of tribalism both in the party and in the society at large. A first step, which got effectively underway in 1957, was to remove the chiefs from political power and to substitute for them a system of elected local councils under the control of the party. Within the party itself Touré turned away from organizing its local units on an ethnic basis, in contrast to the neighboring Parti Démocratique de la Côte d'Ivoire (PDCI) . . . which based itself on ethnic groups in urban centers. Similarly PDG organizers and propagandists, and candidates for office as well, were selected on a non-ethnic basis with the expectation both of strengthening the sense of national unity and of establishing a direct relationship with the party, no longer mediated through the traditional ethnic community.[11]

But as we have already indicated, the success of such unitary political movements is hampered by the recurrence of local demands. That

---

10. Immanual Wallerstein, "Class, Tribe, and Party in West African Politics," in Lipset and Rokkan, *Party Systems*, p. 502.

11. Rupert Emerson, "Parties and National Integration in Africa," in LaPolambara and Weiner, eds., *Political Parties,* pp. 275-76.

these are associated with tribal and linguistic ties makes them all the more pressing, although we must not overlook the significance of conflicting economic interests with a regional base. In this connection, the secessionist activities of Katanga and Biafra are important examples. But even if of less extreme consequences, regional-ethnic parties have been a feature of post-colonial Africa. No matter how unattractive it has been to some leaders, recognition of the enduring quality of regional loyalties, with all that is associated with these, has been a necessary part of successful politics. As Wallerstein has observed, "the nationalist party, if it wanted to be a national party, had no choice but to collect ethnic support."[12]

We need not look so far afield from the politics of western countries to see analogous examples of the strains between national and local interests. They can, for example, be illustrated by class parties. It can be argued, in the best Marxist tradition, that political parties based on class interests, by their very generality, help loosen the parochialism of ties based on region, religion, or similar identities. Marx, of course, prophesied a class struggle that would transform society, but others have been willing to acknowledge the positive contributions of class-related politics without this ultimate outcome. Alford, for instance, has written of the consequences of class cleavages for national unity.

> Under conditions of highly developed industrialism, class cleavages may actually be the cleavages which are most easily compromised and the ones most likely to retain national unity and political consensus (regardless of the level of class voting). Regional and religious loyalties are not easily compromised because they rest on differences of "values", not "interests". Such cleavages may be inherently more disintegrative and less flexible than class ones.[13]

Certainly current history seems more often to provide instances of virulent conflict associated with ties of origin rather than with class. Indeed, urbanization and industrialization, accompaniments of class politics, do not always produce the breakdown of ties of a more primary nature, despite contrary predictions.[14] For successful class parties, however, access to power is through national appeals, in particular those that cut across regional loyalties. In this way, they

---

12. Wallerstein, "Class, Tribe, and Party," in Lipset and Rokkan, eds., *Party Systems*, p. 509.

13. Robert R. Alford, *Party and Society* (Chicago: Rand McNally & Co., 1963), p. 339.

14. This is a theme of Clifford Geertz, ed., *Old Societies and New States* (New York: Free Press, 1963).

can perform important integrative roles, especially if in their governing capacity they are able to equalize opportunities in all regions, or even to encourage population movements that make all parts of the country equally attractive to its citizens. By so doing, regional interests would not be ignored; they would be rechannelled. To the extent that regional cleavages are not the result of "false consciousness," but of objective conditions recognized by their inhabitants, especially when seen in opposition to the interests of other regions, then a class party that does not make efforts to deal with these cleavages is not likely to acquire the strength that comes with support from all regions. Even if such a party were to form a government, it could not deal with the problems of a diversified nation if it persisted in seeing them only in terms of class conflict. For example, in a region dominated by a single industry, efforts to cope with structural unemployment by pitting workers against owners would not be effective where the owners were hardly more advantaged than their workers, and where even government subsidization would not do much more than provide an alternative to unemployment benefits. Alternatively, a move to proletarianize the whole region, creating in this way "class enemies" in neighbouring regions, may be easier to accomplish, given the incidence of colonial-type exploitation patterns by more developed regions.[15] In the long run, however, this would serve to exaggerate regional cleavages and detract from the possibility of national integration.

The paradox of nationally oriented parties is that, if they do not make adequate provision for the representation of local interests and solutions to their special problems, they are soon faced with fragmentation. Parties which operate in the national milieu but are oriented solely to regional interests, often face the obverse situation. They are unlikely to govern, except in highly unstable and conflict-ridden situations. Since they are confronted by limited resources, they cannot, consequently, assign priorities to national tasks. The paradox of their existence is that they are then limited in what they can achieve in the way of local goals.

There is obviously no simple solution to the problems faced by political parties in regionally-divided societies, or more basically, to the problems of the societies themselves. We have indicated some range of alternatives, but never with the thought that any describes

15. Michael Hechter, "Regional Inequality and National Integration in the British Isles, 1801-1921," *Journal of Social History* 5 (Fall 1971): 96-117; A. G. Frank, *Capitalism and Underdevelopment in Latin America* (New York: Monthly Review Press, 1967), pp. 121-42; C. B. Macpherson, *Democracy in Alberta: The Theory and Practice of a Quasi-Party System* (Toronto: University of Toronto Press, 1953).

the ideal. Perhaps parties should be working toward ways of re-organizing their societies so that currently regionally-linked problems would be absorbed by the total nation. But whatever normative judgements we might make on what represents a better form of social organization, what is clear at this time is that, in many societies, regional and national demands simultaneously clamour for attention. In the next section we consider some of the ways in which Canadian parties have dealt with contending interests.

ASSESSING PARTY ACTIONS

The way in which parties respond to demands of a local or national character needs to be tested empirically. To explore it, we suggest six questions, directed to what appear to be the central strains in the process of reconciling national and local demands. These questions have been formulated in terms of the Canadian experience, but they are more general in scope. The fourth question, however, applies only to a federal system of government.

The focus of the investigation is on the accommodative role of parties. It would be possible to approach the assessment of party actions by asking how parties might contribute to a society in which local demands were clearly subordinated to national needs. Or con-versely, how might parties aid in the concentration of power in the hands of regional governments or regional interests? Either of these perspectives could be adopted in the context of the six questions posed, with appropriate adjustments. We have instead focused on the accommodative role of parties because this is responsive to the circumstances of Canadian society, both as they are now and have been in the past. An emphasis on either regional or national domin-ance would also have required more programmatic answers than we are prepared to suggest at this time. But we cannot avoid the impli-cations of alternative arrangements, nor the possibilities of future change. We leave these, however, to the concluding comments.

1. *Do parties get support from all regions?* A national party that performs bridging functions must be recognized as a satisfactory vehicle for the expression of regional interests. At the same time, it should not be seen as the exclusive spokesman of only a few regions, rejected by others. If we use voting as an indication of this support, then we would expect it to be manifested through votes from sizeable proportions of the electorate in all regions and in all elections.

The measurement of widespread electoral support for Canada has, somewhat arbitrarily, been defined as no less than 30 percent and no more than 70 percent in any one region. We set an upper as well as a lower limit, since the former provides the check on whether a party has become too much the vehicle for any one region. If we apply these criteria to the fourteen elections between 1921 and 1965 for the two major parties, we find that neither fulfills our requirements perfectly. The Conservatives were unable to obtain our definition of adequate support in eight elections in Quebec, which must be considered a major failure from the perspective of responsiveness to provincial interests. In addition, they were also unable to get this minimum of support from the Prairies in seven elections and British Columbia in four. In contrast, the Liberal party gained adequate voting support in most elections in the east, but failed to do so in the Prairies in 7 instances, and in British Columbia in 5. For both parties, weakness of support in the west is indicative of the difficulties faced by the major parties in understanding and responding to the special interests and problems of the western provinces. But of the two, the Liberals in total had done a more effective job in the time spanned, mainly because of contrast with Conservative operations in Quebec.

Minor parties by definition do not receive widespread support. We cannot in fairness then use our preceding criteria for evaluating the amount of support they gain. In their case, we suggest that the minimum level be lowered to 15 percent. Comparing ten elections since 1935 for the CCF/NDP, we find that they had been able to achieve this level in all elections in British Columbia, nine in the Prairies, and four in Ontario. In addition, support had hovered around 10 percent in remaining elections in Ontario, and in the 1965 election stood at 8.6 percent in the Atlantic provinces and 12.0 percent in Quebec. For the most part, we would conclude that the NDP was still primarily a regional party in support terms, yet it did seem to have some potential in industrialized areas in the east.[16]

Social Credit has had much narrower support, and that quite uneven. Even its principal strongholds in the west were the scene of no more than two elections in the Prairies and three in British Columbia where Social Credit received at least 15 percent of the vote. In Quebec, they were able to gain more than this level of support in the elections of 1962, 1963, and 1965, yet after September, 1963, the Quebec wing was no longer a part of the national organization. Of the four parties, then, Social Credit had been least successful in gaining dispersed support.

2. *Can parties retain regionally-diversified support?* For a party to perform its functions with continuity over time, it needs to anticipate

---

16. In the 1968 election, however, support for the NDP had dropped to 5.4 percent in the Atlantic provinces and 7.5 percent in Quebec and was only slightly better in the former in 1972.

that some share of the electorate will stick with it through changing
issues, leaders, and candidates. In the context of this discussion, we
are suggesting that these loyal voters should be found in all regions.
If this is not the case, then the bridging function becomes subject to
fluctuating party fortunes, unanchored to a stable base of voter support. Without thought of giving a definitive answer to how this
support should ideally be distributed, we can use our survey data,
previously discussed in Chapter 6, for illustrative purposes. There, in
Table 6-1, we noted the percent of respondents who reported that
they always voted for the same party in federal elections. At that
time we were more interested in characteristics of regions, rather than
parties. In general, we found that loyalty to party declined as we
moved from east to west.

The Liberals benefited from greatest average party loyalty in all
regions. While it is true that their support diminished as we moved
from east to west, ranging from 65 percent in the Atlantic provinces
to 43 percent in British Columbia, they were still left with what, on
the average, we must describe as a stable body of supporters in all
regions. The Conservatives too had a large share of voters who
remained steadfast in their support. At the time of the 1965 election, almost half described themselves as party loyalists. Like the
Liberals, the Conservatives too suffered from weakened party ties
in the west, but they appeared to have even more serious flaws. They
had an even lower rate of stable support in British Columbia, 34
compared to 43 percent for the Liberals, and a less stable hold on
voters in Quebec.

Of the two older parties, then, we would consider the Liberals to
have been in a better position with regard to loyal voters who could
be expected to rally to the party, no matter what. The Conservatives
were less secure in their regional strongholds, in the areas we have
mentioned. Both parties, however, had roots in all regions in a way
that was shared by none of the minor parties. The latter, by their
younger age and the relative infrequency with which they ran candidates in all constituencies, had not built up the same kind of loyalty.
Despite the commitment that we might anticipate to be associated
with support for third parties, they still operated in a highly volatile
political environment. On the average, even in those regions where
they had participated for at least nine elections, only about one-
quarter of the voters in the 1965 election regularly supported these
parties.

3. *Do parties give adequate representation to regions?* Both this and
the first question are related to factors of size and the advantages that
size conveys. While Ronald May discusses these variables in terms
of a federal system of government, they are obviously not confined
to it, but operate wherever there are unequal units.

Two main sources of inequality may be distinguished which affect units' bargaining strengths in a systematic way. One of these is size measured by population and total resources; the other is wealth per unit of population. The first is an indicator of how many votes a unit can wield at the nation level (assuming a system of something like one man one vote) and of its ability to exercise effective sanctions; the second, as an index of "state of advancement," is suggestive of a unit's propensity to produce decision-making elites.[17]

In this discussion we are concerned only with aspects of size as they relate to support for specific parties and the representation that parties in turn give to regions, although it is apparent that they also raise broader issues of the relative power enjoyed by regions.

In the Canadian political system, we have understood the most effective form of representation that parties can give to regions to be through cabinet positions. This form of representation is hence restricted to parties that form the government. We discussed both the principles and facts of equitable representation in Chapter 3, and there is no need to repeat it here. But at least some brief comment needs to be made on how parties, in their formation of cabinets, balance the local concerns of regions with the national interests of the federal government.

On the average, in ten cabinets formed between 1921 and 1965, the Liberals allotted 14 percent of the cabinet positions to the Atlantic provinces. Thirty-three percent went to Quebec, 31 to Ontario, 14 to the Prairies, and 7 to British Columbia. The average Conservative distribution, based on five Cabinets, was 18 percent for the Atlantic provinces, 19 for Quebec, 33 for Ontario, 19 for the Prairies, and 11 for British Columbia. Neither party can then be described as having treated all regions either equally or equitably. Liberal cabinets typically gave undue representation to Quebec and Ontario. Conservative cabinets did the same for Ontario, while they treated almost as populous Quebec as though it were only the equal of the Atlantic and Prairie provinces.

4. *Do parties provide links between national and provincial interests?* Linkage may occur both at the level of party organization and through voter behaviour. Organizationally, common bonds would appear to be furthered by common structures that handle party business, most notably that of selecting candidates and ensuring their election, in both arenas. In terms of voting behaviour, national and provincial ties are reinforced where voters select candidates of the same party, regardless of the kind of election.

17. Ronald J. May, "Decision-Making and Stability in Federal Systems," *Canadian Journal of Political Science* 3 (March 1970): 78.

In Canada, there are separate federal and provincial structures for the two major parties and outside of the Atlantic provinces, for the two principal minor parties. Each is highly autonomous in its own realm.

> . . . we find . . . in all parties . . . provincial structures that differ from province to province, that are constituted autonomously, and that are not in hierarchic relationship to the national party structure. The National Liberal Federation, the National Progressive Conservative Association, the national organization of the Social Credit Party, and even the national organization of the more compulsively structured NDP, are agencies that coordinate rather than integrate parties on a nation-wide scale. This holds true even at the time of a federal election campaign.[18]

To some extent then, it is only the symbolic significance of the same party label that helps establish in voters' minds the sense that they are dealing with parties that can exercise authority at both levels of government. In the case of Conservatives in Quebec, even this is missing. Given the looseness of ties between the two levels of party organization, it may well be that federal-provincial links are not a particular strength of political parties in Canada.

Another possible tie between the two levels can come about as a result of the behaviour of voters. Voters can emphasize the links between the federal and provincial if they support the same party in both spheres. In Table 6–5 we reported the percent who had voted for the same party in the 1965 federal election and the closest preceding provincial election. At that time we noted how support for the same party declined as we move westward for the two older parties, but as we move eastward for the two minor parties.

The range of cross-election supporters for the Liberals extended from 86 percent in the Atlantic provinces to 38 percent in British Columbia. The span was wider for Conservatives—93 percent in the Atlantic provinces and 28 percent in British Columbia. In addition, support in the two elections was lower in Quebec than we would expect if the east-west pattern held consistently. In this instance, the organizational break between the federal Conservatives and the provincial Union Nationale had prevented more extensive consistency in the behaviour of voters. Indeed, since we use vote in the 1965 election as the base for our percentages, and this number was relatively small for Conservatives in Quebec, the 61 percent whom we considered to be consistent across elections was, in absolute terms, a

---

18. F. C. Engelmann and M. A. Schwartz, *Political Parties and the Canadian Social Structure* (Scarborough: Prentice-Hall of Canada, 1967), p. 143.

small share of the Quebec electorate. That is not, of course, the issue here, which is the weakness of the major parties in retaining support across the two kinds of elections in the west, particularly in British Columbia. Secondly, we have evidence from this one set of elections that Liberals in Ontario[19] and Conservatives in Quebec did not, in large numbers, transfer their preferences in national elections to provincial ones.

The NDP had the largest proportion of uniform supporters in British Columbia, 71 percent. Since Social Credit in that province also displayed a high level of consistency (92 percent voted Social Credit in both elections), this suggests that the volatility of major party support was compensated for by the stability of the minor parties. But in terms of the linkage functions of the party system, this still leaves us with some important gaps for the very reason that neither the NDP nor Social Credit were able to perform this function anywhere else. In other words, the ties between national and provincial interests did not operate consistently for any one party insofar as this was manifested in the behaviour of voters.[20]

5. *Do parties contribute a general framework to the views of their supporters that is still responsive to local conditions?* We introduced the idea of parties moulding opinions in Chapter 5. It was our contention that, even in political situations that permitted loose party ties, supporters could adopt consistent viewpoints that would set them apart from other parties. The likelihood of this occurring depends, as we earlier suggested, on the nature of the party, the kind of supporters it attracts, and the political setting in which it operates.

It is a particular role of parties that concerns us here. We look for evidence that party supporters have apparent affinities for each other, with the result that, in the aggregate, there are party outlooks that are national in scope. Yet at the same time, we expect regional boundaries to be associated with fairly distinctive climates of opinion. Supporters of different parties resident in the same region should reveal some effect of this climate by a degree of similarity in outlook that still leaves intact their own partisan commitment. To the extent that they do, we can infer that parties have played an influence appropriate to the needs of a regionally-divided society.

The thesis of this chapter is that national and regional interests exist side by side, and national parties, one way or another, are forced into taking a position on their contending demands. In the discussion and data analysis that follows, we speak of the nationalizing potential

---

19. This has also been found by John Wilson and David Hoffman, "The Liberal Party in Contemporary Ontario Politics," *Canadian Journal of Political Science* 3 (June 1970): 177-204.

20. Full details on the relation between voting consistency and region can be found in Chap. 6.

of political parties. By this we mean that all parties which operate in the national sphere have the potentiality for breaking through primal ties, including those of region, and building new ties that are nation-wide in scope. This is not to say that, having forged these new bonds, parties necessarily operate in response to national interests. It is possible to conceive of such parties adopting policies and programs most supportive of regional demands. The nationalizing aspects of parties emerge when they are able to unify their supporters, regard-less of the substantive bent of the issues.

When we use the term party influences on opinions we mean it to be understood as similar in nature to regional influences. In both instances, what we mean by "influence" is manifested through opinion distributions, in which Aggregate A (made up of residents in a region, supporters of a party, or portions of both) can be distinguished from a comparable Aggregate B. With this, we always keep in mind a conception of the process whereby individual voters become repre-sentative of a region or party, but neither this process nor the indi-vidual respondents are central to our discussion. What concerns us here are the patterns of opinion divided into regional and party strata. These become the data for making cross-regional and cross-party comparisons and attributing differential influences. We use for our empirical test the entropy measures first described in Chapter 5 and used to discuss regional influences in the preceding chapter. These are considered in conjunction with actual response patterns.

Accommodation of interests, in the sense that it is being used here, is demonstrated where party effects on opinions are greater than regional ones. Ideally, we should deal with issues that directly con-cern the balance of interests between nation and region. They should also be explicitly political in content, engaging the attention of politi-cal parties. The best we can do to illuminate party influence on voters' perspectives is to utilize the twenty-five political orientation items. Since they were not originally intended as measures of partisan per-ceptions, they do not necessarily pertain to the operation of political parties. Nor do they always focus on the strains between nation and region in the most pertinent fashion. Until more suitable data are available, what follows is intended to be only illustrative.

Of the possible alternatives, our greatest concern is with situations where the nationalizing potential of parties is maximized. We consider this to be manifested in several ways. One is through partial measures of association (based on entropies), where partials for parties con-trolling on region are larger than those for region controlling on party. Multiple associations, based on party and region, should be mainly attributable to the party effect. A further test comes from an examina-tion of response patterns. Where these are consistent across all re-gions, such that a party always plays the same role in attracting voters with a particular perspective, we add this to our evidence of party influences. Finally, we would expect proportional entropy reductions, for the effect of party within regions, to be relatively high, while proportional entropy reductions, due to region within parties, to be relatively low. That is, for each region and for each party separately we have an additional test of the degree of internal homogeneity.[21] Regional influences can be compared with party influences, using similar procedures. If the former dominate, partial associations for region controlling on party will be greater, as will be the regional contribution to the multiple association. Response patterns of party supporters follow their region's lead, and have little affinity with the views of their fellow-supporters elsewhere. As a last check, proportional entropy reductions due to parties within regions are relatively low, indicating some measure of regional consensus.

While it would be surprising if all of these conditions were fully met, they are at least a model of the contrast between the nationalizing pull of parties and the localizing pull of regions. Where it is not possible unequivocably to attribute greater influence to either region

---

21. The proportional entropy reductions due to region within party are summarized below.

Issue Area	Item	Proportional Entropy Reductions:		
		Liberal	Conservative	NDP
Awareness	Name	.037	.018	.024
	Party	.048	.045	.013
	Own leader	.238	.556	.196
Majority	Very important	.024	.005	.009
	Makes difference	.009	.001	.003
	Would switch	.004	.007	.021
Party differ- entiation	In government	.027	.008	.030
	Between parties	.003	.002	.015
	Exclude some	.030	.009	.020
Authorities	Own MPs	.041	.018	.025
	Lose touch	.033	.038	.044
	Intellectuals	.019	.022	.018
Cynicism	Big shots	.002	.013	.022
	Don't know	.007	.021	.012
	Trust	.006	.034	.019
	Waste	.012	.007	.014
	Crooked	.016	.026	.020
Federalism	Problems	.080	.049	.046
	Self	.008	.015	.058
	Elections	.079	.037	.047
Efficacy	Voting	.002	.019	.019
	Complicated	.018	.012	.039
	No say	.018	.011	.023
	Doesn't care	.065	.018	.068

or party, we will interpret this as an instance of accommodation, although it is not clear that regional pressures are always resolved under these circumstances. In presenting our data, we deal with issue areas rather than single items. This in fact insures that none of our examples fit the theoretical models perfectly, yet the use of a complex of items gives richer substantive content to possible influences from region and party.

Party Dominance

The only illustration of strong party dominance is revealed through concern with majority government. Three items were used to measure this: the likelihood that it had a strong impact on voting, belief that the existence of a majority made a difference in the conduct of government, and the possibility of switching parties in order to increase the chances of a majority. If supporters defined as showing most concern for majority government are assigned first place, the data indicate that there was a single dominant pattern found in all regions. Typically, Liberals expressed most concern about the issue, followed by Conservatives and then NDP. In the remaining one-third of the cases, Conservatives and NDP reversed their positions.

Confirmation of the greater influence of party is provided by partial associations derived from measures of entropy. The partial association for party controlling on region was particularly strong on the issue of majority government affecting respondents' voting decision. Yet we see that in all cases, partials for party were larger than those for region.

MAJORITY GOVERNMENT:	Affected Vote	Makes Difference	Would Switch
Partial associations:			
party/region	.027	.011	.018
region/party	.015	.005	.006
Multiple associations:			
party + region	.033	.014	.019

A check of proportional entropy reductions, first for each region, does not fully support our expectation that these should be relatively high, as a measure of association between party and opinion. In the Atlantic provinces and Quebec, proportional entropy measures ranged from .000 to .008. In the remaining regions, however, they were high on two out of three issues. We do have better evidence on internal homogeneity for parties. With the exception of Liberals on the effect on voting and NDP on the possibility of switching, where proportional entropy measures were .024 and .021 respectively, the remaining seven proportional entropy reductions were low. Looking at the full range of opinion distributions and statistical measures, then, the three related items on majority government do exemplify the dominance of party ties in affecting the views of party supporters. Whatever qualifications need to be made are those suggesting that perhaps regional influences were minimized more by some pressure to a national consensus than by overwhelming party influences.

No other issue area came close to that of majority government in demonstrating party effects. Feelings of political cynicism were all that could be found to even partially illustrate the requirements of party dominance. Cynicism has been measured by five items dealing with the nature of governmental personnel. In each instance, it is the negative view that indicates cynicism: government is run for big interests, there is a lack of understanding, not everyone can be trusted, tax moneys are wasted, and some government personnel are crooked. There was one principal pattern for parties: in 64 percent of the cases, NDP supporters were most cynical, followed by Conservatives and then Liberals. In an additional 20 percent, Conservatives were more cynical than NDP adherents, but Liberals remained in the least cynical category. Liberals were in second place in the remaining patterns.

Measures of association give limited support to an interpretation of party dominance. Only on the issue of trust is the partial association for party high, and there, as on waste and crookedness, multiple associations suggest that there is considerable interaction effect from party and region. In two of the five items, the partial for region is slightly larger than that for party.

CYNICISM:

	Big Shots	Under-standing	Trust	Waste	Crooked
Partial associations:					
party/region	.012	.007	.028	.014	.016
region/party	.008	.012	.018	.011	.020
Multiple associations:					
party + region	.014	.012	.035	.023	.031

High proportional entropy reductions for individual regions were found in ten of a possible twenty-five cells. In an additional six cases, there were moderate proportional entropy reductions ranging from .013 to .017. Proportionately entropy reductions for the three parties were low to moderately low in nine of a possible fifteen cases. Internal diversity associated with party ties was especially prominent in Quebec and British Columbia, but it was of relatively little consequence in Ontario. Strong regional contrasts, on the other hand, were fairly prominent in the Conservative and New Democratic parties, but not in the Liberal. This suggests that our overall results were strongly affected by a single combination of factors—the characteristically low level of cynicism expressed by residents of Ontario and supporters of the Liberals. Party influences were those that stemmed primarily from the Liberal party, while regional influences were mainly the impact of Ontario, and secondly, the Atlantic provinces.

Regional Dominance

Where one lives has been a principal determinant of how one views the federal government. When we examine the relation with party ties, we find that they have some impact, but quite secondary to that of region. Generalizations are based on responses to three questions: the level of government that handles most important problems, has most personal impact, and whose elections are most crucial. Because the largest group of respondents mentioned the provincial level as having most effect on themselves and their families, we have used this category for our analysis throughout. Yet this adds some confusion, because obviously this response is most appropriate to a provincial, and not a federal, orientation. To retain some continuity with previous chapters, as well as to face up to this confusion, we have simply reversed the order in which party supporters mentioned the provincial government. That is, parties are ranked according to the frequency with which the provincial government was *not* mentioned. The dominant pattern occurred only 40 percent of the time. In it Liberals were followed by Conservatives and then NDP supporters in the extent of their federal orientation.

The strength of regional influence was most apparent when we looked at measures of association. Regional partials were invariably high, especially on the importance of the federal government handling problems and in its elections.

FEDERAL ORIENTATION:	Problems	Affects Self	Elections
Partial associations:			
party/region	.004	.009	.018
region/party	.064	.019	.060
Multiple associations:			
party + region	.064	.019	.064

In keeping with conditions we have set for establishing regional influence, we also found that proportional entropy reductions for each region tended to be low, while those for each party tended to be high. The only exceptions to indications of lack of association between party and opinion within region is indicated by proportional entropy reductions of .031 for Ontario on elections and .036 for British Columbia on self-orientation. The latter item also produced relatively low proportional entropy reductions for Liberals and Conservatives. In all other cases, however, proportional entropy reductions for parties were of a magnitude to indicate that party supporters were strongly swayed by the outlooks prevalent in their regions. It is particularly interesting that, despite the propensity of Liberals toward a greater federal orientation, this was not sufficient to establish a clear-cut national pattern.

A trend toward regional dominance was also apparent on issues of political awareness. This was measured by knowledge of the winning candidate's name and party, and the attachment of one's own party leader to one's region. Parties are ordered in a variety of ways, such that no consistent patterns emerged as dominant. Partial associations for region were always greater than those for party, but we also saw a strong party effect when respondent's own party leader was tied to his region. We noted as well secondary influences from party on questions pertaining to candidates' name and party.

POLITICAL AWARENESS:

	Name	Party	Own Leader
Partial associations:			
party/region	.014	.017	.277
region/party	.029	.040	.321
Multiple associations:			
party + region	.035	.043	.333

Because of the extent of interaction of the leader's identification with respondent's region, proportional entropy reductions were high for all regions on this issue, even in the Atlantic provinces and Quebec, where none of the three party leaders had a strong attachment. Otherwise, however, proportional entropy reductions tended to be low. In contrast, they were moderate to large for all parties. We can conclude then, that while party influences had some importance, especially on the more emotional aspects of leader identification, those from region were dominant.

Attitudes toward political authorities also showed stronger impact from regional influences, but there were as well noticeable party effects. For example, in rating own member of Parliament as doing a good job, the partial association for region was .031 and for party, .021. Considerable interactive effect was also manifested in a multiple association of .040. In addition to rating of MPs, evaluation of authorities was determined by feelings that members of Parliament soon lose touch with their electors and complaints that there were too many intellectuals in government. Reversing the order of the last two items, no consistent pattern for parties across regions was found. Even so, Liberals did tend to be more positive in their assessments, ranking seven times in both first and second place, out of a possible fifteen (three items x five regions). Conservatives appeared most critical, ranking second five times and third, nine times. The NDP, as we noted in the preceding chapter, were curiously polarized, ranking first with most positive responses seven times, and third, five times.

AUTHORITIES:

	Own MPs	Lose Touch	Intellectuals
Partial associations:			
party/region	.021	.016	.010
region/party	.031	.036	.020
Multiple associations:			
party + region	.040	.039	.021

We have assumed that regional dominance of political views and weak party effects is also manifested internally by proportional entropy reductions that are low for each region and high for each party. But because of considerable party influence on views of authorities, these conditions were not fully met. Proportional entropy reductions for parties were in fact all high, or at least moderately so—in the case of intellectuals for Liberals and NDP (PER = .019 and .018), and rating of MPs for Conservatives (PER = .018). We conclude from this that each group of party supporters was divided along lines of residence. Within regions, proportional entropy reductions of .010 or less occurred in only five of fifteen cells; three were high, that is, .029 or more; and the remainder were moderate. This is additional evidence of the pull between party and region, especially prominent in Quebec, the Prairies, and British Columbia.

The remaining two issue areas, tapping feelings of low efficacy and perceptions of a differentiated party system, showed on the average more effect from region than party, but results were neither particularly strong, nor patterns clearcut. For example, on three of the four measures of efficacy, partial associations for region ranged from .010 to .019 and for party, from .008 to .010. Only in response to the statement that the government does not care about the opinions of the ordinary voter did a strong effect appear, and it was for region, with a partial association of .050. Except on this issue, regional contrasts appeared moderate for the Liberals, and on all issues for the Conservatives. Within regions, strong contrasts between parties appeared only in British Columbia. Except for the tendency of Liberals to be more efficacious, there was no distinct pattern of party responses.

Party differentiation resulted in slightly more regional effect, with partial associations of .021 on feelings that it makes a difference which party governs, and .022 on the exclusion of some party. Party effects were also more prominent, with partials of .016 and .014 for these two items. There was little noticeable impact from either, however, on the issue of distinguishing between federal parties. Proportional entropy reductions were relatively high on the first two issues for Liberals and NDP, and in the Atlantic and Prairie provinces. This was apparently an issue area that had a fairly general impact across the country, while still having special meaning to particular popultion groups.

On the basis of these twenty-five orientation items, it appears that the nationalizing influence of parties was subordinated to that from region. Yet our evidence certainly is not that parties are unassertive. What we still do not know, because of the limitations of our data, is the extent to which parties play their balancing act. As far as the orientation items are concerned, it is apparently not very effective. The general applicability of these findings is probably doubtful, especially since we are dealing with a very limited sample of issues. Yet they are instructive of the barriers that exist to an accommodation of interests, both because of the nature of territorial claims and the limitations of party ties.

6. *Do parties, through the policies they adopt, actively further both national and local interests, but neither exclusively?* This question is, much like the preceding one, concerned with the accommodation of national and regional concerns. In some respects, it is the most crucial we have raised. This preeminence stems from the overt efforts of parties to deal with contending interests in terms of substantive issues. We described these efforts in Chapter 5, where we were primarily interested in parties as spokesmen for region interests, as manifestations of the advocacy role of parties.

A full description of advocacy failed in Chapter 5 because of our inability to bring together a systematic sample of issues. At that time we focused solely on the advocacy of regional interests, yet even so we could not always distinguish these. In this chapter we have an even more difficult task. When, out of the universe of issues that parliamentary parties face, do they advocate policies that are exclusively regionally or nationally oriented, and when are they conciliatory of demands from both spheres? At first glance, some issues would appear to be totally in one or the other realm, but a search for examples made it clear that it was not the issues themselves that defined the area of interest. It was rather the policies adopted to handle them that determined the impact of territorial claims. We may illustrate with the well-known issue of conscription. If we did not know the history of Canada, we could assume that whatever policy was adopted toward national military service during wartime would serve the nation without conflicting with regional interests. But the problem during both World Wars was not only finding sufficient military manpower, but doing so in a manner that also served local needs and sensitivities. No party was completely successful in reconciling all of these concerns, yet there were important differences in the ways the issue was handled by governments during the two wars. In the first instance, the Union government, a coalition of Conservatives and some Liberals, thoroughly alienated French-speaking Quebec; in the second, the Liberal government managed to retain some support from that province, even though it antagonized other parts of the country. But if we use national unity as our criterion, then partial support everywhere was far better in its long-range consequences than the polarization associated with total support in some areas and total opposition in others.

Not only then are specific policies the touchstone of which interests are being furthered, but it should not surprise us, in view of the regional diversity of Canada, that provinces may define their interests in mutually contradictory ways. Regional interests, in other words, are not all of the same cloth. This makes the notion of contending interests even more complex than our previous discussion may have suggested. Empirically, it seems almost impossible to decide what is local, what is national, and perhaps surprisingly most difficult of all, what can be considered accommodative. Yet, despite these difficulties, we cannot abandon Question 6 entirely. The issues it raises are an essential part of the political processes in societies divided along regional lines. But for the time being at least, its political relevance remains theoretical.

Before leaving the topic of party policies, we illustrate, through provincial responses to medicare, the way in which local and national interests are confounded. If party stands are given only a minor place in the ensuing discussion, it is because they cannot always be separated from their provincial locus.

The consequences of uneven economic development, coupled with insufficient population mobility to compensate for lack of opportunity, have raised barriers to national unity in Canada. The institution of social welfare measures has become one of the recognized ways for coping with such regional inequalities. This was the rationale given for the introduction of a medicare proposal by the Liberals, in which the federal government would pay half the costs of doctors' bills, provided provincial governments instituted medical plans that would cover at least 95 percent of the population. Such plans must pay for all medical services, be publicly administered, and permit portability across provinces.

Opposition to this plan was soon rampant. Most provinces objected to the costs they would have to assume. This included such poor provinces as Prince Edward Island and New Brunswick, whose leaders recognized the benefits that their citizens would gain, but who could not find the means to participate. It also included the wealthy provinces of Ontario and Alberta. The Conservative government in Ontario based is objections on having money raised in Ontario spent in other provinces to put medicare into effect.[22] Premier Manning, the Social Credit leader of Alberta, was quoted as saying that it was "fundamentally unjust" to use public funds to aid those with the means to pay their own bills. He also predicted that non-participating provinces would oppose any increase in taxation that would be used to finance the medicare plan.[23] Poverty and lack of charity then might be said to characterize the principal arguments against medicare, with the latter coming from wealthy provinces that happened not to have Liberal governments. Inter-provincial rivalry was thus augmented by the proposed medicare scheme, even though its very purpose was to dampen such feelings by equalizing welfare benefits.

Hostility became even greater when the Union Nationale government in Quebec voiced its opposition on constitutional grounds, a view that had been previously expressed by the Quebec Liberal government when the federal government introduced a contributory, portable pension plan.[24] This position brought an emotional, and hardly consistent rejoinder from a Toronto newspaper. "The people of Canada have paid a price over the years for Quebec's suspicious nationalism. Now another instalment of the bill seems about to be presented. Many thousands of Canadians in other provinces may suffer preventable, and untreatable disease, even premature death in the years ahead, because of the Quebec government's insistence on maintaining its precious autonomy."[25]

The medicare issue revealed great lack of sympathy on the part of

---

22. For example, after the plan was in operation and Nova Scotia indicated that it would soon join, Premier Robarts predicted that Ontario also would participate. "After all, we can't expect the people of Ontario to pay the health costs of the rest of the country." Toronto *Daily Star* (14 September 1968).

23. Toronto *Daily Star* (3 February 1969).

24. Opposition in both cases was based on interpretation of Section 94A of the British North American Act, which permitted the federal government to make laws on old age pensions without abrogating the right of provincial governments to do the same.

25. Editorial, Toronto *Daily Star* (23 January 1968).

provincial governments for those less advantaged. The federal government could be interpreted as showing greater concern for local
needs, yet its policies served only to arouse antagonism, both against
itself and other provinces. Hostility was undoubtedly augmented by
the activities of two organized groups who attempted to discredit the
proposed plan, the medical profession and the insurance industry.
The alignment of parties on this issue was not entirely consistent. A
Liberal government introduced the plan and it was supported in the
federal house by the NDP. When medicare went into effect in July,
1968, it had only two participating provinces, British Columbia and
Saskatchewan. British Columbia had a Social Credit government, as
did non-participating Alberta. Normally, Liberals supported medicare, even though in the Atlantic provinces they found it difficult
initially to join. Despite the example set by opposition to the Canada
Pension Plan, Quebec Liberal party activists were in favour of the
federal plan. They were highly incensed when a prominent member of
their party, Eric Kierans, opposed medicare on grounds similar to
those of the Union Nationale. In total then, while party stands were
discernible, at the local level they were generally subordinated to
provincial needs.

This issue makes clear that policies which best serve local interests
are difficult to define unambiguously. In the case of Quebec, for example, provincial autonomy was seen as more important than welfare
assistance, although of course federal money was not being rejected,
only federal administration of the plan. In Ontario, a provincially-
supported contributory plan administered by a private agency was
viewed as superior to broader coverage, if the latter meant aiding less
advantaged provinces. From the perspective of the federal government, the importance of a national medical plan outweighed the financial burdens it would place on relatively poor provinces. Yet the
tensions between national and provincial interests, and the conflicting
stands taken by political parties reveal, even in the summary way
they have been pictured here, the major currents in Canadian politics.
Even though we cannot disentangle entwined interests, we are left
with no doubt that national and regional concerns produce an ever-
present tension in the political process. The issue used to illustrate this
tension is not unique, but represents one of an increasing body of
problems requiring joint jurisdictions. It is this which is frequently
the reference in current talks of "co-operative federalism."[26]

---

26. For further illustrations see Neil Caplan, "Some Factors Affecting the
Resolution of a Federal-Provincial Conflict," *Canadian Journal of Political
Science* 2 (June 1969): 173-86; Neil Caplan, "Anatomy of a Federal-Provincial
Conflict," *Journal of Canadian Studies* 5 (February 1970): 50-61; Richard
Simeon, *Federal-Provincial Diplomacy* (Toronto: University of Toronto Press,
1972).

DEFINING INTERESTS

In asking, as we did at the outset of this chapter, "in whose interests should the government be run," we called attention to the pervasiveness of territorial divisions and their interpenetration of the political process. In assembling supportive data to test our six secondary questions, we were forced to acknowledge that there were no simple answers.

With respect to the support they gained from the electorate, all parties had weaknesses. For the Liberals, these were principally in the western provinces, and for the Conservatives, in Quebec. Regional dispersion of support was even more seriously distorted for the minor parties. The continuity of this support, as we were able to discern it through our survey, was quite strong for the Liberals in all regions. The Conservatives suffered some gaps in nationwide party loyalty, while the minor parties possessed what was numerically only a small body of loyal supporters confined to a few sections of Canada.

The representation given to regions through cabinet positions was conferred only by the major parties. Since 1921, the Liberals had overrepresented Quebec and Ontario; the Conservatives had done the same for Ontario, while underrepresenting Quebec.

Links between the national and provincial levels of government are provided through the operation of political parties with the same name. For the most part, organizational ties between these parties are so loose, that solidarity often exists in name only. Linkage provided by voters choosing the same party in both national and provincial elections is highly uneven, being especially weak for the major parties in the west and for the minor parties in the east. Altogether then, the links between national and provincial interests provided by the party system exist in unstable and inconsistent forms.

Party links with opinions could not be precisely described with the data available. From what we could discern, it appeared that parties have some impact, but this is usually secondary to that from regions. The accommodative outcomes that seemed most in keeping with the needs of Canadian society were thus relatively rare.

Party advocacy of regional or national interests remained theoretically important without the support from systematic data. An examination of a few issues did show the play of interests accompanying adoption of a government policy. No conclusions could be drawn on the tendencies of political parties to assume a particular orientation. We failed in this task because of the difficulty of assembling an adequate sample of issues, the equivocal character of specific policies, and the evidence of party inconsistency across provincial lines.

What we conclude from these findings is partially dependent on what we ask from them. If our question is, are provincial divisions important factors in the actions of national political parties, the answer is a definite yes. If we ask, do national political parties act as even-handed vehicles for the expression of regional interests, manifested through such indicators as the support they receive and the representation they give, the answer is clearly no. If instead we wish to know whether parties serve as accommodators of national and regional concerns, then the answer is sometimes. Parties appeared to play this accommodative role in those instances, more often isolated than general, when they gained widespread support, gave regions equitable representation, helped temper regional outlooks with a national perspective, and balanced regional needs against national ones in proposing policies.

We centred on the accommodative role of parties for a number of reasons. For one thing, such a role is directly responsive to past and current circumstances. In addition, even if governmental arrangements should change, as is implied if either national or local interests were to dominate, it is unlikely that the needs of these spheres would themselves alter. For example, it can be argued that a federal system of government has strongly contributed to the continuation of regionalism in Canada. Yet given the social and economic diversity of the country, it is unlikely that a unitary system of government would have much different impact. The political mechanisms, as they exist, certainly reinforce the importance of territorial considerations; they do not produce them, nor need we assume that by themselves they could drastically alter them.

In a sense, our entire argument has been at odds with the evolutionary perspective of Rokkan, who predicts that territorial cleavages will give way to functional-economic ones. The major thrust of our response to the place of evolutionary theories in understanding regionalism is presented in the concluding chapter. At this point we can take issue more specifically with the position, expanded in the paper by Rokkan and Lipset, that as shifts occur in the major cleavages of the society, so too will the bases of party formation.[27] While we have not been particularly concerned with the sources of party origin in Canada, we could not ignore, especially in Chapter 6, the fact that territorial claims were always critical in affecting the kinds of parties that exist. More important, however, is the relation between regional interests and current party operations. This can be demonstrated even using the Lipset-Rokkan adaptation of Parson's system problems.[28] For example, the principal function of the party system,

---

27. Lipset and Rokkan, "Cleavage Structures," pp. 1-64.

28. Mildred A. Schwartz, "Political Parties in Regionally Divided Societies," paper presented to the Eighth World Congress of the International Political Science Association (Munich: 4 September, 1970).

just as of the entire polity, can be viewed as the attainment of socially-defined goals, including, of course, ones defined by party elites. Specific parties are able to carry out this function through their interchanges with other collectivities that respond to the remaining functional problems. Inputs from the adaptive system are resources; from the integrative system, support; and from the pattern maintenance system, legitimacy. Outputs from the party system to each subsystem are services, policy decisions, and responsible leadership.[29] To the extent that inputs are unequal because of regional divisions in the total society, then outputs will in turn be regionally biased. As a result, the effectiveness of parties will be limited in carrying out nationally defined goals. This does not mean that parties cannot operate with some success; that is, they can still provide leadership and decisions, and obtain support, including sufficient to stay in office. But to the degree that they are successful, this will be partly because of their effectiveness in areas that do not touch on regional interests and inequalities.

Once we grant the contemporary significance of territory, then its political relevance looms large. Territorial considerations obviously affect much more than the sources of party formation. Regardless of formative influences, all political parties, even disregarding those with purely local arenas of operation (e.g., in provincial politics), are affected by national-regional tensions. We recognize that the definition of interests can change as regional resources alter in significance or distribution. As such changes occur, we can expect that inputs to the party system will vary with them. Party outputs are also not inflexible, and one measure of party effectiveness is a responsiveness to shifting circumstances. The impetus to change can come as well from within the political system, as party programs and the initiative of party leaders act to create new priorities in national goals. However these alterations in party actions take place, they will reflect the salience of regional interests at a given point in time.

---

29. Parsons treats as a separate output to—*I*, the pattern maintenance system, moral responsibility for the collective interest and the integrity of the political system. Talcott Parsons, "On The Concept of Political Power," in Parsons, *Sociological Theory and Modern Society* (New York: Free Press, 1967), pp. 297-354.

CHAPTER 12

The future of regionalism in Canada

THE CONDITIONS OF REGIONALISM

The relevance of regionalism in modern, industrial society hinges on answers to three questions. Under what conditions is territory politically salient? What are the prospects for deregionalization? What are the consequences of regionalism?

The conditions making for regionalism have been fully explored in this volume. We began in Chapter One by discussing the concept of regionalism in terms of eight inter-related elements, presented with sufficient generality to apply to many societies. They can be reduced, for the sake of simplicity, to three principal components.

One set of components relates to the characteristics and conditions that separate territorial units. These are economic, political, and demographic factors, and the resultant life styles that emerge from their operation. The second component consists of states of mind, ways of viewing reality through regional frameworks. Of critical significance is the emergence of a group consciousness, whereby residents express a regional identity, recognizing their distinctiveness and their special interests. It is this consciousness which helps mobilize regional demands and grievances. Thirdly, regionalism is a product of behaviour. These are the political actions which contribute to the salience of territorial divisions. Such actions may be the result of conscious decisions to further the interests of one or more regions, and are generally part of the behaviour of political leaders. But regional behaviour may be the result of even unanticipated and un-recognized effects stemming from the experience of regionally-defined conditions. This is how we have often treated the behaviour of ordinary voters.

Our Canadian example provides clearest evidence for the impor-tance of structural conditions making for regionalism. We have not been able to establish each factor's relative contribution to regional-ism, but at least three are prominent, and in all instances, show little sign of altering over time. The economy makes its contribution through the continuity of inequalities in resources and in outputs generally. Relevant demographic factors are those tied to imbalances in the economy and those stemming from the uneven distribution of critical ethnic groups. While these demographic features have changed with time, the results are still such as to emphasize regional differ-ences. Finally, the political structure enhances the experience of regionalism through such means as the allocation of power among regions, the responses of political parties, and the existence of a federal system of government. For the most part, regions are political units, and where they are not, they are combinations of such units, with some independence as political actors. This in itself ensures that regionalism will continue to be a political phenomenon.

The frame of mind that accompanies territorial divisions has been described in this volume in terms of subjective evaluations of life in regions and of orientations to the political system. Our survey data provided evidence that the outlooks of voters were at least partially linked with their region of residence. Here, however, we found several limitations in our data resources. Unlike our discussion of conditions, we come nowhere close to exhausting the politically-relevant opinions. We also do not have data covering a time span, by which to evaluate the historical continuity of differences in out-look. Some items, particularly those pertaining to respondents' judge-ments of their own conditions, are especially likely to be time-bound. Even some aspects of political orientations may be influenced by immediate conditions. Most frustrating was our inability to directly measure the strength of regional consciousness. Yet with all of these limitations, we believe some inferences about the importance of the opinions surveyed are warranted. The lack of exhaustiveness of our items is compensated for by their apparent relevance, both to our respondents and to the situation of Canadian regions. The absence of a time series does prevent tracing trends in opinions. Yet given the stability of regional differences with respect to economic, demo-graphic, and political factors, we can anticipate some comparable, though not necessarily identical, stability in regional differences in opinions. Most regrettable is our inability to directly ascertain the extent of regional identification and regional consciousness. For the latter at least, we can do no more than infer its existence from the kinds of response patterns dominant in each region, which indicate that residents vary in their judgements of personal and regional circumstances and of the political processes.

The study of pertinent behaviour in Canada has emphasized voting. This has meant that we have omitted those kinds of political actions that have most obvious and direct links with the continuity of regionalism. Voting is not insignificant, however, since it provides the broadest indication of mass responses to regional pressures, and in the case of our Canadian data, gives persuasive evidence of the continuing political importance of regional divisions. At the same time, we must continue to search for ways to discover and evaluate the broad range of political acts bearing on regionalism.

The political salience of regionalism is partially established through our conceptualization. For example, we have used regionalism not only to describe territorial units differentiated by conditions, outlooks, and behaviour; we also see regionalism as a principle of inequality. That is, differentiation is experienced as a source of relative disadvantage, contributing to regionally oriented feelings and actions. In addition, regionalism is more than the recognition of differences in one or more regions. As we understand it, it is the property of a total society. While actual disadvantages may vary among sectors of a country, and some differences may not even lead to inequalities, where the national emphasis is on differentiation, the total effect is a society, and not just parts of one, in which divisiveness is a principal characteristic.

The determination of actual regional inequalities for Canada was not always easy. The set of conditions with clearest evidence of inequality were economic ones. They distinguished among regions with unequivocal harshness. The nature of these economic conditions was also evident to the respondents in our survey, whose evaluations were dominated by their regional experiences. Demographic characteristics drew our attention mainly in Chapter Two, where we were content to trace uneven regional distributions. There we felt it sufficient to demonstrate differences, rather than establish connections with overt disadvantage. We did so because, while it is true that some groups have suffered through discrimination, an even more general reason exists for the importance of differences in ethnic and class composition of regions. This is related to the ability of such groups to readily acquire a sense of identification and consciousness which can then be transferred to the region where the group has a territorial base. That is, while the uneven distribution of critical demographic groups may or may not be associated with actual disadvantages suffered by these groups, their territorial roots give them an added potential for mobilizing in support of their special interests. Finally, it was apparent as well that political power was not evenly distributed. From the perspective both of the political system and the orientations of voters, each region manifested considerable uniqueness, though this was not necessarily seen as disadvantageous. Yet, particularly in our interpretation of voter orientations, we saw the existence of differences as signs of stress. While we do not argue for the necessity, or even the advantages, of a national consensus in political orientations, the absence of such consensus indicates that there are several competing ways in which citizens can relate to the political system. Competition produces stress, particularly in the integration of Quebec and British Columbia into the political fabric of Canada. But more important is the over-all effect, in which Canada emerges as a regionally-divided society.

We have, we believe, successfully answered our first question. We have done this by providing the guidelines for determining the salience of territory, and the rationale for selecting these. Since this is a book about Canada, and not only about regions and regionalism, we have not felt the need to elaborate our argument beyond what was needed to describe adequately the situation of the country. As a result, we must admit to the limitations always posed by the use of a single case study. The relation among the factors making for regionalism, their relative contribution to its strength and continuity, the possibility that some features have been omitted—these and similar questions require a thorough comparative analysis before they can be answered. At this time at least, we feel convinced that the factors we know to be at issue can be as prominent in mature, industrialized societies as in less developed ones.

THE DECLINE OF REGIONALISM

Two Models of Change

Where regional divisions exist, are they immutable, and the most poignant question of all, must regional inequalities always remain? Change is a feature of all existence and we can expect it to affect regionalism as well. What we need is an adequate model of change to predict the circumstances of declining regionalism.

In several places in this volume, particularly in Chapters One and Eleven, we took issue with evolutionary theories of change. Because of their importance, we shall look at these again, and in more detail. In the context of our abbreviated model of regionalism, they predict that as changes occur in conditions (C), mainly through technological innovation and the pressures that this will bring for urbanization and related demographic changes, these will have an impact on outlooks (O) and behaviour (B), resulting in a lessening of importance attached to regional divisions and an alteration in political behaviour consistent with this (C → O → B). Alternatively, we shall look at a more purposive model of change. This presumes that behavioural interventions are used to alter conditions, which in turn will alter outlooks and then subsequent behaviour. (B → C → O). Because of the attractiveness of evolutionary views, however, it is these which will engage most of our attention.

Evolutionary Change

Herbert Spencer's notions of social evolution, in which all social phenomena are subject to universal, inevitable, and unidirectional processes of transformation from simple to complex states, have long been abandoned by sociology. But the theme of evolutionary development itself has not disappeared, since something analogous to the economists' concept of secular trend so obviously explains a good deal of social change. Parsons, for example, describes the evolution of societies in terms of such processes as differentiation and adaptive upgrading. One crucial result is a shift from ascriptive statuses and concerns to universalistic considerations of achievement.[1] The substantive pressure comes about primarily through technological change, mainly the introduction of industrialization and the large-scale movement to cities. That such shifts would be accompanied by the declining importance of territory was predicted by no less an authority than Durkheim.

> Some have seen [the increase in national homogeneity] to be a simple consequence of the law of imitation. But it is rather a levelling analogous to that which is produced between liquid masses put into communication. The partitions which separate the various cells of social life, being less thick, are more often broken through. . . . Territorial divisions are thus less and less grounded in the nature of things, and consequently, lose their significance. We can almost say that a people is as much advanced as territorial divisions are more superficial.[2]

Despite the plausibility of this general position, one purpose of this volume was to demonstrate, through the example of Canada, that regionalism is not a declining force in the political life of a country that otherwise bears all the characteristics of a modern state. This was

---

1. Talcott Parsons, *Societies, Evolutionary and Comparative Perspectives* (Englewood Cliffs, N.J.: Prentice-Hall, 1966), especially pp. 21-25. See also Richard P. Applebaum, *Theories of Social Change* (Chicago: Markham Publishing Co., 1970), pp. 36-59.

2. Emile Durkheim, *The Division of Labor in Society* (New York: Free Press, 1964), p. 187.

easy enough to do, since the theories we examined did not provide us with contrary evidence. At the same time, since we only discussed Canada, there is always the possibility that it is but a rare exception. The subsequent discussion will not provide much in the way of additional, comparative evidence, but following our critique of evolutionary theories will be a number of possible explanations for their inadequacy. It is these explanations that should provide us with guidelines for predicting the importance of regionalism in other, industrial societies.

Earlier, we reviewed three views of the process of deregionalization. In one, Lipset and Rokkan presented a three-stage model of nation-building that essentially involves a progressive resolution of tensions between national and local interests. While in its outlines this conception is highly compatible with our own perspective, especially since the authors do not see the resolution of tensions as inevitable, our main quarrel was with their judgement that instances where national interests do not come to predominate can be seen as gaps in the process of modernization.[3] Rokkan presents a convincing case for such evolutionary developments in Norway,[4] yet neither he nor Lipset do the same for those apparently modern states where territorial interests still abound.

Similar objections were made to the Lipset and Rokkan formulations, based on Parsons' concept of system-problems, to account for the emergence of political parties. In essence, they argue that at different stages of societal development, different factors will underlie the representation of dominant concerns in the party structure. Thus at early stages, political parties emerge to defend territorially-based cultural interests, while at later stages they will represent nationally-distributed class interests.[5] Although not necessarily disputing their theory of social change, we questioned in Chapter Eleven the adequacy of their conception, in those situations where territorial cleavages remain strong, to deal with the current operations of political parties.

Kevin Cox took a position similar to Rokkan's, but also asked more specifically what in the nature of industrialization brings about a shift from territorial to functional-economic cleavages. He has

---

3. Seymour M. Lipset and Stein Rokkan, "Cleavage Structures, Party Systems, and Voter Alignments: An Introduction," in Lipset and Rokkan, eds., *Party Systems and Voter Alignments* (New York: Free Press, 1967), p. 9.

4. He does not, however, deny their current, if not pervasive importance. Stein Rokkan, "Geography, Religion, and Social Class: Crosscutting Cleavages in Norwegian Politics," in Lipset and Rokkan, eds., *Party Systems and Voter Alignments,* pp. 367-444.

5. Lipset and Rokkan, "Cleavage Structures, Party Systems, and Voter Alignments," pp. 9-13.

isolated four factors, previously discussed in Chapter One. These are information flow, resistance to information, birth-death processes, and relocation processes.[6] We have not been concerned with examining each of these factors in our description of Canada, although we have accumulated considerable data bearing on them. We found, in Chapter Two, that the population of French origin has remained fairly stable over time, and that French and other origin groups continue to be unevenly distributed geographically. Regional differences in urbanization, while changing for the Prairies and the Atlantic provinces in the last few decades, have in general also persisted. Regions differ as well in educational opportunities and in their access to communication. Only in the strong pull of Ontario and British Columbia to migrants do we have evidence that the more advantaged pace-setters may help to alter the population distributions in a direction consistent with the breakdown of regional divisions.

We have no comment to make here about the evolutionary forces set in motion by industrialization. What we have questioned in Cox's theory, and this based primarily on our Canadian materials, is the impact of industrialization on those demographic factors that might influence deregionalization. In considering why demographic changes have not occurred in the expected direction in Canada, we had also to question the developmental character of other changes. This led us to isolate five barriers to deregionalization, potential blocks to the normal process of evolutionary change. These are associated with the growth of cities, economic development, the politics of regionalism, cultural homogeneity, and the dynamics of government. In the following discussion we illustrate each of these mainly in terms of the Canadian experience. They are, however, of a much more general character, and should be usable as guides for assessing the current status of regionalism in any society.

The Growth of Cities

From the perspective of developmental theories, the growth of cities is viewed as a necessary concomitant of modernization.[7] From another, though not unrelated perspective, the tie between cities and regions is so intimate, that eventually regions may be seen as structures of cities. In early stages of development, cities emerge in response to the needs of a region, defined by its available resources. Where

6. Kevin R. Cox, "The Spatial Evolution of National Voting Response Surfaces: Theory and Measurement," Department of Geography, Ohio State University, discussion paper No. 9, mimeo., p. 3.

7. Neil J. Smelser, "The Modernization of Social Relations," in Myron Weiner, ed., *Modernization* (New York: Basic Books, 1966), p. 111.

resource development has been adequate, cities have become self-sustaining, acquiring new links with other cities and fewer with their regional hinterlands.[8] Region in this sense may be a much smaller territorial unit than the kind we have been using, but the connection nonetheless is of the same character. ". . . despite their original dependence on regional economic viability, cities are now the determinants of that viability."[9]

There is some agreement among geographers and economists that the growth of cities becomes a determinant of economic growth; there is probably less agreement on how this affects the continuity of regional divisions. If one takes the position that in later stages of development, region per se becomes less important as links are forged between cities, or even that cities and their hinterlands are placed in a nexus resulting in a totally urban way of life, then Donald Kerr's conclusion is particularly pertinent. He says that,

> Viewed simply as a physical phenomenon, interaction between city and hinterland, and between one city and another, is a powerful unifying force. Urban centres are closely tied by a variety of communications which . . . carry people, information, decisions, goods and services, quickly and easily. Surely this is the very substance of any modern industrial state as it functions on a day-to-day basis. Critical in the whole system is the metropolis from which authority is diffused to which in turn wealth feeds back.[10]

The extent to which such processes have occurred in Canada have been limited by considerations of region. Several forces seem to have been at work. One is the historical continuity of patterns of urbanization, a second derives from the nature of metropolitan dominance, and a third from the conflicts associated with the growth of cities.

In Chart 2–2 we presented trends in urbanization for regions, documenting the narrowing gap among the three most urbanized provinces of Ontario, Quebec and British Columbia. The two remaining regions remain set apart, most dramatically in the case of the Atlantic provinces.[11] Yet even these trends do not fully capture

---

8. N. H. Lithwick and Gilles Paquet, "Urban Growth and Regional Contagion," in Lithwick and Paquet, *Urban Studies: A Canadian Perspective* (Toronto: Methuen, 1968), p. 31.

9. Ibid., p. 32.

10. Donald P. Kerr, "Metropolitan Dominance in Canada," in John Warkentin, ed., *Canada, A Geographical Interpretation* (Toronto: Methuen, 1968), p. 553.

11. Leroy O. Stone, *Urban Development in Canada* (Ottawa: Queen's Printer, 1967), pp. 36-38, 41. The only country evidence, purporting to show a decline in regional divisions, comes from Sanford Labovitz and Ross Purdy, "Territorial Differentiation and Societal Change in the United States and Can-

ada," *The American Journal of Economics and Sociology* 29 (April 1970): 127-47. These writers have used urbanization as an index of technological efficiency, to test the thesis that increases in technological efficiency will lead to the eventual decline of territorial differentiation. To demonstrate this, they compared the United States and Canada in their relationship between urbanization and fourteen other social and cultural variables. Available for the United States, but missing for Canada, were measures of income, race (here French origin would have been analogous), and voting behaviour, three major variables which others have shown to be little effected by nationalizing pressures. With the data they do use, they conclude that Canada is in the third stage of a developmental process. In this stage, "Technological changes cross the boundaries of the developing areas and begin to pervade the whole society. The rural areas specialize and develop, and the territories become more economically interdependent. Consequently, the areas converge on social and cultural characteristics. Rural productivity becomes increasingly closer to urban productivity, and therefore,differentiation decreases among the areas." (129)

If we look at only one principal finding, that differences in levels of urbanization are quite small among provinces, we must ask how such a conclusion could be drawn in the face of everything that has been presented thus far. One possible source of Labovitz and Purdy's unexpected findings is from a consistent error in computing the index of dissimilarity, the statistic used to measure the amount of difference between provinces. It is described in Otis Dudley Duncan and Beverly Duncan, "Residential Distribution and Occupational Stratification," *American Journal of Sociology* 60 (March 1955): 493-503. "The statistic is interpreted as the minimum percentage of individuals with characteristic *i* [e.g., living in urban areas] who would have to move from one territorial unit to another to bring about an equal distribution of individuals with characteristic *k* [e.g., those living in rural areas] among the territorial units." (135). A check on their urban data for one year, 1961, presents quite different conclusions than those they publish. Their index of dissimilarity is 5.7; our computations, using, as far as we can determine, identical data, produce an index of 18.5. If the latter represent the correct results, then they certainly indicate a high level of dissimilarity. Without doing a comparable check on their remaining data, a visual check suggests that levels of dissimilarity in urbanization have *increased* since the turn of the century.

The implications to be drawn from a low index of dissimilarity are also open to question. Interpretations must take into account the actual distribution of residents, and not only the percentages involved. If the index of dissimilarity is 5.7 for 1961, this means that 5.7 percent of the population would have to move from urban areas into rural ones (or vice versa) in order for regional imbalances to disappear. The total population they dealt with, excluding Newfoundland, the Yukon and North-West Territories, was approximately 17,744,000. The appropriate percentage of that total which would require moving is over 1 million, of which 70 percent are urban. A population transfer of this size, while perhaps minor in percentage terms, would be drastic in actual effects. In 1961, only Quebec and Ontario had populations of over five million. British Columbia had over one and a half million residents, and Alberta, one and a third million, but everywhere else, population concentrations were less. In other words, the kind of population movements required to eliminate regional imbalances would simply swamp most provinces, since the least urbanized were also the least populous. Or, if movement were from non-urban areas, it would virtually deplete them. The index of dissimilarity does not of itself then capture the nature of regional imbalances as these reflect inequalities of far-reaching proportions, beginning with the initial population bases of each region.

the nature of urbanization in each region. For example, Ontario has
become highly urbanized throughout southern Ontario, while in
British Columbia urbanization is concentrated in the growth of two
principal cities. These patterns are linked to other aspects of economic development. To Lithwick and Paquet, for example, urbanization was first effect and now cause of the level of regional development.

> . . . whereas cities were largely dependent upon regional
> development for their initial growth, in Canada this process
> has reversed through the dynamic changes in industrial
> structure in the course of economic development. The indus-
> trial focal points of economic growth are found in an urban
> environment, and the economic health of a region is now a
> function of the viability of the city within it. To the extent
> that there are no cities, regions tend to be depressed, except
> where profitable resource activities persist, such as in north-
> ern Ontario, the Prairies, and British Columbia.[12]

The growth of cities in Canada has not taken place in such a way as
to create national bonds cutting across regions. The expectation of
such linkages is based on several possibilities, as in the emergence of
a single primate city, such as London or Paris, that exerts centripetal
pulls; or through the growth of several national metropolitan centres,
interrelated both to each other and to their hinterlands. There are
two national metropolises in Canada, Toronto and Montreal. While
they compete with each other, they are also strongly tied together.[13]
Between the two, they channel the bulk of population movements in
the country. Vancouver, a newly emerging metropolis, also does the
same. The results are not, however, a metropolitan dominance that
links various parts of the country. The channelling effect serves to
reinforce pre-existing barriers of a political, physical, or cultural
nature.[14] For example, the interaction between cities in Ontario and
Quebec resembles a situation where they would be five times farther
apart than they are in fact.[15]

The continuity of regionalism, as it is associated with the growth
of cities, also stems from conflicts among cities, and between cities
and their hinterlands. Careless, for example, relates the growth of

---

12. Lithwick and Paquet, "Urban Growth and Regional Contagion," p. 37.

13. Kerr, "Metropolitan Dominance in Canada," pp. 546-48.

14. James and Robert Simmons, *Urban Canada* (Toronto: Copp Clark
1969), pp. 77-78.

15. J. Ross Mackay, "The Interactance Hypothesis and Boundaries in
Canada: A Preliminary Study," *The Canadian Geographer* 11 (1958): 1-8.

French-Canadian nationalism with the conflict between hinterland and the dominance of Montreal.[16] Kerr suggests that perhaps there is some unifying sentiment to be generated from such conflicts, but he has difficulty convincing himself.

> . . . the metropolitan centre is bound to arouse feelings of resentment and hostility, making its position *vis-à-vis* the hinterland at least an uncomfortable one. The connotation of the "St. James Street Robber Barons" in the past, and the "Bay Street Boys" at present, has been and continues to be widespread throughout the hinterland, to distinguish most sharply the impoverished exploited back-country from the wealthy metropolis. And yet even this may be a unifying force for there has been established from Nova Scotia to British Columbia a common bond which finds emotional satisfaction in carping at Toronto. Substantial unity is rarely built from such negative concepts, however.[17]

The Canadian situation has revealed three reasons why the growth of cities does not always lead to declining regionalism. These in turn suggest the contrasts that would be required for urbanization to contribute to deregionalization. First is a level of urbanization similar in all regions. Second is the development of links among cities, such that they become truly national centres. Thirdly, deregionalization will be aided where cities are well integrated with their hinterlands, rather than foci for conflict.

Economic Development

Although not without its critics,[18] one current theory sees modernization accompanied by sustained economic growth.[19] This theory has little room for instances of uneven regional development. Yet many studies indicate that neither development in itself, nor sustained economic growth, guarantee that existing economic disparities among regions will be removed, or that new disparities will not arise. While economists describing such situations often feel that, in the long run, such inequalities will disappear, the short run may be associated

---

16. Maurice Careless, "Metropolitanism and Nationalism," in Peter Russell, ed., *Nationalism in Canada* (Toronto: McGraw-Hill, 1966), p. 277.

17. Kerr, "Metropolitan Dominance in Canada," p. 553.

18. For example, Simon Kuznets, *Economic Growth and Structure* (New York: W. W. Norton, 1965), p. 232.

19. Harvey Leibenstein, *Economic Backwardness and Economic Growth* (Cambridge: Harvard University Press, 1957); W. W. Rostow, *The Stages of Economic Growth* (Cambridge: Harvard University Press, 1961).

with tenacious regional differences.[20] Many of these discussions are based on the experiences of newly industrializing societies. We must also look to the history of fully developed societies for the relation between economic growth and regionalism.

In Canada, regional economic disparities have endured for over one hundred years. We demonstrated some part of this trend with respect to per capita income in Chart 2–1.[21] Comparisons between Canada and the United States and Australia indicate that all these regionally divided societies manifest continuing gaps between regions, although Canada is outstanding for the stability with which sizeable gaps have endured.[22] In the United States as well, differences remain potent political factors in the life of regions.[23] In Britain, regional inequalities have assumed historic dimensions.[24]

Regional inequalities are not only a feature of newly industrializing nations, as even the few sources cited should indicate. Moreover, such inequalities can continue to exist for a century or more without diminishment. This is not to say that regions will not show absolute improvement in their economic output, but that relative to other regions in the same society, the gaps among them may remain unaltered. While economic development may indeed proceed as an evolutionary process, there is nothing inherent in this process that will necessarily lead to obliterating initial disadvantages, or to preventing new disadvantages arising.

Why do regional inequalities not disappear as a result of development? One theory, constructed to account for the experiences of Latin American regions, argues for the existence of internal colonialism. This assumes that more developed regions continue their develop-

---

20. Gunnar Myrdal, *Rich Lands and Poor* (New York: Harper, 1958); A. O. Hirschman, *The Strategy of Economic Development* (New Haven: Yale University Press, 1958); E. B. Hughes, "Interregional Income Differences: Self-Perpetuation," *Southern Economic Journal* 28 (July 1961): 41-45; J. G. Williamson, "Regional Inequality and the Process of National Development," *Economic Development and Cultural Change* 13 (July 1965) part II.

21. S. E. Chernick, *Interregional Disparities in Income* (Ottawa: Queen's Printer, 1966); Economic Council of Canada, *Sixth Annual Review: Perspective 1975* (Ottawa: Queen's Printer, 1969); Alan G. Green, "Regional Inequality, Structural Change, and Economic Growth in Canada—1890-1956," *Economic Development and Cultural Change* 4 (July 1969): 567-83.

22. Gordon Merrill, "Regionalism and Nationalism," in John Warkentin, ed., *Canada, A Geographical Interpretation* (Toronto: Methuen, 1968), pp. 561-63.

23. Ira Sharkansky, "Economic Development, Regionalism and State Political Systems," *Midwest Journal of Political Science* 12 (1968): 41-61.

24. Michael Hechter, "Regional Inequality and National Integration in the British Isles," *Journal of Social History* 5 (Fall, 1971): 96-117.

ment at the deliberate expense of the less-developed, using them both as sources of raw materials and as primitive markets, in a fashion analogous to colonial exploitation patterns. This argument has been extended to other countries,[25] and has some currency as well in explaining the Canadian situation.[26] Barriers to even development are seen as essentially political, arising from the greater power of some regions. Viewed in this way, the internal colonialism thesis is not a refutation of theories of continuing economic growth, since what it does, in effect, is to say that development is hampered by political considerations. Presumably, with their absence, development would proceed so that regional inequalities could disappear. It does not seem necessary, however, to adopt such a conspiratorial rationale for the continuity of regional inequalities. It is even more likely that economic, rather than political, explanations have greater importance. Physical resources, access to markets, ability to diversify, adequate manpower and similar economic factors are determinants of a region's economic status. We should not, however, completely discard the possibility that power differentials contribute to the continuity of regional economic differences.

Economic differentials may also have some roots in cultural factors. This is analogous to what some writers mean by a "culture of poverty."[27] In the case of regions, the relevant values would be those opposed to aspects of industrialization, such as working in factories, living in cities, or adopting universalistic criteria of evaluation. In this sense, traditionalism has been seen as a major barrier to economic progress in the southern United States. The economist William Nicholls, for example, classifies this traditionalism into five categories: "(1) the dominance of agrarian values, (2) the rigidity of the social structure, (3) the undemocratic political structure, (4) the weakness of social responsibility, and (5) conformity of thought and behavior."[28]

The counterpart of traditional values upholding patterns of behaviour that prevent regions from becoming similar are those values

---

25. A. G. Frank, *Capitalism and Underdevelopment in Latin America* (New York: Monthly Review Press, 1967); Pablo Gonzales Casanova, "Internal Colonialism and National Development," *Studies in Comparative International Development* 1 (1965): 27-37.

26. C. B. Macpherson, *Democracy in Alberta: The Theory and Practice of a Quasi-Party System* (Toronto: University of Toronto Press, 1953).

27. For example, Ulf Hannerz, *Soulside, Inquiries into Ghetto Culture and Community* (New York: Columbia University Press, 1969), pp. 178-88.

28. William H. Nicholls, "Southern Tradition and Regional Economic Progress," in John Friedman and William Alonso, eds., *Regional Development and Planning* (Cambridge: M.I.T. Press, 1964), p. 466.

that result in discriminatory practices. These hinder full participation in opportunities for economic advancement. On the surface, this may appear to be the same as internal colonialism, but we would understand these values and practices to be more diffuse and unlikely to be directed from any one source. Often they would be the result of attitudes toward some category of people who happened to be living in a particular region. Their results would be a blocking of group economic progress, producing in the aggregate a depressed status for the region as a whole.

We have not attempted to evaluate the validity of these factors in accounting for economic differences among Canada's regions. We do not have the tools to make such an evaluation, although there are inklings that all of the factors mentioned have some bearing on the continuity of regional differences.[29] Without presenting completely supportive data, our discussion still suggests that, in the absence of economic handicaps or political and cultural barriers to equalization, the progress of economic development should be associated with only minor regional inequalities.

Cultural Homogeneity

The existence of regional subcultures at any point in time does not preclude their later change. The pervasiveness of the mass media and pressures to a national or even international culture would seem to portend what some already see in existence—a homogenized mass culture. This is predicted as a consequence of modernization.

> . . . industrialization is viewed as a process that creates cultural homogeneity, in that certain patterns of belief and behaviour are necessarily common to all industrial societies. Moreover, commonality is not limited to the single act or norm but applies as well to the configurations into which they are formed, for example, the interrelations among machine technology, division of labor, and authoritative coordination.[30]

But the contrary pull is every bit as evident. It is hardly necessary to document the number of instances in modern, industrial societies in which the basic struggles between groups representing different sub-

---

29. See, for example, the discussion of obstacles to the elimination of economic inequalities in the case of Nova Scotia. Roy E. George, *A Leader and a Laggard, Manufacturing Industry in Nova Scotia, Quebec and Ontario* (Toronto: University of Toronto Press, 1970), especially pp. 132-70.

30. Wilbert E. Moore and Arnold S. Feldman, eds., *Labor Commitment and Social Change in Developing Areas* (New York: Social Science Research Council, 1960), p. 364.

cultures have been the most intransigent examples of internal conflicts. In Canada this is primarily exemplified by conflict between
English and French-speaking regions, but ethnicity and other sources
of cultural groupings also play some role in all regional cleavages.

Several explanations have been offered for the lack of decline in
cultural identities tied to regions. Michael Hechter describes these in
terms of isolation and economic malintegration, but in both cases, he
feels there is sufficient contrary evidence to question the general
applicability of either of these theories. That is, regional cultural
differences remain not solely because of isolation among regions or
lack of complete integration into the economy.[31] Hechter places more
emphasis on the solidarity of regional status groups, and we would
concur, though not necessarily for the same reasons.

Regions as foci of common cultures develop through the existence
of shared characteristics among their residents. The pertinent
characteristics are those that bear on a way of life. Two principal
ways in which shared characteristics come to affect regional cultures
is through the existence of a common language, encouraging communication within regions, and a common religion, leading to distinctive values. These are, of course, not the sole avenues for the emergence of regional cultures. Economic characterictics themselves are
important sources of common life styles and outlooks, as Atlantic
fishermen and prairie wheat farmers illustrate. Whatever current or
historic experiences lead to shared experiences and ways of life, these
will exist as potential sources of a regional culture.

Solidarity in the foregoing instances can be said to arise from the
way a group defines itself. It may also be associated with the definitions of others. Labelling by others, the existence of even covert
prejudice, all help to set the people of a region apart. Where this
is accompanied by discriminatory practices, as we earlier indicated, a
further rationale for separateness is added. Discrimination is a compounding factor where it serves to cause or to exaggerate economic
inequalities, reinforcing in this way regional disparities.

Finally, and perhaps this is most important, regional cultures will
continue to exist where there is an overt recognition of a regional
identity. This may stem from a sense of group deprivation, but it
may also be associated with feelings of group superiority. It is here
that we had most difficulty in making a case from our Canadian
data.[32] This was at least partly due to our inability to generate empirical indicators of regional group consciousness, although we
certainly inferred its existence a number of times. Whether or not the

---

31. Michael Hechter, "Towards a Theory of Ethnic Change," *Politics and
Society* 2 (Fall, 1971): 21-45.

32. See particularly Chapters 4 and 5.

reader was equally convinced is another matter. But at least we can jointly recognize that such group consciousness is an important aspect of regional cultures, and a necessary precondition for organized political action that serves to deal with explicitly regional problems.

If regionalism is often sustained by the tenacity of regional sub-cultures, then forces leading to their break-up should contribute to the contrary effect. These include high levels of both in and out migration involving all regions, in order to prevent the isolation of any one part of a country. Inter-regional contacts would also be ensured by elaborated communication networks and the use of a common language. The population should be almost completely homogeneous with respect to religion and other significant sources of values, or where diversity exists, this should not coincide with any geographic base. In these and other relevant ways, regional subcultures could be prevented from emerging. Once they had emerged, these same policies, though much more difficult to introduce, would also be effective in dislodging subcultural attachments.

The Politics of Regionalism

Our discussion of regions and regionalism has been couched almost solely in terms of the divisions associated with provincial boundaries. We did this to have the means for dealing with regions as political units. In the two cases where we grouped provinces, we based at least part of our justification on the political relevance of the group-ings. The effects of these provincial boundaries on the continuity of regionalism is inestimable. Provinces are the arenas for mobilizing and expressing contending interests. Through their jurisdictions, the lives of citizens are regularly touched in ways distinct from any other level of government. A federal system of government makes routine both the existence of distinctive regional interests and the means for coping with these. Province as region and regions as combinations of provinces daily manifest one of the critical barriers to a lessening of regional ties.

Differences in available resources, in populations served, in prob-lems faced, in historical traditions, and in the political avenues developed for coping with these all set regions apart from each other. Sharkansky has discussed the interrelation of some of these factors for the United States.[33] In Canada, we have documented their political results in tracing voting trends in Chart 3–1. We have also seen their association with the adaptation of the party system, dis-cussed in Chapter 6. No implication of a conspiracy has been used in

---

33. Ira Sharkansky, "Regionalism, Economic Status and the Public Policies of American States," *Social Science Quarterly* 49 (June 1968): 9-26.

Chapter 3 to account for differences in provincial power, to the effect that some provinces are deliberately kept from the influence that is their due. But we have certainly implied that the end result of power differentials is to weaken the ability of a region to gain its special goals within the context of the national government. These differences have some historical continuity, although they are also dependent on the party in power.

In view of the continuity of relative disadvantages, we might anticipate some sympathy for the realignment of provincial boundaries. Despite the apparent gains that would be associated with larger units bargaining with the national government, attempts to alter the boundary status quo are viewed with suspicion. The Canadian Institute of Public Opinion interviewed a national sample about both Maritime and Prairie union. Nowhere did a clear majority advocate union, although one in the Maritimes was more popular than with the Prairie provinces.[34] The sense of separateness associated with provinces, even where there is also a broader regional identity, seems sufficient to block the likelihood of political union in the near future.[35] From this we would assume that deregionalization would come about more readily where regions were not also formally defined political units.

Dynamics of Government

Everywhere the existence of the modern state has been accompanied by the growth of powerful, centralized government. Trends in this

34. Opinions of Maritime and Prairie Political Union.
(percent)

	Approve	Disapprove	Undecided
Maritime Union:			
Maritimes	44	52	4
Quebec	42	35	23
Ontario	44	40	16
West	46	34	20
Canada	44	38	18
Prairie Union:			
Maritimes	29	44	27
Quebec	34	37	29
Ontario	25	57	18
West	26	63	11
Canada	28	52	20

Source: Canadian Institute of Public Opinion, The Gallup Report, 9 and 11 September 1970.

35. Mildred A. Schwartz, "Attachments to Province and Region in the Prairie Provinces," in David K. Elton, ed., *One Prairie Province? Conference Proceedings and Selected Papers* (Lethbridge, Alberta: Lethbridge Herald, 1971), pp. 101-105.

direction could be assumed to be a primary means for weakening the ties of region. At the same time, other tendencies have occurred, perhaps complimentary in their intent, but contrary in their outcome. Two tendencies, which might be seen as in direct opposition, are of special importance since their consequences have been to bolster regionalism. One derives from pressures toward greater efficiency, in particular those associated with assumptions about economies of scale. The second is a compounding of populist concerns with direct democracy and liberal objections to bureaucratization. Both tendencies may operate at any level of government.

From one perspective, there appears to be growing recognition of the functional efficiency of larger units of government and administration. Small towns and even cities are seen as unable to provide necessary services to their residents unless they can find a larger population base, and a larger tax base. Some services, such as theatres and museums, cannot even be considered unless there is a large concentration of population. As a result,

> Most official and nonofficial proposals in the United States, Canada, and Great Britain are for drastic reduction in the number of units of local government. For instance, a Royal Commission has proposed that England (outside of London) be divided into 58 new local government areas each under a single, unitary local authority and three metropolitan areas where responsibility would be divided between the metropolitan council and a number of district councils.[36]

Such moves have already been underway in Canada. For example, the development of a metropolitan form of government for the city and suburbs of Toronto was a pioneering venture in North America.[37] Divisions of provinces into larger subunits has likewise proceeded in Ontario and Quebec, both of which had earlier experience with a second-tier of Government between province and municipalities.[38]

Unions across provincial boundaries have at least been broached in Canada, although opposition from the electorate still remains strong (see table in fn. 34). In the Maritime provinces, however,

---

36. Victor Jones, "Editorial," *Public Management* 52 (April, 1970): 3.

37. Harold Kaplan, *Urban Political Systems: A Functional Analysis of Metro Toronto* (New York: Columbia University Press, 1967); Frank Smallwood, *Metro Toronto: A Decade Later* (Toronto: Bureau of Municipal Research Inc., 1963).

38. Walter R. Fuhrman, "Ontario: Province Implements Regional Switch," *Public Management* 52 (April, 1970) 15-17; Municipal Affairs Department, "Quebec: Teamwork Approach to Regionalism," *Public Management* 52 (April, 1970): 18-19.

union has enough practical implications that, at least at official levels, it is under consideration. [39] One of the immediate benefits would be savings to the taxpayer, who would no longer need to support three provincial capitals, legislatures, and governmental bureaucracies. In the Prairies, union is more remote, but even there it has some appeal as a way of bringing together areas with similar and related interests into what could be a more viable and effective regional government. This is an instance where union is viewed, by some at least, as a way of increasing regional power vis à vis the central government.[40]

None of the American states, as far as we know, is currently contemplating union with another state. While first taken as a great joke, Norman Mailer, in his campaign for mayor of New York City, advocated the creation of a city-state, a proposal that turned out to have considerable merit.[41] Currently, there is also a move to reorganize states into federal regions, not as a way of dissolving existing state boundaries or governments, but as an attempt to increase the efficiency of the central government and ease of access to some of its administrative units. States have been divided into ten regions, each with a regional headquarters, and to begin with, they will provide the basis for organizing field services from the Departments of Health, Education and Welfare; Housing and Urban Development; and Labor; and those from two agencies, the Office of Economic Opportunity and the Small Business Administration.[42]

In all of these moves to reorganize cities, provinces, and regions the continuing theme is concern for the evils of excessive bureaucratization. Each of the changes advocated, in addition to its greater efficiency, is also viewed as providing greater democratization. Or, where such would not be the immediate result, there are parallel proposals for ensuring that local interests be protected. For example, advocacy of broader urban regions is often coupled with pleas for small local or neighbourhood councils that would have the ability to represent local interests and the authority to serve local needs.[43] The argument is also made that the formation of regions as political units

39. Maritime Union Study, *The Report on Maritime Union Commissioned by the Governments of Nova Scotia, New Brunswick and Prince Edward Island* (Fredericton: 1970); J. R. Winter, *Federal-Provincial Fiscal Relations and Maritime Union* (Fredericton: 1970).

40. Elton, *One Prairie Province?*

41. Peter Manso, ed., *Running Against the Machine* (Garden City, N.Y.: Doubleday, 1969), pp. 172-77, 198-207, 212-13.

42. Statement by the President of the United States on restructuring government service system, March 27, 1969; Executive Order 11297, May 21, 1969.

43. Victor Jones, "Editorial," *Public Management*, 2-3.

should begin from the common needs and interests of the residents.[44]

Whatever the rationale for any of these proposals, it is becoming increasingly clear that the dynamic needs of modern government cannot be met simply through greater centralization. While some part of the decentralization proposed now in fact derives from motives for making the central government more effective and efficient, it does not take much imagination to see that the strengthening of regional units, whether these are metropolitan complexes, parts of existing provinces, or broader regional groupings, will heighten the relevance of these units to their inhabitants, and even to the central government, and not necessarily in the ways intended. As an extreme result, the strengthening of regional governments will provide the potential focus for separatist movements, now equipped with the means for carrying through a broad range of governmental functions. This need not be the outcome, of course, as pressures continue to work against separation. But at least the continuing viability of regions themselves seems to be ensured through these means.

Planned Change

Deregionalization as a consequence of economic and other developmental processes is not impossible. But the strength and variety of barriers to it make it difficult. In order for large-scale alterations in the nature of regionalism to occur, deliberate planning is required. The need for such policies has been recognized in a growing number of countries, including those in mature stages of development.[45]

Historically, the equalization of regional opportunities in Canada has been primarily an unplanned consequence of policies with other objectives. Their outcomes have also created pressures from regions, not sharing in the initial benefits, to obtain concessions from the federal government. According to Hugh Whalen,

> Public policy in Canada has been designed traditionally to achieve *national* economic, social, and political objectives. Policies aimed at nation-building were directed to increasing

44. D. C. Rowat, "The Concept of Regional Government and a Proposal for Ontario," in N. H. Lithwick and Giles Paquet, eds., *Urban Studies: A Canadian Perspective* (Toronto: Methuen, 1968), pp. 240-61.

45. For some examples, see Hollis B. Chenery, "Development Policies in Southern Italy," *Quarterly Journal of Economics* 76 (November, 1962): 515-47; S. Wellisz, "Economic Planning in the Netherlands, France, and Italy," *Journal of Political Economy* 68 (June 1960): 252-83; Albert O. Hirschman, *Journeys Toward Progress: Studies of Economic Policy-Making in Latin America* (New York: Twentieth Century Fund, 1963); Lloyd Rodwin, *The British New Towns Policy* (Cambridge: Harvard University Press, 1956); Harry M. Caudill, *Night Comes to the Cumberland* (Boston: Little, Brown and Co., 1962).

the total population, constructing transcontinental rail systems, and creating a viable secondary manufacturing sector behind a national tariff wall. The realization of such national objectives did confer artificial—that is, policy produced—economic advantages on particular regions. For example, the Dominion Lands Act of 1872, with its homestead provisions, was designed to open up the Prairies; the tariff policy introduced in 1879, and the extensive federal outlays on canals in the years after Confederation, favoured the central provinces of Quebec and Ontario; and the building of the Canadian Pacific Railway, completed in 1885, rendered possible the development of British Columbia.

During the last four decades there have been massive public expenditures in the Prairie region on behalf of agricultural development. During the war and postwar years, defence procurement, St. Lawrence River development, assistance to pipelines, and subsidies to gold mining have favoured the central provinces. These policy-produced advantages, even when justified in terms of the nation's development, have inevitably produced demands for compensatory adjustments from other regions which have not been helped. Partly as a counterpoise to national tariff arrangements, for example, a reduction of the railway freight rate structure favourable to the Prairies was introduced as early as 1898, and a somewhat similar reduction was extended to the Maritime Provinces in 1927. To compensate for the Prairie farm rehabilitation projects and gold mining assistance, the Maritime marshland rehabilitation scheme and various federal programs affecting the Nova Scotia coal industry were introduced.[46]

With time, more deliberate plans have increased to ensure that particular regions could meet their economic problems, though still in a piecemeal fashion. As Whalen indicated, early examples of legislative efforts to overcome handicaps of particular areas include the Maritime Freight Rates Act (1927), the Prairie Farm Rehabilitation Act (1935), and the Maritime Marshland Rehabilitation Act (1948). In 1969, the need for comprehensive regional planning and development was expressed in the formation of the Department of Regional Economic Expansion. Its terms of reference state that:

The Governor in Council, after consultation with the government of any province, may by order designate as a

---

46. Hugh Whalen, "Public Policy and Regional Development: The Experience of the Atlantic Provinces," in Abraham Rotstein, ed., *The Prospect of Change* (Toronto: McGraw-Hill, 1965), pp. 102-103.

special area, for the period set out in the order, any area in that province that is determined to require, by reason of the exceptional inadequacy of opportunities for productive employment of the people of that area or of the region in which that area is a part, special measures to facilitate economic expansion and social adjustment.[47]

The Act requires close cooperation between federal and provincial authorities, and what appears to be the initiation of programs from the provincial level. The emphasis is almost solely on economic problems and not on other sources of regional disparities.

Despite the attractiveness of rational planning as an avenue for overcoming regional disadvantages, problems of selecting the appropriate means and goals and the difficulties of instituting them are monumental. For example, Hirschmann discusses the widespread tendency of governments to disperse new projects, as a means of convincing voters that the largest possible numbers are sharing in efforts toward economic upgrading.[48] Political expediency has also been an important factor in Canada. Programs designed to secure votes and those that appear to have immediate payoff have strong attractions. As Whalen describes it,

> Characteristically, the political approach to complex economic problems is to seek simple solutions; but there are more serious limitations inherent in provincial rivalries, federal-provincial tensions, and divided jurisdictions. The British and European regional development experiments . . . have achieved substantial success in large measure because they operate in unitary state systems. But in Canada, by contrast, there has always been a lack of coherence in federal policy with respect to the major economic regions, due in part to interprovincial competition, the inevitability of compromise solutions produced by the need for federal-provincial agreement on outstanding issues, and the continuing frustration and lack of decisiveness in the face of centrifugal forces.[49]

47. Government of Canada Statutes, Government Organization Act, 1969, C. 28, 17-18 Eliz. II, p. 594.

48. Albert O. Hirschman, "Interregional and International Transmission of Economic Growth," in John Friedman and William Alonso, *Regional Development and Planning* (Cambridge: The M.I.T. Press, 1964), pp. 630-35. See also Lloyd Rodwin, "Choosing Regions for Development," ibid., pp. 37-58.

49. Whalen, "Public Policy and Regional Development," in Rotstein, *The Prospect of Change,* pp. 142-43. Provincial governments have also faced great difficulties in their efforts to encourage economic growth. See Philip Mathias, *Forced Growth* (Toronto: James Lewis & Samuel, 1971).

The creation of the Department of Regional Economic Expansion does not seem to have solved these problems. Already there are cries that decisions on economic development are based primarily on political favours, that they are ineffective, and that they are biased either for or against special interests.[50] Whether or not these accusations are true, they underscore some of the obstacles to long-range planning.

Planning then, as a solution to the problems of regional inequalities, is no easier a path than one that waits on evolutionary developments. But while it is difficult, it is also the most necessary form of social change for a country such as Canada.

THE CONSEQUENCES OF REGIONALISM

The Essential Canada

The consequences of regionalism are many: stable regional divisions do not determine a single mode of adaptation to the problems of societal functioning. Of the three possible alternatives which concern us, one presumes the existence of a region that acts as the carrier of the dominant norms and orientations, and hence as the model for the remainder. Through its institutions and values it encapsulates the essential features of the total nationhood. Emulation by other regions occurs but need not result in the disappearance of regional differences. Whatever differences remain, however, must not be at the expense of the dominant institutions and values. Societies of this type require the widespread conviction that only through the existence of these core values and institutions can the uniqueness of all regions survive.

André Siegfried, apparently long fascinated by the concept of nationhood in divided societies,[51] has examined the case of Switzerland. In many respects, Switzerland is even more puzzling as a nation-state than Canada. Its regions differ by language, custom, and religion; and its parts are separated by formidable geographic barriers. Moreover, each of its regions has greater cultural affinities with some neighbouring country. Federation was piecemeal, with cantons joining at different times, so that Switzerland acquired its present physical form only in 1815, and its constitution even later (1874). The

---

50. David Crane, "Party members attack Ottawa over regional aid programs" (Toronto: *The Globe and Mail,* 21 November 1970).

51. André Siegfried, *The Race Question in Canada* (London: Everleigh Nash, 1907).

original areas are viewed as having special qualities, as the model of the final state and the mother of it. Siegfried calls this essential Switzerland *Urschweiz*,[52] and it has in his usage almost mystical properties of a progenitor. This is not to suggest that the *Urschweiz* gave a preeminent identity to the total nation. The principal identity of citizens is to their canton, and many of the institutions of that society coalese to encourage this, legally as well as emotionally. The special properties of *Urschweiz* derive from its creative force. As the origin of contemporary Switzerland, it has provided the focus for nationhood, the guarantor, paradoxical as it may seem, of the unique identity of the confederated cantons.

Siegfried was undoubtedly over-enthusiastic in his assessment of Switzerland's solutions to its internal tensions. We do not, however, wish to test the validity of *Urschweiz*. It is Siegfried's theory of a core area, rather than his evidence, that suggests one form of adaptation to the problems of regional divisiveness.

Does *Urkanada* exist in one or all of the Atlantic provinces? One contender is Nova Scotia, the first colony in New France. Its strategic importance was early recognized by the English as well, who began recurring attacks on Port Royal. The area passed back and forth between the two colonial powers, ending with the cession of Acadia to England. The expulsion of the French would make this part of Canada the first scene of lasting tensions between those of French and English origin. With formal peace between the two groups, Nova Scotia embarked on a course of development that made it rich and powerful. These were attributes that would soon be lost as demands and competitive advantages changed. But initially at least, Nova Scotia incorporated the tensions, positive values, and life styles that would soon be prominent elsewhere. Nova Scotia, and what soon became New Brunswick, were also among the original partners to the Confederation agreements.

Quebec could also be considered at least a segment of the essential Canada. From its beginnings as a French colony, it was the original Canada. After the conquest, Canada became part of its name, whether designated as Lower or East. From this period on, Canadians of French origin were instrumental in shaping the character of the nation. And from their beginnings in North America, they were the pacesetters in establishing this continent's models of explorer, frontiersman, settler, and perhaps least effectively, entrepreneur.

What is now Ontario comes on the scene as a centre of population considerably later. Yet, like Quebec, it too is a portion of the original nucleus that makes up present-day Canada. While the national capital

---

52. André Siegfried, *Switzerland, A Democratic Way of Life* (New York: Duell, Sloan and Pearce, 1950), p. 27.

was established at a point mid-way between the two provinces, it does remain in Ontario, and this gives that province an extra claim to national status. From the nineteenth century, Ontario had asserted its claim to leadership in many areas, claims that others have not been successful in challenging. Ontario embodied the British institutions transplanted to North America, and acted to preserve these from what were seen as alien influences. Its major claim to *Urkanada* would be as the carrier of British institutions, although these have long been transformed and adapted to local conditions and needs.

Of the three Prairie provinces, only Manitoba has a long enough history as a political unit to even approach originating status. Despite this, all of the Prairies have some claim to the essence of nationhood. They do so because they are the west, that geographic locus that was the magnet for the aspirations of both French and English in the beginnings of Canada. It was in the west that new institutions developed, new life styles emerged, and new political philosophies were put in practice. Innovation was the response to conditions of life that could not be anticipated by the manners of Europe or the eastern provinces. The frontier had a great impact on Canadian development, and the Prairie provinces represent both the early and the mature expression of this.

British Columbia, the western anchor of Canada, also represents the frontier traditions, though in different respects from the Prairies. From the first settlement at Victoria, it was the outpost of British imperialism and colonization. The fur trade, and especially the gold rush, needed the stability provided by these British ties to keep from being overwhelmed by alien interests, in particular those coming from the United States. In this sense, British Columbia early experienced the encroachments of population and interests from the United States and the needs to develop ways of restricting these. In other words, it has been the scene from its beginnings of one of the recurring problems of Canadian existence.

In Chapters Seven, Eight, and Nine, we considered orientations to politics through indications of knowledge, feelings about the relations between government and citizen, and judgements about the ways the political system operates. In each instance, we found more or less distinct patterns of orientation for each region. This lack of uniformity posed severe problems of interpretation, particularly in Chapter Eight, where we chose to treat the content of the questionnaire items as issues of legitimacy. If indeed legitimacy means what most scholars understand by this concept, then almost by definition we should expect some cross-regional consensus. In fact, we found little consensus, except for some ties between British Columbia and the Prairies. At that time, we chose to interpret our results as evidence of the lack of a single set of legitimate norms to which citizens could orient themselves. We also considered the possibility that one region might best express the legitimate norms, although we did not feel that we could defend such a view. Our overview of Canada's history adds weight to our original decision, since we see that it is possible to argue for many essential Canadas. Each region expresses at least several of the basic themes of Canadian existence and several of the basic methods of adaptation to the problems of nationhood. As a consequence, there seems to be no *Urkanada*. Whatever the approaches contending claimants may have developed to face recurring problems, these can be used as arguments for their legitimacy. While some may believe that they have greater claim to legitimacy, others could give counter arguments that have at least local support.

Union of Equals

The doctrine of "separate but equal" has been found wanting as an approach to the educational problems of racial groups in the United States. Does this thesis have any greater validity in the life of regions? The answer lies in the way equality (or inequality) is defined. There are some who extend their egalitarianism to a suspicion of all differences, but being equal need not mean being alike. Diversity at the societal level can produce many positive benefits, adding to the variety and strength of the whole nation. The nineteenth century Swiss poet and nationalist Gottfried Keller, wrote, in arguing against a unitary nation.

> What do you want with your Switzerland without her old and new cantons? It would be only an empty barrel. . . . The red uniform of Helvetia with the white cross is beautiful, but equally beautiful are the twenty-two white shirts beneath the uniform, each one different with its own coat of arms. Without the federal tie no Swiss citizen would exist, but without cantons and without their differences and competition, no Swiss federation would exist: this is the cornerstone in our fatherland. We wish that our canton play a leading role in this competition; this depends on the Great Council which we have to elect today. It should be a beacon for the fulfilment of our duties to the federation and to the canton alike, to preserve the fertile diversity of our Swiss land.[53]

Of the many sources of regional differentiation, the two that are associated with serious and far-reaching inequalities derive from the

---

53. Cited in Hans Kohn, *Nationalism and Liberty, The Swiss Example* (New York: The Macmillan Company, 1956), p. 96.

economic and political situation of regions. Of these, political equality
is the most essential. Regardless of how regions differ from each
other, if they are able to enjoy equal power, then their political union
is one where local interests can expect to be treated fairly and equitably, even when demands are not always satisfied. Compromises are
achieved through strength, and not through inevitable weakness, with
a high probability, at least perceived, that some local demands will be
met.

We emphasize political power and equality because of the critical
functions performed by the polity. In the most general sense, the
principal function of the political system is the attainment of the
society's goals.[54] At issue here is the extent to which regional interests
are incorporated into national goals. For example, an attempt at
such incorporation was expressed by President Franklin Delano
Roosevelt when he said, "We have an economic unbalance in the
Nation as a whole, due to [the economic condition] of the South. It is
an unbalance that must be righted for the sake of the South and of the
Nation." Where necessary, a government may introduce changes in
electoral laws and in constituency boundaries. The regular expression
of local demands and support can also be ensured through legal
protection. The distributive and redistributive means at the disposal
of government can be used to protect regional diversity and to re-
channel the allocation of resources and rewards for the equalization
or regional opportunities.[55] While the results may still be imperfect,
for the reasons earlier enumerated when we discussed planned change,
efforts in this direction are extremely important to prevent building
up serious regional grievances. In contrast, the Canadian situation
remains one where regional inequalities in power are still evident. To
the extent that regions and their constituent provinces are not equal
partners in Confederation, either despite or because of the terms of
their union, each is hampered in the fulfillment of its needs and the
nation as a whole is hampered in the expression of the goals of unity
in diversity.

Institutionalized Inequality

In Canada, we have neither a core region nor a union of equals.
Although we have chosen to term the relations predominating in

---

54. Talcott Parsons, "On the Concept of Political Power," in Parsons,
Sociological Theory and Modern Society (New York: Free Press, 1967), pp.
297-354.

55. We rely here on the functions enumerated by Theodore Lowi, "American Business, Public Policy, Case Studies, and Political Theory," *World
Politics* 16 (July 1964).

Canada institutionalized inequality, this should not be interpreted to mean that the former alternatives provide a stress-free setting. No matter what adaptation is achieved in the face of regional diversity, some tension is inevitable. The mere existence of observable differences, despite what may be rationally known about their positive features, inevitably introduces the potential for contrast, and with it, the likelihood that differences will be equated with more or less desirable states of being. Even more basic as a source of conflict is the probability of a scarcity of resources. Along with the pervasiveness of such sources of stress are variations, however, in the ways they are met. Of the three responses to regional divisions that we consider, the existence of a core area and the union of equals are less likely to be associated with serious conflict. In both cases, there are related principles of reconciliation. The existence of a core region means, by the way we have defined this, that there will be shared values among all regions, core or peripheral. Where regions are equal in political power, there is a great premium on bargaining, since no one has the greater advantage. But where regions are linked together in relations of inequality, the conflict potential remains most severe, and most likely to become overt.

Labelling the Canadian situation as one of institutionalized inequality should not come as a surprise. The empirical signs are found in the historical continuity of patterns of inequality. We have generally looked at these for a span of four decades, and even earlier data sources indicate their persistence. In general, we would say that it is such historical patterns that can be used to test the institutionalization response in any society.

Given the institutionalization of inequality, are there ways it can be overcome? Will its continued existence lead to unavoidable civil strife? Some answers are suggested by the literature on political violence internal to nation-states. For example, there is considerable agreement that revolutions are likely to occur when periods of improvement are followed by decline. With expectations on the rise because of past improvements, disappointment is the more bitter when the promise of a better life seemed so close at hand.[56] Neither change nor stability, regardless of the circumstances of life in which most people find themselves, are preconditions of violent conflict, although some disorganized and spontaneous outbursts may certainly occur when situations are particularly oppressive. More important in general,

---

56. James C. Davies, "The J-Curve of Rising and Declining Satisfactions as a Cause of Some Great Revolutions and a Contained Rebellion," in Hugh Davis Graham and Ted Robert Gurr, *The History of Violence in America* (New York: Bantam Books, 1969), pp. 690-730.

however, are experiences of rapid change and the transition between traditional and modern societies.[57]

It was such generalizations that guided our interpretations of the Quebec experience. We remember that our survey was conducted in 1966, in other words, prior to the 1970 provincial election when the Parti Québecois gained one-quarter of the popular vote, whether because of its separatist platform or because it provided a convenient focus for protest. It also preceded the most violent forms of revolutionary separatist activities, manifesting its darkest face in the murder of the Quebec Minister of Labour, Pierre Laporte. Yet it was clear that the rapid changes that had taken place in the province were unsettling many people, from those who felt changes were too slow to those who found them too drastic, and including those unfortunates who had neither the transferable skills nor the personal resources that would fit them into a new social order. We judged the potential for unrest to be great in Quebec, but also considerable in British Columbia. Part of our reasoning was based on the evidence that voters in both regions were not particularly supportive of traditional political mechanisms, while they readily found political channels for expressing their discontent. We contrasted these circumstances with the objectively more serious inequalities suffered in the Atlantic provinces, which while clearly recognized by their residents, had not as yet led to any major questioning of the political system. This implies that the Atlantic provinces still enjoy some of the stability that comes from political traditionalism. Does this mean that if major changes were introduced into the eastern provinces, changes designed to alter the way of life and raise standards of living, the conflict potential would also be raised? The answer might well be in the affirmative, if changes were rapid and development was uneven. What seems to be required is a rapid rise in income, associated with increasing job opportunities, but less in the way of other social changes. In particular, a sharp increase in educational opportunities without

---

57. Ivo K. Feierabend, Rosalind L. Feierabend, and Betty A. Nesvold, "Social Change and Political Violence: Cross-National Patterns," in Graham and Gurr, *The History of Violence,* pp. 632-87. The absence of circumstances described by the Feierabends help account for different developments in Scotland, where regionalism is not accompanied by violence. John E. Schwartz, "The Scottish National Party: Nonviolent Separatism and Theories of Violence," *World Politics* 22 (July 1970): 496-517. For a comparative perspective on separatism, see Ted Gurr (with Charles Ruttenburg), *Cross-National Studies of Civil Violence* (Washington: The American University Center for Research in Social Systems, 1969), pp. 121-30.

an even greater rise in occupational resources seems to be a dangerous combination.[58] It is not that education raises expectations to unrealistically high levels, thus contributing to discontent, but that education inspires people to feel that they can directly effect the conditions of their lives.[59]

It may turn out to be impossible to introduce the kinds of changes that would eliminate the most crucial inequalities. Even if we assume that some measure of improvement is possible, we can still expect vast numbers of people, confined to their territorial base, who will always be among the "have-nots." Should they then go their separate ways, taking their chances on independence, with at worst the outlook of being poor but proud? For some, this may appear the only alternative. For others, and for the sake of Canadian nationhood, we hope the majority, there will be some appreciation of the bonds that tie them together. Perhaps large numbers will continue to emigrate from the Atlantic provinces, but of those who remain or return, most need to be content with a way of life which provides satisfactions not readily available to residents of the great metropolitan centres of central and western Canada. When we remove all the romantic explanations of Swiss existence, for example, the pragmatic benefits of union predominate.[60] Ultimately, the fate of Canada too will rest on such issues. If one can only live as a Quebecker or a Manitoban by virtue of Canadian union, then the benefits of Confederation will become more important.

We end on a restrained note. This is an age when declining numbers are convinced of the inevitability of progress or the benefits of economic growth. It also appears that inequities are not easily eradicated. The best we can hope for is to live in peace, if not in prosperity.

---

58. Ivo K. Feierabend and Rosalind L. Feierabend, "Aggressive Behaviors Within Polities, 1948-1962: A Cross-National Study," *Journal of Conflict Resolution* 10 (September 1966): 249-71.

59. Ted Robert Gurr, "A Comparative Study of Civil Strife," in Graham and Gurr, *The History of Violence*, p. 599.

60. J. Christopher Herold, *The Swiss Without Halos* (New York: Columbia University Press, 1948), p. 134.

INDEX